Urban Transport, Environment and Equity
The Case for Developing Countries

Eduardo Alcântara Vasconcellos

T0330871

from Routledge

DEDICATION

To Mahatma Gandhi, Paulo Freire and Nelson Mandela, and the light of fraternity they have tended.

To people in developing countries who are struggling to be accepted as human beings.

To my childhood friends, in memory of the time when we were allowed to walk, chat and play football on the streets of Brazil.

First published in the UK and USA in 2001 by
Earthscan Publications Ltd

This edition published 2013 by Earthscan

For a full list of publications please contact:

Earthscan
2 Park Square, Milton Park, Abingdon, Oxon OX14 4RN
Simultaneously published in the USA and Canada by Earthscan
711 Third Avenue, New York, NY 10017

Earthscan is an imprint of the Taylor & Francis Group, an informa business

A catalogue record for this book is available from the British Library

ISBN: 978-1-85383-727-2 (pbk)

Typesetting by Composition and Design Services

Cover design by Danny Gillespie

Library of Congress Cataloging-in-Publication Data

Vasconcellos, Eduardo Alcântara de, 1952-.
    Urban transport, environment and equity: the case for developing countries/
Eduardo Alcântara Vasconcellos.
        p. cm.
    Includes bibliographical references (p.) and index.
    ISBN 1-85383-726-1 (cloth) – ISBN 1-85383-727-X (pbk.)
    1. Urban transportation–Developing countries. 2. Urban transportation–
Environmental aspects–Developing countries. 3. Urban transport policy–Developing
countries. I. Title.

HE311.D44 V37 2001
388.4'09172'4–dc21

2001023295

CONTENTS

LIST OF TABLES, FIGURES AND BOXES

TABLES

FIGURES

Boxes

LIST OF ACRONYMS AND ABBREVIATIONS

AADT	annual average daily traffic
ANFAVEA	Associação Nacional de Fabricantes de Veículos Automotores
ANPET	Associação Nacional de Pesquisa e Ensino em Transportes
ANTP	Associação Nacional de Transportes Públicos
ASC	average social cost
BID	Banco Interamericano de Desarrollo
CBD	central business district
CEPAL	Comission Economica para la America Latina
CERTU	Centre D'Études sur les Réseaux, les Transports, L'Urbanisme et les Construction Publiques
CET	Cia de Engenharia de Tráfego
CETESB	Cia de Tecnologia de Saneamento Ambiental
CMSP	Cia do Metropolitano de São Paulo
CMTC	Cia Municipal de Transportes Coletivos
CNG	compressed natural gas
CO	carbon monoxide
CO_2	carbon dioxide
DENATRAN	Departamento Nacional de Trânsito
DERSA	Desenvolvimento Rodoviário SA
DETRAN	Departamento Estadual de Trânsito
ECMT	European Commission of Ministers of Transport
ERR	economic rate of return
FABUS	Sindicato das Empresas Encarroçadoras de Ônibus
FAPESP	Fundação de Amparo à Pesquisa do Estado de São Paulo
GWP	global warming potential
HC	hydrocarbons
HCM	Highway Capacity Manual
IBGE	Instituto Brasileiro de Geografia e Estatística
IIT	Indian Instittute of Technology
ILD	Instituto Libertad y Democracia
INRETS	Institut National de Recherché sur les Transports et leur Sécurité
IPEA	Instituto de Pesquisa Econômica Aplicada
IPPUC	Instituto de Planejamento e Projeto de Curitiba
IPEA	Instituto de Pesquisa Econômica Aplicada

ITE	Institute of Transportation Engineers
ITS-UCD	Institute of Tranportation Studies, University of California at Davis
IUIDP	integrated urban infrastructure development programming
LA	Latin America
LRT	light rail transit
MJ/pass-km	mega-joules per passenger kilometre
MSC	marginal social cost
MTW	motorized two-wheeler
NMT	non-motorized transport
NMV	non-motorized vehicles
NO_x	nitrogen oxide
NTU	Associação Nacional das Empresas de Transportes Urbanos
OD	origin-destination
OECD	Organization for Economic Cooperation and Development
PM	particulate matter
SEADE	Fundação Estadual de Análise de dados
SETRA	Service D'Études Techniques des Routes et Autoroutes
SIMR	Medium to long term road improvement plan
SMT	Secretaria Municipal de Transportes
SO_x	sulphur oxide
SO_2	sulphur dioxide
SP	suspended particles
SPM	suspended particulate matter
SPTRANS	São Paulo Transporte SA
SPURT	Seventh Plan Urban and Regional Transport
SWOV	Institute for road safety research
TB	time budget
TRB	Transportation Research Board
TRLL	Transport and Road Research Laboratory
TTI	Texas Transportation Institute
UN	United Nations
UNCHS	United Nations Centre for Human Settlements
UTPS	Urban Planning Transportation System
VRU	vulnerable road users
WHO	World Health Organization

Acknowledgements

The initial funding for this work was provided by FAPESP – a public agency from the state of São Paulo – who funded my postdoctoral research at Cornell University in the US between 1993 and 1995. At that time I had the patient and generous support of several people, especially Porus Olpadwalla and William Goldsmith, to whom I am deeply indebted. After returning to Brazil, the resulting thesis was published in 1996, in Portuguese in two volumes. The content has recently been reviewed, updated and enlarged to capture the important political and economic changes that have happened in the world since, resulting in the book that is now presented to the reader. I would like also to thank Earthscan for offering me the opportunity to publish the book in English.

Many friends as well as people I do not know personally have helped me with data and suggestions and I am deeply grateful to all of them: Ailton Brasiliense (ANTP, Brazil), Brian Williams (Habitat, Nairobi), Charles Wright (Inter-American Development Bank), Craig Townsend (Murdoch University), João Carlos Scatena (Cia do Metropolitano de São Paulo), John Howe (IHE Delft, The Netherlands), Licinio da Silva Portugal (Universidade Federal do Rio de Janeiro/COPPE), Lisa Kane (University of Cape Town), Livia Salomão Pichinini (Universidade do Rio Grande do Sul), Paul Guitink (World Bank), Paul Barter (SUSTRAN, Malaysia), Pedro P Benvenuto (Cia do Metropolitano, São Paulo), Pedro Szasz (São Paulo), Philippe Bovy (École Polytechnique Fédérale de Lausanne), Rogerio Belda (ANTP, Brazil), Tom Rickert (Access Exchange International) and William A Pereira (ANTP, Brazil). I would especially like to thank Orlando Strambi (University of São Paulo) and Lourdes Diaz Olvera (LET, Lyon) for their detailed criticism on specific chapters. I would like to stress that despite their help and relevant contributions, the final content of the book is my entire and exclusive responsibility.

This work would not have been possible without the love, patience and support of my wife Clarice, my daughter Carolina and my son Eduardo.

PART 1
INTRODUCTION

1 INTRODUCTION

When I was a kid in the 1960s in São Paulo, I used to meet friends on the streets, to run, cycle and play football, like almost all other Brazilian kids. The school, the news stand and the grocery store were all within walking distance. Brazil was already a controversial country, with deep social and economic differences between social groups; but there was a sense of belonging, of community, of nation. Economic modernization began, and opportunities emerged for those with already-acquired educational and economic assets; social differences increased, along with violence. Then the people with cars came – they hit my younger brother, who stayed in hospital for 45 days and they injured and killed many more, among them friends and relatives. They forced us off the streets with our balls; today my son no longer plays there and I have to pay for a private club so that he may play safely. I have to have two cars to address my family's needs. To use public transport is an ordeal, and to use the streets as a pedestrian or cyclist is unthinkable for children. People in automobiles travel freely. Curb-sides are permanently filled with parked cars, and children and the elderly stay inside their homes. Road space has been delivered to other occupants and the city belongs to no one. While the environment is being destroyed and physical violence has become a major cause of urban fatalities, the economic elite is working to benefit from the globalization process and the middle class is struggling to join the venture. Brazil is now a rich country, but a large part of the population is still poor and deprived. It is a very complex development and it is not easy to explain. The only thing I know is that it has not made us happier or more humane.

This book analyses what has been happening in developing countries, taking as its prime subject the urban transport issue. It also discusses ways to improve current and future conditions, which affect hundreds of millions of people in their daily lives.

The interest in analysing transport problems in developing countries emerged in the 1960s and evolved at a fast pace as problems became increasingly severe. Several books and a large number of papers have been published so far. Most, especially in the early stages, were written by people from developed countries benefiting from the knowledge accumulated through experiences in their own countries, and trying to reflect their personal contact with problems in developing nations. People from the developing world have only recently been given the chance to voice their concerns, ideas and proposals; however, despite this large effort – beset by several difficulties – few comprehensive contributions have yet been proposed by them. This books intends to start filling this gap by offering a comprehensive explanation and proposals.

The approach is mainly sociological and political, in the sense of examining a complex set of interrelated factors that escape the strict technical or economic reasoning that forms the core of prevailing thinking. However, it is also technical and economic, in that transport involves important economic issues that require careful, competent technical treatment. It is not easy to combine such different perspectives due to an artificial separation that has been persistently constructed and encouraged between 'technical' and 'social' sciences. Consequently, literature combining them is scarce. One of the main challenges was therefore to combine such different 'knowledge worlds', by examining which contributions could yield a compound, comprehensive approach.

I firmly believe that the production of knowledge is a collective work, fuelled here and there by personal efforts, and that my individual contribution belongs to a never-ending chain. The final content of the book has greatly benefited from a large number of papers and books. The social and political approach to urban transport – and corresponding recommendations – may be understood as emerging from a knowledge-production chain that includes contributions (in chronological order) from Marx (19th century), Weber (first decades of the 20th century), Buchanan (1963), Hagestrand (1970), Illich (1974), Castells (1976), Healley (1977), Cardoso (1977), Kowarick (1979), Appleyard (1981), Harvey (1985), Henry and Figueroa (1985), Preteceille (1986), O'Donnel (1988), Newman and Kenworthy (1989), Dimitrou (1990) and Whitelegg (1997a). In addition to such comprehensive approaches, there are a large number of relevant ideas and proposals published in papers and articles, and extensively quoted in the book. The combination of all such intellectual undertakings and the final shape of the proposed social and political approach is my responsibility and my intellectual contribution.

When referring to 'developing countries' I am aware of all the problems and shortcomings related to such terminology, including the functionalist, 'evolutionary' and linear-thinking prejudice that is implicit in the opposition of 'developed' and 'developing'. Such philosophical and political concerns will not be treated here. For the sake of simplicity, I will use this widely-known term throughout the book. In using the term 'developing countries' I am referring not only to those countries with low average income levels but also to those with middle income levels and poor income and welfare distribution. Most have unstable political institutions and increasing social and economic problems, such as poverty, malnutrition, lack of adequate education and health services and facilities, inflation, unemployment and violence (although these two last conditions are also found in most developed countries). They may be said to correspond to the United Nations (UN) definition of 'less developed regions', whose urban population is estimated at 2 billion for the year 2000.

The reasons for raising concerns about urban transport conditions in developing countries are clear. Conditions remain highly inadequate for most of the population: low accessibility, poor public transport supply, accidents, discomfort, pollution and congestion are all negative features. Unbalanced economic growth and persistent poverty generate chaotic urban expansion, which – together with population growth – poses obstacles to effective urban and transport planning. Structural political and economic conditions maintain social exclusion, poverty and unemployment, and confine the decision-making process to selected groups. Traditional transport planning techniques, applied according to a 'black box' ethic, have been generating transport systems that propagate an unfair distribution of accessibility and reproduce safety and environmental inequities.[1] Private transportation has often been favoured, and local public transportation and non-motorized means have been neglected. These problems have been aggravated since the 1980s, in line with the economic restructuring and the fiscal crisis of the state, which inhibit the organization of an adequate supply of public transportation means for most of the people. They have also been aggravated by increased motorization.

On the technical side, transport infrastructure and services have been selected with the support of methodologies originated in industrialized countries in the 1950s and transferred to the developing world. These methodologies embrace mobility as a prime objective, adopt market and efficiency paradigms, and are used to propose transport solutions for hypothesized future conditions, based on the forecasting of social and economic variables. The results of these modelling procedures in the developing world have been widely disappointing. Presented as supposedly neutral techniques, they have been used as decision tools in closed arenas operating mostly within weakly democratized environments.

Although actual conditions vary significantly among developing countries, the various inequities concerning transportation and traffic conditions can be attributed to some common factors. In addition to the structural factors already mentioned, poor transportation conditions for the majority are maintained by policies supporting the dominance of the automobile at the expense of non-motorized means, and the submission of public transport to a market approach. The dominance of the automobile lies behind safety, environmental and space inequities, which derive from both transport policies (road and transport infrastructure) and traffic management (the division of space). The direct cause of the remaining inequities has to do with the economics of public transport operation, which implies low levels of accessibility and comfort for users.

Current conditions have often been treated as the 'natural' consequences of economic development, of people's choices in a free market context or of social and cultural characteristics such as gender, ethnicity and level of education. Therefore, current conditions are said to be 'fair', and the possibilities of change are said to rely simply on further economic development. Accordingly, increases in automobile or motorcycle use and decreases in public transport use also appear to be natural consequences of consumer decisions, therefore confirming road expansion policies as the most logical political answer to people's desires.

This book intends to provide alternative explanations of current conditions, given that most of the prevailing explanations are inadequate or inaccurate. Most do not fit developing countries' characteristics, and if they continue to be used in the traditional way they will support unfair and inequitable policies. Therefore, the assumptions that sustain traditional planning techniques have to be replaced by others that are better able to support socially and environmentally sound transportation policies. This book offers alternative approaches that emphasize the social and political aspects of transport policy and the use of the urban space.

First, we define how to distinguish a traditional technical approach to the problem from a social and political perspective, and analyse how social groups and classes interact with the environment to fulfil their social reproduction needs, seen as those activities that are needed to live and participate in society. The roles of the most relevant public and private actors in influencing transport policy are analysed – the state, the bureaucracy, the planners, social groups and classes, the private sector, the consultant sector, the real estate industry and the transportation industry. Actual road use is scrutinized through an analysis of the role played by people in traffic (the microphysics of traffic), considering how they interact and how benefits and harms are created and distributed. This analysis proposes several variables, such as accessibility, safety, fluidity, level of service, costs and environmental conditions. Physical and political conflicts that determine the use of the streets are discussed, and consequent limits to public policies are devised.

This book also explores new concepts that support the alternative approach. First, the city is understood as a built environment, to help unveil the relationships between society, space, transport and traffic. Second, the concept of the circulation environment is proposed, encompassing several physical, operational and symbolic features involved in the act of using space. Third, the relationship between social reproduction and transport is defined, with emphasis on the reproduction needs faced by people (related to age, income and gender) and the consequent transportation strategies adopted by them to fulfil their needs. Fourth, accessibility is defined as the main output of transport – and consequently as the main social and political issue to be investigated – as opposed to the simplistic idea of mobility (as expressed, in the technical view, by the number of trips made per person). Fifth, the relationship between the built environment and the means of collective consumption is defined, as a basis for analysing the use of roads as public assets. This particular definition reveals the unfair use of space and unveils the myth that has supported extensive road building based on the supposed collective nature of road use. In the final part of the methodological section, the book discuss the forms of provision, regulation, operation, control and use of transport means, aggregating all previous discussions and concepts into a broad framework for analysis.

Current conditions are analysed through ten dimensions: structural (economic and social developments), political (decision-making processes), ideological (the principles behind policies), economic (poverty and income distribution), institutional (planning agencies), technical (planning tools), technological (mode use), operational (transport supply), social (mobility and space) and environmental (accidents and pollution).

Alternative solutions to current problems are also analysed and proposed. Although long-term solutions rely on complex structural changes – such as the democratization of decision-making processes, the control of urban expansion and better income distribution – an improvement in current conditions may be achieved by several policies that are compatible with the proposed alternative approaches. An analysis of the social, economic and environmental aspects related to equity, urban development and sustainability supports most proposals. For practical purposes, proposals are discussed according to three main fields of intervention – urban planning, transportation planning and traffic management – that are meant to be worked out in a coordinated way. Public agencies should be open to community participation and public accountability, and the definition of transport and traffic programmes should be socially controlled.

The search for the most fruitful contributions has revealed that assumptions about increasing concerns on equity issues are correct, and such concerns are shared by people from all parts of the world. It is proposed in the book that equity is a situation in which people are granted satisfactory living conditions and opportunities in respect to socially-accorded services (for instance education, health and access to the city), irrespective of their individual physical, economic, social, religious or ethnic characteristics. It is different from equality, which represents the mere equalization of a formal right. An equitable condition is therefore superior to a formally equal one and the search for equity in transport is a challenge for planners in developing countries.

The main objective of this book is to offer tools for analysis and action, to help support an equity coalition among those concerned with the future of developing countries. In this respect, I would like to remark first on the countless anonymous people who have been working in their developing countries to confront inequity and injustice, and whose contribution is yet to be properly heard. Although a large number of studies has already been included in the book, numerous other important contributions remain unknown in face of the restricted access to publishing opportunities. I would also like to remind the reader of the work of several people and institutions from all parts of the developed world who have been giving their hearts and minds to the improvement of equity, justice and quality of life in the developing world. We need to develop together a universal, humane approach to guide our common future on Earth, and the work has just started.

PART 2
CURRENT CONDITIONS OF URBAN TRANSPORT IN DEVELOPING COUNTRIES

2 CURRENT TRANSPORT AND TRAFFIC CONDITIONS IN DEVELOPING COUNTRIES

INTRODUCTION

The purpose of this chapter is to provide a broad view of the current transport and traffic conditions in developing countries, drawing extensively on previous research.

These data should not induce in the reader a false impression of similarity between developing countries. As explained in the introduction, developing countries vary in their social, political, economic and cultural contexts, with implications for the decision-making process, transport and traffic policies and the actual travel patterns of people. However, as will be shown, developing countries do share some common characteristics with respect to transport and traffic conditions that may yield a tentative classification. Despite being difficult to summarize, these similarities will be explored in this section and in its conclusion.

The following data display a wide variety of conditions to be found in developing countries' cities. The objective is to highlight the most revealing data, those able to provide a better understanding of the issue. Among them are, on the supply side, road infrastructure and vehicle fleets and, on the demand side, general conditions in accessing the city, such as the use of each transport mode, the purpose of trips, travel times, public transport vehicular internal conditions, transport expenses, speed, accidents and air pollution. Unfortunately there are no detailed or comprehensive data for all such characteristics, and so I have used those that appeared more reliable and pertinent for the purposes of the book.

THE AVAILABILITY OF TRANSPORT INFRASTRUCTURE AND MEANS

The availability of transport will be analysed here in reference to both road infrastructure and to vehicle availability.

Road infrastructure conditions play a vital role in defining transport and traffic conditions, for both non-motorized and motorized means. Although obvious, considering the widely neglected approach to pedestrian needs in developing countries, it is always important to remember that pavements are vital for pedestrians, while carriageways are used by all vehicles.

There are several ways of analysing the quality of pavements in cities: their general provision, their capacity relative to pedestrian traffic, their quality and their upkeep. Unfortunately, there are no comprehensive, city-wide data on this matter as pedestrian traffic has been almost entirely neglected within a motorized, automobile-skewed approach to the issue. What is conveyed by the available literature is the general lock of provision of pavements in developing countries and their poor state of repair. In the absence of pavements, pedestrians use carriageways, often under very dangerous and uncomfortable conditions (Wright, 1992).

Road conditions may be examined through the type of surface and the total road area supplied in a city – as compared, for instance, to its urbanized area. This has several drawbacks, as it is the social and economic conditions of people – and not the urbanized area itself – that determine transport demand, and the actual traffic mix has a direct influence on the roads' carrying capacity. However, as reliable data are seldom available, Table 2.1 summarizes how different are the road supply rates of cities all over the world.

Table 2.1 *Road supply as a percentage of urbanized area*

City	Road space (%)
Developing countries	
Kolkata (India)[1]	6.4
Shanghai (China)[2]	7.4
Bangkok (Thailand)[3]	11.4
Seoul (South Korea)[4]	20.0
Delhi (India)[1]	21.0
São Paulo (Brazil)[5]	21.0
Developed countries	
New York (US)[4]	22.0
London (UK)[4]	23.0
Tokyo (Japan)[4]	24.0
Paris (France)[4]	25.0

Sources: (1) Chakraborti, 1997; (2) Lu and Ye, 1998; (3) Kenworthy, 1997; (4) Kim and Gallent, 1998; (5) author's calculation

Road surface is especially important for public transport use, both in terms of speed and also for safety in bad weather. Most cities in the developing world have low percentages of paved roads; in Logo (in Togo), 37 per cent of streets are not paved and 63 per cent have no drainage system (Akapko, 1998).

Road width is also important for capacity purposes. In most developing countries roads are narrow, especially in old downtown areas, which are frequently the most trafficked; in Hanoi, for example, only 12 per cent of roads are wider than 11m (Cusset, 1997). In the Beijing planned area (650sqm), 60 per cent of roads are less than 7m wide; when all roads are considered (2069km), 750km may be used only by non-motorized transport (Sit, 1996). Peripheral areas are often less well served than central ones, especially when poor neighbourhoods occupy hills and mountains. In Caracas and Rio de Janeiro a large proportion of poor people live in slums built over the mountains, where alleys play the role of streets, most of them less than 4m wide.

The manner in which road infrastructure is used by different modes is another way of assessing the quality of transport systems. Preferential treatment for non-motorized and public transport vehicles is vital for ensuring good travelling conditions; this is virtually absent from most cities in developing countries. One of the most important barriers faced by non-motorized transport is a hostile street environment (Replogle, 1992; World Bank, 1995). As regards buses, most large cities have no priority schemes at all, and the few that have often suffer from coverage and operational drawbacks; in São Paulo, of the 500km of main road with high bus flows, just 43km have priority schemes (CET, 1997).

People in developing countries use a wide array of vehicles. The most basic, humane form of transport is walking. Bicycles and similar non-motorized vehicles are used when distances or the frequency of trips become difficult to manage on foot, provided that people have access to such vehicles. Motorized transport is even less accessible, considering the costs of purchase, maintainance and operation. For such reasons, global mechanization and motorization rates vary widely.

If we take the human body as the main vehicle for transport then the world fleet is basically the entire human race, except for very young children, some people with physical disabilities and some elderly people. As regards the second main vehicle, people make extensive use of bicycles and bicycle-like vehicles, such as the pedal rickshaw in Asian countries. These vehicles are used to carry both passengers and merchandise (Hathway, 1985; Hierli, 1993).

Table 2.2 shows that in some Asian cities, non-motorized vehicles constitute between 50 per cent and almost 100 per cent of the transport. Cycle rickshaws may contribute more than 50 per cent of the transport, as in Dhaka, Bangladesh. In some cities, motorcycles are dominant.

Table 2.2 *Non-motorized and motorized vehicle fleet, selected cities in developing countries with high non-motorized vehicle use*

City	Non-motorized (%)				Motorized (%)		
	Bicycles	Cycle rickshaws	Animal carts	Total	Buses	Motorcycles	Other motor vehicles
Phnom Penh	47.1	4.2	0.2	51.5	0.0	43.6	4.9
Hanoi (Vietnam)	84.6	0.4	0.0	85.0	0.0	10.8	4.1
Dhaka	10.7	53.3	0.0	64.0	1.3	16.0	18.8
Kanpur (India)	54.7	3.5	0.6	58.8	0.1	18.6	22.4
Shanghai	95.9	1.4	0.0	97.3	0.3	0.5	1.9
Surabaya (Indonesia)	40.1	4.6	0.0	44.7	0.3	38.7	16.3
Penang (Malaysia)	49.6	0.6	0.0	50.2	0.0	29.0	20.8

Source: World Bank, 1995

The possession of vehicles by a household is strongly related to income (Rao and Sharma, 1990). In Asian and African countries, where bicycles, motorcycles

and cars are used in most cities, the majority of poor households have no vehicle at all. Motorized vehicles are found in higher quantities in wealthier
households (see Tables 2.3 and 2.4).

Table 2.3 *Vehicle ownership and household income, India, 1988*

Household	Percentage of households with		
Monthly income (rupees)	Cycle only	MTW* only	Car only
<1000	37	12	
1001–2500	13	39	1
2501–5000	11	53	10
>5000	2	64	35
All	13	45	15

Source: Twari, 1997
* MTW = motorized two-wheeler

Table 2.4 *Vehicle ownership and household income, two African cities, 1992*

Vehicle ownership[1]	Poor households (%)		Rich households (%)	
	Bamako[2]	Ouaga[3]	Bamako	Ouaga
No vehicle at all	37	8	21	3
One or more bicycles	25	62	16	48
One or more motorcycles	45	47	59	94
One or more cars	2	5	34	29

(1) Totals may exceed 100 per cent due to multiple household ownership; (2) In Mali;
(3) Ouagadougou in Burkina Faso
Source: Diaz Olvera, Plat and Pochet, 1997

If motorized vehicles are considered separately, wide variations also appear
(see Table 2.5). Motorcycles may dominate (as in Delhi, with 70 per cent), as
may cars (as in São Paulo, with 80 per cent). Trucks are less numerous than
private vehicles, although they represent 41 per cent of the fleet in Beijing.
Public transport vehicles are always a small portion of the transport, although

Table 2.5 *Motorized vehicles, selected large cities in developing countries*

City and date	Fleet (000)	Percentage of the fleet				
		Motorcycles	Cars	Buses	Trucks	Other
Bangkok, 1990[1]	2046	36	29	16	16	3
Jakarta, 1996[2]	3387	52	29	9	10	0
Delhi, 1996[3]	2097	70	23	1	5	0
São Paulo,1997[4]	4350	12	80	1	7	0
Beijing, 1990[5]	0384	29	26	na	41	4

Sources: (1) Du Pont and Egan, 1997; (2) Abubakar, 1998; (3)Twari, 1997; (4) DETRAN,
1997; (5) Sit, 1996, figures adapted from Table 6

Table 2.6 *Global car ownership, 1993*

Region	Cars/1000 pop
South Asia	3
Africa	14
East Asia & Pacific	29
Middle East	45
LA* & Caribbean	68
Central and Eastern Europe	72
OECD (excluding the US)	366
US	561

Source: World Bank, 1997
* LA = Latin America

Table 2.7 *Global vehicle ownership, selected countries*

Country	GNP/capita (US$)	Veh/1000 Pop	Private motorized vehicles (%)		
			MTW	Cars	Total
Japan	34,630	640	20	58	78
US	24,780	740	2	88	90
Germany	23,980	570	9	89	98
France	23,420	520	10	87	97
UK	18,340	410	3	86	89
Australia	18,000	610	3	76	79
South Korea	8260	206	24	33	57
Brazil	4400	190	10	82	92
Malaysia	3140	340	56	34	90
Thailand	2140	190	66	16	82
The Philippines	950	32	26	28	54
Indonesia	810	58	69	15	84
Sri Lanka	600	50	60	13	73
China	530	21	40	24	64
India	320	30	67	14	81
Vietnam	210	27	91	9	100

Source: Mohan and Twari, 1998, for all countries except Brazil (ANFAVEA, 1997)

they have a much greater passenger-carrying capacity. Public transport vehicles display a wide range of technologies and capacities; they may be adapted trucks, or small (mini), medium or large buses.

Global motorization comparisons

When the vehicle fleets of developing countries are compared to those of more developed nations, wide differences appear. Table 2.6 shows that rates of car ownership are very low everywhere except for in the US or other OECD countries, where the car ownership rate may be eight times higher than in Latin America and the Caribbean. Table 2.7 shows that the rate of vehicle ownership also varies widely, showing a strong relationship with income per capita. It also shows that most of the fleet is comprised by either motorized two-wheelers or automobiles, once trucks and buses correspond to a minor share.

Despite the apparently increasing relevance of the automobile, developing countries can usually be adequately classified as either non-motorized (especially in Africa) or basically reliant on motorized modes (as in Asia and Latin America). Within the latter group, the main difference concerns the proportion of public versus private motorization – that is, buses, two wheelers or cars.

MOBILITY AND THE USE OF TRANSPORT MODES

Mobility is measured by the number of trips made per person per day. As mobility increases with income, mobility rates in developing countries are lower than in developed countries. At the global scale, the mobility rate of urban populations in European countries ranges from 2.9 daily trips per person in Austria to 3.6 in Sweden (Bieber et al, 1992), while figures for Brazilian cities settle at around 2 trips per person per day (CMSP, 1998) and those for very low income societies may be just one trip per person per day (Sharma and Gupta, 1998). The higher mobility rates of high-income earners in developing countries (as in São Paulo) equals the average mobility of people in developed countries.

The use of transport modes may be examined by calculating the share of daily trips made using each mode. This is known as the modal split, and it varies widely. Modal splits are related to historical, social, economic and cultural characteristics, but the key issues are the balance between modes, and how the split changes over time (Godard, 1997). In addition, the often biased approach of traditional transport planning neglects or ignores data on non-motorized transport; for example, data on pedestrian trips are either absent or are collected on a limited basis – for example, only for trips longer than 500m – leading to underestimates. Therefore, modal split figures must be treated carefully. Despite such limitations, it is important to try to identify broad patterns and to classify cities into groups, in order to understand conditions in developing countries.

Three main groups may be devised. First, cities with predominantly non-motorized trips: Bamako, Bobo Doiulasso, Beijing, Dakar, Hanoi, Jaipur, Havana, Ouagadougou and Yaoundé. Second, cities in which public transport accounts for the majority of trips: Abidjan, Bouake, Buenos Aires, Caracas, Pretoria and Santiago. Third, cities in which motorized private modes play an important role: Caracas, Hanoi, Ouagadougou, and São Paulo. Cities may also be classified according to the type of private motorized transport they have: Hanoi and Ouagadougou rely mainly on motorcycles, while in Buenos Aires, Caracas, São Paulo and Pretoria, cars play a predominant role. If motorized trips alone are considered, another set of data is available for analysis.

Table 2.9 shows that in the first 16 cities, more than 50 per cent of motorized trips are made by public transport. Few have trains and underground railways, and the bus is the main mode, as is the case in most developing world cities. Care must be taken when analysing the role of the bus, as taxis may refer to shared vehicles that play the same role as buses: they are dominant in cities

Table 2.8 *Modal split of daily trips, selected cities in developing countries*

City	Modal split (percentage of daily trips)			
	NMT*	**Public**	**Private** (motorized)	**Other**
Bobo Dioulasso, Burkina Faso[a1]	87	3	10	0
Alger, Algeria, 1990[2]	67	18	15	0
Jaipur, India[a3]	66	21	12	1
Bamako, Mali, 1984[4]	63	12	26	0
Beijing, China, 1992[5]	62	33	5	0
Havana, Cuba, 1998[6]	57	27	6	11
Yaoundé, Cameroon, 1982[4]	55	22	23	0
Hanoi, Vietnam, 1995[7]	54	4	42	0
Ouagadougou, Burkina Faso[a8]	52	3	45	0
Dakar, Senegal, 1987[4]	50	32	17	0
Douala, Cameroon, 1982[4]	36	37	27	0
Cairo, Egypt, 1998[9]	36	47	17	0
São Paulo, Brazil, 1997[10]	35	33	31	1
Abdijan, Côte d'Ïvoire, 1988[4]	30	58	12	0
Bouake, Côte d'Ïvoire[a1]	27	62	11	0
Santiago, Chile, 1991[11]	20	56	16	9
Caracas, Venezuela, 1991[12]	16	50	34	1
Pretoria, South Africa, 1996[13]	11	57	30	2
Buenos Aires, Argentina, 1992[14]	9	60	24	7

(a) survey date not mentioned in the reference
* NMT = non-motorized transport
Sources: (1) Gueye and Bamas, 1994; (2) Matouk and Abeille, 1994; (3) Hierli, 1993; (4) Akinbami and Fadare, 1997; (5) Spencer and Andong, 1996; (6) Magdaleno et al, 1999; (7) Cusset, 1997; (8) Cusset and Sirpe, 1994; (9) Barge and Chesnais, 2000; (10) CMSP, 1998; (11) Ortúzar et al, 1993; (12) Garcia and Ocaña, 1992; (13) Cameron, 1998; (14) Rivasplata, 1992

Table 2.9 *Modal split of daily motorized trips (%), selected cities in developing countries*

City	Public transport					Private transport		
	Train	Metro	Bus	Taxi	Total	Cars	Motorcycles	Total
Beijing, China, 1992		7	78	0	85	13	0	13
Bouake, Côte d'Ïvoire[a]			57	28	85	15	0	15
Rio de Janeiro, Brazil, 1994	4	3	78	0	85	15	0	15
Abdijan, Côte d'Ïvoire, 1988			73	10	83	16	1	17
Santiago, Chile, 1991		9	67	2	78	22	0	22
Colombo, Sri Lanka, 1995	6	0	63	9	77	23	0	23
Seoul, South Korea, 1991		14	43	18	75	25	0	25
Cairo, Egypt, 1998		17	19	36	72	20	1	21
Mexico City, Mexico, 1994		12	21	39	72	28	0	28
Buenos Aires, Argentina, 1992	8	4	59	0	71	29	0	29
Pretoria, South Africa, 1996	22	0	23	21	66	34	0	34
Dakar, Senegal, 1987			52	12	64	32	2	34

Table 2.9 (*Continued*)

City	Public transport			Private transport				
	Train	Metro	Bus	Taxi	Total	Cars	Motorcycles	Total
Lagos, Nigeria, 1985					63	35	3	38
Caracas, Venezuela, 1991		19	41	0	60	41	0	41
Douala, Cameroon, 1982			27	31	58	22	20	42
São Paulo, Brazil, 1997	3	8	40	0	51	47	1	48
Yaoundé, Cameroon, 1982			16	33	49	49	2	51
Bobo Dioulasso, Burkina Faso[a]				23	23	77	0	77
Hanoi, Vietnam, 1995					9	2	89	91
Ouagadougou, Burkina Faso[a]			6	0	6	12	81	93

(a) survey date not mentioned in the reference
Source: as in Table 2.10 plus Rio (Ribeiro and Balassiano, 1997); Mexico (Cervero, 1998);
Seoul (Kim and Gallent, 1998)

such as Cairo, Douala, Mexico City and Yaoundé. In the last four cities more
than 50 per cent of motorized trips are made by private transport. Car is the
dominant private mode in most cases, while motorcycles are the main mode
in Douala, Hanoi and Ouagadougou. Again, the share of motorcycles must
to be examined carefully, since it appears that in some Asian and African cases
the modal split data may have not included them.

The split between public and private motorized travel shows (Figure 2.1)
that there is a remarkable difference between the cities. While in Beijing 85
per cent of motorized trips are made with public modes, this figure changes
to 51 per cent in São Paulo and just 6 per cent in Ouagadougou, where there
is a large use of motorcycles.

Trip purposes

Trip purpose varies according to several social, cultural and economic factors. Universally work and school seem to be the most important purposes,
regardless of geography and wealth (Table 2.10).

Table 2.10 *Trip purpose, selected cities*

City (country)	Trip purpose (%)			
	Work	**School**	**Work and school**	**Other**
Alger (Algeria)[1]	25	50	75	25
Bangkok (Thailand)[2]	34	18	52	48
Kolkata (India)[3]	44	29	73	28
Delhi (India)[3]	46	31	77	25
Hanoi (Vietnam)[4]	45	19	64	36
Jakarta (Indonesia)[2]	39	20	59	41
Santiago (Chile)[5]	36	32	68	32
São Paulo (Brazil)[6]	41	34	75	25

Sources: (1) Matouk and Abeille, 1994; (2) Shimazaki et al, 1994; (3) Datta, 1998; (4)
Cusset, 1997; (5) Ortúzar and Ivelic, 1997; (6) CMSP, 1998

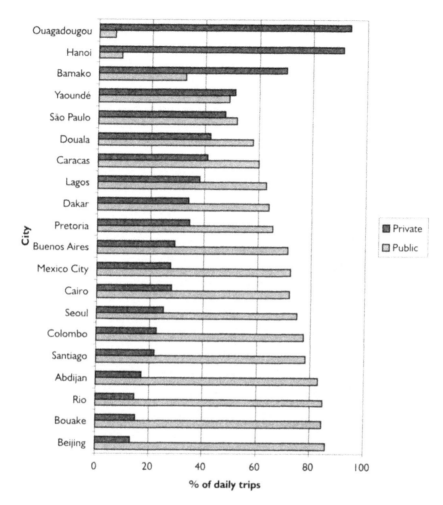

Figure 2.1 *Daily motorized trips by public and private transport, selected cities in developing countries*

CURRENT TRAVEL CONDITIONS

Accessibility

Accessibility, defined as the degree of ease with which people get to desired destinations, is the most direct measure of the positive effects of a transport system. In its simplest form, accessibility can be represented by the number (quantitative) and the nature (qualitative) of the destinations that can be reached by a person. A similar, although indirect, measure is the density of the infrastructure and transport supply that impacts on travel conditions: pavements for pedestrians, public transport lines for captive users, and roads for people with access to private motorized vehicles

In a more elaborate analysis, accessibility can also be evaluated through the computation of the costs involved in travelling, such as money and time. When both cost components are translated into monetary terms (by attributing monetary values to time) one arrives at the 'generalized cost' that represents accessibility, a standard procedure in prevailing modelling techniques (Oppenheim, 1995). When time alone is considered, cost can be represented in a simple form as the total time taken to travel from origin to destination, or by separating the total time into the walking, waiting, travelling and transferring portions of the trip. Both figures are given below for selected cities. As there are no 'ideal' rates, values are depicted by comparing different modes of motorized transport, especially public and private means.

The total travel time between origin and destination varies markedly between motorized modes, depending on the access to each mode and the spatial distribution of activities. The wide array of door-to-door travel times in a large city such as São Paulo makes such differences very clear (Table 2.11). It may be seen that between the motorized modes there is a 1 to 4 ratio for motorcycles versus trains. Trips by private modes always take much less time than trips by public modes, and non-motorized trips correspond to the lowest travel times due to the shorter distances.

Table 2.11 *Door-to-door travel times, all modes, São Paulo, 1997*

Mode	Door-to-door travel time (min) (including transfers)
Train	93
Subway	77
Bus	56
Minibus[1]	37
Auto	28
Taxi[2]	26
Motorcycle	25
Bike	23
Foot	15

1 illegal paratransit
2 individual use only
Source: CMSP, 1998

The automobile is the fastest mode, as the walking time to the vehicle is usually low, travel speeds are high, and average distances are short. As previously seen, the bus is the main public transport mode in large cities in developing countries. Hence, an important performance comparison is between bus and automobile travel times. Table 2.12 shows that the average door-to-door travel time by bus may be double that of the car. It is important to emphasize that trip purposes and distances may be very different between the two modes.

It is also important to compare relative speeds. Average speeds on urban roads depend on several physical and operational characteristics as well as the particular vehicle mix. There is no comprehensive survey of average speed in most major cities of the developing world, unlike European and North American cities. Few large cities have been reporting general traffic speeds.

Table 2.12 *Car and bus travel times*

City (country)	Travel times (min)[a]		
	Bus	**Car**	**Ratio bus/car**
Alger (Algeria), 1990[1]	56	30	1.9
Caracas (Venezuela), 1982[2]	54	36	1.5
Mexico City (Mexico), 1994[3]	50	35	1.4
São Paulo (Brazil), 1997[4]	56	28	2

(a) door-to-door travel times, average for all trips
Sources: (1) Matouk and Abeille, 1994; (2) Ministerio de Transportes y Comunicaciones, 1982; (3) Connolly, 1999; (4) CMSP, 1998

In cities with high road capacity when compared with traffic demand, such as Brasilia, automobile speeds in peak hours may be as high as 45km/h (IPEA/ANTP, 1998). This may be a common situation for most of the medium-sized cities in the developing world with no serious topographic or road restrictions. However, in larger cities conditions are not that good, as a result of increasing congestion. In Seoul, the daily average car speed was 23.2km/h in 1994 (Kim and Gallent, 1998). In Beijing, a survey of the ring roads in 1985 revealed car speeds ranging from 9.3km/h to 28.8km/h. In São Paulo, the average car speed in 1997 was 27km/h (morning peak) and 17km/h (evening peak). In Bangkok, speeds in the central area are close to 8–10km/h (Daniere, 1995). In Shanghai, speeds were about 14km/h in 1995 (Lu and Ye, 1998). Motorcycle speeds are presumably higher, as they have more freedom to percolate through stationary vehicles. Bus speeds usually fall in the 10–20km/h range (Table 2.13).

Table 2.13 *Average speed of buses, peak hours, several cities*

City (country)	Bus speed (km/h)
Bangkok[1] (Thailand)	11.5
Cairo (Egypt)[2]	17.5
Caracas (Venezuela)[3]	16.3
Curitiba (Brazil)[4]	20.5
Havana (Cuba)[5]	18.0
Nairobi (Kenya)[6]	11.5
S C Sierra (Bolivia)[7]	15.7
Seoul (South Korea)[8]	18.4
São Paulo (Brazil)[4]	14.5

Sources: (1) Daniere, 1995 (daily average); (2) Abras, 1999; (3) Sanánez and Da Silva, 1999; (4) ANTP/IPEA, 1998; (5) Magdaleno et al, 1999; (6) Koster and Gerwin, 2000; (7) Figueroa and Pizarro, 1998; (8) Kim and Gallent, 1998

Four important partial times are included in this overall accessibility indicator: walking time to the vehicle, waiting time, running time, and transfer time (in the case of transferring between two services). Walking time reflects the average distance between a person and the vehicle the person intends to use.

Table 2.14 *Spatial coverage of public transport lines, selected Brazilian cities*

City	Population (10³)	Length of streets with transit/ length of all-purpose streets
Santo Andre	400	1:5.6
Campo Grande	700	1:6.3
Porto Alegre	1100	1:3.2
Ribeirão Preto	300	1:4.7

Source: survey made by the author with official local maps

Table 2.15 *Walking and waiting times of bus users according to area of residence, Rio de Janeiro, 1989*

Boarding area	Walking time (min)	Waiting time (min)
Core	10.4	6.4
Immediate periphery	12.8	12.5
Intermediate periphery	17.3	19.1

Source: Câmara, 1994

In the case of public transport, this distance reflects the average distribution of lines and bus/train stops. In the case of private transport, taxis and trucks, it reflects the availability of streets and parking/loading conditions.

Usually, access time to cars is low – around one minute – since many owners have private spaces at home in which to park the car, and parking availability at the destination is also often high (except in dense commercial centres). Access time to buses is always higher, due to the spatial distribution of bus stops and the waiting time at the bus stop. For standard bus-stop spacing of 400 to 500m in a grid-pattern network of bus lines, walking times usually fall in the range of 5 to 10 minutes. For a service frequency of 15 minutes, waiting time is about 7 minutes. Therefore, total access time turns out to be about 15 minutes. Sparsely supplied networks and low frequency services may substantially increase such figures, especially in peripheral areas. In Harare (Zimbabwe), the average waiting time in 1988 was 36 minutes (Maunder and Mbara, 1994). In Nairobi, average waiting time during the morning and evening peaks at selected bus terminals was 16 and 14 minutes for minibuses and up to 26 minutes for regular buses (Koster and Gerwin, 2000). In Delhi, several routes have waiting times well above 20 minutes (Armstrong-Wright, 1993).

Table 2.14 shows the ratio between the supply of all-purpose streets and the supply of public transport lines. The better accessibility conditions for those with access to private transport is clear. This crude accessibility rate shows unequivocally that public transport users face worse general conditions in terms of access to the city space. In addition, the conditions faced by transit users are not evenly distributed. As transit lines are more dense in the central areas, peripheral regions are less well served. Lines linking neighbourhoods are often rare, for most lines connect distant areas to the centre of the city. Hence, people living far away from central areas have their accessibility to transport further impaired. In Rio de Janeiro, a study found that walking times and waiting times to get access to buses are greater for those living on the outskirts than for those living in more central areas (Table 2.15).

With respect to running time, cars travel much more easily through the highway system than buses. The difference is due both to the stop–start nature of bus operation, and to its poor management in most developing country cities (such as lack of enforcement of parking regulations, or passenger-congested bus stops).

Transfer time is also an important part of the problem. In all cities, many people do not find services linking their origin and destination directly. In addition, many cities do not have any physical or operational arrangements for convenient transfers, and so the users must manage these by themselves, which implies discomfort and uncertainty. In São Paulo, a significant proportion of users (22.2 per cent) have to combine two or more modes to get to their final destination, especially when travelling to work. In Beijing, 25 per cent of bus and trolleybus trips require vehicle change, and 37 per cent of total time is spent walking and waiting (Sit, 1996).

The ultimate effect of all transport-related difficulties for captive public transport users is that a long journey is inevitable. This is aggravated in peripheral areas, where many people may spend more than 12 hours outside their homes.

Comfort

As regards walking, the lack of pavements and their poor condition result in highly uncomfortable trips for pedestrians. The same may be said about non-motorized vehicle use, which is severely hampered by the lack of proper right-of-way, appropriate surface conditions and traffic signs.

As regards public transport, to the inferior conditions of overall accessibility, one must add bus loading conditions, which often hinder people from boarding at the desired time and impose extremely uncomfortable trips. Overcrowded vehicles are a daily reality in almost every developing country (Dimitriou, 1990; UN, 1989). While the international figure for daily patronage per vehicle is around 500–1000 passengers in acceptable conditions, in Bombay each bus operated by the main public company carries 2188 passengers per day (UNCHS, 1992) and in Cairo each bus carries 1462 people (Abras, 1999). Although prevailing speeds influence the number of trips that can be made and hence the daily patronage of the vehicle, this is indeed indirect proof of overcrowded conditions. In São Paulo, all private companies providing bus transport in 1984 carried a large percentage of people travelling under unacceptable conditions in the peak hour; some companies carried up to 84 per cent of passengers in such conditions (CET, 1985).

Transport expenses

People may spend money on either private or public transport means. On the private side, low-income earners in several countries use bicycles or motorcycles, while those on a high income use cars. In all cases, the main costs are for purchase, maintenance and operation. On the public side, the most-used vehicle is the bus, and the only cost for the user is the fare.

The costs of owning and using a non-motorized vehicle are usually low. Table 2.16 shows how such costs vary in some Asian cities. The costs associated with the bicycle are very low in several countries, although the purchasing price is high in some of them. Bicycles may be purchased for less than US$100 in several countries. In Beijing, the cost was about ¥300 in 1991, corresponding to the monthly salary of a regular worker (Sit, 1996). Motorcycles are much more expensive, and cars fall into a price range that can be afforded only by the wealthy.

Table 2.16 *General costs to own and use vehicles in Asian cities (US$ 1992 values)*

City	Purchase of a new vehicle (US$)			Annual operating and maintenance (US$)		
	Bicycle	**Motorcycle**	**Car**	**Bicycle**	**Motorcycle**	**Car**
Phnom-Penh (Cambodia)	40	1690	25,100	3	174	600
Hanoi (Vietnam)	36	1660	35,800	n/a		
Dhaka (Bangladesh)	61	n/a	n/a	n/a		
Kanpur (India)	53	1200	6,400	15	349	1000
Shanghai (China)	60	2380	34,000	n/a		
Surabaya (Indonesia)	138	1480	24,600	20	183	820
Manila (The Philippines)	176	1760	31,300	16	147	1130
Chiang Mai (Thailand)	178	1520	19,800	16	239	1280
Penang (Malaysia)	180	2000	16,000	20	380	2230

Source: World Bank, 1995

Considering that costs and fares vary within cities and countries, the best way to analyse transport expenses is by comparing them to family income. Absolute transport expenses increase with income, as higher-income families are more mobile and use faster or more expensive modes. However, most studies show that the proportion of these expenses in total family income tends to decrease with increasing wealth (Kranton, 1991). While low-income families may spend as much as 20 per cent of their total income on transport, wealthy families may expend just 5 per cent.

Table 2.17 shows that in São Paulo, the percentage of transport expenses is low in very low-income households and increases sharply with income, due to the use of cars; the proportion of such expenses decreases with increasing income, within a 1:4 ratio between the extreme income levels. In the case of Accra (Table 2.18), relative expenditures increase between the first and second income strata, and then decrease as income increases.

Table 2.17 *Absolute and relative transport expenses by income level,*
São Paulo, 1997

Income (Reais$/month)	Absolute expenses (Reais$/month)			Relative expenses
	Public[1]	**Private**[2]	**Total**	**(% of income)**
0–250	14.1	34.6	48.7	39
250–500	25.7	60.0	85.7	22.8
500–1000	35.1	112.0	147.1	19.6
1000–1800	44.0	203.6	247.6	17.7
1800–3600	37.9	327.7	365.6	13.5
> 3600	27.6	492.2	519.8	9.6

(1) all modes, considering that 50 per cent of users receive travel vouchers from employers; (2) automobile
Source: CMSP, 1998

Table 2.18 *Transport expenses and family income, Accra*

Earnings/month	Daily expenditure (% of total)
0–10,000	13.7
11,000–25,000	24.2
26,000–40,000	12
41,000–60,000	11.6
> 60,000	4.3

Source: Kwakye et al, 1997

Safety

Traffic accidents are a major problem in both developed and developing countries, and constitute the most relevant environmentally related transport problem in the latter. The traditional approaches to quantifying and analysing the problem in developing countries use inappropriate or misleading rates, as will be discussed in Chapter 15; despite such drawbacks, some general figures about the issue are presented below, to allow for an initial comprehension of the problem.

The first important data from the social point of view are the absolute number of traffic fatalities and their relationship to social data. A large number of fatalities is found in several countries, both developed and developing (Table 2.19). When overall accident rates are analysed, sharp differences appear between the countries. In respect of fatalities per 10,000 vehicles, developed countries present rates of around 3 to 6, while rates in developing countries may be as high as 141, such as in Nigeria in 1980. Such extreme values may refer to particular, short phases of intense vehicle growth. With fatalities per population, the differences are less marked.

Second, recent tendencies are of great concern, especially in countries were motorized transport has been growing rapidly. Between 1968 and 1985, while road accident fatalities decreased by around 20 per cent in developed countries,

Table 2.19 *Traffic fatalities and rates, selected countries*

Country	Fatalities/ year	Fatalities/ 10,000 veh[a]	Fatalities/ 100,000 pop[a]
Developed			
US, 1995[1]	41,798	3	16
France, 1984[2]	11,685	6	21
Germany, 1984[2]	10,199	4	16
Japan, 1984[2]	9262	2	8
Developing			
Índia, 1996[3]	69,800	21	8
China, 1994[1]	66,322	82	6
Brazil, 1995[4]	27,886	11	17
South Korea, 1995[5]	10,323	12	23
South Africa, 1992[6]	10,142	18	32
Nigeria, 1980[7]	8936	141	13
Thailand, 1992[8]	8184	9	14
Poland, 1992[9]	6946	6	18
Mexico, 1994[10]	5115	4	5
Bangladesh, 1992[11]	2317	61	2
Czech Republic, 1997[12]	1600	4	15

Sources: (1) Pucher, 1999; (2) OECD, 1986; (3) Mohan, 1999; (4); Denatran, 1996, correcting original data with additional data from São Paulo; (5) Lee, 1998; (6) Wise, 1994; (7) Barrett, 1988; (8) Tanaboriboon, 1994; (9) Reksnis, 1995; (10) BID, 1998; (11) Quium, 1995; (12) Mikulik, 1999
(a) approximate values; rates compiled from the authors, or computed using UN data on population (UNCHS, 1996)

they increased by 300 per cent in Africa and by almost 200 per cent in Asia (TRRL, 1991). Some large developing countries such as China, India and Brazil have been experiencing high increases over recent decades.

The third relevant question from a social perspective relates to who is harmed by traffic accidents. Studies made with data from the 1970s in four developing countries show that pedestrians, cyclists and motorcyclists are the most vulnerable groups, accounting for 56 to 74 per cent of fatalities (Hill and Jacobs, 1981). This is the main difference between developing and developed countries (Table 2.20).

Table 2.20 *Pedestrian fatalities as a percentage of total traffic fatalities, several regions*

Region	Pedestrian fatalities (% of total)
Europe/US	20
Latin America	60
Africa	45
Middle East	51
Asia	42

Source: Guitink and Flora, 1995, using data summarized by the World Bank

Environmental conditions

Air pollution has already reached extremely high levels in several large cities in developing countries, exceeding the limits recommended by the World Health Organization (WHO) (Table 2.21). The cities differ in the nature of the air pollution, as well as in the excess pollution produced, due to the specific characteristics of pollutant sources and the fuels used. However, in most cases transport is the main source of pollution (World Bank, 1996).

Table 2.21 *Large cities in developing countries exceeding WHO pollution levels*

City	Pollutant concentration exceeding WHO recommended levels[a]					
	Lead[1]	CO[2]	Nox[3]	Ozone	SO[2]	Suspended particles
Bangkok	<2					>2
Beijing				<2	>2	>2
Bombay						>2
Buenos Aires		n/a	n/a	n/a	n/a	<2
Cairo	>2	<2				>2
Kolcata		n/a		n/a		>2
Delhi				n/a		>2
Jakarta	<2	<2		<2		>2
Karachi	>2	n/a	n/a	n/a		>2
London		<2				
Los Angeles		<2	<2	>2		<2
Manila	<2	n/a	n/a	n/a		>2
Mexico City	<2	>2	<2	>2	>2	>2
Moscow		<2	>2			<2
New York		<2		<2		
Rio de Janeiro			n/a	n/a	<2	<2
São Paulo	<2	<2	<2	>2		<2
Seoul					>2	>2
Shanghai	n/a	n/a	n/a	n/a	<2	>2
Tokyo				>2		

(a) Figures show concentration surpassing limits by a factor of up to 2 (<2) or by more than 2 (>2).
(1) 90–100 per cent from transport sources; (2) 80–100 per cent from transport sources; (3) 60–70 per cent from transport sources
Source: World Bank, 1996, and UN, 1996

Most pollutants are related to serious respiratory diseases and to several forms of cancer. One of the most harmful pollutant at the local level is suspended particulate matter (SPM). Table 2.22 shows that SPM concentration is much higher in large cities of the developing world than in developed cities.

Table 2.22 *Average SPM concentration, cities in developing and developed countries*

Developed countries			Developing countries		
Country	**City**	**SPM**[a]	**Country**	**City**	**SPM**[a]
Australia	Sidney	138	China	Beijing	395
Belgium	Brussels	24		Shanghai	240
Canada	Montreal	59	Ghana	Accra	150
	Toronto	62	India	Kolkata	374
Finland	Helsinki	87		Delhi	464
Germany	Frankfurt	36	Indonesia	Jakarta	175
Japan	Tokyo	60	Iran	Tehran	241
	Osaka	47	Malaysia	Kuala Lumpur	136
US	Chicago	79	Pakistan	Lahore	405
	Houston	48	Thailand	Bangkok	198
	New York	62	Venezuela	Caracas	78

(a) in kg/m^3; average for commercial and industrial areas (centre or suburban)

Source: UN, 1996

SUMMARY

Despite large differences between specific conditions, developing country cities may be said to present some similarities. These are outlined below.

Infrastructure supply As regards pavements, there is often a generalized shortage of good infrastructure and in many places people have to use the road, which is dangerous. Road provision may vary from 6 per cent (Kolkata) of urbanized area to 21 per cent (São Paulo), but actual traffic conditions depend on the social and economic conditions of people, as well as traffic mix and surface type. Roads with inadequate surfaces and a lack of drainage systems are common. Especially in central areas, roads may be as narrow as 7m and in peripheral areas alleys have to be used for all traffic.

Vehicle supply In addition to walking, people in developing countries use a wide array of vehicles. Bicycles are the most important non-motorized mode all over the world and bicycle-like vehicles are extensively used in Asia and Africa for the transport of both people and goods. Motorized transport is less accessible, considering the costs of purchase, maintenance and operation. Motorcycles are already a common means of transport in Asia and some parts of Africa, but cars are still limited to the wealthy sectors of society, although in high proportions in countries such as South Korea, Thailand, Brazil and Mexico. Trucks and buses are less numerous than private vehicles, although in the latter case they represent a much greater passenger-carrying capacity. Vehicle ownership within developing countries presents wide variations and is much lower than that of developed nations.

Mobility and modal split Mobility is generally low in the face of low income. Modal splits present large variations and three main groups may be devised:

cities with predominantly non-motorized trips (for example Beijing), cities where public transport accounts for the majority of trips (for example Buenos Aires) and cities where motorized private modes play an important role (for example Ouagadougou). In this respect, cities may also be classified according to the type of private motorized transport they have: Hanoi, Lagos and Ouagadougou rely mainly on motorcycles, while in Buenos Aires, Caracas, São Paulo and Pretoria, cars play a predominant role.

If motorized trips alone are analysed, in most cities more than 50 per cent of trips are made by public transport. Few have trains and metros, and the bus is the main mode. There is a wide range of buses, ranging from 10 seats to 50 seats.

Trip purposes Trip purpose varies according to several social, cultural and economic factors. However, work and school seem to be the most important purposes, regardless of geography and wealth.

Accessibility Total travel time varies markedly between motorized modes, depending on access and the spatial distribution of activities, and reaches a 1:4 ratio between motorcycle and train trips in São Paulo. Trips by private modes always take much less time than public modes, and non-motorized trips correspond to the lowest travel times. Bus speeds usually fall in the 10–20km/h range, and average door-to-door travel time by bus may be 50 per cent higher than by car. Automobile speeds depend on road conditions and the traffic mix. Motorcycle speeds are higher. When total travel time is divided into parts, important conclusions appear. Usually, access time to autos is low. Conversely, access time to buses is always higher. Transfer time is also an important part of the problem. The final effect of all transport-related difficulties for captive public transport users is that a long journey is inevitable.

Comfort Overcrowded and uncomfortable vehicles are a daily reality in almost every developing country.

Transport expenses The costs of owning and using non-motorized vehicle are usually low, while motorcycles and cars are much more expensive. Absolute expenses with transport increase with income. However, the proportion of these expenses tends to decrease with increasing wealth.

Traffic safety Traffic accidents are a major problem in developed and developing countries and a large number of fatalities are found in all cases. Developed countries present rates of around 3 to 6 fatalities per 10,000 vehicles, while developing country rates may go as high as 141 (Nigeria in 1980). Recent tendencies are of great concern, especially in countries were motorized transport has been growing rapidly. Between 1968 and 1985 road accident fatalities increased by 300 per cent in Africa and by almost 200 per cent in Asia. Studies show that pedestrians, cyclists and motorcyclists are at greatest risk, accounting for more than 50 per cent of fatalities.

Environmental problems Air pollution has already reached extremely high levels in several large cities in developing countries, exceeding the recommended limits set by WHO. In most cases transport is the main source of pollution. Available data show that SPM concentration is much higher in developing world cities than in developed cities.

Table 2.23 *Summary of current transport and traffic conditions in developing countries*

Factor or variable	Current conditions
Infrastructure supply	Absolute lack or poor provision of pavements
	Low-quality roads
	Little special treatment for NMT or buses
Vehicle supply	High availability of bicycles
	Low to medium supply of public transport vehicles
	High availability of private motorized transport for medium- to high-income groups
Mobility and transport use	Low average individual mobility
	Large variation on modal split, with a predominance of non-motorized and public transport means
Trip purpose	Most trips made for work and school purposes
Accessibility	Large variation in door-to-door travel times between modes
	Private transport faster than public transport
	Low spatial supply of public transport
	High walking and waiting times to access public transport
	Poor integration of public transport services
Comfort	Low quality of pedestrian and non-motorized trips
	Frequent overcrowding of public transport vehicles
	Medium to high quality in private motorized trips
Expenses	Low-income groups spend a high percentage of earnings on transport
	High-income groups spend lower share of their earnings on transport
Traffic safety	High accident rates
	The most vulnerable (pedestrians and NMT users) are the most damaged
Environment	High pollutant concentration in large cities

PART 3
HOW IT HAPPENED

3

SOCIOLOGICAL AND POLITICAL APPROACHES TO TRANSPORT

COMPARING TRADITIONAL AND PROPOSED APPROACHES

Urban transport in the last few decades has been subjected to a predominantly technical treatment, as an area that was seen as 'naturally' inclined to physics, mathematics and economics. This traditional approach is now subjected to increasing criticism, as its limitations can no longer be hidden. My intention here is to propose a social and political approach, which should not just complement the traditional one but replace it, without minimizing the importance of competent technical treatment in specific phases of the analytical process. In the first instance, I will call this new approach the 'sociology of transport', as it has already been classified by some authors (Yago, 1983; De Boer, 1985).

Considering that such a sociology of transport has a debatable objective in the academic experience, one has first to find out who, and within which conditions, has been following social and political approaches to transport and traffic problems. Another task is to clarify what is understood by these approaches.

To begin with, a distinction should be established at the research level; sociological transport research must be distinguished from descriptive social research (Town,1981). While the latter is limited to the account of social impacts, the former is characterized by the analysis of travel patterns given social, political, economic and institutional constraints. This means that while descriptive social research accepts the trips as a *given*, sociological research asks the basic questions about *why* and *how* trips are made. Also, a sociological approach differs from a social one in the sense that it analyses transport and traffic-related social data in respect to the relative economic and political assets of social groups and classes, as well as their conflicting (or merging) interests. This explains why it is easier to find studies infused by social accountability considerations than to find studies constructed as 'transport sociology'.

Healey (1977) suggests a broader distinction between the sociology *of* transport and sociology *in* transport. While the former could be seen as a pragmatic, quantitative-bound approach limited to the inclusion of some social issues within more traditional transport impact analysis, the latter would imply a more profound analysis of the whole chain of effects on both users and non-users, capturing the impacts on a macro-economic scale. In the case of the analysis of car restraint policies, instead of assessing just the direct positive impacts on environment and public transport modes, sociology in transport would have to capture the whole set of effects on the automotive industry and the related economy.

Regardless of what sort of social and political analysis is used, it is important to understand why and how it was incorporated into transport studies. This inclusion can be related to the legitimization crisis of transport planning which erupted in the 1960s, when many of its assumptions were criticized and even challenged by alternative views. As explained in detail by Healey (1977) with respect to transport planning and by Rimmer (1978) with respect to transport geography, since the 1950s both fields have passed through several phases which could be broadly described as a sequence of description and prediction, rejection, and redirection. During the first phase, the increased use of cars and related rapid urban growth rates led to the organization of sophisticated management techniques that relied on a set of forecasting methods known as the four-step modelling process (see Chapter 9 for a detailed analysis). This phase was characterized by the role of the highway engineer, who worked to accommodate the car. This work was supported by the supposed neutrality and technicality of the methodology, as well as by its supposed use in promoting the best distribution of resources, according to neoclassical market economics. The role of the planner was 'to fit the revealed community aspiration to limited resources, through objective technical expertise' in a context of 'social consensus belief' (Healey, 1977). Therefore, there was no practical need for the use of social and political approaches, transport planning being a technical expertise in its own right. During the second phase (rejection) the most important assumptions of the first phase began to be challenged by reality, including confidence in the market as an appropriate signal and provider of needs, and the neglect of social and environmental impacts brought about the first major crisis. New approaches were called upon and sociology and political science made their first entrance in the field of transport. Cost–benefit analysis started to include social and environmental impacts, and political participation in the decision-making process was formalized. However, transport planning continued to be consensus-seeking, broadly market-based and with a narrow, aggregate and one-way view of cost–benefit analysis that neglected concrete contributions by and interference from the users. These are sufficient reasons for identifying a 'trivialization of sociology', with its adoption for transport planning being only a 'survival tool' (Healey, 1977). Finally, the phase of redirection was characterized by a rethink of transport planning, with sociology being used for the first time in analysing social structure and social change. The analysis of the decision-making process, rather than the decisions themselves, was one of the prime objectives. The ideology of 'community' was replaced by the acceptance of divergence and conflicts in needs, interests and values, inside and between groups and classes. The distributive and equity effects of the policies were investigated, along with economic efficiency. The long-held separation between engineering and sociology was no longer defensible, and planning became politically mature (Healey, 1977).

De Boer (1985) provides a chronological summary of what could be named transport sociology studies, within which there are different denominations such as 'sociology of the street', and 'sociology of the car'. The first intellectual wave attempted to understand the spiralling problems brought about by the increasing use of the private car. Traffic safety was a major concern at the beginning of the motor age (the 1930s in the US and the 1950s in Europe), leading in the case of Europe to an increasing consciousness of traffic accidents as a public health problem. Later, in the 1960s, the major problem appeared to be traffic congestion, related to the rapid increase in city size and car populations. Many studies were made of the influence of the car in society, especially among US scholars.[1] A phase of hidden admiration – and surprise – at the car's social impact was followed by a new generation of studies, which began to ask questions about its potential negative impact. These studies have combined the analysis of the 'suburbanization' effect in the US with the evaluation of those social sectors denied access to the automobile. This latter analysis brought out issues of non-motorized transport, especially regarding pedestrians and public transport.

Two main reasons for the reassessment of this problem in the 1970s can be detected. First, at a micro level, the analysis of travel patterns was turned upside down as most planners became aware of the disconnection between manifest demand and actual needs, and the time and social limits of individual trips. In the first case, many studies showed that the manifest demand, captured through origin–destination surveys, revealed only the 'possible' trips: that is, those possible given prevailing conditions. If other conditions were present, other trips would have taken place. In the second case, research into the daily activities of people in a household made it clear that all individuals were constrained by both personal and family limits, along with limits imposed by the environment and transport supply. These researches, first developed on a systematic scale by Hagestrand in the 1960s in Sweden (Carlstein et al, 1978) and by Chapin in the US (Chapin, 1974), opened a new way of understanding the problem. Finally, all the models were challenged on the basis of their supposed ability to represent actual behaviour and forecast the future (Kanafani, 1983; Atkins, 1986; Dimitriou,1990).

The second major change can be identified at the macro level as the politicization of the transport issue. This is related to the questioning of the automobile's impact, and the parallel inquiry into the nature and scope of public transport policies. Three major movements can be identified with this change. The first movement is conservative, attempting to overcome the worst impacts of the automobile without creating structural limitations to its acquisition and use. Buchanan's essential 1963 report, *Traffic in Towns*, maintained that the main conflict was between accessibility and environment, proposing the reorganization of space to reduce the adverse impacts of automobiles. This ultimately optimistic view was followed by innumerable studies and practical proposals. The second movement is more political, developing a systematic questioning of the privileges accorded to the accumulation interests of dominant sectors in a capitalist society. This is the extensive new school of urban sociology, with its parallel analysis of specific transport issues. The third movement is more practical, in that it uses this new critical approach to develop studies on specific transport problems and related policies.[2] A consequence of these studies is an increasing concern for equity issues in transport, and the reassessment of the prevailing development of auto-oriented cities.

These movements, initiated in the industrialized world, have been disseminated throughout developing countries that were themselves facing increasing transport problems, especially in major towns. Consequently, traditional methodologies imported by the developing countries to help formulate transport policies came in for heavy criticism and reappraisal (Merlin,1985; Dimitriou,1990). This criticism came long after its emergence in the industrialized world, further delaying the adoption of social and political perspectives in developing world transport planning.

THE BASIC OUTLINE FOR A SOCIOLOGICAL APPROACH

The difficulties in linking engineering, sociology and political science can be attributed to several factors. Town (1981) summarizes the reasons for both the lack of interest and the emergence of interest in 'sociologizing' transport.

The lack of interest in the topic is attributed to two factors. First, transport is often seen as a pragmatic action, anchored in technical engineering, construction, and management. Second, sociology often sees transport as only a tool, not an end in itself, with little or no effect in shaping people's values, as opposed to religion and education. Another reason may be added to those given by Town: engineers resist social and political approaches to transport because they believe, as a corporate sector, that transport and traffic issues are primarily technical. This view incorporates an implicit assumption that transport and traffic planning are neutral intervention activities.

Despite these factors, Town stresses that there are two reasons for the growth of interest in a sociological perspective. First, the transport system's distributive effects are related to an increase in car use and a decrease in public transport use. Second, the adequacy of conventional demand models for predicting behaviour, and the models' implicit assumptions regarding fiscal and transport infrastructure impacts, have been increasingly questioned.

From the broadest point of view the most adequate way of approaching the issue of human movement in space would be to search for an *anthropology of movement* (Tarrius, 1989). This anthropology is seen by Tarrius as dealing with three stages of human movement in space, or social rhythms: regional or international migration, which happens according to long time spans; residential mobility inside a city, related to the family life-cycles and social and economic constraints; and daily mobility, related to activities in time and space based on everyday exchanges in the city economy. This anthropology of mobility is intended to analyse the complex pattern of human spatial mobility; the continuity and discontinuity of social rhythms, connecting the practices of people, classes and economic agents to the organization of the space and transport means. This approach has to rely deeply on the time and space budget framework (Hagestrand, 1970), as revealing the interaction between people's conditions and the environmental constraints, and has some similarity to the 'geography of transport' as expressed by Rimmer

(1978). It is indeed the broadest approach possible, for it entails all possible time-movements of human beings. Nevertheless, its amplitude renders it less practical for policy analysis, because the linkages between these three time spans of movement and the construction of the human environment are far from well known.

Considering this difficulty, one has to move to a more modest objective; that of asking why and when one should try to apply a sociological and political approach to transport and traffic, within a more limited time span. In this way, the discussions that follow will primarily consider the last two time spans proposed by Tarrius – mobility related to daily activities, and to housing location/moving strategies based on family or individual life-cycles.

The first point to make is: if such an intellectual effort has to be made, does it have a scientific meaning? Is it related to any broader fields? Initially, one has to question the very existence of an urban sociology which could produce a child called 'transport sociology'. After Castells (1976) proposed (despite denying it) the death of existing urban sociologies, a great deal of debate took place on how to save them from the fire, or how to bury them once for all. The debate will not be reproduced here, nor will its main components be mentioned.[3] The most important criticism of urban sociology concerns the status of the city itself as a scientific object. There is very little support for the concept of the city as a specific entity, as opposed to other non-urban spaces (Saunders,1979). As emphasized by Castells, the existent urban sociologies (mainly of the Chicago school) are in fact sociologies of the capitalist industrial economy, used as integrative sociologies to overcome conflicts. In this sense, they are ideologies of modernity. Therefore, any attempt to create an urban sociology would result in a general sociology that would include every aspect of society.

Searching for an urban sociology opens up the opportunity to search for a sociology of space, which would be free from urban bias. This is more appealing, for it can include regional and rural spaces, necessary for transport analysis. Thus the search for a sociology of transport has to take place within a broader context of a sociology of space – not geographical space in itself, but man-made space, the 'built environment'. Space has to be seen as a product of the lively forces operating inside society; the fourth domain of social relations, along with production, consumption and exchange (Lefevbre, 1979; Gottdiener, 1993). This is the approach that is proposed in this work.

A further comment is necessary. On one side, the term 'sociology of transport' has an important drawback, for it represents a one-way, passive approach, in which users are seen as non-active in the face of a given supply of a particular service (transport). The task implied in this denomination would be that of studying 'how people *are* transported', which is important but insufficient. On the other side, the term 'sociology in transport', applicable to either people or goods transport, is too generic for our purposes. Therefore one has to overcome both problems by including the users' views and practices, and by creating a linkage with the circulation space in which movements occur. This will be done by proposing a *sociology of circulation*, in which the objective is to describe the relationships between the supply, operation and appropriation (use) of circulation structures and means. 'Circulation structure' refers to railways, highways, streets, pavements and terminals, while 'circulation means' refers to vehicles (the human body, as well as non-motorized and motorized vehicles). Supply, operation and appropriation are organized by the state, private economic agents, and social groups and classes, on a cooperative or competitive basis. Decisions of supply, operation and appropriation are constrained by political, economic, social and cultural factors, which vary remarkably in time and space. This proposition also assumes that the central issues for transport and traffic policies are:

- how access is distributed in space;
- how different social classes and groups use the city; and
- what the related conditions of equity, safety, comfort, efficiency, environment and cost are.

Finally, the proposition implies that circulation is a physical necessity related to the reproduction needs of social groups and classes, which in turn are constrained by economic, social, cultural and political conditions varying from one society to another.

The basic outline for an initial approach along sociological and political lines can now be made. Here, I will follow Castells (1977) and Town (1981), adding other elements that I believe are important. According to Castells,

> *The historical conditions for the existence and functioning of means of transport are a function of the logic of the traffic system ... and the economic and political determinants; a sociological study of transport is based on an analysis of the contradictions between the internal logic of a traffic system and the historical conditions of the means of transport through which it must be realised.* (1977, p201)

Castells adds that this analysis has to consider general social contradictions, especially the tendency of capitalist urban development towards spatial segregation. All traffic movement has to be analysed in the face of social, economic and political determinants. Such an approach acknowledges the intimate relationship between movement (traffic) and the means of transport as being a mutually reinforcing dynamic. In addition, I believe (with Town) that the central role of the state and other political forces in shaping transport policies should form part of any transport analysis.

Basic differences between the three main approaches are summarized in Table 3.1, for two examples – urban transport quality and traffic accidents.

With urban transport conditions in a particular road, traditional technical analysis would try to represent the problem in quantitative terms, using well-known speed–density–volume relationships, such as those widely explored in the technical literature (TRB, 1985). Flows and vehicles are understood as a given, and the challenge for the analyst is how to provide enough space and traffic conditions for the manifest demand, through either a capacity increase or traffic management schemes; the elements deserving attention here are vehicles, not people. The social approach would complement such analysis by calculating how many people are travelling on each

Table 3.1 *Differences between prevailing and proposed approaches to transport*

Approach	Typical factors considered in the analysis (examples)	
	Transport quality	**Traffic accidents**
Technical	Vehicle traffic conditions (volume, speed, density)	Number of accidents by type
Social	Vehicle traffic conditions and quantity of people involved	Accidents by type and characteristics of people involved (age, gender)
Sociological	Vehicle traffic conditions and quantity of people involved, analysed in the light of their social and economic characteristics and their access to different transport means	Accidents by type and characteristics of people involved (age, gender) analysed in the light of their social and economic characteristics, their behaviour, their level of education

mode, allowing for an initial understanding of the division of space between people and hence of the social impact of any particular decision. The sociological approach would add to such initial data any information on the social and economic characteristics of people travelling on each mode, their actual access conditions to each mode, and the political determinants of transport and traffic policies that surround the issue. It would therefore allow for the analysis of why space is divided in the prevailing way, why some people may have access to certain transport modes, and how externalities are generated and experienced by those involved with the transport or traffic problems under analysis. It would also allow for the analysis of why people do not use certain transport modes, and what would happen to demand and modal split if different conditions prevailed.

With a traffic safety problem, a similar difference in approach may be devised. While the traditional technical approach would make a quantitative account of accidents by type, the social approach would include some characteristics of the people involved, and the sociological approach would have to add who is using road space, within which conditions, and for what purposes. In addition, it would examine how the accident externality is produced and experienced by people involved.

Therefore, the sociological approach never sees manifest demand as a given, but rather as a product of prevailing conditions, influenced by individual and family characteristics, the existent transport systems, spatial and time constraints, and public policy decisions. It includes the political dimension as an essential component to complement the technical one. Hence, the sociological and political analysis of transport is neither fatalistic – as were the traditional approaches to the 'inevitability' of automobile use – nor naive, in the sense of seeing public transport use as a good in itself.

Considering this, I believe that Town's suggestion for the sociological approach is the most comprehensive and useful. It is based on four main points described below, and summarized in Table 3.2.

1   The analysis of the trip patterns, the social structure, and the general constraints that affect the user's choices.
2   The examination of the transport-deprived and the very concept of deprivation.
3   The analysis of social movements involved in transport issues.
4   The analysis of the planning process itself and the characteristics of the social and political groups that directly or indirectly shape its content. This latter is also emphasized by Yago (1983), who stresses the need to analyse the institutions and processes that constrain people's choices with respect to transport.

Table 3.2 *Essential differences between the three approaches*

Approach	Data used (nature)	Preferred elements for analysis	Preferred focus of explanation	Preferred elements of evaluation
Technical	Quantitative	Vehicles	Individuals	Economic efficiency (cost–benefit analysis)
Social	Quantitative and qualitative	People in general	Individuals	Economic efficiency, with social analyses
Sociological	Quantitative and qualitative	Political beings and their roles in traffic[1]	Individuals, family, social groups and classes	Economic and social efficiency; equity analysis

(1) see Chapter 6

The attempt to further clarify the nature and scope of a transport sociology will be developed first by analysing how agents interfere with and organize urban space (Chapter 4), by evaluating the relationships between social reproduction, the built environment and transport policies (Chapter 5), and by examining how road space is divided between users (Chapter 6).

4

THE ORGANIZATION OF URBAN SPACE

This section provides a general representation of the relationships between agents involved in the organization of the urban space, and also in the functioning of a city. Included in this broad analysis is an examination of how the transport planning process operates and how its outputs are produced.

As stated in the Introduction, I am aware of the difficulties inherent in representing the variety and complexity of conditions all over the world, in both developed and developing countries. Such difficulties are related to the historical, economic, social and cultural conditions existing in any society, at any period. Furthermore, it is not the main objective of this book to dive into a detailed political analysis of political systems and societies. Instead I take a simplified approach to the issue, forming a methodological basis to support the ensuing analysis of urban transport policies, their formulation and implementation.

MAJOR SOCIAL AND POLITICAL FORCES AND CONSTRAINTS

Figure 4.1 is a simplified diagram, containing only the most important features of a complex chain of relationships. It is intended to provide an overall view of cause–effect chains, feedback movements and external influences, complementing other representations in the literature (Deloucas, 1983). The diagram is centred on the notion of socio-spatial organization, which is broader concept than the 'city', in that the social and political aspects required by a sociological and political approach to the issue are considered. It is equivalent to the concept of 'built environment' discussed in the last section.

The first important concept is the state. The state is a dominant apparatus that is formally organized to deal with those issues that society understands as belonging to the public domain, and therefore deserving of attention from public entities. However, the state should not be conflated with an aggregate of public bureaucracies, and should rather be seen as a 'set of social relations that establishes and maintains a certain order via centralised coercive authority over a given territory' (O'Donnell, 1994, p159). This definition is broad enough to encompass many current (and former) states in the world, even accounting for religions, cultural and other differences.

'Political and economic system' refers to the structural rules and codes that define how people may interact in trying to address their economic, social, cultural and religious needs. Example are Western-style states based on

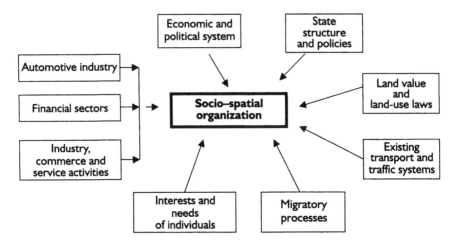

Figure 4.1 *Agents and factors in the organization of the built environment*

a market economy, formal democratic political relationships and a clear separation between civilian and religious power; socialist states; newly democratized states; and states that are deeply influenced by religious or ethnic beliefs and norms.

'State policies' refers to the way in which any particular state formulates and implements public policies relating to its internal structure and political nature. We may identify two extremes: the former socialist states, which have almost overwhelming power to define public policies; and Western, Anglo-Saxon states in which policies are the result of a long, complex political bargain. Within each category we find large variations: for example, the difference between China, which chose to give support to bicycle transport, and Russia, East Germany and Poland, all of which supported motorized public transport (Pucher and Lefèvre, 1996). We can also see important differences in the relative power of the state vis-à-vis private agents, and the influence of welfare concerns; such variations exist between the US and European (mostly Scandinavian) states, expressed in decisions to support either the automobile or public transport. We find further differences in the varying roles attributed to the state apparatus and the private sector; they are evident, for instance, when comparing Japanese and US transport policy formation (Cervero, 1998a; Hook, 1994a). With developing countries in particular, we see a large group of very poor states, in which a small elite controls almost every public policy decision. Even within states with higher average incomes, there may by inequalities within society and a powerful, often well-educated elite working closely with 'modernity-seeking' bureaucracies, as is the case in some Latin American states, especially Argentina, Brazil, Chile and Mexico, and some Asian states, such as South Korea, Thailand and Indonesia. Finally, we also find religiously or ethnically driven states, where cultural beliefs and norms drive public action; examples include some low-to-middle income Asian and Islamic countries and apartheid South Africa. States interfere in a wide range of public issues, from health to the economy. For the purpose of this book, some of these public policies are important:

- Urban development and land-use policies that define how urban space may be settled, organized and occupied, and what sorts of land uses and densities are accepted. Crucial to our understanding are specific decisions concerning the spatial supply of public services such as schools, hospitals, parks and public offices, and the conditions of physical access to them. These policies directly influence land values and therefore people's access to land.
- Transport policies that define road infrastructure, and public transportation infrastructure and means. They regulate the provision of such services and user access to them.
- Housing and construction policies that define where and how people may build their homes.
- Economic policies that define fiscal and taxation measures, interest rates, labour relations, wage levels, and how public resources will be invested on each policy area.
- Traffic policy that defines who has access to vehicles and how the available road space will be used.

States may work on policies separately, which is often the case in developing countries, or they may subject them to some sort of coordination. A division of responsibilities may lead to conflicting actions, leading to a poor performance. In addition, some policies may receive high priority during certain periods, while others may be considered less important for political reasons. States may have highly qualified people, or they may lack skilled workers in most areas; such skilled workers may have the freedom to define policies, or they may just follow directions. In this book, an emphasis will be placed on two layers of state personnel that I think are essential to understand recent transport policy outcomes in developing countries. First, the bureaucrats, in charge of administrative and fiscal decisions; second, the technocrats, in charge of technical decisions.

External forces may come from direct pressures exerted by the formal political system; representatives who may have interests related to the electorate or economic interests. Pressures may also be exerted by social sectors affected by transport policies – local communities, transport-deprived groups, environmental organizations – or by the media. Finally, indirect pressures may come from selected social sectors with direct access to the state, such as the economic elite and the middle class.

Turing to the other factors listed in Figure 4.1, land values directly impact on people's access to land for housing purposes and on investment opportunities for new businesses. Transport supply and costs directly affect travel possibilities. People's interests and needs impact on their decisions concerning how to use space. As explained below, such decisions will be taken within a complex mix of individual and family capabilities and constraints.

Finally, one has to add those organized private agents directly interested in shaping and benefiting from the socio-spatial arrangement. First, the automotive industry, which wishes to sell motorized vehicles. Such an interest depends in large part on the influence exerted on public authorities and public opinion to create adequate conditions for the purchase and use of such vehicles. The industry needs benign fiscal policies, road infrastructure built with public resources, and favourable traffic rules.

Second, the construction sector, which wishes to make profits by building roads and public transport infrastructure. Third, the real estate sector, which has an obvious interest in the outcomes of land-use policies. Such interests may be worked out in concert with the construction sector.

Fourth, there are sectors of industry, service and commerce, which are interested in earning profits from investments in their businesses. These rely deeply on proximity to the market and the availability and performance of transport systems. Fifth, the financial sector, which wishes to obtain profits from the loan of money to other sectors. Sixth, the public transport sector, whether publicly or privately owned and operated. The first interest of the public operators is to provide public services, although the sector's power may be used to extract corporate benefits. Private transport operators also wish to make profits and to protect the industry from competition. In both cases, the interest of related workers' unions and associations are relevant (see Chapter 11).

Seventh, the consultant sector, which is interested in selling its services to public and private agencies involved with the formulation and implementation of public policies. This sector often works in conjunction with industrial and real estate sectors in commercializing solutions and services. These services may be provided by foreign firms, linked to foreign industry sectors willing to sell specific products and services. As analysed in Chapter 9, the urban and transport planning techniques in developed countries were transferred to developing countries by foreign consultant firms. Finally, international lending institutions, which are interested in obtaining financial returns from investments in transport infrastructure and services. They are a very powerful influence on policy decisions, particularly in the use of specific equipment and services that originate in the donor countries. Their work is usually closely related to that of consultant firms, both internal and external.

There is therefore a highly complex network of interests involved in sociospatial organization. It is important to note that such interests will be highly dependent on their access to the state. Every socio-spatial organization will show a specific mix of structures dedicated to production, reproduction and circulation. This mix will lead to a specific distribution of accessibility in space and will generate a pattern of average distances to be traversed, with profound consequences for the transport system.

There are also social forces. Two dimensions of social behaviour are relevant here: migratory processes – very common in developing countries – and the daily pattern of human activities, which is related to family and individual interests and needs. Socio-spatial organization is constantly influenced by rural–urban migration, particularly by the speed of the movement and its magnitude. Social, economic and cultural characteristics will determine reproduction needs, family internal division of tasks and individual use of transport means. These factors are so important that they are discussed in detail in Chapter 5.

LIFE, MOBILITY AND REPRODUCTION

Reproduction needs

In order to continue to live and participate in society people have to ensure its reproduction. They have also to provide for the reproduction of other people who, for biological, social or physical reasons, rely on others for their reproduction. The reproduction process requires several activities, which vary according to social, economic, cultural and political characteristics. It takes place through consumption activities, by which a person obtains goods or services. Despite the overwhelming importance of the relations which reproduce labour skills, other social relations are also important in reproducing people, especially those related to the family, the religion, the school, and the community (Preteceille, 1981). The activities which are undertaken correspond to manifest needs related to the reproduction process.

Figure 4.2 depicts some general relationships constraining reproduction needs and consequent travel behaviour. The movements that will take place in this space will be determined by several factors. No movement corresponds to any sort of 'natural desire' (Preteceille and Terrail, 1985) since all movements are related to the reproduction needs – dependent on individual and family characteristics and the social division of labour, and constrained by the dominant ideology. This constraint is not absolute, given non-economic factors such as cultural perceptions and the value people place on space (Kane, 1997). Hence, the reproduction needs will be formed (and perceived by the person) according to two sorts of factors. First, and most importantly, class, ethnicity and religion; second, gender and age.

Social class – translated mainly in terms of income, and political and educational assets – influences reproduction needs and transport behaviour by defining activities and goals and which means of transport will be employed to achieve them. Religion and ethnicity exert their influence by either defining mandatory activities or limiting other activities. Some elements may work in a dominant way – such as class and income in capitalist societies, religion in Islamic societies or ethnicity in African societies – or in a combined way, such as in several African, Asian and Latin American societies. The relative importance of these factors will vary markedly. Class, age and gender can be said to be key factors everywhere, while ethnicity is undoubtedly a major factor in the US as it was in apartheid South Africa. Ethnic and religious factors are of prime importance in Asia and Africa.

Second, reproduction is influenced by the family life-cycle and its internal characteristics. Life-cycle influences reproduction according to the age structure of the family, whether adults and children living together, an adult couple living alone, or a house with children, adults and elderly people. Gender influences reproduction and transport in terms of the division of tasks in the family. In addition to such major factors, it is important to mention the social division of labour, which influences reproduction through the separation of those who perform managerial work and those who perform physical work. The technical division of labour – differences in levels of skills – also

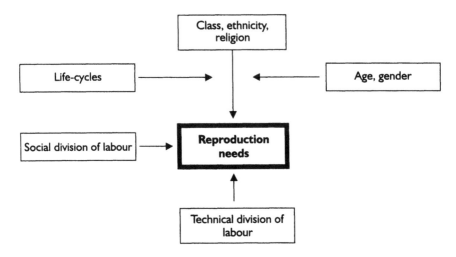

Figure 4.2 *Elements influencing reproduction needs*

influences reproduction, especially by defining educational and training re-quirements. Several of these factors may be seen in the actual occupation of urban space, generating divisions and 'clusters' with similar class, ethnic or religious characteristics. For instance, in the US, 80 per cent of people have as neighbours people of the same ethnicity (Goldsmith and Blakely, 1992). In several Arabic cities spatial ethnic segregation is a common reality (Abu-Lughod, 1996). Latin American cities have clear 'clusters' of middle- and high-income people, whether inside large low-income settlements or com-pletely separated from them.

Therefore, each adult individual will perceive his or her reproduction needs and will act accordingly. Physically, most of these needs have to be fulfilled through transport between points in space, and the set of movements that will take place on a typical day forms the 'network' of the daily activities of each person. As most people live in family groups, the sum of all individual networks could be described as the family network of activities. However, as individuals have to consider others' needs to some extent, the final result is not the exact sum of individual networks, but a different sum resulting from some individual accommodations to others' needs. In most cases, younger and older people will conform to working adults' needs, and 'non-productive' (eco-nomically inactive) people will conform to 'productive' people's needs.

The network of activities will consider four major constraints: personal or family economic resources, personal or family time availability, the location and the operating hours of the desired activities, and the available transport means. Every individual will contrast his or her reproduction needs (as well as the family's) with these four constraints and decide how to negotiate the network. This is the moment at which two key events occur: a mode choice is made for every possible trip – the feasible (possible) trips – and the needs which cannot be fulfilled for any reason – the non-feasible (impossible) trips – are acknowledged. The latter are then fulfilled by other means, replaced by alternative activities, or suppressed indefinitely.

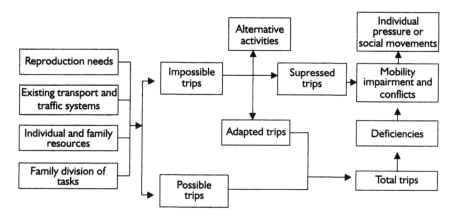

Figure 4.3 *How transport demand pattern is formed*

The set of feasible trips forms the origin–destination (OD) pattern of trips in the space. This OD pattern reflects the set of feasible trips that are performed every day, through a mix of non-motorized and motorized means which is a function mainly of family income and the physical arrangement of the built environment. That is why the OD survey, despite being extremely important and helpful to a sociological approach to transport, has an important drawback: it does not show (directly) the deviated or suppressed demand.

The dynamics of change

The description made so far is of a stable system of relationships. However, despite the fact that daily trip patterns are quite constant, the system is permanently subjected to disruptive pressures and to evolutionary changes (see Figure 4.4). The pressures come from three main sources: political dissatisfaction, urban and economic evolutionary changes, and external changes in the economic or political environment. They may also arise from society and state internal sectors.

Political dissatisfaction may arise from a daily experience of costly, uncomfortable or dangerous trips, or from a need to fulfil suppressed reproduction needs. These latter pressures are not just a feature of working classes or transport-deprived poor people, but can originate from any segment of society; for instance, the automobile-dependent middle classes are the source of permanent pressure to improve conditions of automobile use.

Pressures may be limited to individual complaints or may come from formal organizations or social groups, with a broader emphasis on the provision and management aspects of the problem. Other pressures may originate within the state. As analysed in Chapter 7, these internal pressures are directly related to the nature and interests of the bureaucratic and technocratic sectors.

Evolutionary changes can arise from the need to adapt space to economic development or migration, to accommodate changes in labour market (the feminization of labour), to cope with new reproduction needs (increase in

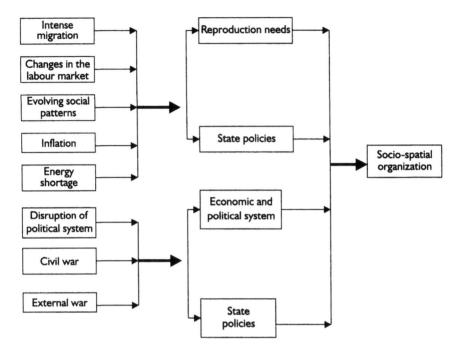

Figure 4.4 *Structural and external factors influencing socio-spatial organization*

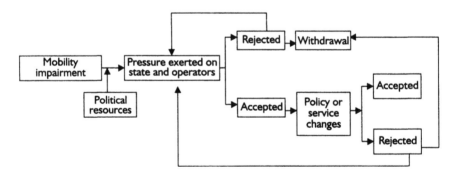

Figure 4.5 *Conflicts, changes and adaptations*

schooling), or to address catastrophic external influences (such as an energy shortage). At a micro scale, households are always changing from one life-cycle to another, breaking the equilibrium of demand and supply. They are also subject to a continuous process of adjustment, which may be slow in the face of inertia, lack of information or habits (Goodwin, 1981).

External changes may be caused by inflationary processes which limit or deny access to transport means or by a fiscal crisis, which may decrease state investment or support for the poor. External changes may also be brought about by sudden political disruptions that modify political alliances, and change state policies, and by war.

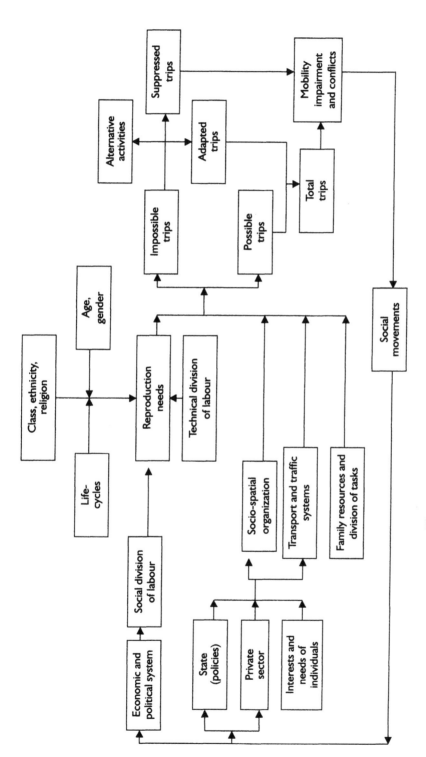

Figure 4.6 *Comprehensive view of agents and factors*

Therefore, the whole system is permanently subjected to considerable forces. The possibility of exercising influence on policies depends on the political system and the structure of the state. Some pressures are either repressed or diverted, while others are negotiated, leading to a change in public policies. This can affect any of the major policies mentioned above (see Figure 4.5). Figure 4.6 groups all aforementioned relations into a single diagram, picturing the complex relationships between them. The most important factor is the state, a central focus for policy formation and implementation, which will work to help the reproduction needs of the most powerful social groups and classes, or those whose reproduction is most important for the endurance of the economic and political systems. State intervention may be directed to ensure better reproduction conditions for certain ethnic groups, dominant religious strata or selected middle-class and elite sectors. That is why many cities of the 19th-century 'First World', and of the 20th-century 'Third World', were adapted to the reproduction needs of the middle classes, as the most powerful and important social group to support the organization/modernization of the capitalist system. And that is why the alliance between the middle classes and the bureaucrats is so powerful. As it will be seen in Chapters 6 to 9, the supposedly 'neutral' traditional traffic management techniques and the set of transport models used in recent decades were very important tools for this process.

5 THE CITY, THE CIRCULATION SYSTEM AND URBAN TRANSPORT POLICIES

THE CITY AS A BUILT ENVIRONMENT

An alternative approach to the urban transport problem requires a correspondingly alternative view of the city, which will overcome the traditional, functionally based view of the urban space as a physical arrangement of buildings. Many authors working with urban sociology concepts have attempted to advance alternative proposals, such as that by Dear and Scott:

> in each individual city a complex spatial system materialises, comprising an interdependent assembly of (private and public) functional areas and locations. These ... can be categorised as either production space (in which the accumulation process proceeds), or the reproduction space (in which the regeneration of labour is accomplished). Both of these spaces are mediated by a third subjacent space, devoted to circulation needs. (1981, p10)

Dear and Scott's view that circulation space mediates between the other two spaces has to be tempered by replacing its rigid functional separation of the three areas by a more holistic, integrated view. The key element combining these three areas is space, used to support economic activities through its specific physical arrangement. The spatial arrangement of a city may strengthen productive forces and speed up accumulation; space is then used in the very same way that a machine is used in a factory (Lefevbre, 1979). Space is a distinctive, straightforward feature in Western capitalistic societies; however, it is infused by cultural, ethnic and religious characteristics in Asian and African societies (Chen and Pavish, 1996; Abu-Lughod, 1996; Gugler, 1996).

The central concept of this alternative approach is of the city as a built environment, made consciously and composed of a myriad of physical structures designed to sustain the development process. This built environment is not static, but subjected to ongoing constructive and destructive processes in conjunction with the external and internal migration of people and economic activities. In practical terms:

> [The] built environment is a vast, humanly-created resource system, comprising use values embedded in the physical landscape, which can be utilised for production, exchange and consumption. (Harvey, 1982, p233)

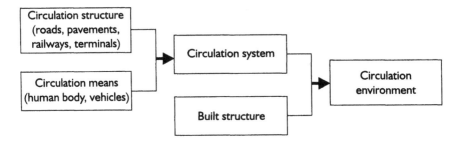

Figure 5.1 *Circulation structure, means, system and environment*

Such distinctions will be essential when analysing recent development processes in cities in developing countries, and especially in the making of
'middle-class cities' whose built environment is adapted to efficient use of
automobiles (see Chapter 12). It is important to note also that this concept of
space is being reassessed now in the face of recent globalization processes
and the impact of new communication technologies, but no clear picture has
yet emerged (Castells, 1999; Cervero, 1998a).

Focusing directly on the circulation issue, it is important to define the *circulation structure* as the part of the built environment that allows the physical
circulation of people and vehicles: streets, pavements, railways and terminal
facilities. The circulation structure is the physical support for circulation itself, whether by foot or vehicle (*the circulation means*). The combination of the
structure and the means constitutes the *circulation system*. The circulation
structure links all spatial components of the built environment by allowing
for the movement of goods and people. The movement of goods is usually
effected through the use of vehicles. Human movement can take place with or
without vehicles. Both movements are essential for all urban activities and
are often subject to public regulation. The combination of the circulation system and the built structure (buildings, public spaces) is called the *circulation
environment* (Figure 5.1).

REPRODUCTION AND TRANSPORT

The use of the space depends heavily on where people live and perform activities. There is a complex relationship between social and economic factors
that lie behind the selection of a place to live, a place to work and places to go
to (Tolley and Turton, 1995). Especially in developing countries, reproduction strategies rely to some extent on a hierarchical decision process, entailing
housing, employment and transport (Trani,1985; Pacheco, 1985). Selecting a
place to live seems to be the first decision that has to be made, followed by the
decision on where to work and how to get there. As stressed by Trani, when
facing the housing and job markets people have to respond to two needs that
are not necessarily convergent; consequently, most poor people will face severe accessibility restrictions.

Second, the level of consumption, and hence the trip pattern, is not fixed by
biological factors (Gough, 1979). It is determined by social, political, religious,

cultural and economic factors, which vary in time and space across social classes and groups, regions and countries. In this respect, production cannot be conceptualized in a functionalist manner, as being only a means of satisfying needs; needs are also related to the production process, which shapes them in a continuous movement of conflicts between social classes, groups and dominant sectors. Nobody 'needs' dozens of different models of cars or motorcycles to choose from; such product proliferation results from competition between manufacturers and their need to survive in a capitalist economy, not from 'natural consumer desires' (Amin, 1992). The use of a particular transport mode may not be seen as a 'natural' desire, but as a decision constrained by the conditions.

Third, although constrained by individuals' actions, the trips are also highly dependent on general household and individual characteristics (income, age, gender) which limit an individual's circulation choices; it is also constrained by external factors, such as the time windows (opening hours) of desired destinations and the available transport means. This is the main reason why personal transport data have increasingly been analysed on a household basis, connecting the family trip pattern to the city structure (Hagestrand, 1987).

Fourth, transport demand, captured through the actual trips made by people, does not always represent their actual needs. These trips are the 'feasible' trips; if other conditions were present, other trips would be made. Hence, there are 'impossible trips' that are either fulfilled by non-desired means (walking instead of taking a bus), replaced by alternative activities (watching TV instead of going to the movies) or suppressed indefinitely (giving up going to school). The acknowledgement that only feasible trips are captured does not diminish the importance of the use of OD data. In addition to basic information regarding the actual appropriation of the circulation system, other relevant information can also be obtained by indirect means, such as analysing which activities or trips cannot be performed by people due to external constraints (eg a lack of transport connections).

Mobility and accessibility

The reproduction process implies physical mobility. It also implies the availability of transport means, either non-motorized and personal or motorized. Finally, it implies an appropriate connection between the transport means and locations of desired activities. Therefore, the reproduction process depends on a combination of personal conditions, the conditions of the circulation system, and the spatial distribution of desired destinations. Hence, the first important task is to clarify the differences between a technical, simplistic view of personal mobility and a social, more comprehensive view of accessibility.

There are several views of mobility and accessibility. Mobility may be seen as simply the ability to move, a function of physical and economic resources. In this sense, in a city with equal physical access to transport means, poor and elderly people with disabilities would be placed at the lower extreme of a mobility scale while wealthy and healthy people would be placed at the upper extreme. It is clear that mobility alone is just a technical computation that fits engineering, production-based calculus. It is therefore a very limited concept for transport policy analysis because it does not indicate why and how mobility is exercized (or not). Hence it is possible (Moseley et al, 1977), to arrive at a more meaningful definition of mobility and accessibility. The latter is seen as 'mobility for opportunities', that is, mobility which allows the person to get to the desired destination. That is why accessibility is not just the ability to overcome space but the ease of getting to a destination (Portugalli, 1980). What matters is access and how transport may contribute to it, not mobility in itself; a consequent relevant question for policy purposes is actual versus potential accessibility (Tolley and Turton, 1995).

This definition has three important consequences. First, it is user-related; that is, it reflects the user point of view (rather than the place point of view, as in the case of place accessibility). Second, it allows for the analysis of family, rather than individual strategies to organize joint trip schedules, using the available time, money and vehicle resources. Third, it leads to the analysis of accessibility as an important spatial output of transport systems (Reichman, 1983). This complex of conditions makes accessibility a much broader concept than mobility and the only one capable of capturing the travel pattern in its entirety; hence, accessibility becomes an essential tool for analysing transport and traffic policies.

The political analysis of mobility and accessibility requires three further considerations. First, social, economic and political differences deeply influence both mobility and accessibility conditions. Second, the relative importance of mobility and accessibility must be understood within the structural constraints of the development process. In this respect, the priority given to mobility in contemporary societies is deeply embedded in the process and ideology of capitalist development, where the concept of time as a value is increasingly relevant (Sachs, 1992; Harvey, 1985; Whitelegg, 1997a). Third, the analysis of mobility and accessibility conditions entails the discussion of equity issues and the welfare state in contemporary societies, using the questions raised in Chapter 3, concerning how space is used by people.

Strategies for reproduction

While circulating, the user develops desired or needed activities interrelated by a time and space network. This network is composed of origins and destinations spread over the space, and the traveller must consume time in order to reach any one of these spatial points. The daily operation of this network is comprised of people's mainly personal techniques for optimizing time and cost. The trips that are generated in this context are necessary, compulsory or discretionary. Necessary trips are those that fulfil economic and social needs, such as travelling to work or shopping. Compulsory trips are those made as a part of other people's trips (a child who has to follow its parents). Discretionary trips are those made at will, for cultural and social purposes. Some trips can be a part of other longer trips, in the sense that they share the same mode and are integrated in time and space. Connections between trips form 'trip chains', related to individual or family strategies to optimize available resources.

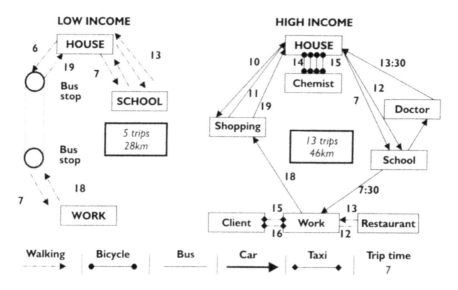

Figure 5.2 *Travelling patterns of two different families*

The set of trips requires a certain amount of time (time budget) and consumes a certain amount of distance (space budget). The analysis of these two budgets is essential to understanding reproduction processes (Zahavi,1976; Goodwin,1981). This analysis also has to consider two key factors: the purpose of the trips, and the travel mode. In addition, they have to be separated according to economic characteristics (income), social characteristics (age, level of schooling) and gender, ethnic or religious factors, whenever necessary and pertinent. Hence, the basic elements for the analysis are time budget, by mode and purpose, and space budget, by mode and purpose, according to selected social groups and classes. An example of how people use space is provided in Figure 5.2. It shows that the low-income family used bus and walking modes to perform 5 trips (not counting trips back home) which added up to 24km. The middle-class family used two automobiles and two bicycles to perform 13 trips (not counting trips back home) which added up to 46km. Should any particular condition be altered, travelling strategies would change accordingly. In the case of the low-income family, if the bus becomes too crowded or involves longer waiting times, another bus line may be selected or informal transport may be used. If school shifts are modified, the adult escorting the children may have to make additional trips at other times. In the case of the middle-class family, if parking is prohibited close to the office, the employed adult may have to rethink his or her journey. If the doctor has to be changed, the new doctor may be so far away that the escorting adult will have to find a way of gelling there. Even deeper changes may occur in the case of external forces such as unemployment or sudden income decrease.

THE BUILT ENVIRONMENT AND TRANSPORT POLICIES

The analysis of how people use space entails the analysis of transport modes. The differentiation between private and public modes and between the level of regulation that is related to any particular mode becomes crucial.

A particularly significant aspect is the increasing intervention of the state in the provision of physical conditions for production and reproduction, and consequently in the level of regulation of transport. This state intervention is directly related to the scale of consumption in increasingly complex urban structures, to the unwillingness of private agents to provide services, and to the changes brought about by the 'commodification' of social relations – that is, the process of progressively submitting such relations to monetary transactions.[1]

Families in the pre-capitalist period provided for their own basic consumption needs, such as water, wood, rubbish disposal, transport and housing (O'Connor,1973). In the face of deep transformations in the production sphere – the separation of labour from means of production, the complex social and technical division of labour – the individual or family satisfaction of consumption means was no longer possible and some forms of the socialization of consumption began to develop (Preteceille, 1981). The state began to intervene through the provision of public services like water, sewage collection, electricity and public transport.

As regards commodification, two cases must be identified. First, individual payments to the state for public services such as water and electricity (when essential services such as education and medical treatment were provided free). Second, payments to private suppliers for schools, medical services and private transport. This latter form reflects a sort of 'elitization' of consumption and is crucial to understanding the increasing use of the car (and motorcycles, to a lesser extent) for the new middle classes, as part of economic modernization in developing countries.

Developing countries may be classified according to their position within this historical process. There are very low-income societies which still have individual provision of subsistence means, especially those based on non-motorized transport. There are also medium-income societies in which the state already interferes in public services. There are medium-to higher-income societies in which public services are directly related to a well-established state that interferes in the provision and regulation of public services, where both public and private transport play important roles. Such a simple division is obviously not exhaustive. Current neoliberal reforms are prompting a change in the state role, but the process is slow in most developing countries and the state still retains a large responsibility for supplying or regulating services related to public interests. This way of approaching contemporary consumption needs gives rise to two important concepts. First, the *nature of consumption*, whether collective or individual. Although such a distinction is difficult to delineate, it is useful as an initial approach to the issue.[2] Unlike individualized consumption – which is mostly submitted to market rules – collective consumption refers to the socialized forms of consumption, submitted in a high degree to collective rules emanating from the state. Hence, it calls for an analysis of equity issues in access to products and services, in which the state plays a vital role. The way consumption is materialized implies the analysis of the *means of consumption* as expressing those facilities and tools which allow for the physical consumption of products and services – water distribution systems, electricity transmission systems, schools and, in our case, pavements, streets and vehicles. A crucial consideration for urban transport analysis is that, roads being public assets, their use is always subjected to some form of regulation. The same happens with transport vehicles.

From the above discussion, several questions arise concerning the socialization of consumption and related transport policies:

- Who plans, finances and provides for the means of consumption and under what conditions?
- What are the physical and symbolic characteristics of these means?
- How are they regulated, operated and controlled?
- Who appropriates them and under what conditions?

The provision (supply) of the consumption means can be accomplished by the state, the private sector, the individual, the family or the community. The actual relative participation of all these sources will vary dramatically in time and space, despite the overall tendency towards significant state participation, replacing investment by capital. Considering the usually unprofitable nature of infrastructure, roads and public transportation facilities (railway terminals) are supplied by the state, while vehicles may be provided by individuals or by the private sector. Recent privatization tendencies did not substantially change the overall pattern.

Regulation is vital to understanding the limits and constraints imposed upon the provision and the appropriation of the means of consumption. It is a public activity in itself. Traffic (the use of roads) is always subjected to regulation while public transport is often subjected to some form of regulation; in some cases, it is not subjected to any regulation at all (as with informal bus services in some Asian, African and Latin American countries).

Operation refers to who is allowed to operate the means of transport and which resources are available to accomplish the task. Circulation infrastructure is operated directly by the government; private modes are operated by individuals subjected to public regulation on traffic rules; public transport systems can be operated by either public or private agents.

Control refers to the power to enforce rules that govern supply. It is often exercised by public authorities but it can also be exercised by private agents, through the delegation of power. Appropriation of the means of consumption reveals the actual practices of consumption, represented by the acts of circulating and using streets and vehicles. These acts are performed by the users themselves through the organization of strategies to optimize time, cost and convenience. Appropriation also entails two other important considerations: the difference between the projected and actual clientele of the service that is provided, and the non-consumption strategy that is represented by alternative forms of consumption which are engendered by social groups to better address their needs (as in the case of informal public transport). The physical and symbolic characteristics of the means of consumption are also relevant aspects. Physical conditions are relevant as a way of understanding the nature of the product or service delivered and the spatial and time coverage of the supply; from an economic point of view, physical conditions are also necessary for measuring outputs against costs. Symbolic characteristics are relevant because the actual meaning of consumption is socially and culturally determined (eg the consumption of motorcycles as opposed to bicycles, of cars as opposed to buses). All the aforementioned characteristics are summarized in Table 5.1.

Table 5.1 *Main characteristics of urban transport policies*

Action	Content	Instruments, resources
Supply	Organization of infrastructure and circulation means	General laws: pavements, carriageways, vehicles and terminals
Regulation	Definition of rules of access and usage	Codes and regulations
Operation	Functioning of infrastructure and circulation means	Resources, rules and logistics
Control	Monitoring operation; enforcement	Resources, rules and logistics
Appropriation	Measuring impacts, actual use of infrastructure and circulation means, and symbolic characteristics as seen by users	Quantitative and qualitative data on users, transport and traffic conditions, and users' perceptions

6 THE USE OF ROADS: THE MICROPHYSICS OF SPACE

INTRODUCTION

Space is an essential element for analysing urban transport through a socio-logical and political perspective. This is because roads are public assets, to be used by anybody legally allowed to do so, and also because main roads – which carry most of the traffic – are built and maintained with public resources. The way road use and space organization have been handled by traditional techniques is reflected in 'traffic engineering' and its practical, operational branch, traffic management. Traffic management has long been viewed as a comprehensive and technical means of organizing city traffic optimally. Traffic engineers have developed quantitative techniques to deal with circulation-related considerations such as street capacity, geometric features, vehicle dimension and operation, and human physical and psychological characteristics, and have used them to decide how street space will be distributed between users. Implicit in this is the idea that this division may be decided neutrally, allocating equal benefits to everybody. This belief is deeply imbedded in a planning tradition that stresses quantitative approaches and underestimates the social and political aspects of urban circulation. The standard approach becomes especially problematic in developing countries where the political and social conditions differ widely from those in the developed world.

The main objective of this section is to evaluate the role of traffic management in distributing the circulation space. This evaluation requires the investigation of traffic conflicts and the social and political aspects of circulation, which in turn implies examining the limits of neutrality.

THE TRADITIONAL APPROACH TO TRAFFIC MANAGEMENT

Traffic management can be considered as the allocation of street space. In this respect, it can be said to pertain to a larger field – traffic engineering – which includes the work of building the street infrastructure itself; this is a part of an even larger field – transport engineering – which deals with the planning and operation of transport facilities of all modes.

The best definition of traffic engineering comes from the Institute of Transport Engineers (ITE),[1] as quoted in McShane and Roess (1990, p3):

Traffic engineering is that phase of engineering which deals with the planning, geometric design and traffic operations of roads, streets and highways, their networks, terminals, abutting lands, and relationships with other modes of transport.

That is to say, the traffic engineer works with technical tools – mostly mathematical and physical ones – in order to better organize the circulation of people and goods given the available structure of streets and the means of transport. The political characteristics of users, as well as the political dimension of space utilization, are believed to pertain to fields other than traffic management itself:

... whenever confronted by different opinions and political interests around the problem, the information that is given by the traffic engineer, based on essentially technical approaches, *allows the Public Administration (Government) clear guidelines for the determination of final decisions.* (Soares, 1975; emphasis added)

Hence, this view of traffic management as a 'technical' action assigns the task of dealing with differences in interests to another sphere of the state – the 'public administration'. In other words, this approach poses a clear distinction between the technical and the non-technical, the latter pertaining to a separate sphere of the state, distinct from traffic engineering. Following this approach, traditional traffic management considers the urban circulation problem as a given, 'natural' result of human activity, without analysing its nature; consequently, traffic engineering is considered a pragmatic, rational and neutral activity concerned with the physical optimization of the movement of people and goods within the given environment.

The current framework was developed in the US in the 1920s and experienced a rapid expansion throughout the world.[2] This expansion was related to the growth of the automotive industry and the congestion-related problems associated with the increasing use of the car. Especially in developing countries, traffic management has often been disconnected from other urban intervention techniques such as urban planning and transport engineering. This is so because traffic management constituted itself as a powerful independent branch, in terms of its importance in managing daily problems, and the commercial interests related to the outcome of its decisions. Despite this overwhelming dominance, the traditional approach has been criticized on many grounds. The following section summarizes some of the most important criticisms.

Criticism

The political nature of traffic policy and the political characteristics of users have been emphasized by many authors, although not in the same way as here. The first (indirect) approach can be traced to Mitchel and Rapkin's seminal book on urban traffic:

It seems apparent that some individuals travel about a city in highly specialised capacities; physicians make their rounds of calls, salesmen call on customers, businessman call upon bankers, housewives do the family shopping ... conceivably, the conflicting roles of individuals may become apparent also in their travel patterns, and may have considerable influence in determining them. Certainly in the design of any research on the motivations of travel, the influence of the status of an individual and of the single or multiple roles in which he is acting should be taken into account. (1954, p57)

To my knowledge, this statement is the first attempt in the traffic literature to relate traffic studies to traffic roles. Surprisingly, it disappeared from the usual definitions of traffic management that dominated in practice.

The second essential criticism came with the Buchanan's report (1963) that proposed a broader view of the urban transport problem. His report changed the traditional approach by attributing vital importance to the relationship between land use, traffic and the automobile. He questioned the actual benefits of the increasing number of private cars in modern towns, and proposed an analysis of the causes of urban movement. In addition, the report identified accessibility and environment as the basic conflicting objectives related to traffic management. Buchanan stresses that accessibility and environment 'tend to be in conflict' and acknowledges that it is difficult to work both out together; sacrificing accessibility would interfere with the functioning of the city, while sacrificing environment has already been done 'without solving the accessibility problem' (1963, p40). It is very important to note that this new conflict replaces the traditional one – safety and fluidity – with a much broader perspective, which creates a linkage between traffic management and both urban planning and transport engineering.

Other authors have also acknowledged the conflicting nature of traffic management decisions. Whol and Martin (1967) refer to the different interests of social groups. They ask two vital questions: Whose objectives are being considered? And what is the planner's point of view? This approach incorporates the values and interests of the social groups connected with the problem, as well as those of planners and politicians. Plowden (1972, p24) also addresses the political issue:

The most important misunderstanding ... is the idea that we have a choice between a policy which involves some restriction and a policy which does not. There is no such choice.

Whol and Martin (1967) also criticized the priority placed on fluidity and, implicitly, on car traffic. They questioned the pragmatic focus on eliminating congestion and proposed a broader view, which would shape a circulation system responsible to overall community goals and expectations. As stressed by Thompson:

Most cities have treated the car as a sacred cow ... in support of the car some highway engineers have become amateur philosophers, politicians and economists, proclaiming that people have a right to use their cars freely on the roads ... and that the economic survival of the city or nation depends on it ... they have spread the belief that the volume of traffic must always be accepted, cannot be resisted and is necessarily more important than any thing that may stand in its way ... (Thompson, 1977, p263)

Furthermore, Plowden comments on the conflicts involved in the use of space by drivers, pedestrians, cyclists, and bus and truck drivers, comparing the relative benefits and disbenefits of certain traffic management schemes.[3]

Finally, another approach proposes tackling the traffic conflict problem through research into the quality of life in residential environments and the impacts of traffic and transport on them (Appleyard, 1981). Appleyard's research makes an important contribution to the development of a sociological approach to the study of traffic relationships. The report breaks with a long tradition in the field by including the systematic analysis of the roles, conflicts and interests emerging from people's use of circulation space. This approach centres on a basic conflict similar to that of the Buchanan report. As Appleyard (p1) states, 'the street has always been the scene of this conflict, between resident and traveller, between street life and the threat of traffic', suggesting an inherent conflict between accessibility and environment. At first glance, this conflict is related to the increased and indiscriminate use of the automobile:

The pavement of roads ... has encouraged the intrusion of a new menace – the motorized vehicle. Today, traffic and its by-products have steadily and inexorably invaded the streets of our cities. (Appleyard, 1981, p3)

Appleyard reminds us that particular conflicts are also present. For example, traffic control devices on residential streets, while yielding immediate positive results, 'can generate strong opposition from residents, parallel streets, business, public service vehicles ...' (p10). Furthermore, the report stresses that the needs, values and expectations of residents differ, and depend on social, economic and cultural characteristics. This emphasis on social factors challenges the idea of a 'community of equal people', so important to traditional traffic engineering. Finally, the report introduces some preliminary notions about the roles played in traffic. In explaining the process of residential adaptation to the impact of traffic on neighbourhood life, Appleyard stresses that the suggested explanatory model is interactive, but

simplified, because 'travellers' and 'residents' are not always separable: residents also drive, and travellers reside. These are in fact the roles that people play. In the residential neighbourhoods people can think as drivers or residents, and can value either mobility or livability; this can lead to personal as well as social conflicts. (p32)

The contributions of all these authors can be said to have transformed the prevailing concepts of circulation space distribution. Nevertheless, they present some important drawbacks. Buchanan ultimately sees the automobile as desirable and neglects the social and political aspects of both using traffic space and formulating transport and traffic policies. In addition, he sees physical scarcity of circulation means as an independent variable, not society-related. Appleyard takes a limited view, street-based, and highly dependent on the US view of what a street should be. Finally, none of these different approaches go so far as to propose a new framework, because they deal only in passing with the concepts of roles, interests and conflicts. The next section proposes a comprehensive framework that is meant to overcome these drawbacks.

IN SEARCH OF A NEW APPROACH

For a better understanding of circulation space and related public policy, it is necessary to analyse the nature of traffic roles and conflicts, and the political aspects of the distribution and use of circulation space.

Traffic roles

The above approaches often consider only two basic roles: the driver, and the pedestrian, viewed as static identities. However, the outcomes of traffic policies are related to a larger and more dynamic number of roles. This set of roles is not explicitly mentioned by the traditional approach, and is instead referred to simply as 'people'. The first task is therefore to define these roles and their relevance for traffic policies.

To accomplish this task I will consider these roles in relation to two features: the use of mechanized transport, and passive or active relationships to traffic. Movement by foot is the only equally distributed means of overcoming space. With the exception of young children, old people or disabled people, everybody is capable of walking. The use of any sort of mechanized tool to overcome space introduces a sharp difference in capability that can be identified as a dividing boundary. This difference is larger when the mechanized tool is also motorized. Once this new tool is introduced, access to it is not equally distributed (Illich, 1974). This is true in any society, at any time. Nevertheless, it is important to define more precisely the relevant social and political consequences of the introduction of mechanized traffic. There are two basic differences to be addressed: accessibility and safety.

With accessibility, motorized means increase the average speed of overcoming space, thereby dramatically changing its consumption for those who can afford to buy the transport means. Needless to say, the actual access to these mechanized tools in developing countries is deeply constrained by personal, economic and social differences, thereby introducing immense inequality. Motorized transport implies heavier weight in motion, at higher speeds, and with higher kinetic energies in comparison with pedestrian movement, with obvious safety implication. The consumption of space includes the possibility of physical 'conflicts' in the form of traffic accidents, with often serious health consequences. These accidents are much more violent and likely to be fatal when pedestrians are involved; in most large developing country cities, the majority of people killed in traffic accidents are pedestrians. The political consequence is that some people with access to motorized transport may threaten other's health and life. Where impunity is the rule – such as in most developing countries – this possibility turns into a practical right.

The second feature mentioned above, the active and passive relationship to traffic, may be used as an analytical tool to differentiate between active and passive roles. The active role is characterized by a *movement* and hence the need to use road space. Conversely, the passive role is *stationary*: it doesn't traverse space but is affected by the active use of space by others. We can now propose a classification of traffic roles.

Table 6.1 *Traffic roles*

Role condition	Roles enacted
Non-mechanized and active	Pedestrian
	Escorted pedestrian
Non-mechanized and passive (stationary)	Resident
	Visitor/guest
	Owner/employee
	Customer
	Public facility user
	Waiting public transport user (bus stop)
Mechanized and active: non-motorized	Cyclist
motorized	Motorcyclist
	Car driver
	Taxi driver
	Truck driver
	Bus driver
	Car passenger
	Bus passenger
	Taxi passenger
	Truck worker
Special role (enforcement)	Police
Indirect role planning and regulating	Traffic planner/regulator
	Urban and transport planners
Indirect interests	Real estate agents and land developers
	Construction sector
	Automotive and related industries

This classification represents the diversified set of possible traffic roles and illustrates how simplistic is the approach taken by traditional traffic engineering, which considers only the fixed roles of 'drivers' and 'pedestrians'.

Most active and passive roles are related to social, economic and cultural characteristics, which restrict or impose limits on the use of space and vehicles. Some of the major factors are outlined below.

- *Income*: the access to expensive vehicles and to some sorts of public transport (fares) are restricted by income; even access to motorcycles – which have a lower purchasing and operating cost – is constrained by income, such as in Asian and African countries.
- *Age*: poses mental or physical limits to the use of roads and vehicles, as in the case of children, youngsters and elderly people.
- *Gender*: poses constraints that arise from the division of tasks among the household members – which varies according to different societies and are reinforced by traditional transport planning procedures.
- *Culture*: may limit access to some sorts of vehicles or place incentives on the use of others, in a way usually directly related to income and sociological determinants; it is often related to ethnicity.
- *Ethnicity*: may impose limits on the access to vehicles. The most famous cases are the separate school bus systems operating in the US until the late 1950s, and the recent spatial and transport separation between 'whites' and 'non-whites' in apartheid South Africa (Cameron, 1998).
- *Religion*: imposes limits on the access to vehicles and places. This gives rise to parents not allowing their children to attend schools that receive pupils from other religions, such as in Iran and India (Hallak, 1977).

Table 6.2 *Traffic roles and individual characteristics*

| Role | Frequency in performing roles according to individual characteristics | | | | | | | | |
| | Income | | | Age | | | | Gender | |
	high	middle	low	children	young	adults	elderly	male	female
Active									
Pedestrian	L	M	H	H	H	H[1]	M	M	H
Cyclist	L	M	H	L	H	H[1]	L	H/M	H/M
PT pass	L	M	H	L	H	H[1]	M	H	H
Motorcyclist	L	M/H	L/M	–	M	H[1]	M	H	L/M
Auto driver	H	M	L	–	–	H[1]	M	H	L/M
Passive									
Resident	M[2]	M[2]	H	M[3]	M[3]	M[4]	H[5]	M[6]	H[7]
Visitor	H	H	H	L	H	H	M	M	H
Customer	H	H	M	L	M	H	M	M	H
Owner	H	M/H	M/L[8]	–	–	Var[1]	Var[1]	H/M	M/L[8]
Student	H	H/M	M/L	H[9]	H[9]	H/M			

H = high frequency; M = middle frequency; L = low frequency; Var = variable
(1) Depends on specific conditions related mainly to income
(2) High- and middle-income people are more mobile and may spend more time in outside activities
(3) Children and youngsters spend several hours in school
(4) Adults spend several hours working outside home
(5) Elderly spend more time at home
(6) Men have more outside activities than women
(7) Women spend more time on home activities in most societies
(8) Informal businesses may be frequent within some societies and may be run by women
(9) Mainly schooling activities

BOX 6.1 *Road capacity problems are vehicle problems*

Conventional traffic engineering has developed sophisticated methodologies to deal with road capacity problems. With uninterrupted flow conditions, the most important example is the large literature developed in the US, epitomized by the famous capacity manual, the TRB's *Highway Capacity Manual* (TRB, 1985), first published in 1965. The difference in the depth and extent of treatment of vehicle and pedestrian capacity is astonishing but not surprising considering the prevailing travelling environment; the US has a 'pedestrian-deprived' travelling environment. The same difference affects bus traffic, although the 1985 edition included a fairly good chapter on the issue, along with a chapter on pedestrian capacity problems. With interrupted flow conditions, international literature is more diversified, as European literature has been added to that developed in the US. While the *Highway Capacity Manual* included procedures fitted to US traffic conditions, European literature proposed procedures better suited to developing countries (Webster and Cobbe, 1966; SETRA, 1973), including more detail on parking-related effects. However, all of them kept neglecting pedestrian needs, and remained immersed in the world of vehicle road-capacity analysis. Another important aspect is that capacity analysis refers to vehicles not people, and all vehicles are transformed into 'car equivalents', since cars are the most numerous vehicles in the traffic stream. Pavements are consequently kept away from the capacity analysis. Space is something that belongs to vehicles, reinforcing the strong fetishism surrounding cars. Developing countries need, instead, a *People's Capacity Manual*.

The actual distribution of these roles according to such characteristics is specific to each country or society, and can be analysed accordingly. Table 6.2 makes an initial classification of the frequency of the most important roles. From several active and passive roles, I have selected those that are either more frequent or more important for the proposed social analysis. Three individual characteristics were chosen – income, age and gender – which I think are the most important in determining travel choices.

Owing to different needs and interests, these roles involve several conflicts that are analysed in the following sections.

Travel needs and traffic management objectives

Two objectives have been extensively used in traditional traffic management studies: fluidity, and to a lesser extent, safety. Despite their importance, a better understanding of urban circulation must consider additional objectives that reflect other traffic conditions: accessibility (macro and micro), public transport service levels, cost, and environmental quality. Therefore, we should consider seven objectives, instead of two.

Accessibility, can be subdivided into two types. The first, *macro-accessibility*, refers to the ease of crossing city space and access to buildings and urban equipment. This objective relates to the spatial coverage of pavements, streets and public transport services, and reflects actions taken at the transport planning level, where physical circulation infrastructure is defined. It can be worked out operationally by traffic management, through one-way streets and the sequential connection of previously unconnected streets, which dramatically increases the connection possibilities. The second, *micro-accessibility*, refers to the relative ease of direct access to vehicles and buildings (bus stops and parking). These notions are based on an interpretation of Buchanan's accessibility concept and desegregate types of accessibility in a way not explicitly formulated in his work. Quantitatively, macro-accessibility can be expressed by the time spent walking (in walking-only trips) or, in the case of vehicle trips, by the sum of four travel times: the time taken to get access to the vehicle (micro-acessibility); time waiting (in the case of public transport); time inside the vehicle; and the time taken an arrival at the final destination, after leaving the vehicle (micro-accessibility again). A fifth time should be added in the case of transfer times between different vehicles or modes. The walking times to access vehicles are part of the general macro-accessibility, but they need to be isolated as traveller behaviour and mode selection are directly impacted by them (Kanafani, 1983; Oppenheim, 1995). Accessibility may also be translated in monetary terms, when it expresses transport costs.

Safety represents the level of danger experienced by people when using streets. It is measured by either the number of accidents, or by fatalities per number of vehicles or population.

Fluidity represents the rapidity and the smoothness of travelling throughout the space. It is measured by the average speed or any similar speed measurement. It is by far the most-used objective in traffic management, virtually mandatory in any single study, since it is related to the consumption of time, the most important variable for the traditional approaches.

Public transport service levels represent the average conditions offered to users. This is an essential consideration in developing countries, where theoretical assumptions of convenient supply are negated by reality. It has to be translated mainly through the passenger density (pass/m^2) and average comfort conditions inside the public vehicle (seating and standing facilities), since access and waiting times are already included in the accessibility computation.

Cost represents the direct (out-of-pocket) costs, such as fares for public transport users and fuel and parking for motorized vehicle users. In a more elaborate computation, it may include other costs such as travel time, taxes and maintenance, up to a point where an overall 'generalized' cost can be computed.

Environmental quality represents the level of air and noise pollution, and compatibility between traffic patterns and the local environment. It is also an objective reflecting actions taken at the urban planning and transport planning levels, as stated in Buchanan's concept of accessibility and environment conflict. Nevertheless, traffic management can directly and deeply effect environmental conditions.

Based on the above objectives, adequate safety conditions would be met by an absence of accidents, and adequate fluidity by an optimal average speed with few interruptions. Adequate macro-accessibility would be measured by a greater ease of moving around the city; adequate micro-accessibility by the possibility of having direct access to public transport and to parking. A good public transport service would be represented by the availability of seats in out-of-peak periods and of comfortable space in peak periods. Affordable transport would be represented by low-cost bicycle use, low-fare public transport and low-cost private motorized transport. Finally, an adequate environmental quality would be measured by little or no air and noise pollution, as well as by a compatible relationship between traffic nature and urban land use. These seven objectives should be considered in all traffic studies because they are included, directly or indirectly, in all circulation problems.

An important question is why only two objectives (fluidity and safety) have been pursued. There are two main reasons. First, the functional approach to urban management has kept urban planning, transport planning and traffic management isolated from each other; while land-use issues are supposedly dealt with by urban planners, and the provision and operation of public transport is thought of as being under the control of transport planners, for traffic managers the sole function left is to keep traffic moving. Second, when pursuing this limited objective, traffic managers commit themselves to the ideology of mobility at any price; nothing can remain stationary, because to move is essential. Hence, fluidity is the prime objective, while safety is pursued as a secondary priority.

The dynamics of roles and needs

As previously mentioned, everybody plays several roles when circulating, regardless of wealth levels and mode of transport. It is therefore worthwhile to analyse in detail how these roles and the associated needs develop when circulating, and the political consequences for policy purposes.

If we take the example given in Chapter 5 (Figure 5.2), now depicted in a different way in Figure 6.1, the characteristics of different roles become clear. In the low-income family, the daily movement of the worker using public transport could be represented as follows. He or she leaves home early in the morning, walks to the bus stop, waits for the bus, travels to the bus stop near the work place and then walks to work. During lunch time he or she eats inside the building. After finishing work, he or she walks to the bus stop, waits for the bus, takes the bus to the bus stop near home and then walks home, where he or she stays all night. This person has been out of the house for 11 hours. The daily movement of the middle-class male is different. He drives to a nearby school and escorts the children to the front gete. He drives again and parks at the office. At lunch time, he walks to a nearby restaurant. In the middle of the afternoon he leaves the office by taxi to attend a meeting, returning by taxi to work. Late in the afternoon, he leaves the office by car and, before getting home, stops at the shopping centre. Then he drives home and parks there.

This detailed but simple description of daily activities reveals the complex pattern of roles and needs. In this case, the worker enacted five different roles during the day: resident, pedestrian, waiting bus passenger, bus passenger and worker. He or she changed his or her needs ten times, each time he or she changed from one role to another. Considering just the out-of-house activities, this yields an average of about 2.75 hours per role (excluding the resident role) and 0.9 changes of interest per hour. The longer-lasting roles are obviously the stationary ones – resident and worker – due to the length of

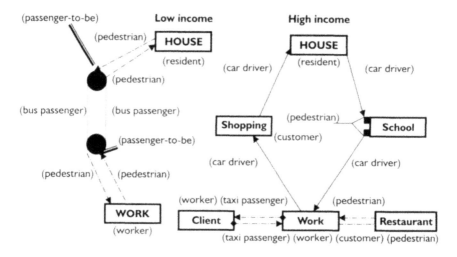

Figure 6.1 *Roles in typical journeys, according to income and mode*

time committed to them. The second longest is the active travelling role, followed by the active pedestrian and the waiting pedestrian.

The same description could be made of the daily activities of the middle-class male. His daily activities are more numerous and involve the use of private transport. They include the transport and escort of children. Therefore the number of roles is even greater, as well as the changes of needs. In this case, the man enacts seven roles: resident, pedestrian, driver, employee, customer, taxi passenger and visitor. He changed needs 16 times. Considering just the out-of-house activities, this yields an average of 1.83 hours per role (excluding the resident role), and 1.4 change of interest per hour.

In any given situation, people are in conflict with the roles played by others who share the same space, or who affect the individual's living or working space. These conflicts are not strictly class-based; that is, they involve all types of people, regardless of their class. Nevertheless, the severity of the conflicts and their related impacts, as well as their actual management, vary significantly.

Traffic roles and traffic conflicts

Urban circulation occurs in a physical space that must be distributed between those who want to use it. People and goods do not always have sufficient space and therefore must negotiate. The rules for this negotiation are determined externally by the traffic code, and internally at the traffic scene through minor decisions taken by the users. There is a certain level of flexibility in this negotiation. Traffic management organizes the circulation space and mediates the conflicts through physical and symbolic communication tools (signs), relying on the user's respect of traffic rules. Nevertheless, traditional traffic management deals only with the physical characteristics of conflicts. It is necessary to broaden this view, and think about the political content of these conflicts. Under which conditions do people negotiate the available space? Is anybody favoured? The political and physical analysis of traffic conflicts may help us to understand urban circulation problems. To do this, active and passive role enactment must also be considered. The best way to approach these relationships is to examine them as sets of roles representing typical traffic situations. Examples are given below.

Pedestrians and drivers at crossings

When crossing the street, the pedestrian is concerned with safety, while the driver wishes to travel as fast and fluidly as possible, with few stops or delays. At a street crossing, the pedestrian has to find time gaps in the traffic stream in order to cross safely. In this case, the driver's fluidity is optimized at the expense of the pedestrian's safety and fluidity. Conversely, a traffic signal installed for safer pedestrian crossings is at the expense of driver fluidity.

Residents and passing drivers

While a resident desires safety and environmental quality for his or her family, the non-resident passing driver desires fluidity. This case is similar to the street crossing case but has additional characteristics in the resident's desire to play or walk safely on the street, and to be free from traffic intrusion, and air and noise pollution. This conflict emerges when local streets are used as alternatives to congested routes. The residents either adapt to the prevalence of passing traffic or react against it in several ways. When residential streets are used as alternative routes, the optimization of the driver's fluidity and accessibility is made at the expense of residents' safety and environmental quality. If traffic authorities divert the passing traffic to other routes, they either damage the passing driver's accessibility (if the new route is a longer route to long-distance destinations), or they just transfer the problem to another street. If impeding obstacles are installed to slow down the passing drivers, local safety and environmental quality are imported at the expense of the driver's fluidity. Many drivers are also local residents and therefore are on both sides of the problem. In São Paulo, for instance, residents have demanded obstacles to slow down passing drivers only to request later that they be removed (Vasconcellos, 1995). Similar conflicts can emerge when the passing vehicles are buses.[4]

Shopkeepers, customers and passing drivers

The shopkeeper desires maximum accessibility to his place of business. This requires adequate parking or convenient bus stops for customers. The shopkeeper also needs sufficient space for loading and unloading delivery trucks. Conversely, passing drivers need fluidity. Therefore there are two conflicts: the first between three sorts of micro-accessibility needs – parking, loading and bus stop facilities – and the second between these micro-accessibility needs and the fluidity of passing drivers. If parking and loading restrictions are adopted, this can benefit the micro-accessibility of public transport passengers at the expense of private drivers' micro-accessibility. Conversely, if parking or loading operations are facilitated, this can severely damage the micro-accessibility and traffic fluidity of public transport passengers.

Public transport passengers and car owners

Public transport passengers require state intervention to improve bus speeds or to reserve circulation space for optimal bus fluidity. The car owner desires driving fluidity and accessibility to destination points. Therefore, there is a major conflict of political and technical priorities in state policies. If the traffic authorities reserve space for buses, public transport fluidity is provided at the expense of automobile and truck circulation. If it does not, the buses suffer a reduction in average speed and an increase in operational costs, which may eventually be transferred to passengers.

CONSEQUENCES FOR POLICY ANALYSIS

Several consequences for policy analysis can be derived from this discussion. They are outlined below.

- In changing roles and needs, the user makes different demands in time and space. As the user travels throughout the space, he or she may demand fluidity, accessibility, safety, comfort or environmental quality. At the same time, other users have other needs and place other demands. They are inherently conflicting and they have to be negotiated.
- The higher the number of activities, the higher the number of roles and the higher the frequency of need changes. As the number of activities is directly related to the income level, middle- and upper-class people have a much greater interaction in traffic, therefore making more varied demands.
- People who take on active rotes are much more likely to have their needs attended to. However, their are different kinds of active role. The car, motorcycle and taxi driver are much more influential than the pedestrian and the cyclist, because they embody the ideology of speed and movement as progress. Nevertheless, some stationary roles are politically important, for example the resident role and the business person. The resident's role is relevant because people spend a large part of their time in home. It is related to the family's quality of life, to children's safety and to a sense of territory, that should not be undervalued (Appleyard, 1981). The shopkeeper is also important politically because profitability is directly related to the customer's access conditions.
- All roles are theoretically possible. Nevertheless, some roles are played more efficiently, safely or conveniently than others. As the satisfaction of all needs is impossible, and as traffic management decisions are not neutral, every circulation space is physically marked by past policies, revealing the dominant interests that shaped them. The physical arrangement of most large cities in developing countries is proof of the shaping of circulation space for the most powerful roles, especially the driver, and, more directly, the middle-class driver. Cities were adapted to the convenient circulation of automobiles at the expense of other interests, especially pedestrians and public transport users. However, the organization of these aggressive built environments did not prevent the weakest roles from finding their space. No role is totally rejected, or limited on a city-wide scale,

but the weakest have to submit themselves to the needs of the strongest. Hence poor people in general, and poor children and elderly people in particular, are the most affected by restrictions to safe and convenient access to the urban space.

- The daily trajectory of a person has to be analysed on a household basis, because families define strategies for circulating, given external and internal constraints. The analysis of all the individual trajectories allows the computation of time and space budgets which reflect, respectively, the time allocated to travel and the space consumed in travelling. This combined analysis reinforces the conclusions set forth regarding the complexity of space appropriation and its relationship to social, economic and cultural characteristics.

Principles for a new approach to traffic management

The analysis made so far poses several fundamental principles for a new approach to urban circulation and traffic conflicts.

First, two types of traffic conflicts govern the division of space:

1   The *physical conflict* of two bodies trying to occupy the same space at the same time. This type of conflict is the concern of traditional traffic management rules and techniques.
2   The *political conflict*, representing the users' needs and interests, as political actors inside a specific society. This conflict is the concern of a political approach to traffic management.

The joint consideration of these two sorts of conflict changes completely the approach to traffic management. First, traffic is not made by people divested of their social and political characteristics, but by *political human beings with different needs and interests*. Therefore, the political approach to traffic management is not just a new proposal, it is the only possible proposal for a responsible policy analysis.

Second, *there are no fixed roles in traffic, because people play many roles*. Despite the tendency of social characteristics to restrict one's roles – like the middle-class male who, while circulating, generally assumes the role of driver – human activities make it necessary to play almost every possible traffic role. Therefore, if someone is a driver between home and office, he or she may be a pedestrian at lunch time, a driver when going back home and a resident at night. He or she may also be a public transport passenger, a taxi passenger, or a customer. Therefore urban traffic is a very complex arena, in which conflicting roles are constantly competing.

Third, *needs change in time and space*. Before boarding, public transport passengers desire accessibility to the bus; when travelling on the vehicle they desire fluidity; when approaching the destination they desire accessibility again. A middle-class driver desires accessibility to the car and fluidity in driving conditions; however when leaving the children at school he/she expects safety and when arriving at work he/she again desires accessibility to parking. As needs and interests change, *there is a great deal of variation in the demands placed on traffic authorities* by the conflicting needs of different people.

Fourth, as roles, needs and interests change in time and space, *no single issue should determine traffic policies.* The fundamental political consequence is that there are no strong social movements mobilized around traffic, because there is no single actor or single issue. This does not mean that traffic policies are neutral, or that they originate solely in the heads of planners. In addition to being influenced by the press – traffic is a highly political issue, especially with respect to congestion – planners are political beings, committed to perceptions of reality and to political beliefs. Moreover, they are deeply committed to the interests of the middle class, not only because they often are middle class, but also because they share the same support for capitalist modernization and social mobility.

As a consequence, *it is impossible for the state to resolve all the demands simultaneously.* To install a pedestrian crossing means an increase in pedestrian safety but a decrease in driver fluidity.

Hence, the political nature of human activities along with the conflicting nature of space use makes traffic engineering not only a technical, *but also a political act.* It uses technical tools to distribute a limited space between political players with conflicting needs and interests, and different levels of access to the decision-making process. Therefore, it cannot be viewed as a 'neutral' activity. State intervention is always a compromise that will distribute benefits and disadvantages between the users according to their relative powers. Consequently, any analysis has to consider the essence of the movements as social and economic activities along with the relative position of the users.

Finally, it has to be acknowledged that *traffic management has been largely reliant on two myths.* The first is the ideological myth of neutrality in traffic management. This belief is driven by the strength of technical tools in shaping people's view of public policies, and by the political strength of the technocracy, represented by traffic planners. Traditional traffic management tends to see circulation analysis as a neutral activity, supported by a reliance on computation and forecasting. People are either 'pedestrians' or 'drivers' and the planners have only to use their neutral expertise to decide the optimal division of the space. Then there is the spatial myth. This assumes that conflict may be eliminated by constructing a conflict-free physical circulation space. Buchanan, Thompson and Plowden seem trapped within such a myth. Buchanan (1963) imagines a conflict-free space made of connected environmental areas. His report suggests the redevelopment of cities (with all the related costs), reduction of the basic of conflict through land-use control (a technique called 'traffic architecture'), and diversion of through traffic. The report emphasizes the organization of 'environmental areas' by accommodating only the amount of traffic compatible with environmental capacity (Hillman, 1983). For Thompson (1977) the problem is economic and all aspects of the problem can be solved, or 'almost solved', given enough money. Finally, Plowden (1980) imagines that conflicts are always car related and that a public-transport-oriented policy would avoid them. These views neglect the changeable nature of traffic roles and the ultimate impossibility of constraining them in fixed structures. Physical, let alone political, conflicts cannot be overcome completely. The physical elimination of circulation conflicts can be accomplished in only a limited number of places, not only because of the costs involved but also because of the fluid nature of human activities in traffic. And political conflicts may be negotiated, not eliminated.

CONCLUSION

A reassessment of traffic management requires a recognition of the political nature of the division of circulation space. Second, it requires the consideration of a more complex set of variables that better explain the needs and interests that occur around any traffic activity. Finally, it requires the analysis of the political roles that are played in daily traffic, as well as the changing character of these roles and their needs and interests.

These political elements have to be considered in the light of state action – the public policy of urban circulation – and the political powers that influence this action. Since it is impossible to simultaneously address all needs and interests, it is necessary to ask which role is being favoured by the intervention, and which is being harmed. The final balance of this evaluation will reveal the policy substance.

7 THE POLITICAL ISSUE: AGENTS IN URBAN TRANSPORT POLICY

Although globalization and other profound social and cultural changes are transforming the way the state functions, and redefining its relationship with the private domain (Castells, 1999), current urban transport conditions in developing countries have to be analysed in the light of the way the state has been operating in those countries in recent decades. Globalization is still in its initial phase, and despite changes in the way investment and development are conducted, many of the former conditions still hold true in a highly conflicting political environment. Whatever changes globalization brings I believe the state will continue to play a key role in defining and monitoring public policies.

Political issues in urban transport policy will be analysed in light of the conditions found in developing countries, particularly the structure of the state, the profile of the decision-making process and the main agents involved.

The analysis of the state will place emphasis on its role in recent decades and the characteristics of the political process, including the level of political representation and the state of democratic institutions. Throughout, one must remain aware of the particular social and historical characteristics of each country.

Two main analyses will be made. First, the role of the elite, the middle classes, the bureaucracy and the technocracy; second, social movements related to urban transport.

THE STATE AND THE DECISION-MAKING PROCESS

The fundamental characteristic of society and state relations in developing countries in recent decades is the relative political autonomy of the state with respect to economic and social spheres, creating conditions for broader state action and the self-expansion of its apparatus (Martins, 1985). Furthermore, the characteristics of peripheral capitalist development give the state a structural function as well as a role in guiding the development process and participating directly in the production effort. The state organizes the accumulation of capital, conducts the relationships with the core, mediates external influences, and legitimizes the actions of the bureaucracy. Although public policies are considered to be 'collective' actions, the state is the focal point for most of the key decisions; transport infrastructure is provided mostly by the state, and public transport services and users receive legal or financial support during critical phases, when adequate provision or affordable access is threatened. This central role of the state continues despite recent neoliberal policies that deregulate or privatize public services and infrastructure provision.

Second, the state is neither impenetrable nor homogeneous – it does not act in exclusive accordance with the interests of dominant groups. Despite its function in supporting the reproduction of dominant economic relations, it acts through a set of agencies with different resources and levels of autonomy, loosely attached by institutions and representing the 'crystallisation of interests' of several social groups and the bureaucracy (Martins, 1985). Its action is full of contradictions and is based on a conflicting set of loyalties to different interest groups.

Finally, economic development does not presuppose the search for equity; that is, it can be pursued by simply creating a small, but reliable, market. The tension between accumulation and legitimization (O'Connor, 1973) is resolved in a politically astute way. This sort of development 'leads to the creation of islands of wealth inside a context of poverty'. These islands are sustained, on one hand, by the importation of technology and equipment, and on the other hand, by the formation of a consumer class (Cardoso, 1977). Such unbalanced growth has been occurring in all developing countries in recent decades to varying degrees and is directly related to the emergence of middle-class families who see motorization as a necessity.

New political systems and democracies in developing countries

Political representation and its position in the decision-making process is a major issue. Recent democracies that have developed in developing countries are named 'democracies' in the sense that they admit the coexistence of multiple levels of decision and influence. Nevertheless, they are not 'representative' in the European style, but are rather 'delegative' (O'Donnell, 1988). This sort of democracy is largely personality-based, as one person governs without the need for manifestos or adherance to a political party. Consequently,

> *Legislative and judicial powers are intrusions … the mere idea of accountability with respect to public or private agencies and organisations appears like unnecessary impediments to the unambiguous authority he has received.* (O'Donnell, 1988, p31)

For instance, Daniere (1995) points out that political scientists see Thai people as literate and increasingly urbanized, but generally indifferent to national policies, believing in a system of status according to religious belief, and the patron–client relationships that characterize economic activities.

This comparison between delegative and representative democracies rests on the notion that the latter are founded on a set of democratic institutions, which constitute the focal points of the decision-making process. They are based on the acceptance of a superior interest, leaving individual or group strategies and needs to one side (although not denying them). They operate on the basis of a 'competitive cooperation', which facilitates political bargaining and ensures the sequential accomplishment of the political agenda, strengthening mutual acceptance and increasing the value attributed to the institutions (O'Donnell,1988). Therefore, the political institutions are indeed a decisive means of mediating and aggregating structural factors on the one hand, and social needs and interests on the other (the latter being represented by social organizations).

Delegative democracies are seen as having a restricted scope, weak and low-density institutional relationships, and strong non-formalized institutions, including patronage and corruption. They are characterized by exclusive and personal access to policy decisions. This personal access denotes what Da Matta called the 'relational citizenship', in which personal relations are much more important to policy formation than formal Western-style citizen's rights (Da Matta, 1987).

From a practical point of view, unlike representative (or 'institutionalized') democracies in which decisions are made after a long process of discussion, in delegative democracies policy decisions are formulated rapidly, thereby carrying the possibility of substantive errors and implementation problems.

Brazil is an example of a country in which local governments usually experience high levels of autonomy (Pahl, 1977a). Mayors in Brazil are considered to have a 'discretionary and irresponsible' power, in the sense they are free to choose the path of policies and are not accountable except in the most formal and bureaucratic ways (Nunes, 1991). The mayor is the central focus of all issues pertaining to the public sphere, and chooses the actors who will participate in the policy-making process. New social movements sometimes impinge on policy decisions but the mayor still has a large discretionary power. Legislative power is limited by restrictions on its power to deal with budgetary issues, as well as by the fact that some legislative politicians will have a personal interest in issues being handled by the mayor. There is a coalition of patronage between the executive and the legislative, which has profound effects on social demands, actors, and conflicts. Demands are fragmented into specific issues, and patronage conveniently disguises private interests.

In most developing countries, the public sector is formally in charge of planning, a task which performs inadequately because of the fragmentation of agencies and institutional overlap. One can imagine the conflicts that emerge concerning the role and jurisdictional limits of the public agencies that cope with transport policies. In most cases transport issues are dealt with by two or three levels of government: local, regional or federal. The features of the transport system that are formally attached to each of these levels overlap. Therefore several conflicts arise, both between the political interests behind each transport system, and within the agencies themselves. Most major cities in the developing world experience these problems.

Two other aspects must be emphasised. First, most democracies are fragile and are subject to external and internal destabilization pressures, which leads to constant disruption of the political system. Second, the understanding of political citizenship is weakly developed, a situation made worse by deep social and political differences between social groups and classes.

AGENTS IN THE DECISION-MAKING PROCESS

Despite the state's overwhelming power, especially at the local level, other actors also play an important role. All these actors have different and often conflicting interests. Not all of them participate in all the discussions, and when they do, they seldom have equal leverage. In institutionalized democracies policy discussions incorporate several powerful actors (Lupo et al, 1971; Whitt, 1982); in developing countries there are fewer actors since the process is highly exclusive.

Bureaucracy, technocracy and the middle classes

The bureaucracy and the technocracy have to be analysed both in respect to their internal ethos and to their relationship with social and pressure groups.

Prevailing pluralist approaches to the analysis of these agents are inadequate, since pluralism believes private action to be a free force compatible with the public wellbeing, leaving politicians and the bureaucracy to select important public issues. In addition, pluralism sees no contradiction between social classes and private action, and minimizes the influence of market failures and of capital concentration (Alford and Friedland, 1985). The best way to analyse state structure is to combine elite (managerial) and classist approaches. The managerial approach is based mainly on Max Weber's analytical tradition which has become increasingly relevant in the face of the growing importance of state intervention and the bureaucratic control of society. Weberian criticism of the classist approach is rooted in the notion that although economic conditions are important for class formation, other noneconomic elements are essential in determining people's interests. The way rewards are acquired and distributed in the market is crucial (Fainstein, 1997) and 'stratification by prestige, based on occupation, consumption and style of life [is] particularly important in capitalist societies' (Abercrombie and Urry, 1983, p7).

The state must be able to deal with the inherent conflicts between dominant sectors, which requires a minimum level of internal independence. The bureaucracy – and more recently the technocracy – may be capable of performing this role. Therefore, in any specific situation, one has to enquire into the relative freedom of the bureaucracy with respect to dominant sectors (Offe, 1981).

In this respect, Carnoy and Levin (1985) argue that bureaucrats are members of the dominant class; in the case of developing countries, the 'elitist' origin of the bureaucracy is even more pronounced. Daniere (1995) points out that in Thailand the elite is educated and conservative. As educational access is limited by income and class, there is a 'gate' to the access to bureaucratic positions.

Cardoso (1977) also points out that capitalist modernization in developing countries is supported by some portions of the bureaucracy, especially the technocracy, which directs its actions according to the most important interests of capital.

However, despite their strong relationship to the dominant sectors, most bureaucracies and technocracies seem to be closely associated with specific social sectors, especially the middle class. They have common roots in the economic development of the 20th century, especially the monopolistic phase of capitalism after the 1930s (Carchedi, 1975). A differentiation in functions and the development of complex hierarchies occurred at the same time (Wright, 1976). A new stratum of managers and professionals who were qualitatively different from the traditional working class was formed (Howe, 1992).

An understanding of the function, interests and political behaviour of the middle classes is essential to understanding economic development and motorization in developing countries. Their function in the production system could be broadly defined as controlling work tasks, reproducing the system, and developing the conceptualization of the work process; they can be also seen as a new class of 'knowledge producers' (Howe, 1992). These are essential, not accessory, functions of the system, which places the middle class in a privileged position. The notion of an independent middle class can be related to the previously-discussed relative independence of the bureaucracy. Welfare bureaucracies are run by as well as for the salaried middle class (Gould, 1981), which is 'politically equipped to defend the benefits if and when they are threatened' (Ginsburg, 1992, p4). As stated by Cardoso (1977, p33),

> It is a fact that state bureaucracy and the technocracy will turn themselves into strategic points to be used by the middle classes in their struggle to have access to decisions regarding the development process.

The political behaviour of the middle class is therefore variable; it is reformist, in the sense of pursuing changes without challenging the system, and individualist, in the sense of emphasizing personal mobility (Gould, 1981; Poulantzas, 1975). The middle class has a commitment to a new style of life, a new and diversified consumption pattern, and a new way of using city space. Despite the necessary relationship between this new lifestyle and new sources of income, the middle class will identify more closely with other agents who have the historical, educational, cultural or economic background that enables them to benefit from modernization, to engage themselves in the new urban life and experience social mobility. In Brazil, the new pattern of social reproduction of the middle classes is related to four main commodification processes, each with profound implications for travel patterns: education, health, personal services and leisure. The replacement of public by private schools, the inclusion of special educational activities for children (foreign languages, arts), the replacement of public by private healthcare, the use of new personal and leisure services (physical fitness, sports) all characterize the new middle class. Private transport is an inseparable part of this new lifestyle, especially in face of poor public transport.

Social movements

Transport and traffic conditions affect people's daily life, often resulting in complaints and discontent. Here we will analyse political participation in transport and traffic problems. This participation does not necessarily challenge the prevailing process and may lead to manipulation.

In any particular situation people will try to use the circulation structure in such a way as to address their needs as conveniently as possible. This attempt to reach a balance between needs and supply requires three particular conditions which can contribute to the emergence of any sort of political pressure.

First, as previously discussed, the difference between possible and actual trips is defined by personal and external limits. A suppressed demand might form the basis of a particular political movement.

Second, the conditions of the circulation structure may lead to discomfort and discontent, as in the case of poor public transport services and poor traffic conditions. Third, the continuous innovation in production inherent in a capitalist economy is accompanied by innovations in consumption, which entail changes in physical infrastructure and spatial forms. Hence, reproductive activities and related lifestyles are constantly changing, leading to changing trip patterns in need of different transport supply patterns. As stressed by Harvey, '... the ferment of urban politics and the diverse social movements contained therein is an important part of such an innovative process' (1985, p126).

Five main practical problems lie behind people's unhappiness with transport conditions: access to desired destinations, trip comfort and safety, and time and monetary costs. The balance of these variables in any particular situation will depend on objective as well subjective appreciation. Although clear objective conditions may lead to a negative evaluation and hence to a complaint or conflict, the formation of consciousness about the actual conditions in the light of subjective social and political evaluations is the most important factor for long-term political effects (Kowarick, 1991). Therefore, everyday experience is essential in forming individual or collective judgements, and has profound effects on people's perception of their living conditions.

Types of participation

Political participation can be analysed in several ways. My analysis focuses on three main aspects: political nature, individual or collective expression and practical development.

In terms of political nature, participation can be initially classified as reformist or structural (Castells, 1977). The former intends to change conditions without changing the political decision-making process, while the latter intends to change both. In terms of individual or collective expression, these movements may be classified as user-level or collective-action level (May and Ribeill, 1976), as well as state-level. The user-level movement denotes an individual complaint. Collective action is characterized by formal organizations or social groups. The collective nature of this action leads to a broader emphasis on the provision and management aspects of the problem. State-level participation is directly related to the nature and interests of the bureaucratic and technocratic sectors and the corresponding conflicts.

These movements should be understood as either open or hidden, and as demanding or reactive. Open movements are those that operate through explicit forms of pressure, with success depending heavily on their political visibility. An example would be the attempts of poor neighbourhoods to improve public transport services. Political conditions will lead these movements to use either peaceful or violent means. Hidden movements are those that operate through indirect forms of pressure from within the state. Demanding movements press for improvements in actual conditions, such as new public transport lines, higher bus frequencies or road infrastructure. Reactive movements protest against changes in actual conditions, for example an increase in bus fares, the opening of residential streets to local traffic, or motorway construction.

Open political movements can be either demanding or reactive, peaceful or violent. Hidden movements are mostly peaceful and demanding. This is related to the balance between needs and available means in organizing political pressure. Especially in developing countries, individuals and neighbourhood organizations do not have much access to the decision-making process. Conversely, formal organizations linked to dominant and middle-class sectors have direct access to the state, and can exercise pressure either directly or indirectly. The main characteristics of such movements are summarized in Table 7.1.

Table 7.1 *Social movements and urban transport*

Type of movement	Main characteristics	Example
Level of organization		
Individual	Individual complaints	Change in bus stop
Group	Social complaints	Fare decrease
State	Interests inside state	Public transport regulation
By nature		
Demanding	Demand changes	Public transport improvement
Reactive	Resist changes	Road construction revolt
By logistics		
Open	Direct (public) pressure	Community demonstration
Hidden	Indirect (hidden) pressure	Elite and middle-class influence on state decisions
By tactics		
Peaceful	Peaceful means	Community reunions
Violent	Violent means	Destruction of buses

Analysis of political movements

We may now summarise the most important questions regarding political movements:

• What is the relationship between people's conditions and transport and traffic political movements?

- What influence do such movements have?
- How do they conflict with or reinforce each other?

One must remember that individuals face different conditions and may have different views of a problem, a constraint pertinent to any social issue. This particular feature is further enhanced by the singularity of road use; there are conflicting needs attached to each role, placing different pressures on the transport and traffic authorities. There is no single actor, because people play many roles in circulation. In addition, there is no single need or interest and hence no single political conflict. Political movements around traffic problems tend to be limited to emergency situations where dramatic conditions generate violent protest. In this respect they are transitory, making it very difficult to sustain mobility and participation after the achievement of the initial objectives (Boschi, 1987). These characteristics of circulation consumption, as opposed to other consumption needs like water and housing, suggest that circulation is not an issue that divides clearly along class lines. Circulation implies many physical conflicts that affect everybody, regardless of class. However, circulation also implies *political* conflicts.

First, conflict is present when open movements demand better public transport. The supply of transport services is often left to the market and transport costs (fares) come out of the worker's wages (in the absence of subsidies). As long as the actual transport conditions are accepted, capital has no reason to improve them. However when conditions are inadequate, open movements may arise. Although normally aimed at the state as the provider, these movements reflect the conflict between capital and labour. In practice, the solution may be provided either by capital (in the form of a salary increase) or by the state, using public resources to provide or improve transport conditions, and so freeing private capital from another expense.

The second way in which conflicts present themselves is through the use of the circulation structure and the transport means. The simplistic approach which views the conflict as the choice between a car and a bus is inadequate. The conflict is a product of the conflict between the middle classes with access to private transport, and the remaining social groups. It concerns the appropriation of circulation space, and hence the efficiency of social reproduction. In contemporary capitalist cities, the larger the road system and the easier the purchase and use of cars, the better the reproduction of the middle class. Conversely, the larger the spatial and time coverage of public transport networks, and the cheaper the fares, the better the reproduction of other social groups. As a general rule, the circulation structure of contemporary cities in developing countries is much more easily appropriated by the middle class with access to private transport means.

Open movements for better public transport have not led to any significant change in prevailing supply conditions in most developing countries (Dimitriou, 1990).

Open movements to protest against high fares or residential neighbourhood intrusion by traffic have been far more effective. One special case is the neighbourhood movement against speeding thru-traffic (Vasconcellos, 1995). In these cases, residents blocked street traffic with bricks or holes. These movements have important characteristics. First, they happen as a violent protest against fatal accidents, generally involving children hit by passing cars, and therefore have a powerful emotional content which contributes to swift collective organization. Second, they are highly effective in impeding traffic and aiming protest at local traffic authorities with an actual problem-solving capacity. Third, they are short-lived movements which disband after the successful rearrangement of local circulation. Finally, they disguise the conflicts between residents: for instance, limiting traffic benefits some interests (safety and environmental quality) and harms others (fluidity and accessibility).

The most successful movement is indisputably the hidden movement to adapt the cities for private transport. It is a long-term movement embedded in capitalist modernization. It is performed by the bureaucracy and technocracy, along with technical sectors outside the state (consultants) and dominant political and economic groups. Because it addresses dominant interests, feeds the middle-class ideology of modernization, and is rooted in actual and permanent access to the decision-making process, it is by far the most powerful movement. It has already occurred in many Latin American cities and is now under way in developing countries all over the world, especially in Asia. It results in a travelling environment that severely harms the objectives of public transport and non-motorized users, further limiting the efficiency of their supporting movements.

THE INSTITUTIONAL ISSUE

URBAN POLICIES AND DEVELOPMENT

'The institutional issue' refers to how the state, society and private agencies define and implement transport-related public policies. As stressed in Chapter 4, several public policies influence socio-spatial organization, including urban development, land use, housing, labour relations, investment, taxation, transport and traffic. For our purposes, three main areas are relevant: urban planning, transport planning and traffic management. These are associated with three objectives: land, circulation structure and means, and circulation patterns. The identification of these three areas differs from the traditional literature, where urban planning and transport planning are considered to be the most important public actions. Traffic management is often considered to be of secondary importance, related to more technical, simple objectives that should be dealt with by engineers. However, the assumption proposed in the book of the use of space as a central issue for policy analysis renders such activity as essential as the other two.

While urban planning is mainly concerned with land use and the physical provision of public services (water, sewage collection, schools, medical services), transport planning involves the definition of the circulation infrastructure and means, and traffic management works with the division of road space. Despite a hierarchical relationship between the three – with power decreasing as one passes from urban planning to traffic management – there are clear interrelations between them, as well as overlapping areas. The attempt to depict them as separate areas is of analytical use only.

URBAN PLANNING

Urban planning involves the definition of land occupation patterns according to different purposes (residential, commercial, industrial). It also defines how public services will be distributed in space. In defining limits to land use, it constitutes a conflict-ridden political arena, and in defining the physical distribution of public services it directly interferes with accessibility, equity and efficiency.

Urban planning begins during periods of intense urban growth which throw up related conflicts surrounding land use, the provision of public services, the environment, energy consumption and quality of life. The complexity of the production system and the interrelationships between production, exchange and consumption make planning inevitable as an attempt to manage conflicts. It is a means by which the state tries to overcome contradictions, compensate for increasing imbalance and risks, and minimize conflicts (Castells, 1975). However, it can be a precarious way of rationalizing the relations of power (Jamarillo, 1993). The result is a built environment that ensures minimum conditions for the reproduction of the system, but is subject to disruptive tensions.

Urban planning is the tool of a technical rationality that is expected to conciliate divergent social interests, guided by the economic efficiency criteria and directed at social transformation; it is grounded on the belief that scientific rationality (Winner,1977) is in itself indisputable and criticism free (Dupuy, 1978). These characteristics occur in traditional transport planning, which has been intensively used in developing countries.

Some questions can be posed in the light of these structural constraints.

Is urban planning possible in developing countries?

The unbalanced and often disruptive growth experienced by developing countries poses severe limits to urban planning. High levels of migration from rural areas or small towns, persistent poverty, low educational levels, and the lack of adequate infrastructure contribute to an uncontrolled and highly conflicting organization of urban areas. It is unrealistic to attempt to organize urban planning in a permanent, comprehensive basis under these conditions. However, some countries and cities have done, or are doing it, despite immense obstacles.

Is urban planning desired by the prevailing political forces?

Urban planning implies defining limits and constraints, and therefore affecting established interests. Often, dominant sectors do not want such controls to be exerted, and they create obstacles to them. This should be taken into account with several large cities in the developing world. However, specific conditions may persuade dominant private interests to lobby for controlling urban growth in particular areas if economic benefits may be acquired, such as in urban renewal projects.

How can the planner work autonomously?

Planners face many conflicts of interest between social groups, investors, the construction sector and landowners. Several authors have proposed that, as the state ultimately expresses the interest of the dominant class, urban planning cannot be an instrument for social change, but remains a tool of domination, integration and the regulation of contradictions (Lefevbre, 1979; Harvey, 1985). Many criticisms can be made of this position. The importance of dominant interests in driving public policies should not be neglected, but their power is not overwhelming. In many instances dominant interests have to compete with the influence of other social groups, and in others they can be avoided or bypassed.

Dominant sectors may have to deal with the relative independence of planners. Many planners, as state employees, are strongly attached to the middle-class ideology and lifestyle. They are, in fact, the middle class within the state. Despite internal conflicts, both the bureaucracy and technocracy are intimately identified with the middle-class project, sympathetic to capitalist modernization and social mobility. The formulation of public policy is therefore influenced by these sectors. The planners mediate between external forces, delaying the implementation of actions and utilizing state resources to countervail pressures or to redirect previous decisions. In some cases this power will be used to extract class benefits and privileges, but it can also be used to join other interests in a common pursuit.

In the case of developing countries, the built environment is produced by a combination of dominant interest and a myriad of 'micro-powers' (Ball, 1986), which escape state control. These micro-powers are related first to poor people who occupy the peripheral or depressed areas of the city; this pattern of occupation has dramatic effects on the environment as well as on demand for infrastructure. Second, irregular or illegal land use in support of business activities by the elite imposes heavy burdens on transport demand and related externalities. Contemporary cities in developing countries can therefore be said to have two built environments: one organized by urban planning interventions and the other independent of them. Often the latter is larger than the former. In Latin America, it is estimated that 30–50 per cent or the urban population lives in illegal settlements or slums (Schteingart, 1996). In these cases the power of urban planning is limited, to say the least.

In the case of public transport supply, the planner's power can be ignored or bypassed by the autonomous production of transport (Tarrius, 1989). This may or may not be complementary to existing systems. It can be illegal, and is not always coupled with professional transport suppliers. This is the case with informal transport systems in Asia, Africa and Latin America (see Chapter 11).

How do social classes and private interests interfere in the planning process?

How do middle-class sectors manage to influence transport policies when they are not exerting explicit pressures, or organizing social movements? The answer is given by Gramsci's concept of 'organic intellectuals'; people belonging to social groups that operate at the highest state level elaborate the ideology of the dominant class and transform it into a conception of the world that penetrates the entire social body (Portelli, 1977).

In the case of transport planning, professionals linked to transport studies may give support to the development project of the dominant class, which is directly attached to the capitalist modernization. As stressed in Chapters 6 and 9, the use of traditional transport and traffic planning techniques has been one of the most important ways in which this task has been accomplished in developing countries. This development project finds a powerful ally in the middle class, which sees in the modernization the way to social and economic mobility. In most developing countries, modernization implies a new development style: the concentration of income; repression of social movements; a diversification of activities in time and in space; an increase in economic production and consumption. All of these impose new pressures on transport structures and space utilization. Middle-class cities have recently developed in Latin America, as a physical expression of the new lifestyle enjoyed by selected social groups with access to cars. The same sort of built environment is now being organized in several developing countries (see Chapter 12). Therefore, one may conclude that public policy decisions within authoritarian or weakly democratized developing countries are made by the elite, within and outside the government, supported by groups of intellectuals and planners who translate and diffuse the dominant ideology.

Other major interests interact with the planners' activities. Business interests become involved when the division of the space is under consideration; that is, when major studies are expected to generate proposals that will affect local business interests. An example is the traffic study, specifically a study which concerns the pedestrianization of central streets, or major parking restrictions. In these cases business interests are represented by local organizations, which can interfere with policy decisions either directly – using government agencies – or indirectly, using the media. Business interests tend to be well organized, and hence are much more influential. Business may also mobilize in the event of new major transport infrastructures which have a potential effect on rent or land values; both the real estate and the construction sectors can exert an important influence on such decisions. Private investment in real estate along railway lines in Japan is one of many examples (Cervero, 1998a).

Industrial sectors participate in different ways. In addition to the government, the transport industry plays an important role in reproduction capitalist relations in contemporary peripheral states. In several developing countries, governments are attracting and giving fiscal support to new automobile and motorcycle factories (Pucher and Lefèvre, 1996; Cohen, 1996). The mass transport industry has also been receiving continuous support, because rail technologies from developed countries are constantly being marketed.

Finally, it is essential to consider the role of private consultants. The relationship between the state and private consultants became intimate during the most recent phase of capitalist modernization. Many former public agencies were transformed into so-called 'mixed economy' agencies, with much more freedom to hire labour and technical services. These agencies proliferated, followed by an expansion of the consultant sector. Due to the lack of independent forms of control over public affairs, state agencies and the private consulting sector work together to define the state agenda and budgetary commitments. In fact, in many countries consultants behave like para-statal agencies, using public money with little or no controls. Contract tendering is a closed arena, with negotiations taking place between the executive (either federal, regional or local) and the private sector. Despite the existence of bidding rules, especially for public works, transport planning is considered to be a 'technical' issue, requiring high levels of expertise and therefore generating a highly limited selection of entitled bidders. This means that important economic and technical decisions are taken behind closed doors, cloaked by an aura of 'advanced technology'. This image has been propagated since the 1970s, when foreign expertise from developed nations was hired to employ 'modern' forecasting and modelling tools. These conditions have been essential to the propagation of 'closed' and high-energy technologies (Illich,1974). There is no guarantee that this use of public money has led to a more efficient allocation of resources.

TRANSPORT PLANNING

Transport planning deals with the definition of the circulation infrastructure – pavements, roads, railways and terminals. It also covers the physical and operational characteristics of public transport.

Road provision is often a state responsibility. In urban areas, local government is responsible for planning and building roads; in rural areas, regional authorities perform this task. Recently, road privatization in both urban and rural areas has been pursued all over the world, and more intensively in developing countries, but in most cases roads are not attractive to private investors; the World Bank classifies local roads as having 'low potential' for private financiers (World Bank, 1996). Rural highways face similar problems, since they need high AADT (annual average daily traffic) to be attractive to the private sector. In the case of public transport, road-based services benefit from existing roads, while railway services need special infrastructure. Again, the cost of such structures and the time taken to make a return on investment makes their provision a public responsibility. In both cases, infrastructure planning is performed by technical and bureaucratic agencies that develop short- and long-range investment plans, using forecasting techniques. Major forces that act in parallel are the construction sector, the real estate sector, automobile users, and the public transport industries.

The planning of public transport supply is often a public task. It can be organized within a lightly regulated market, in an unregulated one as in most Asian, Latin American and African countries, or in a highly regulated market as in Brazil or China. In lightly regulated markets the transport sector is either managed by individuals or organized by several types of association; for example, the driver's cooperative. The nature of this collective supply creates permanent 'cycles of irregular investment and supply patterns' (Figueroa, 1991). Private operators may exert a powerful influence on governmental agencies, either by threatening street blockages, as in Jakarta (Hook, 1998), or resisting the reorganization of services as in Seoul (Kim and Gallent, 1998). They may also promote the monopolization of services against the public interest (Mandon-Adelehoume, 1994).

In regulated markets like that of Brazil, suppliers are medium to large enterprises that have a form of geographical exclusivity, and are legally protected from competition. Public authorities define supply characteristics and fares. Inflation and competition from illegal operators constitute the two most important threats to these enterprises (see Chapter 11 for a detailed analysis).

Differential political representation by users is important. Public transport users in developing countries, in contrast to those in some developed countries, are not as influential as bureaucrats and private operators. Unlike the middle class, who are represented through the state technocracy, captive public transport users (the majority of the population) face several barriers to representation. The first is their lack of representations in the upper bureaucracy and technocracy, because most of them lack formal education. Second, popular movements have been repressed by dictatorial and authoritarian governments, making it extremely difficult to organize permanent and solid movements (Kowarick, 1979). Third, transport is only one of a number of major problems faced by the public. Therefore, the state must mediate between independent political conflicts. A further element has to be considered: in many developing countries, public transport is provided by loosely regulated private operators, and captive users have to negotiate directly with them, with little success (unless a competitive alternative appears). In Yaoundé, people from the Eba neighbourhood, confronted by the denial of a regular taxi service, turned against the illegal vehicles that were providing alternative services when they decided to raise fares (Ngabmen, 1997).

TRAFFIC MANAGEMENT

Traffic management defines how the available circulation space will be distributed between users. Traffic management has traditionally combined three areas of expertise: engineering, education and enforcement, known as '3E'. It has also been based on another rigid triad: man, vehicle and road.

Engineering, is performed by technically trained people, who have little (if any) concern for social and political issues. The traffic engineer has many instruments to deal with technical concerns, and may become immersed in a technical world that avoids social concerns. Education is performed, in order of importance, by policemen, socially concerned engineers and social scientists. Policemen are frequently involved since they are often in charge of traffic control. Engineers (or planners) may become involved when a wider structure is available. Social scientists become involved only when the social approach to traffic is already highly developed. Enforcement is always performed by policemen. This may mean the civil or military police, in coordinated or uncoordinated efforts with engineers. When joint work is performed, traffic operation and control are improved; when separate work is done, severe conflicts may arise.

The sociological approach to road usage unveils the conflicts that lie behind people's movements. Differences in access to motorized transport dramatically influences space consumption, introducing immense inequality. Urban circulation occurs in a physical space that must be distributed between those who want to use it. Traffic management organizes the circulation space and mediates conflicts through physical and symbolic communication tools (signs), relying on user respect of traffic rules. The impossibility of solving all demands is clear.

HOW THE THREE INTERVENTION TECHNIQUES COEXIST[1]

Having considered the characteristics of each form of intervention, it is important to analyse their similarities and differences, in trying to establish whether they can coexist in coordinated public policies. As stressed by Dimitriou (1990), the coexistence is made difficult by different perceptions of the problem by engineers, planners, social scientists and politicians. In addition, there are several conflicts that place professionals and particular interests in conflict with each other.

Urban planning requires that decisions concerning transport infrastructure should be addressed jointly. The definition of land use greatly affects the generation of trips and therefore transport and traffic needs. Similarly, public transport supply and traffic management interventions can, in the medium term, lead to changes in land use.

Some of the ways in which actions in one field can interfere with others are briefly explained below.

- *Land use and urban density.* The way land is used and occupied directly influences transport demand, both quantitatively (traffic volume) and qualitatively (traffic composition).
- *Roadway characteristics.* Roadway design, the width of streets, and the type of pavement all influence traffic modes and related operational characteristics, such as average speed and level of service.
- *Transport means.* The level of public transport provisions, coupled to its level of service, influences its share of transport modes. In developing countries, low income makes most people captive to these modes. Similarly, the level of access to private transport, coupled to the ease with which it can be used on a daily basis (parking policies, petrol prices), influences choices.
- *Circulation patterns.* The preferential status of a particular road in respect to others, coupled with its circulation pattern (one-way, two-way) greatly influences the pattern of traffic conflicts and the quality of movement of people and goods.
- *Traffic laws.* The rigour of traffic codes and regulations, along with the quality of enforcement, influences human behaviour in traffic.
- *Education for traffic.* The level of formal education of traffic users, coupled to the characteristics of enforcement, influences behaviour in traffic as well as traffic quality.

In practice, the three areas of expertise can work jointly or separately. Nevertheless, especially in developing countries, there are particular limitations to joint work. First, the 'emergency' nature of daily transport and traffic operation makes it difficult. Second, the political conflicts around land use make it difficult and often impossible to have an active urban planning agency. Finally, the lack of resources results in an informal, inadequate organization of services in adapted agencies, especially in smaller towns. The possibilities of coexistence will now be analysed in the light of several political and technical issues (see also Table 8.1).

Action time spans

While urban planning operates in the long term, transport planning works in the middle term and traffic management in the short term (Gakenheimer, 1993). This leads to different perspectives. Time spans may be as long as 20 years for planning land use, and as short as one week for a traffic-management signal timing proposal.

Approaches

The urban planning field uses a broader social and political approach, in the face of a much more complex political environment. The other two fields are more keen to use only technical approaches. Traffic management is deeply tied to strict technical approaches.

Political environments and forces

The political environment surrounding urban planning is complex, since it involves land property rights and economic and financial interests. It also involves dealing with social and cultural differences between social groups and classes. It is more responsive to coordinated – although often hidden – political pressures from particular groups, but the long time span and the variety of interests divides pressures into myriad focal points. Transport planning is subject to complex political environments, although more limited than those surrounding urban planning, in face of shorter time spans and less influence on property rights. It deals with specific economic interests, either road-building enterprises or the transport industry. Conversely, traffic management faces more individualized pressures related to the roles played in traffic, although coordinated pressures may also occur, as in the case of shopkeepers and parking policies.

Different technical problems

Each field faces different technical problems and challenges, requiring different means of solving them. Urban planning deals with complex analyses of land use and economic development, entailing permanent forecasting difficulties (which do not prevent the irresponsible use of forecasting tools). Transport planning deals with technological decisions and with consumer choice modelling, which is also a difficult task in the face of uncertainties about people's behaviour. It also involves forecasting and so possibly unreliable results. Traffic management works with mathematics and physics techniques to divide space and organize traffic. It appears to have much more control over its domain although, as previously stressed, it often ignores the social and political aspects of dividing space.

Social pressure

The only field in which there is frequent pressure for action is traffic management. Most pressures come from inadequate circulation conditions, as in the case of congestion, the most visible traffic problem. These pressures are voiced loudly by most of the media. The agencies in charge of the problem have to be prepared for prompt action and often get the feeling that short-term action is their priority, enhanced further by the mobility interests of automobile users and their efficient pressure tools. Transport planning may be subject to pressures for emergency action or for middle-term action, such as designing a new transport corridor. Conversely, urban planning reacts to problems in a much more long-term way, as in urban renewal projects to rehabilitate depressed areas.

The time taken to get results

While people involved in urban planning rarely have the chance to verify the results of interventions, transport planning sees impacts in a few years and traffic management in a few months (even days). This contributes to a sense of despair among urban planning people, and excitement among transport and traffic management people.

Table 8.1 *Different characteristics in the three fields of urban policy*

Characteristic	Urban planning	Transport	Traffic
Traditional approach	Economic/social	Economic	Technical
Typical political environment	Large diversity of sectors and interests	More limited sectors and interests	Individual conflicts in face of conflicting roles
Nature of human resources	Urban issues, social sciences	Engineering, architecture, economy	Engineering
Typical actions and proposals	Land use and supply of public services	Transport infrastructure and services	Division of road space
Technical tools	Forecasting and urban and economic modelling techniques	Forecasting and transport modelling techniques	Capacity, efficiency and safety analysis of road use
Time span	Long range (up to 20 years)	Middle range (up to 10 years)	Short range (up to 3 years)
Technical issues	Highly complex and unpredictable	Complex but partially predictable	Simple and partially predictable
Feedback time	5–10 years	2–3 years	weeks/months

CONFLICTS IN POLICY COORDINATION: EXAMPLES

The complexity of power relations precludes joint work if it is considered undesirable by dominant sectors.

Few cities in the developing world have planning agencies. When resources are available, they are directed to more practical actions related to the daily management of traffic and public transport. Many important examples of conflicts in the planning process illustrate the issue.

Bangkok has been examined by several authors because of its dramatic transport conditions, and institutional interpretations have dominated some conclusions. Du Pont and Egan (1997) start by pointing out that many studies have recently been made by Western and Japanese consulting firms, but most have forgotten the crucial institutional issue. Daniere (1995) says that in 1991 there were 11 agencies involved in implementing transport planning under the authority of either the Ministry of Transport and Communications or the Minister of Transport. There were four agencies dealing with road construction, five involved in public transport and three in traffic management. The first comprehensive long-term transport study was made in 1975, resulting only in the building of major motorways. It appears that other transport measures were not accomplished because they were not included in the national plan. In 1984 the Sixth National Plan (1987–1991) proposed several roads and public transport investments. In 1989 a major study added proposals concerning institutional coordination, demand control and road user taxation. In 1991 another was developed to support the Seventh National Plan (1992–1996), which added several light-rail lines and land-use control. It also included a suggestion for a single metropolitan authority for land use and transport, which received little attention because of the need to transfer power among agencies. According to Daniere, Bangkok faces two main problems: first, the lack of technical capacity in most agencies; and second, that agencies have different cultures and missions and want to pursue their own objectives. They have no mandatory commitment to implement the national plans. The structure of the Thai state, the behaviour of its elite and the interests of foreign investors must be considered when examining policy outcomes. Daniere (p40) points out that the Thai elite

> *tends to act in ways which will preserve its power and prestige at the same time as it adopts Western concepts and knowledge ... the end purpose of modernization ... has not been to transform the traditional system but to preserve it and strengthen it.*

For Du Pont and Egan (1997, p25) the 'basic barrier ... is how to build a political consensus that will permit the implementation of a coordinated set of policies...'

Mexico City has also been much analysed, both for its physical size and the magnitude of its urban transport problems. There are many conflicts between transport policies. There are four levels of government dealing with the issue, from local authorities to federal ones, and agencies have overlapping and sometimes conflicting responsibilities (Molinero,1991). Transport policies are an important issue for the federal government, in the light of the political and economic interests attached to it. With the rapid growth of the city in the 1960s and the transport crisis that followed, attentions were focused on organizing a comprehensive mass transport system (Benitez and

Roldán, 1999), which originated the construction of the first three subway lines between 1967 and 1970, with French technical support (Henry, 1997). Shortly afterwards, the economic problems brought about by such huge investments led to the suspension of the new underground lines, following deep political struggles in the federal government (Davis, 1994). The metro lines had to provide services in an environment dominated by thousands of private operators with little or no control from governmental authorities and with a strong political position. Increasing conflicts between government and the private operators came to a head in 1981, when all bus services were taken over by one bus company that eventually evolved into a large organization backed by a strong union (Connolly, 1999). There were several attempts to organize a metropolitan transport coordination agency, subject to strong conflicts and to the specific political and economic interests attached to the federal government. In 1995 the bus company was dismantled after charges of corruption and inefficiency and the public transport system was again operated by about 60,000 individual drivers with minibuses. At the beginning of 2000, a new public bus company was formed and the cycles of regulation–deregulation–regulation have started again.

São Paulo is also a clear example of critical, extremely complex institutional conflict. The history of the São Paulo metropolitan area, which includes 39 cities including São Paulo itself, is of a remarkable collection of policies that propelled the region towards unsustainability. Until the end of the 1990s, a large portion of the suburban railway system was controlled by the federal railway company, which also controlled similar systems in other major Brazilian towns. Differences in objectives and goals have prevented the coordination of federal and regional railway systems. Very low levels of service brought permanent chaos, undermining public confidence and ultimately contributing to the current rejection of suburban trains. At the regional level there has been a historic disconnection between metropolitan-level transport problems and local transport policies. Despite the formal existence of a metropolitan authority, a political conflict remains over the issue of who has the power to pronounce on regional matters. The State Department of Metropolitan Transport ran with the subway system, the suburban railway and all intercity bus services within the metropolitan area, but mayors are jealous of their legal power to control local issues. The problem is especially serious in the case of São Paulo. The city accounts for 60 per cent of the regional population and 70 per cent of the regional automobile fleet. Urban, transport and road-building planning are conducted by three different departments. Major urban plans do not consider properly the knowledge and the opinions of transport expertise. Inside the transport agency, public transport and traffic are two different departments. While one deals solely with the legal and administrative issues concerning private bus operators, the other deals with all traffic issues (planning and operation). The split led to uncoordinated policies. This narrow approach is aggravated by conflicting political interests; as car owners are usually politically powerful, the priority is to pursue traffic fluidity. Needless to say, bus priority schemes have been scarce. At the road side, planning and construction have historically been separated from urban planning and traffic agencies. This has led to absurd situations in which major roads are projected and build without consideration for the objectives and suggestions of the traffic department. The final results of such a history are a permanent decrease in public transport use, rapid increase in automobile use, record traffic fatality rates, severe congestion and severe environmental problems.

Other large cities in the developing world also present severe institutional conflicts. In Seoul, responsibility for coordination transport is spread across several agencies, federal and local (Kim and Gallent, 1998). The Ministry of Construction and Transport is in charge of long-range planning, the National Police Agency is in charge of signs and traffic safety devices, and local construction and maintenance is performed by local agencies with financial support from the Ministry of Home Affairs. Within the Seoul municipal government, several agencies deal with planning, management, financing and controlling. Therefore, metropolitan coordination is defective and mismatches between urban development and transport are common. The creation of a multifunctional agency is controversial and remain unrealized due to the required transferring of power, in the very same way that happened in Bangkok and São Paulo.

Even in former socialist countries, despite centralized control over most public issues, several problems were detected. According to Pucher and Lefèvre (1996) land use and transport policies seem to had been surprisingly uncoordinated. This appears to have happened as a result of conflicts in the government apparatus over two key policy decisions. First, the attempts to solve the serious housing problem by building large complexes on the periphery led to long commuting distances and hence expensive and inefficient public transport services. Second, by failing to coordinate suburban industry and local public transport services massive cross-commuting was encouraged.

Such experiences reveal the extent of the challenge to achieve coordinated urban, transport and traffic policies. Next, we must consider how to deal with the problem at two institutional levels, local and metropolitan.

9 THE TECHNICAL ISSUE: TRADITIONAL TRANSPORT PLANNING

INTRODUCTION

The systematic analysis of transport demand in developing countries has been performed using procedures that originated in the developed world. These were grouped under the heading 'urban transportation planning system' (UTPS), which was organized to forecast future transport demand and to define the best ways of coping with such demand. The process has been used in most major transport studies since the 1970s, with few or no adaptations to local conditions. The UTPS was directly related to crucial decisions in these countries concerning investments in transport infrastructure, resulting in controversial economic, social and technical outcomes.

Here, our objective is to analyse the political use and the actual consequences of these techniques in a developing country context. This effort should enable us to better understand the shortcomings of the process and hence options for its continuing use.

THE TRADITIONAL TRANSPORT PLANNING PROCESS

UTPS was first developed in the US in the 1950s (Gakenheimer,1993). It may be dated more precisely to the 1962 Highway Act which was concerned with the construction of a large interstate highway system (Reichman, 1983). UTPS was widely exported to developing countries during the 1970s, with support from international agencies, private consulting firms and universities (Dimitriou, 1992). From the 1960s onwards there had been concern about the 'disruptive social and environmental impacts' of traffic capacity increases, and about the need to balance financial, environmental and social costs (Gakenheimer, 1993). Professionals started to openly confess their own reduced confidence in the long-range forecasting capability of UTPS and began advocating a more operational approach, oriented towards a day-to-day support for decision making. In addition, there was an increasing criticism of its use of aggregated data and its indiscriminate transferral to developing countries.

The reassessment of UTPS occurred in several stages (Jones, 1983). In the 1960s, a fourth step was added to the prevailing three-step modelling process (generation, distribution and assignment). Modal choice considered the trade-offs between private and public transport means. Correspondingly, the basic unit of analysis changed from vehicle trips to person trips. The single-sided travel time analysis was replaced by a broader concept, the 'generalized costs of travel', which included all time and money resources allocated to travel. In a subsequent phase, the changes were more political, including the analysis of the needs of specific social groups and the consideration of non-conventional transport modes. More emphasis was placed on local short-term planning, as well as on direct community participation. From the scientific point of view, a major change in basic assumptions occurred in the 1970s, when the analysis of family and external constraints on trip-making first re-placed the isolated analysis of individual trips. This change characterizes what Pas (1990) calls the 'human activity analysis era'; human interactions and constraints, rather than the trips themselves, were placed at the centre of the analysis.[1] However such change has not yet yielded systematic, practical procedures that could be incorporated into the modelling process (Kitamura et al, 1997).

General assumptions and objectives

UTPS may be seen as a 'scientific' way of planning urban transport demand in certain stages: observing current travel behaviour, advancing hypotheses concerning the relationship between urban land use and movement, testing the hypotheses, forecasting demand and ultimately recommending additional transport capacity (Dimitriou, 1992). Several general assumptions underlie this reasoning: that decisive relationships exist between all modes of trans-port, that transport systems both influence and serve the development of an area, and that the transport process is ongoing and requires continual read-justment. It is also assumed that it is possible to predict and evaluate, comprehensively, a balanced distribution of urban space at some future time (Hutchinson, 1974).

The process entails a systems approach that can be split into seven phases:

1   *The definition of the system* itself, its boundaries and environment, which is a difficult task considering interactive effects.
2   *The definition of the problem,* entailing subjective valuations about what the problem is and which corresponding objectives should be defined; in most cases the single objective is to reduce total travel time; however, qualita-tive objectives such as increased accessibility, safety and environmental quality have been introduced.
3   *The generation of alternatives,* limited to private motorized transport or rail mass transit. Bus and non-motorized transport (such as bicycles and pedestrians)are seldom included due to the lack of modelling tools.
4   *Modelling and analysis of the alternatives,* which is the 'core' of the whole process. The set of models is constructed into four steps: *trip generation,* which studies present trips and their relation to social and economic char-acteristics; *trip distribution,* which considers the destination of these trips; *modal choice,* which forecasts the transport modes that will be used, con-sidering the 'generalized cost of travel' for each trip and deriving mode

choice functions; and *trip assignment*, which assigns trips along existing alternative routes. Sometimes modal choice is performed prior to trip distribution.[2]

5   *Evaluation and selection of alternatives*, by estimating future charges on the transport infrastructure and defining the supply of facilities and transport to cope with them. This decision yields one or several proposals that are selected according to a cost–benefit rationale, which may be straightforward but may include a complex multi-criteria analysis.

6   *Project*: in a subsequent phase, the selected alternative is detailed with respect to its technical and physical features.

7   *Implementation*, at which point the resources needed and the actions to be taken are defined.

Many actors play an important and direct role in the planning process (see Figure 4.1 in Chapter 4). First, the government, including all the institutional levels and expertise responsible for the urban and transport systems being analysed. Second, the politicians with interests in either the geographical area or the issue itself. Third, the private consulting enterprises contracted to perform the studies. Fourth, some indirect actors, such as the private businesses that would be influenced by the outcomes of the planning process, the private sector interested in the businesses related to these outcomes (transport industry, real state) and neighbourhood or social organisations that would be impacted by the decisions. These actors can have diverse effects, depending on the specific conditions and the social and political environment.

CRITICAL APPROACHES TO CONVENTIONAL TRANSPORT PLANNING

The technical shortcomings of the UTPS process are important, but other problems arise from the use of UTPS in developing countries. A crucial distinction must be made between the models and the planning process. Modelling deals with micro-economics (consumer behaviour) and social information (population, income); it requires statistical tools to manage the data. Models are vulnerable to uncertainties and human errors. The planning process is political, in that interest groups are negotiating solutions in a conflicting arena. In some cases both modelling and planning are performed by a single group of people, and in others there is a clear separation of duties. Hence, criticism may initially be split into 'technical' (the models themselves) and 'political' (the planning process) and then re-examined by analysing the impact of the interaction of the two areas.

Technical criticism

Technical criticism of the process is common. UTPS is criticized for its narrow view of the urban process as a whole, as well as its project-oriented approach. Traditional urban transport planning 'took for granted that transport planning should be guided for, and thus facilitate, existing trends as projected into the future' (Hoover and Altschuler, 1977, p21), rather than seeing it as a policy question to be addressed by the planning process. Other problems are the lack of an interdisciplinary approach, and the reservation of system planning to 'masterplans'.

The problem of forecasting variables should also be stressed. Models are a simplified representation of selected aspects of reality, not a completely faithful representation of it. There are several possible sources of errors in the process, and each sort of error has different effects. Some increase with the complexity of the model: a 'more realistic model is not necessarily a more accurate one' (Willumsen, 1990, p293). In addition, the sequential nature of the four-step modelling procedures may propagate errors whose effects may not be calculated. Errors in specification introduce further inaccuracies in the behaviour of variables such as population, employment and GNP growth (May, 1991). Further problems arise when travel data comes from too narrow a time span, meaning that changes in travel patterns and behaviour are not incorporated.

The micro-economic assumptions of modelling can also be criticized (Kanafani, 1983). The rationale of the modal-choice phase has been based on consumer demand theory since the 1970s; several assumptions are controversial when applied to transport demand. Examples are the hypothesis of perfect market conditions, the stability and consistency of consumers' preferences and the 'insatiable' nature of consumption. Stopher and Meyburg point out that 'perfect competition rarely occurs and the prevailing market situation is one of imperfect competition' (1975, p49). Kanafani (1983) adds that suppliers are often not well defined, making it difficult to analyse their behaviour; there are non-monetary aspects of supply that are even more important than price (comfort, time, accessibility and reliability). The evolution of supply depends on many factors, including available technology, operational strategy, institutional requirements and constraints, and user behaviour. The travelling passenger is subject to many more uncertainties than he or she would experience from other consumption activities, including route and mode choices.

In addition to these general problems, there are also some specific problems with the four-step procedure and with of each of the steps themselves:

- The four-step procedure follows a rigid sequence, and does not use interactive procedures or feedback (Domencich and McFadden, 1975). The actual decisions made by the user can also occur in a different sequence. Further, it 'is not based on any single unifying rationale that would explain or legitimise all aspects of demand jointly ... it lacks a behavioural interpretation' (Oppenheim, 1995, p18).
- Trip generation does not admit that the existing transport system affects travel demand. It may be used to impose mobility increases assuming that needs will have to be satisfied in the future. This results in models that provide more transport for the higher-income groups and less for the lower-income groups. New traffic that will be generated by a link is seldom considered in the computation; this undermines the expected increase in travel speed and hence time savings. Furthermore, the estimated deterioration in travel speed if roads are not expanded is exaggerated, since people will find alternatives (Hook, 1994b).

- Trip distribution assumes that demands (and hence different destinations) are independent, which is a clear simplification. Also, residential and ethnic segregation in urban space, as well as the coexistence of formal and informal labour markets, may hamper the reliability of trip distribution models (Merlin, 1985).
- Modal choice faces difficulties in dealing with the random influences and inconsistencies in the user's behaviour and assumes a supposed stability over time of some trip-making aspects (Kanafani, 1983). The costs of travel, which ultimately determine the outputs of the model, may rise or fall as a result of unforeseen changes in legislation or in resource costs (May, 1991). In addition, trip distribution and modal split are usually not integrated (Oppenheim,1995).
- Trip assignment assumes that people select a route based on minimal total travel time, thereby ignoring other factors that might affect the complex nature of the trip-decision process.

Therefore, models 'replicate the results of conditions existing at the time of the survey' (Domencich and McFadden, 1975, p21). There is no interaction between transport system performance and the proposal of competing alternatives.

Strategic criticism

A first critical point is that the process is forward-seeking, attempting to satisfy a specific demand level defined by the model estimations, with no space for a goal-seeking strategy. Second, infrastructure transport proposals often do not allow for adequate funding during the lifetime of the project (Hutchinson, 1974). The goal and policy formulation stages of the UTPS are the least formalized parts of the process. If there is no implementation strategy, for example, or no definition of the staged implementation programme, the proposals often become unrealistic. Furthermore, the process is simply intended to generate additional transport capacity, without analysing what would happen if nothing was done, and without asking what would be the result of using existing transport means more efficiently (Dimitriou, 1992).

Political Criticism

The political criticism draws attention to the relationship between policy outcomes and the decision-making process. It can be separated into two sorts of claims: those related to societal participation and those related to the relationship between politicians and planners within the process. This entails a discussion of the role of the technocracy. Models are built and managed inside a field of economic rationality, where the computations comparing demand and supply are unambiguous. This sort of procedure frees the process from political arguments over value concerns and ideological manifestations. Therefore, the rational computations appear to be neutral and rigorous, devaluing political participation. Furthermore, often the decision-making logic is that plans are proposed by politicians first, and then validated by the work of experts; 'planning is an adjunct of the political process'

(Dimitriou,1992, p17). Dimitriou emphasizes that the history of UTPS shows that its generalized assumptions are:

> *more reflective of normative (sometimes wishful) thinking and the use of conveniently untested hypothesis, rather than based on well understood empirical evidence and practice.*

For Ralph Gakenheimer, 'the transport sector has been artificially carved out as a separate area of study' avoiding political constraints (Dimitriou, 1990, p101). This isolation gives planners the exclusive use of sophisticated modelling techniques.

Ideological criticism

This type of criticism challenges the very nature of the UTPS process and its practical use. The process, rather than being applied to urban transport problems, is directed to the circulation of automobiles, oriented towards the enlarged reproduction of the highway-oriented economic system. The UTPS modelling process grew out of an

> *optimistic and prosperous period characterised by booming car ownership ... thus ... land use/transport studies tended to be strongly associated with planning for roads and cars rather than a balance of transport modes ... once such land use is in place the only transit that can serve it is an inefficient bus service.* (Newman and Kenworthy, 1999, p139)

Therefore, the models have been used in a conservative way to reproduce the present situation, which happens to be based upon the assumption that mobility and car ownership will increase in the time-horizon of the planning process. Whitelegg (1997, p15) recalls that

> *thirty years of traffic forecasting and statistical modelling have failed to incorporate the feedback mechanism that links new road construction to the generation of yet more new traffic.*

As Cervero (1998a) points out, in California between 1973 and 1990, every 10 per cent increase in lane-kilometres led to a 9 per cent increase in vehicle-kilometres. The use of such forecasting tools has a crucial economic and social impact. As stressed by Hillman (1983, p107),

> *to some extent, an optimistic forecast can be seen as a self-fulfilling prophecy, for it is clear that more traffic is generated by a network of roads designed to accommodate high levels of car ownership.*

THE TRANSPORT PLANNING PROCESS IN DEVELOPING COUNTRIES

Searching for the most relevant criticism

It could be considered that all of these criticisms are equally important to developing countries. Nevertheless, we have to ask about the specific consequences of the different shortcomings of the UTPS process in the developing world. Technical criticism is by far the most common. However, despite the problems derived from technical shortcomings, the most important criticism concerns the use of models inside the planning process, and their actual impacts. This does not mean, however, that technical drawbacks are not important.

Technical issues

The most important technical shortcoming worth mentioning is the difficulty, or even impossibility, of making sound and reliable forecasts, either due to the lack of appropriate data or to the unstable socioeconomic environment in developing countries. The most important data – population, employment, school enrolments, average individual and household income, and auto ownership – either do not exist, are highly inaccurate, or may not be reliably disaggregated.

Unstable socioeconomic environments are quite common in developing countries, related to rural–urban migration, intra-urban migration, inflation, unlawful land occupation, and changes in job market structure and size. The population of Bangkok increased from 7.8 million in 1985 to 10.5 million in 1992 (Daniere, 1995). African cities have been experiencing intense urban growth due to rural migration, leading to severe urban infrastructural deficiencies (Halfani, 1996), which have direct impacts on people's ability to travel. In Cameroon, the government decided to make drastic changes in social programmes, infrastructure investment and tax bases, and lowered salaries twice in 1993. Thus, 93 per cent of households experienced a decrease in income, and 74 per cent a decrease in savings (Ngabmen, 1997). These new conditions led to a change in the travel habits of the poor, especially the suppression of trips, mostly for social purposes; the re-chaining of trips; the relocation of children to nearby schools, frequently at the expense of educational quality; and submission to a condition of 'localized mobility', compatible with walking distances. Problems are also caused by continuing inflation and sudden changes in people's income. Between 1970 and 1995 Brazil experienced monthly inflation rates ranging from 10 to 20 per cent, with short periods of hyper-inflation at 60 per cent. It is important to emphasize that such changes may affect low-income people who walk or use public transport, and middle-class people using private transport.

Changes in vehicle fleets also impact on mobility in unpredictable ways. In Seoul, the number of cars and taxis increased from 207,000 in 1980 to more than 2 million in 1995, while passenger trips increased 108 per cent between

1980 and 1993 (Kim and Gallent, 1998). In Bangkok, the vehicle fleet grew from 275,000 in 1970 to 2 million in 1990 (Du Pont and Egan, 1997). In Kolkata, the number of vehicles increased from 92,043 in 1970 to 560,000 in 1995 (Halder, 1997). In Shanghai, the number of bicycles increased from 0.8 million to 6 million, and the number of automobiles increased from 10,000 in 1984 to 200,000 in 1995 (Lu and Ye, 1998). In Manila, estimated daily trips increased from 10.97 million in 1980 to 13.08 million in 1985 and to 17.65 million in 1990 (Villoria et al, 1997).

In São Paulo, economic changes and spatial-related factors increased the average mobility rate from 1.1 trips per person per day in 1967 to 1.5 in 1977 (the period of the so-called 'Brazilian economic miracle'), and later decreased this rate to 1.3 trips per person per day in 1987 (CMSP, 1987). The 1997 OD survey revealed a further decrease in motorized mobility, to 1.2 trips per person per day, while the number of automobiles increased by 50 per cent (CMSP, 1998). During the Brazilian 'Cruzado economic plan' in 1986 (when inflation dropped to zero over four months), the state highway system in São Paulo experienced an average increase of 15 per cent in overall traffic – a figure seldom found in transport textbooks. São Paulo also experienced the greatest congestion in 15 years, when the average time spent by cars in the main arterial system (during peak periods) increased by 30 per cent compared with 1985. Both of these effects disappeared some weeks after the collapse of the economic plan and the return of the inflationary process. To consider a longer period, the main roadway system in the state, linking the metropolitan area to the port of Santos (the largest in Brazil), has been experiencing a highly fluctuating flow pattern since its opening in 1974; first, a steady annual increase of nearly 6 per cent in the 1974–1979 period, then an annual decrease of 2 per cent from 1980 to 1983, an annual increase of 3 per cent from 1984 to 1985, a sharp 15 per cent increase in 1986 during the 'Cruzado' economic plan, a return to previous levels in 1987, and a final 1–2 per cent increase during the 1988–1990 period (DERSA, 1992). Recently, the system has been alternating between small and zero annual growths. The final shape of the annual volume curve defies any forecasting technique. As described by Atkins (1986) and Mackie and Preston (1998), similar forecast problems have been experienced even in developed countries, where the economy is stable and social and demographic changes are rather modest. Tolley and Turton (1995, p294) acknowledge that

> an examination of 41 recent road projects in the UK revealed that about half had traffic forecasts within 20 per cent of the flows that materialised, but that the rest had forecasts ranging from 50 per cent above to 105 per cent below.

A comparison between predicted and actual demand figures in developed countries demonstrates that long-term studies are not faithful in these conditions, let alone in developing countries. Therefore, long-term forecasts in developing countries represent an irresponsible practice that should not be treated as a decisive input to modelling. From a practical point of view, the figures are useless unless applied to devise theoretical 'ceiling' limits, along with prospective scenarios. But the most problematic acknowledgement is that they have been used to support important investment decisions. Many of these investments represent a waste of scarce public resources. Contrary to the view of Lewis et al (1990) that the 'limited view of planning failures' is translated into the provision of less than optimal facilities,[3] the main planning failure in developing countries is the use of traditional techniques to support underutilized or unnecessary transport infrastructure. Therefore, one has to ask why such infrastructure was proposed and built.

The second major drawback is the lack of procedures to model non-motorized and public transport demand, which reflects the environment in which the models were generated. Both these transport modes are essential to developing countries, and such a lack gives rise to questions over the very utility of the modelling package. This has a related drawback, concerning the inadequacy of traditional capacity-analysis procedures to deal with a typical traffic mix in cities of the developing world.

The third major technical drawback is the reliance on market-based supply assumptions for public bus transport, in the few cases when it is considered. Actual market conditions in the transport sector are far from competitive, constrained by a complex relationship between the government, the bus owners, the bus operators, and the users. Furthermore, sudden behaviour changes in response to economic changes or inflation are quite common, which impacts on supply. Therefore, the forecasting of public transport trips reveals little about how the supply will really be organized and maintained.

The fourth major technical shortcoming occurs when planners disregard non-conventional factors that lie behind travelling decisions. Information from OD surveys is not used to analyse the complex trip decision-making process, and the suppressed demand generated by social and economic constraints. The way in which low-income people evaluate time and money in developing countries is far from being well understood, and is not properly addressed by traditional procedures. The increase in the number of non-nuclear families further compounds the problem. The increasing participation of the informal labour market in the urban economy has reinforced this. Mobility cannot be reduced to single measures of the number, cost and time of trips, because its determinants fall well beyond the exclusive consideration of income. The segregated spatial development of cities also directly affects the provision of infrastructure and facilities, therefore changing mobility constraints. This allows for the coexistence of different sorts of transport, from the highly privatized middle-class circulation pattern to formal and informal bus services, and high pedestrian and bicycle flows in some areas. This criticism can be summarized in a 'household mobility economy' model: the difference between developed and developing countries could then be identified by the existence, in the latter, of a family strategy to optimize space, time, production and consumption for survival, which leads to different patterns of mobility and use of available transport means (Henry and Figueroa, 1985).

Strategic issues

From the strategic point of view, the use of modelling in the planning process has been generating unsustainable and unrealistic proposals in the face of unstable social and political environments that bring permanent changes to the groups with access to the power and their approaches to transport policies. Economic instability has to be considered, as it often precludes or radically changes projects. One additional problem is the lack of adequately trained expertise to conduct the implementation and re-evaluation phases.

Long-term complex proposals do not include any definition of the financial and administrative supports that would ultimately help to ensure proper implementation, or to minimize risks. Besides, little or no attention is paid to the intermediate evaluation of the process, which would help it to adapt to unpredicted social and economic changes. Indeed, several major transport proposals that have taken place recently in developing countries were just not feasible. They were either postponed, partially implemented or implemented in full with money borrowed from abroad or from other, postponed, infrastructure proposals. The problem occurred with both automobile-based and public mass transport-based projects. The reasons for this discontinuity are either economic or political. Even when a formal budgetary commitment to a particular project is made, the ultimate decision is taken at the highest political level. The related conflicts are also embedded in the ongoing struggle between the long-term perspective of the planners and the short-term perspective of the politicians.

Political issues

The UTPS process, from the very beginning, has neglected the political reality in developing countries, prefering the straightforward transference of assumptions adopted in developed countries. This was possible because local political and technical forces imported and supported the process with little discussion. The state is the focal point for most major policy decisions, and the strength of the state is related to the strength of its technocratic and bureaucratic sectors, which are often free from any accountability. 'The transport planning process is one of the most inaccessible public sector planning mechanisms ... whose expertise seems beyond the grasp of the average person...' (Williams, 1998, p4). One important tool for the success of such a closed decision-making circuit is the use of many cost–benefit studies after decisions have been made and political commitments to proceed with the project already exist (Wright, 1992), leaving little – if any – space for alternative proposals.

Ideological issues

The process is inherently conservative, resulting in a static projection of the present situation. When an increase in average income is forecast, it is assumed that it has to translate into an increase in auto use, neglecting the impact of transport alternatives for those having a higher income. This means that the process is based on the ideology of unlimited auto mobility for all who can afford it. Furthermore, it is also committed to the ideology of more transport and more motorized transport, instead of less transport and less motorized transport.

Second, the use of modal choice models is controversial. They were constructed in developed countries where people may choose between private and public transport, and where they have been used constantly to evaluate policy proposals that are intended to encourage people to switch from private to public transport. However, in developing countries most people do not have the choice of motorized public transport, let alone a choice between public and private transport. Models that are able to analyse modal choice in different types of non-motorized transport, unconventional public transport means and private modes, have yet to be developed. Even when there is some degree of freedom to choose between transport modes, the rationale underlying the decision is complex, including several non-economic factors and poorly understood behaviour constraints that are not included in traditional procedures.

Third, the forecasting process is supposed to be neutral, but in fact it makes many political assumptions, and tends to benefit dominant political interests. Hence, one has to challenge the very nature of forecasting exercises, as pointed out by Blanchard (1976) and Atkins (1986). Why submit crucial decisions to unreliable forecasts? Who is paying for the costs incurred by forecasting errors, and who is benefiting?

A fourth important problem relates to the neglect of walking, cycling and public transport. Traditional transport planning has ignored some people, such as children, women, pedestrians, cyclists and rickshaw pullers. In Bangladesh, the livelihood of 4.5 per cent of the population depends on rickshaws, but during the second five-year plan (1980–1985) not one transport project in 300 was concerned with them (Whitelegg, 1997). Travel time impacts on non-motorized transport are often ignored: it is as though such people are not worth one minute of the attention of the expert to estimate how many minutes he or she loses or gains under the proposals. Further, even when UTPS is applied to places with high incidence of non-motorized vehicles, slow-moving vehicles are considered to cause 'friction' to faster vehicles, when in fact the opposite is often true (Hook, 1994b). Finally, bus transport – by far the most important public transport mode in developing countries – has been given a poor technical treatment, much less detailed than that devoted to cars. Considering their historical origin in the US, most models are not prepared to adequately consider bus travel demand, let alone to make sound proposals on bus transport supply.

Appraisal issue

The way traditional planning deals with the appraisal of proposals is also highly controversial. The first major drawback relates to environmental evaluation. If actual environmental impacts were considered, conclusions would be completely different and 'road construction would not show the positive results that often now emerge from narrower balance sheets' (Tolley and Turton, 1995, p297). Road proposals do not properly account for the safety impacts of motorized traffic. They neglect urban and social disruption (the 'barrier effect') and do not properly consider the costs for non-motorized users. Furthermore, standard environmental impacts related to air pollution are not properly considered.

The second important drawback concerns economic evaluation, which is performed by analysing economic rates of return (ERR). The major problems relate to the computation of costs and benefits. Costs are initially computed for investments in infrastructure – roads, railways, terminals – and also vehicles, in the case of public transport proposals. They have to include vehicle operational costs or individual costs (fares) and land or building costs when de-appropriation is required. Costs must then be estimated for some key impacts such as accidents, air pollution, ecological damages, and urban disruption. The serious, often insurmountable problem is that placing a monetary value on such things is controversial. The cost of a human life is the prime example of a highly controversial issue (Wright, 1992; Mackie and Preston, 1998). Some methods compute their lost future production (gross or net earnings, after expenses) or take the 'willingness to pay' approach, in which an indirect measure such as life insurance or the willingness to pay to avoid or reduce the risk of an accident is taken to deduce the value that the person attributed to his or her life (the VSOL – the value of a statistical life). The former method may – in the case of young children, elderly people or jobless people – yield negative results (Wright, 1992; Verhoef, 1994). As stated by Maddison et al (1996) 'the fairly obvious objection to this approach is that the death of a disabled person or anyone past retirement age is apt to be counted as a benefit.' In the case of the latter method, apart from the problem that most people in developing countries do not have private insurance, for those who do have it its value depends on monthly contributions, which depends on income and other factors; the WTP approach is also highly dependent on the characteristics of people. We are actually facing a philosophical problem; the value of life cannot be translated into monetary figures, which makes transport project appraisals much more complex. In Europe, value placed on accidents in 1993 ranged from UK£13,100 in Portugal to UK£2.1 million in Sweden (Maddison et al, 1996). Costs of injuries are not so controversial but are very difficult to estimate in developing countries, in the face of unreliable data. Many injuries become permanent disabilities, making the cost even more difficult to estimate.

In the case of the environment, similar problems arise; how should we value people's health? The difficulty in pricing environmental goods is so great that it leads to weird conclusions; as Chichilnisky (1997, p203) puts it:

> ... *if all the water of the US was to dry up next year, using standard cost-benefit tools one may only register a 2 per cent drop in national income, and this would only be because we would account for the fact that plants need water.*

In developing countries, in addition to the philosophical problem of attaching a value to human life, we may add the practical problems of estimating environmental damages and costs. Few developing countries have consistent data on transport-related environmental impacts such as air pollution, noise and natural resource depletion. Furthermore, there are few – and often unreliable – data on the health effects of such environmental impacts. Therefore, initial errors in estimating quantitative impacts are exacerbated by the difficulty of attributing monetary values to such impacts. Again, such a difficulty is both philosophical and practical; who knows how much it costs to treat respiratory disease in a patient in an hospital in developing countries, where actual access to services is highly constrained by geographic and social reasons, service quality differs between areas, and accounting procedures often simply do not exist or are adulterated by inherent biases? These difficulties lead to cost estimates that have high levels of uncertainty. In Cairo, mortality costs for particulate matter (PM) exposure were estimated as ranging from US$186 to US$992 million, while correspondent morbidity costs varied form US$157 to US$472 million; mortality benefits from a 20 per cent reduction in lead, PM, SOx and ozone in Bangkok were estimated in the range of US$429 to US$2,785 million (Pierce, 1997). The question is what sort of decision may be based on such appraisal computations.

Travelling benefits have then to be estimated. The standard benefit is a reduction in travel time, and most of the initial appraisals were limited to this. The first problem is to estimate the travel time changes brought by new proposals. Several problems arise. Initially, the computation itself is subject to considerable errors, especially regarding new traffic that may be attracted to the new facility or service (Bonsall, 1996). Second, traffic conditions in developing countries are very different from those in developed ones, with a complex mix of vehicles that make conventional speed–volume curves such as those

Box 9.1 *The magic traffic signal*

The attempt to place monetary values on travel time occasionally leads to weird results and to unusual, misleading conclusions that are often used to justify a project. Imagine a signalized intersection of two six-lane arterial roads, with an hourly capacity of 700 equivalent cars per hour, per lane, and operating at full capacity at peak hours. Both arterial roads serve 120 buses per hour at peak times, on reserved curb-side lanes, with 50 passengers each. Automobile occupancy is 1.5. If the traffic signal cycle and green/red times are optimized, a four-second delay reduction per vehicle results. Applied to all people using the intersection (20,400 per hour), this yields savings of 22.7 hours per hour, which applied to six equivalent peak hours per day yields savings of 136 hours per day. Considering an average hourly wage rate of US$5 abated to one-third according to the traditional approach, this yields savings of US$227 per day and US$56,700 thousand per year (assuming 250 equivalent days per year). Considering project implementation and maintenance costs (US$4000), net savings are US$52,700 a year (disregarding other minor details for simplicity). Thus, the improvement is 'worth' the same as four new, high-standard pieces of traffic signal equipment, or one new 45-seat diesel bus. Hence, should traffic engineers manage to get similar results at 500 signalized intersections in São Paulo then we would 'raise the money' to buy 2000 new traffic signals, or 500 new diesel buses per year, and the bus system would solve half of its fleet-renewing needs.

developed by the *Highway Capacity Manual* (TRB, 1985) difficult – if not impossible – to use. Finally, the attempt to estimate travel time-savings leads to nonsensical results. Signal timing calculations often result in the weird conclusion that a few seconds gained per vehicle will yields annual enormous economic benefits.

The second problem is the attempt to place a value on time. This is an issue that goes far beyond the transport problem, being deeply embedded in the economic evaluation of almost all aspects of all societies since the 18th century (Thompson, 1967; Harvey, 1990). In transport calculations, time is valued directly – according to wages – or indirectly, using the values that people seemingly place on their time. The latter is calculated by two techniques: revealed preference, when people's actual travel choices are analysed, and stated preference, when people are asked to give their opinion on hypothetical transport options.

Important theoretical and practical problem arise. Some argue that only the time involved in 'productive' trips (such as travelling for business) should be considered (or should be given a higher value), devaluing other trips. Second, wages vary across social groups. Third, the way taxes and fringe benefits are included leads to a wide variation in the final figures.

The values attributed by people demonstrate interesting characteristics and variations. The value of travel time varies with several individual and trip characteristics, especially income and trip purpose (Gunn et al, 1996; Arruda, 1996). Values increase with individual income (Calfee and Winston, 1998) and are often higher for business and work trips. In developed countries, the value of time was found to vary from 20 per cent to 100 per cent of the gross wage rate (Small, 1992). When comparing data from revealed and stated preference techniques for the same group of people, different results emerge. The actual estimate of travel-time values often leads to wide confidence intervals, making the average value highly uncertain (Ortúzar, 1997). Finally, specific social, cultural, religious and economic conditions introduce factors that are not well understood.

These characteristics reveal how controversial is the attempt to value time, and how unrealistic or inequitable policy decisions may be. For instance, in poor and deprived environments people usually place a low value on time and a high value on direct transport costs, what does not mean that they could then be forced to accept unfavourable transport conditions in exchange for low fares. As explained in Chapter 5, people organize their daily travel activities considering several individual, family and external constraints, and the resulting trip pattern fulfils the individual and family's reproduction needs. All activities – and not just those formally 'productive' – interfere with each other and are an indivisible part of such reproduction, all having an inherent value. The attempt to restrict computations to formally productive time is debatable.

The use of different wage rates to evaluate transport proposals is also debatable, related to different approaches to the 'individual' (private) and 'collective' (social) values of time (Quinet et al, 1982). It is clear that actual wages interfere with purchasing decisions (including trips) and that marketing studies have to consider such income differences. The approach is adequate

Box 9.2 *Sorry, poor people must yield*

The use of strict, traditional economic approaches makes it difficult to support investments in the poorer sectors of society. Suppose we use traditional procedures to evaluate a traffic management scheme directed to improve bus speed on a congested arterial road, which decreases an individual bus user's travel time by the same amount as it increases that of an individual car user. If we suppose that the average hourly wage rate of the car driver is six times higher than that of the bus user, the number of bus users on the road would have to be six times that of car occupants on the same road, for the project to be warranted (not considering additional details, for the sake of simplicity). On arterial roads with three lanes in each direction and 700 cars per lane per hour, this would be the case only when bus hourly volume exceeds 210 vehicles (assuming 60 passengers per bus and 1.5 passengers per car), a situation that occurs only on a limited number of road links. The practical result is that few such projects would be ever warranted, which is another aspect of the conservative nature of traditional procedures that help to reproduce current inequitable conditions. Therefore, the 12,600 bus users will have to yield to the 2100 people using their cars until they manage to make more money or get a car.

to estimate how many people will shift to a new, improved bus service with a higher fare, or to estimate how many auto drivers will try to escape a new toll road using secondary roads. However, the same approach is not acceptable when one has to evaluate how public resources should be invested. Appraisal cannot be based on strict economic computations related to market opportunities and relations, but has to be based instead on how public resources are distributed within society. In addition to such an essential difference in approaching the issue, the relevance of this discussion arises from the fact that the use of different wage rates makes it difficult to justify investments in poor people and so perpetuates inequity. Most transport project appraisals that compare automobiles and buses 'prove' that it is economically sound to improve only automobile traffic.

The traditional approach to cost–benefit appraisal in developing countries has been summarized by Wright (1992, p6):

> *Cost–benefit studies have as a rule focused on individual projects, neglecting the overall picture. They have often overestimated the benefits and underestimated the costs of bad projects and neglected to formulate better alternatives. Considerable mathematical skill has been employed to produce unrealistic predictions of the number of trips and the value of travel time that would supposedly be saved by some proposed boondoggle. The numbers and values give the impression of being sufficiently elastic to justify whatever is being proposed.*

Non-motorized transport usually refers to walking and cycling. The analysis of such modes allows a straightforward approach to equity and environmental problems, since these means are the most vulnerable and the most environmentally friendly forms of transport in contemporary cities.

PEDESTRIANS

Walking is the primary human transport mode, available to all except babies and those with walking impairment disabilities. Yet dehumanization brought about by motorization is so profound that traditional transport planning often ignores the activity. Even in developed countries walking has not been properly treated, leading to the publication of an important report in the 1970s entitled *Walking is transport* (Hillman and Whaleey, 1979). Of people who walk when buses are full, Tolley and Turton (1995, p174), for instance, say 'But (these) reluctant walkers are still travellers in the urban system and planning must recognise that walking is, and will remain, a perfectly valid form of transport for most people.'

In all cities walking is an essential means of transport. In wealthy cities such as London and Amsterdam, 33 per cent and 26 per cent of trips respectively are made by foot (Pucher and Lefèvre, 1996). In large developing world cities with medium incomes such as São Paulo, walking accounts for 35 per cent of trips. Obviously, in low-income cities – which form the majority – walking is often the predominant transport mode (Figure 10.1), complemented by its faster substitute, the bicycle.

Walking is a mode of transport in itself, but it is also a complementary mode for all motorized trips; few such trips can be made without walking. Public transport trips require walking trips of about 500 metres at each end. Private transport trips require people to walk to and from their vehicles. When longer distances walked by people are taken into account, the importance of walking becomes even more apparent. Average figures for São Paulo are given in Table 10.1.

China probably has the largest share of non-motorized trips in the world. In Beijing, pedestrian and bike trips are an essential part of the everyday travel pattern. Most people making pedestrian trips are between 16 and 55 years of age. Those under 15 years comprise 9.2 per cent of pedestrians and those over 55 years correspond to 7 per cent (Table 10.2). The gender division shows a female share of 53.4 per cent and a male share of 46.6 per cent. Most trips are

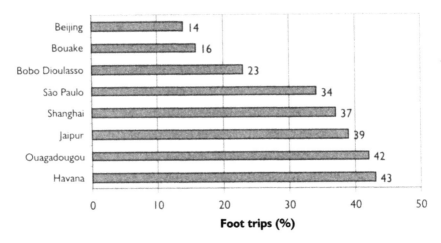

Source: Shimazaki et al, 1994

Figure 10.1 *Walking as a component of daily trips, selected cities in developing countries*

Table 10.1 *Overall distances walked by people, in walking-only and access trips, São Paulo, 1997*

Mode	Trips/day	Distance (km/day)	Share (%)
Foot			
Foot only	10,812,000	10,890,944	6
Access to vehicles[1]	–	9,866,303	5
Total	–	20,757,246	11
Public	10,473,000	98,533,656	51
Private	10,147,000	74,141,841	38
Total	31,432,000	193,432,744	100

(1) Trains, metro, buses and cars

Source: CMSP, 1998

Table 10.2 *Age of people making pedestrian trips in Beijing*

Age	Share (%)
<15	9.2
16–20	16.6
21–25	14.1
26–35	22.0
36–45	15.4
46–55	15.8
56–65	4.9
>65	1.9
Total	100

Source: Qian and Tanaboriboon, 1994

prompted by working, shopping, going to school and getting access to public transport (Table 10.3).

Table 10.3 *Purpose of pedestrian trips in Beijing*

Purpose	Share (%)
Work	22.7
Shopping	22.8
School	15.2
Access to public transport	15.1
Recreational	9.8
Other	14.5

Source: Qian and Tanaboriboon, 1994.

Pedestrians face several problems, constraints, impairments and dangers. The problems faced by pedestrians may be categorized as follows (after Gunnarsson, 1995; Kane and Seck, 1996; and Hillman, 1997):

- Transport-related factors, not involving vehicles. Poor pavements, dirt, physical obstacles, barriers and street vendors.
- Factors related to vehicle traffic. The threat of accidents posed by vehicles when pedestrians are crossing in inadequate conditions; the wait to cross roads; and pedestrian overcrowding due to narrow or below-capacity pavements.
- Sandy surfaces with very high temperatures, especially in Africa.
- Climate conditions.
- Air and noise pollution.
- Falling objects.
- The threat of assault.

The severity of these problems varies between developing countries according to their particular conditions, but the unsafe, inconvenient and uncomfortable conditions of pedestrians may be considered to be universal; in most developing countries walking is a challenge. Unfavourable conditions do not affect all pedestrians in the same way; children, the elderly and handicapped people are much more affected than others, in terms of both the physical difficulties and the accident threat.

Travel time is also an important characteristic of pedestrian trips (Table 10.4). In Beijing, pedestrian trips account for 13.8 per cent of all trips (and bicycles for 50.3 per cent; Qian and Tanaboriboon, 1994), while in São Paulo the corresponding figures are 34.4 per cent (walking) and 0.5 per cent (bicycles) (CMSP, 1998). Although in Beijing the duration of the average walk is greater than in São Paulo, in both cases average values are low, demonstrating the physical limits of walking. This is a common characteristic of walking trips all over the world.[1]

The main problems faced by pedestrians may now be summarized:

- The disregard of policy makers and transport planning techniques. Traditional planning techniques do not even consider pedestrians and bicycles.

Table 10.4 *Time of walking trips, Beijing and São Paulo*

Time (min)	Beijing		São Paulo	
	Trips (%)	Cumulative (%)	Trips (%)	Cumulative (%)
1–5	4.5	4.5	24.8	24.8
6–10	14.7	19.2	29	53.8
11–15	17.8	37	18.1	71.9
16–20	16.7	53.7	11.4	83.3
21–25	9.6	63.3	2.9	86.2
26–30	12.4	75.7	8.6	94.8
31–45	10.1	85.8	2.9	97.7
>45	14.2	100	2.3	100

Source: Qian and Tanaboriboon, 1994; CMSP, 1998

In Nairobi,

> *Road transport planning … is by and large motor-vehicle oriented. The general policy statement on urban transport in Kenya has tended to ignore non-motorised transport: walking and cycling … the existing road networks in Kenyan urban areas … do not meaningfully cater for non-motorised modes (Khayesi, 1997, p5).*

- The lack of appropriate infrastructure, both pavements and crossings. In several developing world cities, roads are heavily disputed strips of spaces. When a government decides to improve traffic conditions, the central part of the space may be paved, but pavements are seldom constructed and pedestrians continue to dispute space with even poorer conditions, under threat from increased vehicle speeds. Even when pavements are built, they are often narrow, irregular and of poor quality, making walking trips difficult and dangerous. Crossing facilities are also inadequate; zebra crossings are rare, and signals rarely consider pedestrian needs; in such cases, pedestrians are seen as something that might be 'stacked' until some gap is available in the traffic stream: 'second class citizens' have to wait until first class ones exert their rights to use roads.
- The differential speed with respect to vehicles and the safety consequences. Pedestrians travel at about 4km/h, while the next-slowest vehicle (the bicycle) travels at 12km/h. Motorized vehicles run at up to 80km/h in cities and much more on regional roads. Once their weight is considered extreme differences in kinetic energy are the result, making accidents very dangerous for vulnerable human beings.

The physically disabled

'Physically disabled' refers to people who, by reason of accident, disease or congenital condition, find it difficult to move around, and sometimes to see, hear or understand (ECMT, 1999). The difficulty may be permanent or temporary. A broader view would include those who have a temporary, specific impairment like heavy loads or small children; this is a frequent occurrence in developing countries.

In developing countries the circulation structure is not constructed for pedestrians, let alone for physically disabled people, who face even worse problems while circulating than pedestrians. Blind people or those with walking difficulties face the most severe problems. The main barriers are pavements and public transport vehicles – the same as those faced by the average pedestrian. However, physically disabled people may also find it difficult to surpass physical obstacles like curbs and stairs. They face specific access problems related to the internal architecture of public transport terminals, bus and train doors and stairs, and inadequate internal space on public transport vehicles. Blind people also face severe problems in crossing roads, as virtually no special signal device is supplied.

CYCLISTS

Bicycles are the most important non-motorized mode all over the developing world (Table 10.5). Bicycles easily outnumber cars in countries such as China and India, and are more frequent than cars even in wealthy countries such as The Netherlands and Japan.

Table 10.5 *Bicycle and automobile fleet, several countries*

Country	Bicycles (millions)	Cars (millions)	Bicycle to car ratio
China	300	1.2	250
India	45	1.5	30
South Korea	6	0.3	20
Egypt	1.5	0.5	3
Mexico	12	4.8	2.5
Tanzania	0.5	0.5	1
Argentina	4.5	3.4	1.3
The Netherlands	11	4.9	2.2
Japan	60	30.7	2
Germany	45	26	1.7
Australia	6.8	7.1	1
US	103	139	0.7

Source: Hierli, 1993

In cities with a high proportion of non-motorized means, bicycle ownership may present a wide variation, from 909 per 1000 people in Hanoi to 99 per 1000 people in Ouagadougou (Table 10.6).

Bicycles are responsible for a large share of the daily trips in a large number of countries, especially in Asia and Africa. As with walking trips, bicycle trips are essential in most Asian countries; in Shanghai and Hanoi, non-motorized vehicles account, respectively, for 87 per cent and 64 per cent of vehicles in traffic (Kuranami, Winston and Guitink, 1994). In many Asian and African countries bicycle trips account for as much as 50 per cent of all trips (Figure 10.2).

It is important to emphasize some characteristics of bicycle use. People using bicycles in developing countries tend to be in the lower-income stratum,

Table 10.6 *Bicycle ownership rates, selected cities in developing countries*

City (country)	Bicycles/1000 pop
Hanoi (Vietnam)	909
Shanghai (China)	865
Penang (Malaysia)	528
Kanpur (India)	227
Phnom Penh (Cambodia)	156
Surabaya (Indonesia)	129
Chiang Mai (Thailand)	100
Ouagadougou (Burkina Faso)	99

Source: World Bank, 1995 for all cities except Ouagadougou (Diaz Olvera et al, 1997)

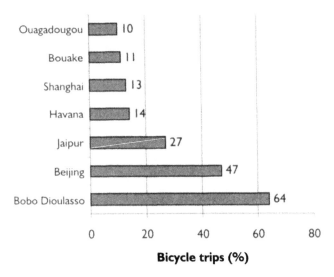

Source: Shimazaki et al, 1994

Figure 10.2 *Bicycle trips as a component of total daily trips*

since the bicycle is the first cheapest mechanized mode. The use of a bicycle implies biological limits and safety concerns, preventing some elderly persons and very young children from using it. Most cyclists in Shanghai are between 26 and 45 years, comprising 64 per cent of total cyclists. Very few are under 15 years of age or over 65 years of age (Table 10.7). In addition, most are men (60 per cent).

Bicycles are used for several purposes – mainly work – and mostly for medium-length trips; in Beijing, the average length of bicycle trips is below 6km (Sit, 1996), while in Delhi about 70 per cent are less than 15km (Replogle, 1992). However, as Replogle has shown, in India average trips may be shorter in smaller cities; about 65 per cent of trips in Jaipur are equal to or less than 5km long. A survey of three residential areas of Baoding (a city of 590,000 inhabitants in 1989) in China, where there are 2.4 bicycles per household,

Table 10.7 *Age of cyclists in Shanghai*

Age	Share (%)
<15	1.0
16–20	3.8
21–25	9.5
26–35	27.8
36–45	36.8
46–55	13.0
56–65	7.3
>65	0.9
Total	100

Source: Tanaboriboon and Qian, 1994

revealed that the bicycle is used for very short trips (100m) and that they become more frequent than pedestrian trips for those trips which are longer than
300m (Kubota and Kidokoro, 1994). Another important characteristic is that
bicycles may be used to complement public transport, but this is highly dependent on the facilities available to integrated services. As a consequence of
trip distances, bicycle travel times tend to be short. In Shanghai, 44.5 per cent
of trips take less than 20 minutes and 73.7 per cent take less than 30 minutes
(Tanaboriboon and Qian, 1994). In large Indian cities such as Jaipur and
Hyderabad, the average cycling times were found to be 22 and 33 minutes,
but this value was 49 minutes in Delhi, which is larger (Replogle, 1992).

Main problems with non-motorized vehicles

Most authors who analyse NMV problems in developing countries agree that
the key barriers to NMV use are affordability, the hostile street environment,
theft, negative social and governmental attitudes to NMVs, and excessive and
inappropriate regulation (Replogle, 1994). Other important problems are
culturally related; in some African cities, using a bicycle is seen as a sign of
poverty. Furthermore, the bicycle is seen as a mode used by devalued rural
people, and also as a 'backward' mode (Cusset, 1997; Pochet and Cusset,
1999). In some countries there are objections to women using bicycles for ethnic or religious factors (Peters, 1998).

The first relevant problem refers to the difficulties faced by NMV users on
the roads. As stressed by Kenworthy (1995), in Bangkok, pavements are in a
poor condition, there are no bicycle facilities, and local streets are narrow with
narrow pavements. Roads that link residential areas with trunk roads are
congested with cars and motorcycles. In urban Africa, poor safety conditions,
the lack of bicycle facilities and the levels of motorized transport make cycling dangerous (Howe, 1994).

Another key aspect is regulation. Taxes, import duties, fuel taxes, licensing and financing all have a direct impact on the purchase and use of an NMV.
Such regulations may be used to support or to suppress NMVs, but the latter
is more common. In Africa, bicycles have been classified as luxury goods and
are heavily taxed, inflating the purchase price (Howe, 1994). As explained by

Replogle (1994), in the case of Bangladesh, the combination of restrictions on the import of bicycles to (supposedly) help local industries, and low taxation of the import of motor vehicles, helped the wealthy and damaged the poor.

A third important issue is regulation that restricts or bans NMVs. All over Asia there is a rising opposition to their presence on streets, based on the argument that they result in slower traffic – understood here as motorized traffic – and in several cities they were banned. There is a desire to clear the way for the private car (Whitelegg, 1997). In Bangkok, thousands of rickshaws were thrown in the river; in Kolkata, the 60,000 rickshaw pullers are constantly submitted to pressures for their removal, to be replaced by cycle-rickshaws or even by motorized means. Such conflict represents an extreme case of the struggle between social classes in defining the use of space in general and road space in particular (Sen, 1997).

This attempt to clear streets may also be the result of proposals to encourage public transport. In Beijing, Sit (1996, p266) says that

> *the massive flow of bicycles has led to a declining average speed of motorized traffic and serious congestion problems…problems of mixed traffic on roads and at road junctions had contributed a 30–40 per cent reduction in flow capacity of the road network. Bikes use twice the space of a bus when stationary and ten times more when moving. It is not a good choice.*

A comprehensive set of issues concerning non-motorized vehicles in Asian cities was provided by Kuranami, Winston and Guitink (1994). The following list is based on their text, with some adaptations:

- The lack of appropriate NMV facilities such as separate rights of way, inadequate signing, and poor enforcement of existing facilities.
- The low priority accorded to NMVs, as compared to less efficient modes such as automobiles. A related issue is the neglect of the role of NMVs in the local economy; they can represent 23 per cent of the job market, as in Dhaka.
- The lack of compliance with traffic regulations by NMV users, resulting from three factors: the inadequacy of traffic laws, unfamiliarity with the rules, and the lack of a trained police force.
- Inappropriate pricing and tax policies in the urban transport sector, translated into low costs being imposed on motorized vehicles compared to the externalities that they cause, and high costs imposed on the purchase of NMVs. Also, the unavailability of loans to buy these vehicles, affecting their affordability.
- Congestion caused by extensive NMV use, as in Shanghai and Hanoi. More efficient public transport modes would cause less.
- Safety problems are an increasing concern.
- Theft represents a barrier to NMV use, as poor people cannot afford to lose such a relatively expensive item.
- Land-use changes, leading to increasing distances and to decreasing use of NMVs, as they tend to be replaced by public transport (or motorcycles).

- Biases against NMVs on the part of policy makers, driving urban transport planning towards a motorized system. Such an approach includes the imposition of limits on NMV use (over-regulation) and even the banning of NMVs.
- Lack of funds, data, analytical techniques and engineering guidelines for NMV facility improvement.

To those important issues, one should add three more:

1 Cultural barriers, such as those in African societies, on the use of bicycles by women (Grieco et al, 1994).
2 The terrain and road conditions, particularly steep hills and muddy roads, which may pose serious limits to NMV use.
3 The lack of integration with public transport, which severely limits the use of bicycles as a complementary mode to trains and buses.

11 PUBLIC TRANSPORT

Public transport in developing countries is at the centre of a conflict between its nature as a matter of vital importance for many people, and the difficulties inherent in an often poor economic environment. This chapter provides a detailed analysis of the issues. Current conditions are analysed according to institutional, supply, economic and travel characteristics. The analysis is performed by depicting, first, the patterns of public transport supply cycles in developing countries and then discussing policy issues concerning supply and regulation.

GENERAL CHARACTERISTICS

Developing countries have many different kinds of institutional arrangements. Private transport is usually controlled by the market and subject only to traffic regulations. However, public transport supply and use is always subject to some sort of regulation, even if it is a private responsibility. There are cities with an exclusively public transport supply (as in China), cities with an exclusively private supply and cities with a mixture (Table 11.1). There are essential differences between rail and subway services and bus and shared-taxi services; rail and subway services are mostly publicly owned and operated, while bus and taxi services are usually privately owned and operated.

Table 11.1 *Public and private ownership of public transport, selected cities*

City	Public transport mode and ownership				
	Rail	**Subway**	**Bus**	**Minibus**	**Taxi**
Alger, Algeria[1]	Public	–	Mixture	–	Private
Beijing, China[2]	–	Public	Public	Public	Public
Manila, The Philippines[3]	Public	–	Private	Private	Private
Mexico City, Mexico[4]	–	Public	Private[a]	Private	Private
São Paulo, Brazil[5]	Public	Public	Private[a]	Private[b]	Private
Seoul, South Korea[6]	–	Public	Private	Private	Private

(a) Large public bus company that has recently been privatized; (b) legal operators on metropolitan lines and illegal operators in local systems

Source: (1) Matouk and Abeille, 1994; (2) Sit, 1996; (3) Villoria et al, 1997; (4) Molinero, 1991; (5) CMSP, 1998; (6) Kim and Gallent, 1998

Public transport may be provided by individuals or by small, medium or large firms, and several types of vehicles may be used. In Manila in 1997, there were 437 minibus operators with 9282 vehicles, but while 263 operators had 10 or fewer vehicles, 19 had 100 or more vehicles (Villoria et al, 1997). As stressed by Henry and Figueroa (1985) in the case of Latin America, Gómez-Ibáñez and Meyer (1991) in the case of Asia, and Mandon-Adolehoume (1994) in the case of Africa, the most common pattern in private supply organization is the cooperative of operators. In some cases new operators are freely admitted, in others not. The most common entry restrictions concern the number of vehicles and the choice of route (Chojoh, 1989; Table 11.2).

Table 11.2 *Entry regulations for public transport services*

Location	Entry regulations
Jakarta, Indonesia	V, R and F
Bangkok, Thailand	V, R and F *
Hong Kong, China	V, R and F(p)
Manila, The Philippines	V, R and F
Kuala Lumpur, Malaysia	V, R and F *
Singapore	R and F
Istanbul, Turkey	V and F
Cairo, Egypt	self-regulated
Buenos Aires, Argentina	self-regulated
Tegucigalpa, Honduras	none
San Juan, Costa Rica	V, R and F
Caracas, Venezuela	V, R and F
São Paulo, Brazil[1]	V, R, and F

V= vehicle; R = route; F = fare; * areas where regulation is not always effective; (p) = partial fare regulation; (1) Brazilian cities have regulated bus services, as opposed to other Latin American countries

Source: Chojoh, 1990, table 2 (except São Paulo)

'Pirate' buses are common; in Lima, they accounted for 42 per cent of all public transport vehicles in 1990 (not including taxis) (ILD, 1990).[1] Their routes and service frequencies are seldom systematically planned; instead, they are determined by the operator's knowledge and by the manifest demand in densely trafficked corridors. Fare and service integration are also very scarce, with the exception of bus–subway services in Caracas and the bus system in São Paulo.

Vehicle supply

The bus in all its variations is by far the most common mode of public transport. The number of buses per head of population varies widely in developing countries. As a general rule, the figure is highest in Southeast Asia, followed by Latin America, South Asia and Africa (Kranton, 1991). Typical values cluster around one to two buses for every 10,000 people, but differences in vehicle capacity hinder direct comparisons.

Buses vary widely, from the standard bus with 40–50 seats to minibuses, with 10–25 seats. The description of the bus supply is a difficult task, since data are not always available and there is often confusion between ordinary buses and shared taxis, which may or not be used for public transport (Table 11.3).

Table 11.3 *Bus fleet, selected cities in developing countries*

City, date	Fleet		
	Large/regular	Mini	Total
Accra (Ghana), 1997[1]		9700	9700
Ankara (Turkey), 1985[2]	1100		1100
Bangkok (Thailand), 1985[2]	4950	12,000	16,950
Beijing, (China), 1991[3]	4877		4877
Kolkata (India), 1985[2]	3300	950	4250
Curitiba (Brazil), 1997[4]	1636		1636
Delhi (India), 1996[5]	2665		2665
Instanbul (Turkey), 1985[2]	2460	3800	6260
Jakarta (Indonesia), 1985[2]	2490	3365	5855
Karachi (Pakistan), 1985[2]	2110	3980	6090
Lima (Peru), 1998[6]	21,550	13,841	35,391
Manila (The Philippines), 1997[7]	9282	89,304	98,586
Mexico City (Mexico), 1994[8]		100,005	100,005
Santa Cruz de la Sierra (Bolivia), 1998[9]		3200	3200
São Paulo (Brazil), 1997[4]	11,000		11,000
Shanghai (China), 1996[10]	7453		7453

Source: (1) Kwakye et al, 1997; (2) Armstrong-Wright, 1986; (3) Sit, 1996; (4) ANTP, 1997; (5) Kulkami, 1998; (6) ILD, 1990; (7) Villoria et al, 1997; (8) Cervero, 1998a; (9) Figueroa and Pizarro, 1999; (10) Lu and Ye, 1998

Productivity

The productivity of bus services can be analysed through several operating characteristics. The main productivity factors concern the number of daily passengers and revenue earned, plus costs, for example operational expenses and labour costs. The daily distance travelled by buses lies in the range of 180–220km. Each 50-seat bus carries 500–1000 passengers per day, while minibuses carry 150–180 (Figueroa and Pizarro, 1998). Such conditions yield, for large buses, a figure of 3–5 passengers/km. Costs are greatly influenced by salaries; the number of employees per bus ranges from 5 as in most private Brazilian bus companies (ANTP, 1997) to 11.5 in Mumbai (Datta, 1998), 16.5 in Cairo (Abras, 1999) and 28 in Accra (Armstrong-Wright, 1986).

Cost recovery

Buses often charge fares that are too high for potential users, due to the low average income in most developing countries. Consequently, bus fares are the focal point for political and economic struggles involving users, suppliers and regulators. In strict economic terms, publicly operated systems have controlled fares and are usually unprofitable (Figueroa, 1985; Dimitriou, 1990).

Private systems can either be profitable – as in the case of most Brazilian firms – or unprofitable, due to excess supply (in deregulated markets), management deficiencies or excessive or undue control by local governments. Table 11.4 provides some evidence that cost–recovery ratios for public transport services vary according to the city and the nature of the service.

Table 11.4 *Profitability of bus services, 1983*

City	Buses[1]	Ownership	Operating revenue/total costs
Ankara	899	Public	0.48
Bombay	2325	Public	0.77
Cairo	2454	Public	0.5
Karachi	646	Public	0.43
São Paulo	2631	Public	0.41[2]
Accra	665	Private	1.37
Guatemala	1600	Private	1.55
Hong Kong	2392	Private	1
Puerto Alegre	1492	Private	1.17
Seoul	8310	Private	1.04

(1) Buses belonging to the principal corporation or group of private operators covered by the survey; (2) privatized in 1995
Source: Dimitriou, 1990, Table 2.2, p61

As a consequence of the struggle over fares, supply is permanently subject to instability in a conflict between revenues and costs (White, 1990; Figueroa, 1991). This instability affects both public operators and regulated private operators. One of its most remarkable effects is the tendency towards fleet dilapidation, which has direct impacts on passengers' comfort and safety as well as on the availability of vehicles for daily operation. Figueroa (1985) reported an average age of 10.4 years for Santiago buses in 1984. In Quito and Lima, 77.9 per cent and 69.2 per cent of buses, respectively, were more than 7 years old in 1982 and 1983.

Armstrong-Wright (1985) found large differences between the fare–recovery ratios of public and private bus operators. They range from 12–100 per cent for public companies and from 110–140 per cent for private companies. Recent research in Indian cities showed that the fare–recovery ratio varied from 39 per cent in Kolkata to 85 per cent in Mumbai (Kulkami, 1998). These low ratios are similar to those found in developed nations, which they range from 22 per cent (Italy) to 60 per cent (Germany; Pucher and Lefèvre, 1996).

The differences in profitability between public and private operators are clear but care must be taken when drawing conclusions. The lower average efficiency of public operators has several causes. There is a tendency to overemploy, to disregard market opportunities and to waste human and material resources. However, it also has three main sources of extra costs: the need to maintain low fares that its customers can afford; the need to provide minimum services, particularly in non-profitable areas; and the need to regulate private operators who are working with government permission. In addition, as is demonstrated by the Brazilian experience, public bus companies are given a secondary priority in local transport policies and are permanently subject to political interference from the mayor and the local elite (Brasileiro and Henry, 1999). They are also subject to pressures of patronage emanating from specific decision-making processes in poorly democratized societies.

The more efficient operation displayed by private companies is the result of better administrative and technical management, and of a closer attention to market opportunities. However, this efficiency is also driven by a cruder rationale, which does not hesitate to lower the level of service or even eliminate supply to ensure profitability whenever it is threatened. Moreover, in certain cases, the efficiency is caused by longer working hours and the avoidance of mandatory social costs. Therefore, a better cost–recovery ratio may conceal disrespect for social legislation, and a lower level of service.

Hence, strict comparisons between public and private operators are misleading. All comparisons should take into account the conditions of the service and the actual costs.

Traffic conditions of public transport

One of the most important attributes of a public transport system is its reliability. This depends heavily on the actual conditions of buses while they are circulating. The average speed depends mainly on road characteristics – the volume–capacity ratio and the number of signals and bus stops per kilometre. It also depends on the bus system's operating performance. Automobile traffic may severely damage bus performance where no enforcement and no priority schemes are available, as is often the case in developing countries. Thus bus speed is normally very low (Table 11.5).

Table 11.5 *Average speed of buses, peak hours, several cities*

City (country)	Bus speed (km/h)
Bangkok[1] (Thailand)	11.5
Cairo (Egypt)[2]	17.5
Caracas (Venezuela)[3]	16.3
Havana (Cuba)[4]	18
Santa Cruz de la Sierra (Bolivia)[5]	15.7
Rio de Janeiro (Brazil)[6]	17.5
São Paulo (Brazil)[6]	14.5

Source: (1) Daniere, 1995 (daily average); (2) Abras, 1999; (3) Sanánez and Da Silva, 1999; (4) Magdaleno et al, 1999; (5) Figueroa and Pizarro, 1999; (6) IPEA/ANTP, 1998

The increase in car use has brought severe congestion problems to several parts of the developing world. A study made in ten cities in Brazil in 1998 demonstrated that automobile-related congestion severely impacts on the bus system's efficiency and reliability in large towns. Congestion imposes an additional 16 per cent operating cost on buses in São Paulo, and 10 per cent in Rio de Janeiro (IPEA/ANTP, 1998). Annual extra costs may be estimated, respectively, at US$125 million and US$30 million. In the former socialist economies, public transport has also been severely damaged by automobile-based congestion: bus travel times have increased by 18 per cent in the former East Germany and it was estimated that buses in Warsaw were travelling at 8km/h in 1996. This 'reduces the perceived quality of service and discourages yet more passengers' (Pucher and Lefèvre, 1996, p151 and p153).

CURRENT PUBLIC TRANSPORT FORMS – AN OVERVIEW

Current conditions

Actual conditions for public transport operation vary widely. This section will provide a summary of interesting experiences in Asia, Latin America and Africa.

In Asia, Kolkata, Manila and Seoul present three different cases. In Kolkata, the rail and tram systems built under British rule were the most important public transport mode until India's independence. In 1948 a bus system started to operate and by 1960 it already had a higher share of the market (60 per cent) than trams. Buses became the most important means of public transport, followed by suburban rail (Halder, 1997). The first subway line was opened in 1984 but it serves just 2–3 per cent of daily trips in the area (about 200,000 passengers; Basu, 1997). Private bus operators are controlled by unions and political parties, who distribute quotas for routes and set fares (Bhattacharyya, 1995 and 1997). An important strategic problem is that bus companies have the ability to bring the city to a standstill by withdrawing service, which the public sector is powerless to control. Private companies work according to their own interests, depriving passengers of their legal entitlement and exploiting workers. Also, there are claims that the 20,000 taxis frequently refuse passengers, tamper with meters and charge exorbitant fares. The recently introduced auto-rickshaws seem to operate without any regulation, refusing to use meters and overloading vehicles.

In Manila, public transport is provided by several modes with very different market shares (Villoria et al, 1997). The state-owned rail system (Philippine National Railway) has an insignificant share, and the lone light rail system is responsible for just 3 per cent of demand. Buses carry 34 per cent of demand, and minibus 63 per cent. Manila has 9000 buses and 89,000 minibus in operation. Some are driven by their owners but the majority are operated through a boundary system, under which the driver pays an amount which may be fixed per day or week, or proportional to the daily revenue. Recently, traffic congestion has severely damaged service performance, increasing turnaround time and decreasing the number of trips and the revenue. As most drivers do not own their vehicles but instead pay boundary fees to owners, most face severe deprivation. Fierce competition, unsafe driving and poor vehicle maintenance are the direct consequences.

In Seoul, public transport is provided mainly by a rather large subway system (163km long) which accounts for 14 per cent of motorized trips, and by buses, which account for 43 per cent. In 1990, 90 private bus companies operated 450 lines, providing more than 10 million passenger trips per day.

Buses face competition from cars and from the new subway system, and operate with low fares due to governmental limits. With no subsidies, poor services and overcrowding are common; vehicle occupancy is 30 to 50 per cent above the 'safe' level (Kim and Gallent, 1998). Recent attempts to change the transport system have faced opposition from bus operators; reorganization to avoid overlaps with subway lines was not accepted because bus operators feared a loss of revenue, and the integrated transfer system failed because of disputes over fare levels.

According to Mandon-Adolehoume (1994), since independence African countries have attempted to provide public transport through public companies. However, problems such as inefficiency, an inability to cope with increasing demand, the need to provide large subsidies, and structural economic adjustment, have often led them to give up. Informal forms of transport have developed at a fast pace in several countries, and have become, in practice, the main public transport service. For instance, in Dar-es-Salaam, Lagos and Brazzaville, at the end of the 1980s, informal transport provided by individuals represented, respectively, 90 per cent, 98 per cent and 95 per cent of the market. Considering the social effects (employment and transport supply) and the political risk involved in suppressing such services, most authorities allowed informal transport to develop outside formal regulation.

In Yaoundé (Cameroon), the public bus company was closed in 1995 and temporary permissions were granted to private operators on selected lines. These operators started to provide services using small buses, driven by the owners themselves or hired out to others. Daily net revenue was dependent on high earnings and low expenses. The first objective was pursued through vehicle overloading of up to 200 per cent, long working hours and forced route sectioning. The second was pursued by failing to take out any insurance, using smuggled fuel, reusing old engine oil, using false vehicle certificates to avoid paying taxes, and using vehicle parts handmade by local people. Yaoundé experienced some important conflicts involving private operators and travellers. For instance, people from the Eba neighbourhood (300 families) realized that the prevailing bad road conditions were affecting their accessibility. Faced with the refusal of taxis to serve the area, they started to work on road maintenance, but steep grades and constant rains made the work difficult to maintain. Irregular taxis (*clando*) started to operate, and were chased by the police. When the *clandos* decided to raise fares after road improvements were made, the community turned against them and threatened to walk instead of using their vehicles. A public meeting with the mayor ended in a return to previous fare levels. However, it seems that the Eba people will have to accept fare increases, as fares in other areas are higher and *clando* drivers may prefer to serve other lines (Ngabmen, 1997).

In El Dar-el-Beida (Casablanca, Morocco) an important privatization process was launched in the 1980s, to supplement highly deficient bus public services with private ones (Oulalou, 1994). This decision did not arise through strategic planning, but because of an emergency situation caused by a severe economic crisis, which prevented the supply of services. Public bus operation was characterized by a poor level of service, with just 68 per cent of the fleet available for use and frequent overcrowding. The crisis was worsened by poor taxi services, operating in anarchy, characterized by long queues, overcrowding, overcharging and the refusal to take passengers on some routes.

Privatization began in 1985, when five private associations were set up to provide special bus services, with seated passengers only and a fare 50 per cent higher than that of public services. The first important consequence was the high occupation rate of the new buses – up to 85 per cent – which changed the taxi share of the market. However, the demand on public buses continued to increase, proving that the new services were catering for a middle-class clientele and were not solving the public transport problem. Despite these differences, competition between the public and the private sector emerged. The public company began to reorganize services and to renovate the fleet by importing new buses from Sweden. Both sectors seem to have adopted more aggressive measures, such as speeding, making unscheduled stops, over-crowding, and concentrating on high-demand corridors to capture the competitors' passengers. In the private sector, labour conditions deteriorated rapidly, with both employers and employees adopting irregular or illegal practices to protect their interests. The conflict between the public and private sectors was aggravated by the freezing of fares despite increasing costs.

In Latin America foreign railroad and tram companies had, since the beginning of the century, had permission to provide public transport services (Figueroa et al, 1993). After the Second World War, competition from buses and adapted trucks made it impossible for these companies to provide competitive services in the newly urbanized areas. Later, they were progressively dismantled and replaced by either public or private bus operators. Few efforts were made to provide large-scale mass transport systems. Consequently, all the major cities in Latin America (except Mexico City and Buenos Aires) evolved public transport systems that were highly dependent on private bus operators, with poor rail systems (Henry and Figueroa, 1985). Urban transport policies crystallized the inequalities; bus systems were in permanent crisis, and automobiles occupied increased portions of the available space, creating sharp differences between those with and without access to private transport. Despite large differences between the countries, most experienced the abandonment and dismantling of rail systems, coupled to the enlargement of road systems (Barat, 1985).

Two different patterns of bus supply emerged from this process. In all countries except Brazil, the most common pattern of private supply is the cooperative of operators, which gathers individuals and their buses in bus corridors. As a consequence of this deregulation a broad array of services developed, with several sorts of vehicles (mostly minibuses with seating capacities of about 25 people) and different fares (UN, 1992). Lima, Santiago and Mexico City are clear examples of such development. All have large fleets of medium-sized vehicles in operation. In Lima, informal transport is the only service in operation, with 34,980 vehicles controlled by 411 organizations (ILD, 1990). In Santiago, public transport is also provided by the subway, although it has a small share of the market (4 per cent), while minibuses accounted, in 1991, for 48 per cent (Ortúzar et al, 1993). In Mexico City, although the subway has several lines, it accounts for just 12 per cent of motorized trips, as compared with 60 per cent for minibuses and shared taxis (Cervero, 1998a).

Santiago has been intensively debated in the literature because it underwent the first large-scale bus deregulation experience in Latin America (Figueroa, 1990; Darbéra, 1993; Koprich, 1994). Deregulation started in 1979, when the unrestricted entry of new operators was allowed. Complete fare deregulation was adopted in 1983. Oversupply led to imposition of entry controls that lasted until 1988, when the market was completely opened up. As summarized by Figueroa (1990), the consequences of deregulation in Santiago were: a doubling of vehicle supply, with a slightly lower increase in seats; the number of lines increased by 36 per cent; the average bus age almost doubled, from 6.95 years in 1980 to 12.1 years in 1988; fares increased by 169 per cent for buses and 103 per cent for shared taxis; the annual number of passengers per vehicle decreased by 56 per cent for buses and 30 per cent for shared taxis; the share of pedestrian trips in the city increased from 17 per cent in 1977 to 31 per cent in 1990. On the institutional side, the most important conclusion is that public regulation was replaced by private regulation, once individuals organized in cooperatives and restricted entry to their areas of operation. Private monopolies were formed around lines.

Mexico City, as one of the largest cities in the world, has long been experiencing severe urban transport problems. Until the 1960s, the city was served by 7000 buses and a few tram lines (Henry and Kuhn, 1996). The first metro line was opened in 1967 and eight others followed, always capturing a small portion of the total demand. In 1990, when eight metro lines were operating, the city already had more than 15,000 urban and suburban buses and 60,000 minibuses, the latter operated by cooperatives. The largest bus company was the publicly owned Ruta Cien, with 6569 vehicles, created in 1981 out of 19 private companies (Molinero, 1991). Ruta Cien captured a large share of the market until the end of the 1980s, when severe problems started to jeopardize its existence. As explained by Davis (1994) and Connolly (1999), overstaffing, high wages and benefits, increasing subsidies, inefficiency, and corruption brought the company to its knees. From 1988 to 1993, vehicle supply and patronage declined by half, while investments were captured by company employees, organized by a powerful union. During one of Mexico's political and economic crises, conflicts between the federal government, the district government and the Ruta Cien labour union led to escalating violence and assassinations, which resulted in the closure of the company in 1995 (Connolly, 1999). Currently, all services are provided by private associations or cooperatives, although a new public bus company has just been organized to provide feeder services for the metro terminals.

Conversely, in Brazil, bus services are regulated and provided by medium-sized or large enterprises, with fixed routes and schedules and charging predetermined fares. In urban areas this system is operated by nearly 100,000 large diesel buses and is responsible for about 95 per cent of public transport (with the exceptions of rail and subway systems in a few large cities). Supply is organized by enterprises that enjoy a monopoly once contracted by the government. No subsidy is provided in most cases. In recent decades the system has experienced several problems related to the conflict between fares and profitability, a permanent disregard for users' needs, and to the support given to cars. As in São Paulo, this regulated system prevailed until 1995, when it started to be severely challenged by illegal transport providers, backed by dissatisfied users, politicians, the media and multinational van manufacturers.

The most noticeable exception in Brazil is Curitiba, where a network of structural bus corridors was implemented along with changes in land use which allowed for denser occupation, adjusting city structure and growth. The planning process in Curitiba goes back to the 1960s, when the city masterplan was first proposed, and the institutional issue was solved by creating a special agency – the IPPUC (Curitiba Institute for Urban Planning and Research) – with the necessary legal power to conduct the process. The IPPUC also managed to control urban development, public transport, housing, and environmental and health issues, representing a large interventional scope not found in any other large city in the country. It is important to emphasize two historical features. First, between 1955 and 1958, city authorities promoted a radical change in public transport by creating 9 areas of operation and forcing 150 private firms to amalgamate into13 firms, later reduced to 9, to serve them. In parallel, public transport was regulated, with the government defining routes, schedules and fares. Second, the intense economic growth experienced by the state of Paraná, and the linkages between the state elite and the authoritarian federal military regime, combined to ensure economic resources to improve infrastructure in the state, including its capital city Curitiba (Brasileiro, 1999). Land occupation was organized along newly built structural corridors, combining high-density use and public transport supply. Motorized traffic was prohibited or controlled in the central area, and pedestrian zones were created in 1971. The new structural corridors consisted of an express bus corridor with two side roads for local traffic, and two parallel roads for long-distance, fast traffic. The bus corridors were later connected to bus terminals from which feeder bus lines operated. In 1979 bus lanes linking 28 districts to each other were created, to improve overall accessibility. The final network at that time was formed by 53km of express bus lanes, 294km of feeder bus lanes and 167km of district bus lanes. In 1991, special lines with fewer stops (one every 3km) were created, with special boarding stations at which the user pays in advance. In 1992, a new bi-articulated bus with a total capacity of 270 passengers was put into use in these special lines. The Curitiba bus system now operates with 1300 buses and serves about 1 million passengers per day. This high-quality, innovative and highly integrated system is the basic reason why Curitiba has not been challenged by the illegal transport that is now plied all over Brazil. Important as it may be as an example, the Curitiba case implies a frustration: its transport conditions are unlikely to be transferred to any other major city in the country.

The Brazilian and African experiences are very different, but both demonstrate that it is not easy for the public sector to benefit from private efficiency (Mandon-Adolehoume, 1994). Private capital does not guard the public interest, because its single motive is capital profitability. In Brazil, tight regulation and an organized transport industry also favour sector oligopolization, which reflects on service quality and supply. This results in the appearance of informal services to cope with unattended demand. In most countries, deregulation and the self-organization of the sector led to new forms of transport, and opened the way to self-interested actions that do not cope with all the needs of the users.

Analysis of current conditions

The negative consequences of the public operation of transport have been extensively portrayed in the literature. Mismanagement leads to inefficiency, service unreliability, crowded vehicles, passenger discomfort and underused equipment. Political interests and union pressures frequently lead to overstaffing, placing further pressures on costs. Disregard for market opportunities prevents the creation of new services. Inappropriate subsidization channels resources to those who need them least, or to the support of corporate interests. The need to define fares and control private operators given scope for collusion. Corruption may cause severe financial and credibility problems, often leading companies to bankruptcy. Cases of extreme disruption and decay, such as the large bus public companies in São Paulo and Mexico City, are clearly negative examples. However, a very important distinction has to be made between public ownership and operation, and public surveillance. The former has been subjected to increasing criticism and has been replaced by private operation in most cases. The latter is still being debated, since the regulatory and surveillance roles of the public sector are inescapable consequences of the public nature of the service.

Informal transport has also been subjected to intense debate. Most of the time, the entrepreneurship of informal transit providers in developing countries is enthusiastically praised by experts from developed countries. Reality, however, is very different. The rapid increase of informal transport leads to savage competition and degenerating working conditions and then to the evolution of private monopolies. The history of informal public transport tells us that when transport is seen as a market issue, a strict market logic starts to operate, as in any normal business. Operators understand that they now have a private business that they have to run according to their own best interests. Any public interference is seen as an intrusion. Any sort of tool is used to protect their interests, be it legal or illegal, peaceful or violent.[2] The immediate consequence is that those who are able to pay are served, and those who cannot pay are not. In Lomé (Mandon-Adolehoume, 1994), a drivers' union was formed to control service provision and line terminals. In Santiago, route associations began to block any new entrants who refused to join the association (Figueroa, 1990). In Dakar, in the face of savage competition, revenue was threatened and several irregular forms of behaviour were observed, such as the bypass of terminal lines and sudden changes to itineraries. During peak hours, individual drivers concentrated on high-demand routes, while in low-demand areas users had to rely on public services (Mandon-Adolehoume, 1994). Contrary to some expectations, deregulated markets often result in an increase in fares, since operators try to maintain revenue levels despite a decrease in patronage. In Santiago, fares more than doubled (Koprich, 1994; Gómez-Ibáñez and Meyer, 1991). In Bogotá, Colombia, the daily patronage of public transport vehicles decreased from 180 people in 1988 to 122 in 1995, while fares increased by 167 per cent and daily revenue increased by 71 per cent (Figueroa and Pizarro, 1998).

Decreasing revenues lead to poor vehicle maintenance and low fleet availability. In Santa Cruz de la Sierra (Bolivia), it is estimated that 30 per cent of the 3200 minibuses in operation do not run on a typical day due to malfunctioning (Figueroa and Pizarro, 1998). In Lomé, the struggle to get more passengers leads operators to disrespect traffic rules and signals; this is common in all unregulated transit systems. Only 40 per cent of shared taxis have licences to circulate (Akapko, 1998).

Service integration, vital to improve overall accessibility, can seldom be achieved. The coordination of transport policies is always difficult, considering the public and private agents involved and their specific interests. However, in a deregulated market, such difficulties may be insurmountable, because of the nature of political conflicts and the sheer numbers of private operators. In addition, as stressed by Cervero (1998a, p392) when discussing Mexico, 'no district authorities have the resources to enforce rules among some 100,000 licensed paratransit operators in the city, much less the tens of thousands of unlicensed ones'. It is also difficult to promote technological changes or to enforce compliance. In Jakarta, minibuses – which are significant contributors to pollution – are part of the cooperative sector, which threatens to block traffic whenever the government proposes to impose vehicle emission controls (Hook, 1998).

Informal transport has a limited seating capacity. When minibuses are used, overall capacity increases but the nature of the operation – which is often highly aggressive – causes constant traffic gridlocks on major corridors. That is why several people see informal transport as having a supplementary role in regular bus operation. The general criticism directed at informal transit in deregulated markets in developing countries is correct. However, the criticism based on their role in congestion has to be properly addressed. It is not correct to say, as do Tolley and Turton (1995, p180), that informal vehicles 'pass substantial congestion costs to the community, because of the obstruction to other traffic caused by frequent intermediate stops in the nearside lane'. And Cervero (1998b, p9) correctly points out,

> *restricting paratransit as a way of enhancing the automobility of the middle class is often a price the poor pay as it undermines their collective mobility ... traffic engineering consultants from abroad often take a myopic and cynical view toward paratransit, recommending the removal of slow-moving vehicles in order to expedite traffic flow.*

The negative consequences of deregulation have been mentioned by several authors. Cervero (1998b, p8) acknowledges that

> *paratransit services generally receive high marks for service frequency, speed, full loads and cost efficiency, and low marks in terms of service regularity and reliability (except during peak hours), safety and level of comfort ... besides clogging up streets, paratransit drivers ... are frequently criticised for reckless and aggressive driving.*

Gómez-Ibáñez and Meyer (1991, p26) recall that 'route associations may also act to limit competition in undesirable ways, however, such as by restricting entry or fixing fares'. The World Bank acknowledges that in an unregulated market, profit may be sought

> *through the creation of a cartel of operators, as occurred in the bus indus-*
> *try in Santiago, or by the combination of operators with suppliers of*
> *vehicles or terminals to exclude competitors from access to crucial sup-*
> *plies or facilities ... regulatory institutions shall be created to prevent*
> *such effect.* (1996, p36)

The problem is that the possible outcomes mentioned by these references are in fact inevitable, as demonstrated by the examples above. No system remains unregulated for a long time; if public regulation is banned, sooner or later (probably sooner rather than later) the private operators will call for some sort of regulation by the government, or will develop their own regulation based on the violent exercise of power. It should also be emphasized that

> *the most important [conclusion] by far, is that benefits depend critically*
> *on whether effective competition can be established and maintained in*
> *the industry ... without competition, such reforms may bring little im-*
> *provement and conceivably even a degradation in service or (as in*
> *Santiago) unwarranted increases in fares and excess capacity as route*
> *associations abuse their monopoly positions.* (Gómez-Ibáñez and Meyer,
> 1991, p35)

Again, the problem is that it is not possible to ensure competition without creating severe negative externalities and also power concentration and private monopolization by those who ban competitors, often using violent means. This is especially serious in developing countries, where route associations often constitute power in themselves, free from public surveillance and legal controls.

The creativity of the informal operators is fascinating at a first glance. According to Cervero (1998b, p9), 'driven by the profit motive, minibus and minibus drivers aggressively seek out new and expanding markets, contain costs and innovate when and where necessary'. The question that should be addressed is: Who benefits from this aggressive behaviour? The author tells with joy his own story of being efficiently driven across Jakarta through congested streets by one of these 'entrepreneurs'. However, we are not told about the personal cost to him and to the driver, or the social cost to other road users. We are also told that in Hong Kong, unregulated minibuses operate in areas that are unreachable by bus. As stated earlier, drivers take care of their market and 'adjust fares up and down according to market conditions. During torrential downpours, fares can very well double in price, reflecting whatever the market will bear' (p9). Again, the question is: What if somebody cannot pay the higher fare?

The most important conclusion about the cycles of informal transport supply is that whatever the prevailing cultural and economic environments, individual suppliers protect their newly acquired business in the same way, and never hesitate to use violent means, or to disregard any social contract they have established with users, to protect their profitability. Conversely, public ownership implies broader objectives that surpass market limits and require mandatory surveillance by public authorities. The inevitable consequence is that all private operators have to accept some level of restraint on their businesses. Another is that government has to define some rules and control results, opening a conflicting, permanent negotiation.

A GENERAL FRAMEWORK OF PUBLIC TRANSPORT REGULATION

The previous discussion poses two key questions: Who should have the responsibility for providing public transport? and Who should govern such provision?

The discussion that follows will consider the cycles of public transport supply, the public-versus-private supply issue, and the regulation issue.

Public transport supply cycles

Public transport in developing countries appeared in the first decades of the 20th century, along with the spread of urban areas and an increasing use of motorized transport. It appears that a common cycle of supply phases may be identified. One was suggested by Gómez-Ibáñez and Meyer (1991, p17). It starts with individual private operation that is eventually subject to regulation, overtaken by the public sector and then returned to the private sector again, in the following order:

1 Entrepreneurial phase; individuals start offering services, often only a few vehicles.
2 Consolidation of private supply, with merging or consolidation into a few dominant companies or associations.
3 Regulation of fares and franchises by the government, to control routes and entry.
4 Gradual decline in profitability of the private business.
5 Withdrawal of capital and services from the transport business.
6 Public takeover of the private services.
7 Public subsidies to cope with increasing demand and maintain reasonable fares.
8 Declining efficiency and rising unit costs.
9 Dilemma of subsidy cuts, fare increases and service cuts.
10 Return to private operation.

As stressed by Gómez-Ibáñez and Meyer, this cycle has been experienced in a very similar way by both developed and developing countries. They also point out that the starting point of the cycle varies according to the country or city. I believe that the proposed cycle is a very useful tool for analysing such a complex issue.

However, the cycle has two drawbacks. First, it assumes that regulation is ultimately the cause of the disarrangement and demise of the system, in that

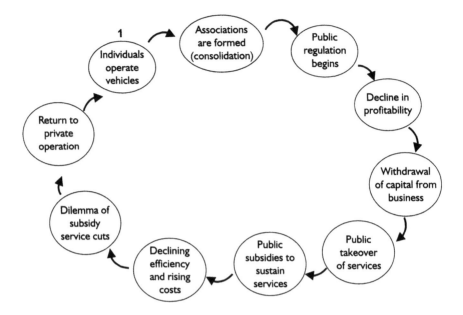

Figure 11.1 *Public transport supply cycle*

the state, after irresponsibly embarking on such venture, is finally convinced to return supply to the more responsible private sector. Second, it does not explore critical phases of the cycle, which may open the way to complimentary analyses. Although there have been several cases of unsuccessful regulatory experiences, regulation is necessary when public transport is seen as a public issue. What matters is what sort of regulation is applied, and under which circumstances; and, in the event of unsuccessful results, what the reasons may be. Three missing links may be added to the cycle. The first depicts the dynamics of individual private operation in a competitive market; I will call it the 'savage cycle'. It may replace or complement the second phase of the Gómez-Ibáñez and Meyer cycle. It may be described thus:

1 Individuals start operating in the face of unattended demand.
2 The first individuals to enter the market benefit from high revenues.
3 Profitability attracts other individuals, increasing vehicle supply.
4 As the elasticity of demand in relation to supply is low, average revenue per vehicle starts to decrease after a certain period.
5 Some individuals give up, but most continue. Those who continue face a dilemma: how to cut costs and increase revenue.
6 Most opt to cut costs by decreasing the level of service, through not repairing the vehicle; overloading the vehicle; using low-quality or illegal vehicle parts; contracting child labour; avoiding vehicle taxes and ignoring labour rights; changing schedules and routes to increase earnings at short notice; fiercely competing on the street with other drivers for customers; reckless driving; and cutting existent services that are considered to be less profitable.

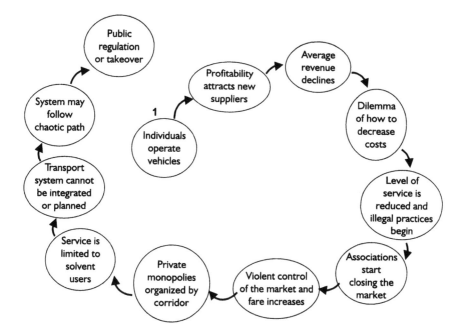

Figure 11.2 *The 'savage' public transport supply cycle*

7 Others increase revenue by forming associations and cooperatives, excluding those who do not want to join, and by banning new individuals from entering the market. Such cooperatives are organized, in most cases, with the support of policemen and, in several cases, with the support of illegal businesses (gambling, drug trafficking).

8 The operators group around corridors of high demand. Once the market has been protected, fares are increased to recover revenues, as in Chile (Koprich, 1994). Monthly amounts are charged to drivers for access to the market. Those who refuse to pay are expelled and those who try to enter are violently prevented.

9 In several cases, cooperatives exist simply to sell entrance rights, with support from bureaucrats and politicians.

10 The final result is that the market is divided between 'mafias' who may or not manage to coexist peacefully. The public monopoly is replaced by private monopolies organized along routes or areas.

The second missing link depicts the dynamics of the deterioration of the service offered by a public company. I will call it the 'corporate' cycle. It may be taken as complementing step 7 of the Gómez-Ibáñez and Meyer cycle:

1 A public company is formed to provide public transport.
2 Political pressures and lack of social control, in some cases worsened by an economic crisis, allow a steady increase in the number of employees and the lowering of overall efficiency.

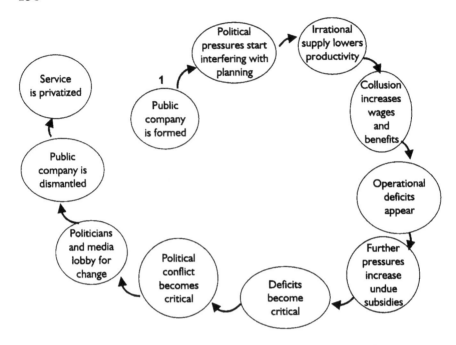

Figure 11.3 *The 'corporate' public transport supply cycle*

3 Continuous political pressures increase the supply of services in a irrational way, decreasing system productivity.

4 Labour movements, or collusion between the technocracy and labour unions, increase wages and benefits while ignoring efficiency considerations. Such pressures are often supported by ideological discourses attributing to the public transport company the status of a 'vital public interest', thereby justifying the appropriation of benefits from workers.

5 Continuous decrease in performance and efficiency leads to sharp increases in operational deficits and to pressures for more money; the system starts its decline towards unsustainability.

6 Critical conditions and external pressures eventually lead to the dismantling of the public company and the transferral of services to the private sector.

The third 'missing link' describes the deterioration of a privately operated service when submitted to a regulated environment. I will call it the 'irresponsible' cycle. This is the case in Brazil, which deserves special analysis. The Brazilian urban public transport system is probably the largest privately operated, highly regulated service in the world. It is estimated that there are 100,000 large buses operating in urban areas, serving 60 million trips per day (ANTP, 1997). Supply is organized by medium and large enterprises, with fixed routes and schedules and under fixed, predetermined fares. The long relationship between the public sector and private operators has led to the organization of a strong transport industry linked to one of the largest bus manufacturing sectors in the world[3] (FABUS, 1997). The industry has been working under increasingly sophisticated administrative and logistical procedures (Henry, 1999) although parts of it follow traditional management techniques. The typical situation involves a city served by one operator, according to contracts that are valid for ten or more years. In large cities such as São Paulo, Rio de Janeiro and Belo Horizonte, several private firms operate, often in geographically divided areas.

The regulated marked in Brazil began in the 1940s, while all other Latin American countries maintained unregulated markets (UN, 1992). The relationship between the strong constitutional power of the mayors and the increasing organization of the bus industry gradually evolved to form a stable bus public transport industry that consolidated all over the country in the 1970s. Few cities had public operators, and even within these the public sector was responsible for a small part of the supply. Private services were always subject to regulation concerning routes, schedules, fares and vehicle conditions, with few – if any – exceptions. Contracts gave market exclusivity to private operators, but illegal competition from small vehicles always served a small part of the demand. The system was permanently threatened by two major conflicts: tensions caused by continuous economic inflation, with a direct impact on fares and profitability; and conflicts related to weak enforcement, with an impact on users' evaluation of the service.

The 'Brazilian cycle' may be summarized as follows:

1 In the 1920s, individuals start to operate small buses, trying to capture the tram market. The first bus firms are organized, very similar to the cooperatives appearing in other Latin American countries.
2 Uncontrolled urban growth and conflicts between the public sector and a Canadian tram company results in a rapid increase in bus services, which gradually start to dominate the market.
3 The strengthening of the Brazilian federal state after the 1930 revolution translated into an increasing influence of the public sector in all aspects of Brazilian society. After the Second World War, the democratization process that occurred alongside the continuing power of the state sector, resulted in the formation in 1947 of a large public bus operator in São Paulo, the CMTC.
4 Until the end of the 1970s joint public and private operation continued, threatened by the permanent pressures of uncontrolled urban growth. Tram services were progressively dismantled until they were ended in 1967, and CMTC gradually lost market share, from 86 per cent in 1949 to 21 per cent in 1977. This generated a privately operated market, with 66 firms and 6420 large buses (SMT, 1978). Private operation was first regulated in 1967. In 1977, the city authorities defined 23 geographical service areas including the CBD, and began a bidding process that induced private operators to form larger groups to operate in such areas. CMTC was granted the licence to operate certain lines.
5 The new system resulted in a lowering of efficiency because of profitability disparities, deficient enforcement and inflation-based tensions. Several private operators, especially those in less profitable areas, started cost-lowering practices that severely harmed level of service, reliability and

accessibility. Deficient enforcement by the public sector and permanent conflicts around fare levels gradually placed the system in an unfavourable position, and these conditions deteriorated even further through the lack of bus lanes and continuous investment in supporting car use. CMTC services started to be disputed by union and corporate pressures on employment and wages, overall inefficiency and corruption (see the 'corporate' cycle).

6   Such decaying conditions were fostered by the 1991–1994 left-wing city government in two ways. First, the permanent conflict between fare level and service supply was managed by paying services according to distances run, but without proper efficiency incentives and enforcement, generating increasing deficits. In addition, local government was unable to cope with union pressures and allowed CMTC to keep pursuing the same destructive path. The way to unsustainability was already traced.

7   In 1994, with the city government in the hands of neoliberal political forces, CMTC was privatized and was given some efficiency parameters. However, public transport remained a low priority, because demand was seen as captive. After 1994 inflation was gradually lowered, but sharp increases in automobile ownership and large investments in motorways fostered automobile use, causing the largest traffic congestion in the city's history. This further damaged bus reliability, and peak-hour speeds dropped to just 12km/h (IPEA/ANTP, 1998). Meanwhile, global and regional structural economic changes, along with the evolution of a tertiary economy, changed transport demand and opened new market niches. Informal public transport, which had always played a minor role, started to be very attractive to individuals. Deficient enforcement, overall dissatisfaction with regular services and the freeing of vans from import duties fostered the appearance of a powerful informal supply, which was supported directly by the media and politicians, and indirectly by foreign van manufacturers who gave financial and legal aid to the organization of cooperatives of operators. Federal government turned a blind eye to the illegal use of vans as public transport vehicles.

8   In 1999, 15,000 vans were in operation in São Paulo alone; 11,000 large buses gradually lost their patronage, and unemployment in the formal sector started. It is estimated that vans captured about 20 per cent of bus passengers, and an equivalent part shifted to automobiles.

9   Inherent legal and economic conflicts led the new city government to react against illegal van transport. Facing such reactions, van operators started a street war. They started blocking bus operations and blocking roads to capture passengers. The first fatal accident involving a van started to change public opinion. Route/area groups were formed, most of them including military policemen who were supposed to enforce illegal transport. Entry to the market was now controlled by such groups. The 'savage' cycle depicted above had started.

10 Bus burning and general violence escalated to the point at which most people began to support stronger police action. Local and regional governments managed to coordinate their efforts and severe measures were taken in the first months of 2000. Most vans were forced off the streets,

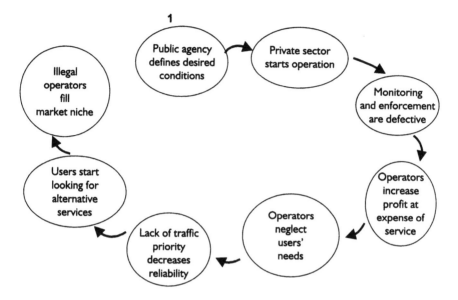

Figure 11.4 *The 'irresponsible' public transport supply cycle*

although a large group continued to operate in peripheral areas. An attempt to reorganize the regulatory environment is now under way.

Public or private responsibility

Contrary to traditional progressive beliefs, there is no mandatory relationship between public responsibility for public transport and the protection of public interests. By the same token, contrary to neoliberal beliefs, there is no mandatory relationship between private responsibility for transport and the protection of public interests. What is at stake is not merely the old 'public versus private' discussion but how social needs are met (Godard, 1990) and within which equity frameworks. In this respect, an inefficient public transport company which absorbs public subsidies in exchange for poor services is as bad as a well-organized private enterprise which submits its employees to illegal working conditions and irregularly lowers the quality of contracted services as part of a strict profit-seeking approach. Both approaches are questionable because public transport is a very special form of service and a very special sort of 'business'. Koprich (1994), Santos and Orrico (1997) and Henry (1999) provide interesting discussions on the peculiarities of public transport. The following is drawn from their work, with specific points added:

- Operation takes place on public goods, such as streets and terminal facilities; moreover, this operation implies no (direct) payment to the state.
- The product that is delivered – the trip – cannot be accumulated if it is not sold at the moment that it is offered; this implies that it is important to find time and spatial coincidence between the user and the seller.

- Most of the demand is captive, as most people have no access to private transport. This dependence lies behind the low elasticity of public transport with respect to fares; people need the transport, whatever the price (although there is an absolute maximum). The most important practical consequence is that public transport is a low-risk business, with a highly predictable revenue, provided that no predatory[4] competition is present and no uncompensated cost increases occur.
- The operation of vehicles generates externalities, especially air pollution, congestion and accidents.
- Users have no information on when/if the next service will come to the bus stop, and therefore are virtually unable to exercise their supposed market freedom.
- Due to the physical characteristics of the road system, to the rather stable OD pattern of trips, and to the cyclical pattern of demand, transport service may be organized along corridors, in which vehicles are scheduled in regular intervals. Hence, the idea of free competition is impractical, ultimately leading to formal (or informal) agreements between operators (as in most deregulated systems).

The experience of several parts of the developing world led some researchers to develop models of the micro-economics of the sector. Working with the internal constraints of the transport 'business', Henry (1999) proposes the interesting idea of 'analytical funnels' representing stages in the process of supplying public transport as a business. He shows how the individual transport supplier, working initially in a 'self-production' mode (the first level of supply), becomes increasingly constrained by external factors such as the automotive industry, the prices of vehicle parts and fuel, and the availability of roads, and has to define alternative – and variable – strategies to keep the business running. The operator may then evolve towards a more 'professional' production, with managing techniques that impact on labour conditions and training, vehicle maintenance, and, depending on the organization of cooperatives, the access to lower prices for vehicles and parts. This second level of business organization may then evolve into a third stage, when supply is organized in medium to large firms and capital is invested in garages, offices and management procedures to ensure the continuous supply of services, according to a standard capitalist production procedure. While the first and the second stages correspond to past and current conditions in all Latin American countries (except Brazil) – and I may add Asian and African countries as well – the third stage corresponds to the Brazilian bus transport industry.

Some general conclusions may be derived. On the one hand, the business of public transport cannot be analysed through neoclassical economics. The consumers are not free, transport causes externalities, information is defective, and the risk is normally low. Hence, there is no basis for taking a market approach. On the other hand, public transport cannot be treated as an exclusively public domain. The complexity of the relationships between demand and supply, coupled to the ever-changing nature of urban environments (especially in developing countries), renders it impossible for planners to forecast and control everything. It is not realistic to submit all decisions to this supposed planning capacity. Hence, there is no grounds for limiting public transport supply decisions to either planning agencies or public operators.

The above conclusions do not mean that a state of laissez-faire should prevail.[5] As clearly demonstrated by the aforementioned examples, oversupply, congestion, inefficiency and violent conflicts are the inescapable consequences of deregulation. Moreover, there is absolutely no basis for eliminating all public control of the system. If private operators are called upon to provide most of the services, public regulation remains essential and irreplaceable for three main reasons: transport uses public goods; it generates externalities that the market will not take care of; and it is an essential service for society and the economy.

Considering the prevailing analyses, four sorts of decisions are key to understanding how current conditions may be improved, and inequalities may be minimized. They are: the regulation of transport supply, the subsidization of transport services, the selection of technologies, and the use of available streets.

Regulation and deregulation of transport supply

Regulation is the broadest form of state intervention in the transport market. It can affect several aspects of the service – fares, routes, vehicles, working conditions – and can be based on the establishment of both quantitative and qualitative limits or requirements. Conversely, deregulation entails the elimination of barriers and restriction rules in order to let market forces organize transport supply.

Formally, according to neoclassical economics, regulation is acceptable only when market failures occur. These failures may include: the exploitation of market power to distort the market; the generation of externalities (pollution, congestion, accidents); and lack of transparency or information for consumers (Bayliss, 1992). The World Bank acknowledges that there are three reasons for retaining some public regulation of the right to supply transport: indivisible infrastructures (roads, railways) whose duplication would be wasteful or impractical; the danger of the duplication of schedules, potential excess capacity, dangerous operational practices and perceived losses in service stability and reliability; and when social services are needed and it is known that the unregulated market will not provide for them (World Bank, 1996, p37). Hence, from a social point of view, regulation is justified by the rationale that the market alone is not capable of providing a comprehensive and convenient transport supply. This is so for three main reasons: first, private operators follow a strict market rationale, with no space for providing social services; second, deregulation often leads to fare increases, as a result either of service specialization or of operators' collusion around shared transport corridors; third, competition increases congestion, traffic indiscipline and accidents, mainly in highly trafficked corridors, due to the oversupply of vehicles and the tendency to use smaller buses. Hence, regulation is introduced to: protect users against bad or lacking services; protect operators against unequal competition; or protect the public from service externalities (CEPAL, 1988).

The simplest form of regulation is the fixed-route, fixed-fare system. Private operators are contracted to run fixed routes, offering a certain level of service and receiving a pre-defined fare. This system prevailed in all Brazilian cities until the end of the 1980s, when its drawbacks started to be acknowledged by transport authorities: inflation raised costs without compensation, and private operators adjusted supply to ensure profitability.

An alternative form of regulation relates to contracting services by distances run, as opposed to the traditional fare-rewarded operation. Brazil has had a long experience with these new contracts and Barat (1992) and Orrico and Santos (1996) provide comprehensive evaluations of this experience. The system has three main positive aspects. First, there is a formal separation between the fare charged to the user and the payment to the operator, giving the state more political relief in the face of the political nature of fare increases; this is facilitated in the Brazilian case by the use of the *vale transporte*, a public transport ticket bought by employers and delivered to employees, who in turn have no more than 6 per cent of their salaries discounted.[6] Second, the system allows a great flexibility in allocating vehicles to routes, and in creating new or temporary services, which fulfils public social planning needs. Third, a flat-fare system avoids the problems derived from profitability differences between routes, a permanent source of conflict between government and operators with low-profitability services (in fact, a sort of a compensation mechanism operates between services). However, the system presents two main drawbacks. First, once service is paid by distance, the operator loses interest in enforcing fare collection, which leads to a slow but permanent decrease in revenue, unless specific controls are organized. Second, operators tend to force increases in the distances run, and to use more sophisticated equipment, in order to increase their payment. Both drawbacks may drive the system to financial instability. Considering the advantages and drawbacks, experience shows that the system is viable, provided that rewards are also based on the number of passengers carried; if subsidies are needed, they must be delivered directly to the users (as the *vale transporte*); the compensation mechanism is managed by the operators themselves, and not by the government; and government has actual enforcement capability, supported by efficient mechanisms to verify the quality of the service, distances run and patronage.

Deregulation is based on the opposite rationale, that of leaving the decisions about how the supply should be organized to the market. The market is understood as a superior mechanism for resource allocation, as in conventional neoclassical economics. In addition, deregulators argue that regulation has many drawbacks (CEPAL, 1988; UN, 1992): first, it implies surveillance costs that have to be paid by the users (or society), and these costs are always higher than the supposed benefits; second, regulatory activities are seen as inefficient and subject to corruption or collusion between regulators and suppliers (Carbajo, 1993); third, regulation discourages competition and innovation, by ensuring too much stability to suppliers; fourth, in the case of public suppliers, their cost is seen as much higher than private operation costs;

fifth, by increasing overall supply costs, regulation discourages entry, further enhancing the protection of existing suppliers; finally, formal or centralized planning is assumed to be too complex and faulty, while the market is assumed to be much more efficient. As in the case of regulation, deregulation can affect one or all of the characteristics of the service. The most common items submitted to examination are entry conditions, vehicles, trip intervals and fares. In any case, a common assumption should be avoided: 'privatization', as it appears in many recent studies, has nothing to do with deregulation, being just a transfer of the responsibility for the operation from a public to a private entity. It can be done without major changes in the regulatory environment.

As previously summarized, international experience shows that most systems in operation in the world are submitted to some sort of regulation. Many studies have been made about these experiences, and conclusions are heavily dependent on the analyst's point of view. The analysis always implies values, in addition to welfare and equity considerations. Nevertheless, it is possible to summarize some conclusions that are supported by most of the studies:

- Highly regulated urban transport markets, with public operators serving all or most of the demand, experience severe deficit problems and low levels of service, with periodical crises revolving around fare levels and subsidy needs.
- Regulated markets based on private operation with controlled fares also experience cyclical crises, related to the fluctuation of the revenue/cost ratio, which is highly dependent on price inflation. The struggle evolves around a conflict between government, operators and users over fare levels. The results are instability of supply and the ageing of the fleet, up to a 'limit' point where tensions threaten the survival of the system, leading to fare increases or more subsidies to operators.
- Highly deregulated markets experience an increase in service provision but at the expense of higher fares, congestion and pollution; moreover, there may be an 'elitization' of supply and the organization of private local monopolies, sustained by violent forms of control. The Chilean experience shows very clearly the drawbacks of such radical deregulation.

Therefore, the peculiar nature of public transport renders both radical regulation and deregulation ineffective in social terms. The most attractive solution will be found by mixing the public regulatory surveillance role with private operating and marketing efficiency. Regulatory decisions will depend on the specific conditions of the local public transport market.

CONCLUSION

However complex the public transport issue may be there is one simple way to analyse it: how public transport is seen within society. There are two possible visions.

First, transport is seen as a market problem, a service that has to be provided according to market rules. This allows operators to make decisions about supply, location, marketing, pricing and service levels. Second, transport is seen as a public issue, that is, a service which has to be provided according to rules emanating from a political consensus concerning public interests and needs. In such cases, rules concerning the nature of the service and surveillance and enforcement by public authorities are inescapable.

Market regulation implies that services should be deregulated to the maximum extent, preserving (if society believes it to be necessary) only safety limits. The consequence is that only those who can afford to pay are served. System integration, land use and transport relations, and social and environmental concerns become meaningless; the role of public transport authorities is limited to issuing basic permits for driving vehicles.

The public approach implies that regulation is necessary, and the only flexibility allowed concerns the level of regulation and control. Discussion follows extremely complex philosophical and ethical issues and becomes a challenge for everyone involved in it. Efficiency considerations become essential but social constraints may require both subsidization and non-market approaches to service provision. Consequently – and this is at the core of the informal versus formal transport debate – all agents involved with the supply of services have to accept the prevalence of public control, a condition which is never accepted by the informal sector (unless it hopes to induce the state to protect it from undesired competition). It is important to note that in this respect informal suppliers are no different from any large private supplier; the difference resides in the capability of state and society to define limits to such behaviour and to protect public interests.

Three essential conclusions are clear. First, regulated markets based on the acceptance of the principle of public interest may end up contradicting this interest if mismanagement, corruption or collusion occurs. Second, even deregulated markets end up regulated in some way, either by cooperatives or 'mafias', which define geographical and market limits. Therefore, there is never a truly deregulated market. Third, in the case of informal transport, entry to the market is cynically denied to protect the business: 'competition', as an ideological keystone, cannot face reality and return to the textbooks of business administration courses.

The approach to public transport may also be seen as evolving from two different views: collective and public. Collective transport is available to the public under market rules; public transport is available to the public under social rules defined by society. The market may deliver collective transport, not public transport; only a publicly planned and monitored system may deliver public transport as an essential service to society.

The public approach is preferable for guiding transport policy in the developing world. Ultimately, in extreme cases, a public monopoly is preferable to a private one. Whatever difficulties such an approach may pose, this is one of the essential steps towards social and environmental equity.

ROOTS OF THE ISSUE

In the last three decades, the rapid growth of cities in the developing world has been followed by a growth in car ownership, profoundly changing the traffic circulation conditions within these cities. Similar growth has occurred with motorcycles in several countries, especially in Asia.

Transport planners seem to be headed down a dead-end street. The increasing use of private transport and especially the car seems unavoidable, as it appears to be something that people naturally desire attached to symbols of status, power and self-affirmation. Consequently, there is a debate about how to deal with this trend. This debate has intensified recently, in the face of the economic globalization process and enlarging markets for motorized vehicles.

The issue is very complex and leads to intriguing questions. When discussing the reasons behind such a rapid increase in automobile use, Cervero (1998) asks 'has humankind been lulled by some unexplained force into a prodigious way of living and travel, seemingly oblivious to the long-term consequences? Unlikely'. Whitelegg (1999, p18) uses an interesting analogy to the Faust myth. The obsession with the car is related to the Faustian bargain, in the sense that the car

> *can liberate the self-imprisoned soul from its perceived boredom ... it can confer strong feelings of power, external signs of material wealth, sexual mastery and status ... (but) the ability to crave and enjoy the benefits and the inability to recognise the severity of the price that has to be paid is Faustian in character.*

The objective of this section is to search for a complementary explanation of private transport and especially the automobile's increasing use in contemporary developing societies. This is not an academic issue but rather a practical one in the light of its consequences for transport policy proposals. Complementary to prevailing views of the automobile, a more revealing sociological approach is proposed. This approach sees transport technology as being embedded in the contemporary pattern of urban social reproduction and, for several reasons that will be discussed later, associates the use of the automobile with the middle-class lifestyle and connected interests, as part of capitalist modernization in developing countries.

Current use of private transport in developing countries

The UN estimates that vehicle population in the world could grow from 580 million in 1990 to 816 million in 2010, excluding motorcycles (UN, 1997). In 1993, OECD countries had 70 per cent of the world automobile fleet, with the US at the top of the list, with 561 cars per 1000 residents (World Bank, 1997). In the developing world, vehicle ownership is much lower, but it is increasing at a fast pace. One of the major concerns is that the growth is expected to concentrate on urban areas, where negative effects such as congestion, accidents and pollution may escalate to intolerable levels, as already happens in Bangkok, Mexico City, São Paulo and Delhi. Specific negative consequences will depend on the rate of growth as well as on the traffic mix and the corresponding traffic conflict pattern.

Whatever the differences between countries, there is a common tendency towards individual motorization. This tendency has been occurring at all social levels. Longer distances and large urban agglomerations have made motorized public transport necessary, especially diesel buses. Social and economic factors have encouraged the use of motorized two- and three-wheelers and automobiles.

In sub-Saharan Africa, the average annual growth of vehicles in the 1970–1987 period was between 2.6 per cent (Zimbabwe) and 15.9 per cent (Nigeria). In Nigeria alone, the number of cars increased from 119,400 in 1976 to 394,893 in 1985 (a 230 per cent increase) (Akinbami and Fadare, 1997). In Asia, several countries and cities have been experiencing the same phenomenon. In Beijing, the number of cars and motorcycles increased from 8836 in 1970 to 202,357 in 1990 (Sit, 1996). In Latin America, São Paulo experienced a six-fold increase in its automobile fleet between 1970 and 1997, from 640,000 to 3.5 million (Vasconcellos,1996a). Recently, the increase has continued; from 1991 to 1996 the motorization rate has increased from 189 to 250 in Buenos Aires and from 90 to 138 in Santiago (Figueroa, 1997). Most large cities in the region have motorization rates around 200 to 300 vehicles per person.

Table 12.1 *Motorized vehicles ownership rates, Latin American cities*

City (country)	Veh/1000 people
Buenos Aires (Argentina)	250
Caracas (Venezuela)	218
La Paz (Bolivia)	100
Lima (Peru)	58
Medellin (Colombia)	148
Mexico City (Mexico)	158
Santiago (Chile)	138
São Paulo (Brazil)	317
Rio de Janeiro (Brazil)	216

Source: Figueroa, 1997

In the former socialist countries, the increase has been dramatic in recent years (Table 12.2).

Table 12.2 *Increase in auto ownership, Eastern Europe, 1980–1992*

| Year | Cars/1000 people | | |
	Poland	**Hungary**	**East Germany**
1980	67	95	150
1985	98	135	199
1988	119	163	225
1990	138	189	296
1992	169	217	415

Source: Pucher and Lefèvre, 1996

Motorcycle ownership is already very high in Asian countries. Table 12.3 shows that their share in the motorized fleet may be as high as 72 per cent (Chiang Mai) and that the motorcycle ownership rate may be as high as 430 per 1000 people (Chiang Mai). Recent trends reveal a sharp increase in some important cities such as Beijing, where the number of motorcycles increased from 4998 in 1970 to 112,984 in 1990 (Sit, 1996) and Hanoi, where it increased 5–10 per cent annually between the mid-1980s and 1995 (Griffin, 1995).

Table 12.3 *Motorcycle ownership and share in the overall motorized fleet, Asian cities*

| City | Motorcycles | |
	Share (%)	**Mot/1000 pop**
Chiang Mai (Thailand)	72.3	430
Phnom Penh (Cambodia)	43.6	145
Surabaya (Indonesia)	38.7	125
Kanpur (India)	18.6	77
Dhaka (Bangladesh)	16.0	18
Hanoi (Vietnam)	10.8	116

Source: World Bank, 1995

THE DEMAND FOR PRIVATE TRANSPORT – A SOCIAL AND ECONOMIC APPROACH

Conventional views of the automobile

The meaning of the automobile in modern societies is multifaceted; no single facet alone can explain why it has so profoundly influenced our lives. I believe that four conventional views encompass most conceptions about the car.

The first conventional view – anthropological – sees the automobile as a symbol of power, status and wealth. The second view – political – corresponds to symbols of freedom and privacy. The third vision – psychological – corresponds to the ideas of youth and athleticism, self-reliance, and personal pleasure. The anthropological view of the automobile as a status symbol is pervasive among scholars. Pucher and Lefèvre (1996, p144) argue that in the case of East Germany after reunification, the possession of a Western car acted as a symbol of status and 'served a psychological need for East Germans who are trying to catch up with the much higher standard of living in West Germany'. The authors extent their argument to Central and Eastern Europe and the countries of the former Soviet Union, arguing that sociologists and transport planners agree that the demand for automobiles 'far exceeds what is actually necessary to meet mobility needs' (Pucher and Lefèvre, 1996, p147). A similar analysis was made for a completely different social and cultural environment, that of Africa. In Ouagadougou (Burkina Faso), more than 90 per cent of people interviewed declared that they see the automobile as an agent of free movement. Most believe that the car is safer, and 63 per cent think that it is admired by other people. The car, then, seems to have many virtues and one drawback: its price (Diaz Olvera and Plat, 1997). Analysing the case of Calcutta, Bhattacharyya (1997, p39) thinks that

> it appears that poorer countries of the world in general have accepted private car ownership as an index of their progress while the Western world has rejected this notion following its own experience over decades.

In the Maghreb region, Mankouch (1997) says that, despite all the enormous infrastructure costs related to the increased use of the automobile, it remains a model that culturally dominates all social classes.

Motorcycle ownership has also been analysed. In Ouagadougou the same survey revealed that most of the reasons for purchasing and using such vehicles were related to the ease of making trips anywhere, any time (92 per cent of people); 88 per cent declared time economy to be the main reason, 57 per cent aid that they wanted 'to be seen' on the streets, and 40 per cent wanted to save money (in relation to using collective taxis). Although status is indeed important, the freedom to circulate at will and the possibility of saving time were more important. This reinforces the hypothesis that private transport in developing countries is utility-oriented (as a conscious reproduction decision) more than status-oriented.

Flexibility is also mentioned as an important characteristic. To perform several different activities in time and space requires frequent trips, and the car is probably the best-suited technology (Diaz Olvera and Plat, 1997). This means that the car is used to a greater extent than other modes in those trips classified as 'other purposes' (aside from the dominant purposes of work and school). In Tunis, autos are used firstly as transport to work (45 per cent of trips) and secondly for other purposes (28 per cent) (Mankouch, 1997).

Other approaches relate automobile use to a wider set of factors. Stone (1971, p99) recognizes that the attractiveness of the car can be explained because 'the random route system approximates a door-to-door transport system'. For Weber (1991, p274), 'people everywhere are attracted to cars not because they are lovable nor because they are prestigeful, but because they offer better transport services'. Orfeiul (1994, p39) stresses that for developed countries 'suburbanization is rational at the individual level'.

For Tolley and Turton

> *(car) popularity is explicable in terms of its flexibility, personal conve-*
> *nience and status that ownership confers ... its advantages are augmented*
> *by powerful social and economic pressures that have made the car a sym-*
> *bol of wealth, choice and success.* (1995, p175)

The anthropological, political and psychological views are integrated in the discourse of daily life, especially by the media. As stressed by Wright (1992, p7)

> *The automotive industry's propaganda has been more effective in exert-*
> *ing subliminal pressures on the public, researchers, administrators, and*
> *legislators. The private car is pictured ... [as] ... a symbol of cleanliness,*
> *freedom, adventure, power, youth, health, sex.*

While the anthropological (group symbolism) and psychological (personal pleasure) views are the most superficial in explaining auto purchase and use, the political view (mobility as freedom) is more powerful as an explanatory tool, related to the very essence of the ideology of economic modernization.

In addition to these three widely adopted views, a fourth one – the economic – is related to the utility of the car, a technology that allows for an unprecedented mobility and provides the most efficient trip-linking organization. The decision to buy a motorized vehicle – and the resulting rejection of public transport – is seen as a consequence of a rational comparison between the benefits and costs of several transport choices. This vision is supported by a large economic literature (Button, 1993; Small, 1992). It represents an important change because it supersedes the drawbacks of the superficial approaches described before by proposing the actual utility of the car as the main factor explaining its valuation. By implying time savings and unrestrained spatial accessibility as the ultimate objectives of private transport use, the economic explanation is indeed the most powerful, connected to the nature of consumer society and corresponding rational decisions.

Despite the relevance of such approaches in explaining private transport use in some circumstances, they are insufficient in explaining the degree of either private transport purchase or usage in the developing world. First, the expansion of the industry and the large volume of automobile and motorcycle purchases are not solely a consequence of marketing efforts or of the industry's communication ability, but must derive from more structural reasons. One cannot imagine that this success was caused by people's 'irresistible' attraction to such goods. The decision to buy such an expensive commodity, often requiring years of monthly payments, cannot be compared to the decision to buy a shirt. There must be other reasons and they must relate to both the specific conditions within which this technology is offered and the way people think that the car can address their needs. Second, the use of the economic approach is inappropriate in developing countries, since the prevailing spatial arrangement and income distribution prevent most people from having a choice beyond public transport. Therefore, consumer choice models are meaningless. In addition, even when such modelling procedures are used to analyse the case of the selected groups with access to private transport, abounding market failures preclude a clear analysis. Third, the statement about the 'obvious utility' of the car is a truism. It either ends the argument or leads the analyst in the wrong direction, that of concluding that if people 'demand' cars we should therefore just provide them with cars, and also streets and parking facilities, without considering the complex relationship between land use, social and economic factors, and transport demand.

Therefore, it is important to analyse other dimensions to understand the motives that shape the significance of the automobile. Who sees private transport as a utility and under which conditions? How do the built environment and the prevailing transport infrastructure influence the need to buy and use private transport? How do cars compare with alternative public transport means? To accomplish this task, a sociological approach to private transport, and especially the automobile within contemporary society, is needed. It complements the economic approach by combining the idea of the utility of private transport with the urban, social and political contexts in which it is offered as a transport technology.

The proposed approach

For the specific analysis of private transport consumption, transport technologies have to be analysed in respect to a given urban structure shaped within specific social, economic and political contexts. In addition, the analysis has to uncover the large, uniform set of 'consumers' and reveal the internal social and economic differences among social groups and classes (their needs and interests) and the context within which the technology is offered: the car (or the motorcycle) does not run itself, and one has to analyse who, and within which conditions, has decided to purchase and use it. I focus mainly on those countries that already have a large industrial base and already use a large fleet of motorised vehicles, such as Brazil, Mexico, South Korea, Indonesia and Thailand, where economic modernization and global integration have been pursued intensively in the last decades, and also on those countries that are now pursuing the same path, such as the former socialist countries and China and India. Nevertheless, specific conditions in each country have to be considered in order to adapt the proposed analysis whenever relevant and convenient.

Urban growth and private transport demand in developing countries

Urban activity networks are becoming larger and motorized transport means are becoming dominant. Motorized two-wheel vehicles and the private automobile are by far the most efficient ways of optimizing network performance from the individual point of view, given their flexibility. Some authors have already scrutinized the issue taking a sociological approach. For Whitelegg

(the) car ... shapes the whole lifestyle (and) ... creates a subtle depen-
dence on itself (emphasis added) ... in many parts ... it is not possible
... to reject car ownership ... the car is the center of a complex web of
lifestyle organisation which sets it apart from many other consumer
durables. (1981, p155)

Reichman (1983, p100) also acknowledges that 'many factors support the idea
that the car implies a whole lifestyle and mobility strategy' and Bernard and
Julien (1974, p100) stress that the use value of the car 'is not explained by an
abstract preference for this mode ... It is the form that urban space is organised
which confers the automobile its use value'. These views get closer to a more
delimited sociological approach to the car because they manage to relate its
ownership and use to social and political characteristics of the economic
development model in which they are immersed, and to the urban structure
as well. To understand the distribution of accessibility in urban areas of developing countries, and the role played by the automobile, it is necessary to
analyse how cities were adapted by the capitalist modernization process of
the postwar period. This will be done by using Sao Paulo as a representative
case and other major cities as secondary cases. Economic modernization entails profound changes in the technology of production, with large impacts
on land use, urban structure and travel patterns. It also requires new educational and technical skills. Considering the prevailing social and economic
discrepancies between people in the developing world, the closed nature of
the political systems, and the limited amount of investments, modernization
is not open to everybody and will be limited (in its full impacts) to selected
groups.[1] The new pattern of investment can only economically sustain selected social sectors (in addition to the elite). These social sectors are called
'middle classes'. Therefore, instead of a strictly income-related economic concept, I am using here a broader concept of middle classes, as being those sectors
that have the cultural, social and economic conditions necessary to commit
themselves to and to benefit from the modernization process.[2]

How do these middle classes relate to the recent urban changes in the
developing world? Large cities in developing countries have recently experienced intense growth related to economic modernization and migration. In
addition, they have experienced an intense process of physical reconstruction and the adaptation of the road system to an increasing number of
automobiles. In São Paulo, transport planning directed some of its most important actions to the enlargement and adaptation of streets and highway
systems to guarantee comprehensive spatial interconnections, while traffic
management used modern technologies and tools to yield high levels of fluidity. These changes were supported by the ideological commitment to the
process of modernization. Accordingly, these policies were carried out along
with a rapid increase in the number of automobiles, from 160,000 in 1960 to
1.9 million in 1980. The availability of cars, despite being limited to selected
sectors, was facilitated by economic policies in two ways: the financing of car
acquisition, and the organization of vehicle 'consortiums', in which people
contribute monthly payments for two or three years to save up for a car. Urban policies also worked to ease car use, as new land-use laws allowed the

building of middle-class housing and apartment complexes in areas where the state provided adequate infrastructure and appropriate traffic and parking conditions. Conversely, public transport captive users (the majority) were subject to poor transport conditions.

The reshaping of the urban space corresponded to a new lifestyle, characterized by new and increasingly complex patterns of consumption and social relations. People's daily activity networks increased and diversified, adding new destinations often at greater distances. In São Paulo, this change led to a 122 per cent increase in the average number of motorized daily trips between 1967 and 1977, as opposed to a 45 per cent increase in population. However, the largest increase has occurred with auto trips, whose proportion within the total number of trips rose dramatically; they almost tripled in the period, compared to a 100 per cent increase in bus trips (CMSP, 1978). Between 1977 and 1987, the private transport share again increased more than public transport (36 per cent versus 6 per cent).

The large increase in auto trips was related to broader economic and urban changes that deeply affected middle-class lifestyles. The daily activity network incorporated new trips, primarily related to private education, private healthcare, sports, leisure and shopping, with a profound impact on transport needs. Before, these activities were not performed at the same level of intensity, or they were performed freely, often within walking distances. Before modernization, most middle-class children attended neighbourhood public schools and used local public health services, and played on the street. Shopping was done at small local markets and stores, and distant out-of-town trips, most of them made by intercity bus or railway, were limited to national and school holidays. Modernization increased these activities, distances and costs, both direct (payments for the new services) and indirect (related to the means of transport needed to accomplish these new activities). Now, middle-class children go to private schools,[3] often located far from their home and requiring escorted automobile trips. Private medical services are also spread over the space, shopping is increasingly concentrated in large regional shopping centres, and streets are closed to leisure activities, as parked and passing cars occupy all the available space. Leisure is provided in private clubs or in shopping centres, and in the few remaining large regional public parks. In addition, weekend trips are now common, supported by a modern highway system linking the São Paulo metropolitan region to other cities.[4] These new forms of consumption derive from the 'commodification' of social relations that occurs alongside capitalist modernization. The most important political consequence in the Brazilian case was the definition of a dividing line between the middle classes and the working classes, enhancing their social and political differences. The working classes continue to walk to nearby public schools and medical centres (no longer used by most of the middle class), use transit on longer trips, and play (unsafely) in the street. The differences are summarized by differences in mobility rates (see Table 12.4).

Table 12.4 shows that mobility rates for higher-income groups are twice as high as those for lower-income groups and more than four times higher when just motorized trips are considered. This increased mobility translates into a more diversified travel pattern for the highest income levels, for whom frequent additional trips are possible. The different travel patterns are associated with different forms of using the space, as the use of transport means is also highly differentiated. The four lowest income sectors travel predominantly by foot or public transport. Conversely, people at the two upper income levels make motorized trips predominantly by car (motorcycles have a very small share, as in most Brazilian cities). These latter households account for approximately 25 per cent of the total number of households in the metropolitan area and represent the social sectors for whom the car is essential. When compared to the availability of the automobile to the family, daily mobility increases from 1.6 trips per person when the family has no car, to 2 trips per person when one car is available, and 2.5 trips per person when two or more cars are available.

Table 12.4 *Mobility and use of transport modes according to income, São Paulo metropolitan area, 1997*

Family income (R$)	Trips/person	Trips by mode (%)		
		Foot	**Public**	**Private**
< 250	1.16	56	31	13
250–500	1.47	49	37	14
500–1000	1.76	42	38	20
1000–1800	2.07	34	37	29
1800–3600	2.34	23	29	48
>3600	2.64	14	19	67

Source: CMSP, 1998

In respect to the spatial coverage of trips, journeys to school are also a clear demonstration of the differences between the social strata (Table 12.5). Lower-income people walk to nearby public schools and higher-income people use private transport to travel to mostly private schools.

Table 12.5 *Journey to school according to income levels, 1987, selected districts,*[1] *São Paulo metropolitan area*

Monthly family income[2]	Transport mode (%)			Average distance (km)
	Foot	**Public**	**Private**	
< 240	97	3	–	0.65
> 1,800	–	18	82	2.94

(1) Three survey areas for each income level. Children under 16 years old only. (2) In US dollars

Source: CMSP, 1987

When different transport modes are compared, average travel time by car was half that of the bus in 1997 (Table 12.6). In addition, access times to either buses or parked cars (micro-accessibility) were also remarkably different.

A portrait of travelling differences between income groups can be revealed by analysing daily activity networks. Shown below are the daily trip patterns of two different families, representative of overall patterns captured by the

São Paulo household survey. The first is a working-class family with a monthly income of about US$360 and no car. The second is a middle-class family with a monthly income of US$2400 and two cars.

Table 12.6 *Access time and travel time by mode of transport, São Paulo metropolitan area,1997*

Mode	Access time (min)[1]	Total travel time (min)
Auto	2	29
Bus	12	57
Metro	12	77
Train	18	93

(1) Calculated by adding both ends of the trip
Source: CMSP, 1998

Table 12.7 *Daily travel patterns of two different families, São Paulo metropolitan area*

Data	Middle-class family	Working-class family
Persons	7 (one housemaid)	5
Autos	2	0
Income[1]	2400	360
Trips	20	8
Modes used	Car, carpool, foot	Bus, foot
Purposes	Work	Work
	School (private)	School (public)
	Shopping	Doctor (public)
	Leisure (at night)	
Distances (km/day)	51.8	18.3
Time (min/day)	210	255
Speed (km/h)	14.8	4.3

Examples drawn from the 1987 OD survey
(1) Monthly income in US dollars

Table 12.7 shows the large diversity in activities and travel conditions. The middle-class family made an average of 2.9 trips per person, compared to 1.6 by the working-class family. Trips for the middle-class family included escorting a child to attend a special class 2.9km away, shopping and carpooling with other middle-class families to transport children to a private school 5.7km away, plus leisure activities at night 3km away from home. Trips for the working-class family were restricted to a work trip (the father), a visit on foot to the neighbourhood public health office (the mother) and walking to the nearby public school (the children). The availability of a housemaid in the middle-class household allowed the mother to go out while keeping a nine-year-old son at home. In the working-class family, the one-year-old daughter was left at home with an older brother (12 years old) while the mother was away at the doctor. In 82 per cent of the time spent by the working-class family, the middle-class family covered three times as much distance. The corresponding average speed is about four times higher. The most important conclusion is that the attempt to replace auto trips by bus (or non-motorized) trips would make the daily schedule of the middle-class family unfeasible,[5] hampering the performance of activities which are perceived as necessary for their reproduction as middle-class people. To accept such changes, the father would have to take one hour to get to the workplace by bus, the children would have to attend local public schools, shopping would have to be done on foot nearby, night leisure would no longer be possible, and the housemaid would probably be fired. These people would no longer be middle-class people, which they will never accept.

The data analysed so far demonstrate that activities and travel conditions in the city vary remarkably with income. The most important point with respect to Brazilian conditions (and other developing countries) is that actual conditions establish a dividing line between those with and without access to private transport. Access to the automobile, limited to selected sectors, generates large differences in accessibility, convenience and comfort. Accordingly, any attempt by automobile users to replace auto trips by bus trips would result in unreliability and discomfort, and would significantly increase the total travel time required, rendering unfeasible the current middle-class schedules.

Therefore, transport and traffic policies helped to crystallize sharp differences between those with and without access to private transport. These differences result from efficient actions to support the increase in the number of automobiles, through the provision of adequate circulating conditions, and from the disregard for public transport. The combination between the reorganization of the space and the increasing use of private transport represents the successful undertaking of a definite political and economic project: the *building of the middle-class city* (Vasconcellos, 1996a) while subjecting most of the people to poor transport conditions. Other Brazilian cities, especially in the more industrialized regions, experienced similar changes. Space was reshaped in central areas, while the outskirts were progressively occupied by low-income people in unfavourable physical and environmental conditions. The final result of these changes is that São Paulo, as with many other large and medium Brazilian cities, was transformed into a space where the middle class, acting as the role of driver, was granted adequate conditions to reproduce itself. Other social groups were less fortunate and remained subject to the negative consequences attached to the roles they play: traffic accidents, while in the role of pedestrians, and travel inefficiency and discomfort, while in the role of public transport users.

The demand for cars: A sociological conclusion

The analysis helps us to understand why the restructuring of space and the deficient public transport supply placed the automobile in a unique position as the sole means of transport capable of guaranteeing a minimum level of efficiency to cope with the middle-classes' new needs. Therefore, the decision to use the car, for those who could afford it, was rational, but deeply influenced by prevailing conditions. In these specific contexts, the purchase and use of the car must therefore be seen primarily as class decisions, not individual ones in the narrow sense of the term. Even if personal preferences are activated to select the product, the major decision is whether to buy and use the specific technology. This decision is socially determined, in the sense of fulfilling the perceived needs of a particular group. If other conditions were present, other purchasing decisions would be made. Consequently, in sociological terms, one can say that the automobile is itself a means of class reproduction, a vital tool to the very existence and reproduction of the new middle classes generated by the income concentration process. Therefore, for the middle classes described here, the decision to buy an automobile is similar to decisions about enrolling children in private schools, paying for private medical care, studying foreign languages, going to restaurants, making weekend trips and even travelling abroad. These are all class decisions, to concerning activities that are believed to maintain and reproduce people in the way they think they must reproduce and maintain themselves and their children in order to remain members of a class or to achieve social mobility. Moreover, these activities are believed necessary because they clearly separate the middle classes from the working classes. Considering prevailing spatial arrangements and the supply of public transport, the automobile is the sole means that can combine these activities efficiently, in a 'trip chaining way', and the decision to use private transport follows logically.

In addition, the class nature of the choice is reinforced by the lack of choice for most of the people. Since its inception, the Brazilian automotive industry has never been organized as a mass industry, as the average incomes of most people are totally incompatible with automobile prices. The monthly minimum wage has been around US$60 for the last two decades, while the less expensive cars have been priced between US$7000 and US$10,000. Therefore, most Brazilian people cannot even think about buying a car. Even if the 'desire' to buy a car may be voiced by ordinary people, and fuelled by the media, it is almost as impossible as buying a boat, and impossible desires do not belong in policy analysis.

In the case of Brazil, the market was organized by generating conditions for the emergence of a middle class corresponding to the ideological and economic project of the proposed development model. The new middle classes played a vital legitimizing political role, especially during the authoritarian period from 1964 to 1982. Key to the objective of market generation was the income concentration process (Bacha and Klein, 1989). The development project envisioned middle sectors committed to a new lifestyle who would then use all tools thought to be necessary to drive to a better future. In this sense, one can talk about a *symbiosis* between the middle class and the automobile, for one cannot survive without the other. It is the longest-lasting and happiest marriage of our times. In addition, one can talk about a mutual sustaining relationship between the built environment and the automobile. Here I return to Cervero's assumption about people not being 'lulled' by some unexplained force into a wasteful way of living and travel. They were not lulled in the psychological sense, but sociologically powerful forces were activated inside a complex process. It is more like a *trap*, within which the middle class was born and guided from its inception to understand that the dream of social mobility would be possible only with the automobile.

Hence, simple explanations of the success of the car related to issues of status, power, sexual strength and privacy are superficial. Even considering that the car may be used as symbol of status in particular conditions, the decision to buy a car is socially determined and is seldom based just on status or power. There are no psychological motives which explain why so many people commit a significant share of their budgets, for such a long time, to buy such an expensive technology. These single factors are secondary and derive their power from manipulation by the media. The car is a tool whose use is deeply embedded in social, political and economic constraints. Behind the wheels are political beings with needs and interests, and with a definite view of society. In addition, the valuation of the car is explained by the particular urban, economic and transport policies promoted in developing countries; these policies have been shaping the contemporary space in the developing world in a way that induces the need for the car, while making alternate public transport means impractical. Considering the prevailing built environment, the ease of automobile use and the poor supply of public transport means, the middle class has no alternative but to purchase and use the car intensively. If other conditions were present, fewer people in the developing world would commit a substantial part of their incomes to cars, and the use of the automobile would be more selective. Hence, the decision to have and use cars is based on its utility. However, the demand is deeply constrained by the actual physical (urban space, transport supply), economic (transport costs and convenience), and political (class consciousness) conditions that surround the decision, enhancing the need for a broader sociological approach.

A final remark is necessary. Although widely referred to in the literature, it is not accurate to label such cities 'automobile' cities, as if automobiles were animated beings. This 'technical' labelling disguises the political and social determinants of the process; we have been building cities for selected social sectors using a specific technology – the car. The only proper label is 'middle-class cities'. This does not mean that other social sectors are excluded from the city; all have their share, which is used (legally or illegally) through several forms of consumption. However, the middle class is the sector that is able to enjoy the city and its space to its fullest extent.

Box 12.1 *'Cars are people': car fetishism*

The car is so deeply immersed in our culture as an ideological 'being' that it replaces human beings in people's minds. It is like a powerful fetishism. When I was waiting at the crossing with a friend in São Paulo I decided to test how this phenomenon had also affected his perception. There were several automobiles, buses and trucks around us and I asked him: 'What is coming from there? You have three guesses.' He said: 'Well, a car!' I said: 'No, take your second guess.' He looked and said: 'A vehicle.' I said: 'No, and now you have your last chance.' And he answered, angry with me: 'An automobile.' I still wonder when he will realize that what was coming was a person, inside a metal case, and that there is no reason whatsoever for that person in the role of a car driver to have priority over us standing on the sidewalk.

STATE, INDUSTRY AND MIDDLE-CLASS INTERESTS

The sociological approach to the automobile also applies to the role of the automotive industry in contemporary capitalist economies. The expansion of the automotive industry would not have happened without the creation of a market for its products. The increasing use of automobiles and motorcycles has been supported by direct government incentives to manufacture or import vehicles. In the case of new plants, support is justified by the economic importance of the industry. In the case of lowering import duties, it is justified as a means of forcing local industry to lower purchasing prices. In Jakarta (Hook, 1998) and in Bangkok (Kenworthy, 1995), the rapid increase in the number of cars and motorcycles is linked to the importance of Japanese manufacturers. In Brazil, the direct support of the federal government helped the organization of several multinational automotive industries and recently has helped other industries to install major plants in the country, generating one of the largest automotive complexes in the world.

The most important recent case is unquestionably China. The Chinese government pursued rapid industrialization and specialization during the reform period, and one of the most important decisions concerned support of the automotive industry. In Shanghai, Volkswagen began to manufacture the Brazilian 'Santana', with tariff protection and a guaranteed market in the initial years. 'The combination of bureaucratic support, investment funds, and foreign technology made the venture the most productive and profitable automaker in the country' (Wu, 1996). In addition, as stated by Doulet (1997), several measures were taken to transform the auto into a family commodity, by encouraging people to purchase them and by adapting laws to facilitate automobile consumption. Figures are impressive: the number of automobiles in China increased from 1.55 million in 1979 to more than 8 million in 1993. Annual increase rates were 7 per cent between 1980 and 1993, peaking at 18 per cent between 1992 and 1993 (Doulet 1997) Increased use of motorized transport may also apply to taxis, which may act as a substitute for cars. In Beijing, for instance, there has been a sharp increase in the number of taxi trips (as compared to car trips), which multiplied by seven between 1990 and 1994 (Doulet, 1997).

The increase in motorized two-wheelers has occurred for several reasons. The two most important seem to have been the association between industry's marketing efforts and government's fiscal support of the purchase and use of such vehicles, and the deficiencies of regular public transport. The latter may be especially relevant in congested cities where motorcycles have several advantages over public transport and can also park easily. For instance, in Ouagadougou according to Cusset and Sirpe (1994), the high share of motorized two-wheelers may be explained by several factors, among them the lack of bus transport until 1984, the poor services provided by them, fare increases by existent collective taxis, governmental support for the creation of a national motorcycle industry (with assembly lines of French and Japanese vehicles) and the freedom to buy and drive such vehicles (no licensing or insurance required). In Vietnam, the motorized two-wheeler fleet increased rapidly in the 1990s, in face of economic changes and the easing of vehicle imports (Cusset, 1997) and poor public transport in Hanoi may be seen as standing behind the increasing use of motorcycles (Griffin, 1995). Similar processes may be identified in several Asian and African countries.

Box 12.2 *How to get a girlfriend by getting rid of public transport*

Two teenagers are standing at a bus stop and look at each other with delight. She starts to imagine them together but the first scene that pops up in her mind (in a cartoon-type balloon) is of them chatting inside the oncoming bus, and a disgusting feeling comes. In the meantime, he also starts to think about her and his cartoon-type balloon shows a new scooter. When she sees that image, she smiles and they finally get together (advertisement on New Delhi television, July 1999).

THE USE OF PRIVATE MODES: URBAN AND TRANSPORT CONDITIONS

To purchase a car is one decision; to use it is another. Private transport use is highly influenced by the actual conditions faced by owners while travelling. Such conditions may be related to economic and spatial constraints. Even when income and auto ownership are high, the actual use of the vehicle is highly dependent on such constraints. Table 12.8 shows that Europeans have higher incomes per capita and travel less by automobile than US citizens. The wealthy Asian countries have a 20 per cent lower income than the US and travel seven times less by car.

Many people suggest that automobile dependence is an inevitable consequence of wealth and that this will in turn lead to sprawling cities (Newman and Kenworthy, 1999, p128). Although there is an obvious impact of wealth

Table 12.8 *Income and car usage in wealthy regions*

Region	GRP/capita (US$/year)	Km car/person/year
US (13 cities)	26,822	10,870
Europe (11 cities)	31,721	4519
Wealthy Asian[1]	21,331	1487

(1) Singapore, Tokyo and Hong Kong

Source: Newman and Kenworthy, 1999.

on land use and the use of transport modes, such a relationship is not automatic. The differences in urban density and automobile use between Europe and the US or Australia are clear enough. In particular cases such as Bangkok, Kenworthy (1995) has shown how private vehicle use is not related to wealth alone but to several factors. Bangkok is a densely populated city, with a poor provision of roads, but with a relatively high supply of parking spaces in the CBD, much higher for instance than Singapore and Hong Kong. Vehicle ownership (cars and motorcycles) is close to the European average (296 against 341) but much higher than average Asian cities, with correspondingly higher vehicle kilometres per person and a higher share of daily trips, with lower use of public transport. Therefore, the 'vehicle population ... is higher than is to be expected if wealth were the only factor involved ... and ... there are clearly more factors than wealth at work in urban automobile dependence' (1995, p34).

Discussing the reasons for such a high private motorized use, Kenworthy recalls that Bangkok clearly has poor public transport, serious problems in using NMT and the lack of governmental intention to change trends, in addition to the existent close links with Japanese car and motorcycle manufacturers. Especially in the case of buses, low speed, lack of air-conditioning and crowding hardly make them an option for the growing middle class. He also recalls that Asian cities who capture middle-class travellers use high-quality trains and impose disincentives on car ownership and that although road provision is relatively low, this is not the real problem, since other cities with low road provision and higher income work well with good conditions to use public transport and NMT.

Relating increasing automobile use to public transport decline is another way of explaining the phenomenon. In former socialist countries, car ownership had been increasing rapidly before the political changes and some authors maintain that car use increased at a slower rate once there were both incentives to use public transport and disincentives to use cars (high maintenance costs and parking fees). While this period witnessed a dual increase (in car ownership and public transport use), the overthrow of socialist economies witnessed two contrary movements: the increase in car ownership and use and the decline in public transport use. The latter decline was also related to the poor conditions of most services and to the inefficiency of most operators, brought about mainly by the reliance on permanent subsidies and the captive nature of demand (Pucher and Lefèvre, 1996). However, some public policies seem to have been important: authorities raised public transport fares by a factor of ten between 1990 and 1992 and decreased the price of gasoline, in such a way that the price of a litre of gas became lower than the cost of a public transport trip, whereas it had cost nine times more in the period of the socialist economy.

The use of transport modes is also highly dependent on traffic conditions. With automobiles, travel time between origin and destination, average speed and parking facilities are very important in defining use. In Beijing, urban and transport changes are causing new and complex conflicts between those using streets, especially pedestrians, cyclists and auto drivers. City authorities are reluctant to address these new challenges, and conflicts between local and central government start to appear, threatening the opening of the internal market to the automobile industry (Doulet, 1997). The central government has issued laws in 1994 stating, for instance, that 'no local institution or department may use any economic or administrative measures to impede the use of automobiles legally acquired' and that measures should be taken to support and protect the use of such vehicles.

Differential speeds between private and public transport also greatly influence mode choice for those that can choose. Bus speeds are always lower than private transport speeds, not only because of operational limitations (bus stops) but also because of automobile-based congestion and a disregard for priority measures for public transport. The more such an imbalance is maintained, the less reliable and attractive are public transport services. This is the case in several large cities in the developing world, such as Bangkok, Jakarta, Seoul, São Paulo and Caracas.

Parking conditions also exert a strong influence on the use of the automobile and hence on the patronage of public transport. Not being able to park the car or having to spend too much money doing so are severe problems for drivers. Conversely, plenty of free or low-cost parking spaces constitute a powerful incentive to use cars.

Subsidies

Direct and indirect subsidies to private transport play a key role. In the most motorized country in the world – the US – the subsidy to low-density single-family housing, together with subsidies to employees, may be compared to the taxable expenses with public transport, as a clear sign of the decision to provide overall subsidy to private transport (Wright, 1992). The estimated daily subsidy for employee parking ranges from US$1.2 to US$4. Direct and indirect subsidies to cars in the US are estimated by some at the US$2.4 trillion level and portray a very different condition to that in Europe, where the ratio between roadway taxes and expenditures is much greater than 1 and petrol price and sales taxes are much higher (Cervero, 1998). Investments in roads are also a key factor in supporting automobile use. In the US in 1994, US$74 billion was spent on roads, seven times more than on public transport; in Eastern and Central Europe from 1989 to 1994, three major international lending institutions spent 60 per cent of their money on roads and 5 per cent on transit. World Bank investments have been directed primarily to roads – 60 per cent – as compared to public transport (17 per cent) (Cervero, 1998).

In developing countries, the main subsidy is that of road provision. Considering that private transport – especially the automobile – uses much more road space, and that higher-income people travel more, roads end up being a public asset mostly consumed by those with access to cars. Taxes raised on such consumption in developing countries, when they exist, are often very low.

THE MAKING OF NEW MIDDLE-CLASS CITIES

In developed countries, the same relationship between transport policies, urban structure, social issues and automobile dependence has been emphasized by several authors. For example, McShane, Koshi and Lundin (1984, p104) stress that the publicly financed housing complexes in postwar Sweden were 'located on the fringe of the cities, far enough from downtown centres to make the provision of other than public transport service expensive and impractical. Consequently, car ownership became a necessity'. In the US, the conjunction of economic prosperity, automobile subsidies (direct and indirect), urban residential policies and public transport policies made transit impractical. The main reasons for the growth of suburbanization were increased crime, social unrest and deteriorating school districts, not the 'innate love affair with the car' (Cervero, 1998, p26). As emphasized by Vuchic (1999, p219), even conservatives acknowledge that in the US 'the dominance of the automobile is not a free-market outcome, but the result of a massive government investment on behalf of the automobile'.[6] The built environment demands the use of the car as a survival tool, and relying on public transport is irrational. Rosenbloom, analysing why North American families need cars, stresses that '…it is hard to see how any other option …(than the car)… could serve the complex travel needs of such families.' (1991, p39).

In European countries, the postwar increase in car ownership also led to pressures on space availability. Although the rate of automobiles per capita is about 50 per cent less than that of the US, the use of the automobile is very different, because of traffic restrictions, higher petrol prices, high taxes on car sales and high parking fees. In addition, transport policies share a more transit-oriented approach that derives from both different historical and urban conditions, and from different political environments. Large public transport systems – subways and railways – have long provided good transport services. Moreover, governments have for a long time subsidized public transport and supported non-motorized means. In addition, the much higher urban land use densities historically found in Europe were maintained in new urban developments, for governments have been consistently supporting high-density occupation served by public transport means (Pucher and Lefèvre, 1996). These policies reflect a different approach to transport issues, and can be said to be directly related to the a more complex political arena, in which radically different views of society coexist.

The specific links between the automotive industry in Brazil and the middle classes can be compared with the Mexican, Argentinean and Venezuelan cases. However, it cannot be compared with very poor countries and to some developed countries that adopted different industrial models (such as South

Korea). The adoption of the automotive alternative was particularly aggressive in Brazil, as part of a large development project that dismantled the railway system and neglected public transport systems. The symbiosis between the middle classes and automobiles in Brazil seems to be the strongest in Latin American countries.

Many Latin American and Asian countries have experienced similar changes. Caracas is remarkably selective from a spatial point of view, with hills occupied by poor people – often illegally – and valleys occupied by the middle class generated during the 1950s oil boom. The road plan was devised in the 1940s by foreign consultants coordinated by Robert Moses (Casas, 1999), who had had a vital participation in New York parkway and expressway systems. The resulting arterial plan was also highly selective, based on a motorway network directed to improve accessibility for private transport, while keeping public transport users dependent on low-quality, poorly integrated private services. The motorway network also worked to rearrange space according to the new consumption needs, such as supermarkets, theatres and private schools (Marcano, 1981). Buenos Aires has experienced profound urban transformations in the last decade, because of neoliberal privatization policies. After steadily replacing rail-based transport by road transport provided by buses and cars in the 1930–1980 period, the city transport system has been recently enlarged by the construction (or completion) of a road network financed by private funds against future toll-based revenues. Land use along such expressways was also changed to accommodate large apartment, commercial and office complexes, physically segregated and directed at the middle- and upper classes, and so dependent on automobile availability. This new urban structure is being superimposed on the old one, creating a new space that further aggravates social exclusion (Vera, 1999).

Some Asian and African cities are also facing the same space appropriation by middle-class sectors and their automobiles. Despite social and economic differences, the process of readapting space for a new circulation pattern is similar. Some important Asian examples are Seoul, Jakarta, Bangkok and Beijing. The main differences in Asia are, first, that private transport is pursued using cars and motorcycles and, second, that automobiles are forcing out not only pedestrianized movements but also long-used non-motorized vehicles, such as the rickshaw and the pedicab (Barrett, 1988). Car ownership (and motorcycle ownership, to a lesser extent) has been confined to selected sectors and public transport services have been subjected to permanent crisis. Sharp differences in trip patterns – with and without automobile – have been identified, reproducing the same differential forms of using the space for circulation. As stressed by Banjo and Dimitriou

> ... *by adopting a transport planning approach which favours motorised traffic so indiscriminately, the elite of these cities is thus in effect acting no differently from their colonial masters in encouraging separate development.* (1983, p108)

Some of the most important transformations are now occurring in Chinese cities. As Chen and Parish note (1996, p85), economic reforms have created uneven opportunities for the different social groups in the sense that 'those in the private sector have got rich quick, while an increasing number of state-sector employees, including the recently retired, have seen their standard of living stagnate'. Such changes, along with revisions of unemployment and old age assistance, will make cities and towns 'highly fragmented, with different workers and citizens subject to very different life chances'. Corresponding impacts on transport demand are stressed by Doulet (1997); economic reforms will lead to radical changes in the production and organization of the urban space, as long as the prevailing urban settlement pattern that was based on the proximity between home, services and workplace, has been changing quickly. Now the main forces are specialization and spatial dispersion, creating new travel patterns. The decentralization of workplaces towards peripheral areas precedes changes in house location, and creates new and large daily movements of workers. New luxury housing complexes are now being opened in peripheral areas, clearly related to an automobile-owning clientele. The automobile then starts to be used in a context of ever-longer distances and diversified trip purposes.

A similar process can be identified in the former socialist countries, where automobile increase has been growing rapidly (Pucher and Lefèvre, 1996). It is clear that economic liberalization forged economic and social differences within previously homogenous social groups, generating new social strata able to benefit from economic modernization and therefore seeing private transport as a vital tool for their reproduction. Therefore, the sudden increase in auto use seems to have happened in a moment of profound social changes, which led people to adopt completely new consumption habits, expressing both their expectations and their need to signalize a clear position in the incoming society. However important such psychological motives have been in the beginning of the economic transition, deeper social and economic motives related to the reorganization of the labour market and the rearrangement of people in social strata seem to better explain people's behaviour in a permanent way.

Therefore, in several developing countries, a new set of middle-class cities is being organized, as a product of different sorts of capitalist modernization processes. Some may reproduce the same broad characteristics of Brazilian cities and others will have physical and transport patterns constrained by different ethnic or religious factors. Two main aspects have to be considered: the spatial distribution of social classes and ethnic/religious groups, and who has access to which type of private motorized transport, cars and/or motorcycles.

The careless, vague mention of a supposedly generalized phenomenon of 'people desiring cars' as justifying automobile-supporting investments is recurrent in the literature. For instance, a recent analysis of the reasons for increasing transport problems in Chinese cities lists several relevant factors; however, among them is also included 'Intense desire for auto ownership and use. According to government surveys, Chinese families are likely to be prepared to spend 2 years' income for a car' (Gakenheimer, 1999, p673). Again, the questions that should be asked are: Among the 1.2 billion Chinese, how many 'desire' the car? To which social strata do they belong? How many will have money to purchase it in the next, say, ten years and how many will be able to use it on a regular basis? Finally, What are the needs of people that will not have access to cars, who are close to 90 per cent of the population?

The most important conclusion for policy purposes it that private transport and especially automobile demand in these countries should not be seen as a consequence of a generalized 'natural consumer desire', or as an 'inevitable outcome of progress'. The demand for private transport should instead be related to the specific social and political conditions of such countries, and to the regional, urban and transport policies that shape space and transport supply. Especially in the poorer countries, and in countries with highly unbalanced income distribution, the access to the automobile will be related to the creation of limited middle-class sectors, who will be able to join and benefit from the economic modernization. They will see the automobile (or the motorcycle) as vital for their reproduction as social classes, and they will make large efforts to purchase it, establishing a mutually reinforcing relationship with the automotive industry. Accordingly, they will try to use private transport as extensively as possible, reacting against old, slower transport modes, as well as against any restraint by traffic authorities. In these countries, modernization will change travel patterns and a new balance between modes will result, changing living and travel conditions for everybody. The final position of the automobile and the motorcycle in the transport market will be related to how the elite and middle classes will conform and influence policy decisions and to how excluded sectors will manage to have their travel needs attended to by existing non-motorized and public transport means. The costs and benefits of all these complex changes have to be analysed in every case, for every particular condition. The sociological approach to car demand can be taken in developing countries, in former socialist countries and in developed countries as well. The challenge for transport analysts is to reconsider existing interpretations of the demand for cars as expressing natural consumer desires, and search for better explanations of how the social, economic and political conditions in these countries influenced people's transport decisions.

13 MOBILITY

MOBILITY FACTORS

When the data on daily travel demand are investigated, several important characteristics of mobility appear. They have been intensively examined and reproduced in the specialized literature. The main factors impacting on mobility seem to be income, gender, age, occupation and educational level. The availability of motorized transport also has a strong effect, however: it may be considered an impact associated with income. The most important observations and conclusions are summarized below. First, mobility increases with income. Second, mobility varies significantly with social and economic characteristics. Finally, men usually travel more than women. Those of adult age, and involved in working activities, travel more than the very young and the elderly. People with a higher educational level travel more than those without. Adults with regular work travel more than those with an unstable occupation. The differences in mobility result in differences in the use of transport modes. Very young children travel only with the help of older people. Children at school use streets as pedestrians and are sometimes allowed to cycle. Youngsters may cycle or use transport. Adults and the elderly use motorized means but also walk or cycle; their use of private motorized means is highly dependent on income. In general, the use of motorized modes is heavily dependent on the position of the person within the household and family structure. For instance, men often use more motorized transport means than women (Cusset, 1997; Williams, 1998), the older people more than the younger, the active more than the inactive.

Family size and structure

Family size directly affects overall household transport demand, not only because of the number of people travelling but also because of the mutual interdependence which decides who will travel and how. Family structure also affects transport demand, in the light of the internal division of tasks. Cultural and religious aspects may introduce further elements of complexity into the family decision-making process. Households in developing countries differ from those in developed ones mainly through the number of people and the family structure, which includes extended and polygamous families in some countries. If we take the 'standard' occidental family of four to six members, an adult couple and children or the elderly, the pattern of transport demand will be very different from that found for instance in Bamako (Mali) or Accra (Ghana), where the average family has, respectively, 11 and 8.6 members (Diaz Olvera et al, 1997; Turner and Kwakye, 1996).[1]

This static picture of the family and its travel pattern may be changed by the dynamics of the family lifecycle; households expand and contract because of the medical and educational needs of rural relatives who come to town, the fostering activities of other family members and the seasonal absence of people working in rural areas. The same happens in several parts of Brazil, where poverty and living conditions create complex family structures, linking close relatives and also acquaintances or members of friendly families.

Mobility and income

Within any specific society, mobility increases with income. This may be called a universal phenomenon, regardless of geography and social conditions. This means that in a particular city those with higher incomes will travel more than those with lower incomes; the ratio between the mobility of the higher and lower income strata may be 3 or 4. In Ouagadougou, both overall and motorized mobility rises with income, respectively from 3.5 to 4.5 and 1.5 to 4 (Diaz Olvera et al, 1997). In São Paulo, differences between lower and higher income mobility are 1:2.5 for general mobility (and 1:4 for motorized mobility) (Table 13.1).[2]

Table 13.1 *Mobility and income, São Paulo metropolitan area, 1997*

Family monthly income (R$)	Trips/person/day
< 250	1.16
250–500	1.47
500–1000	1.76
1000–1800	2.07
1800–3600	2.34
> 3600	2.64
Average	1.87

Source: CMSP, 1998

Immobility, as expressed by the quantity of people not making trips in an average day, is also an important aspect of how people interact with space. In São Paulo, 36 per cent of people are immobile. Immobility decreases with income, from 50 per cent at the lower level to 25 per cent at the higher level.

Mobility and transport mode

The use of different transport modes is highly constrained by income. Low-income people mostly enact the roles of pedestrians, cyclists and public transport users, while higher income people often enact the roles of drivers (of motorcycles and cars) or passengers. Income has a strong influence on mode choice even within poor communities. In Accra (Ghana), fares collected by the collective taxi are double the *trotro* (minibus) fares, but the share of taxi trips in total daily trips increases from 35–40 per cent in the lower-income strata to 55–60 per cent in the higher-income strata, while the share of *trotro* trips decreases from 40 per cent to about 30 per cent (Turner and Kwakye, 1996).

Mobility and age

Age has a direct impact on mobility, related to the ascribed, accepted or expected duties of people, according to societal characteristics. As mobility is primarily related to working activities, those of 'productive' age – from 20 to 50 years old – are often more mobile. As schooling is the second most important trip purpose in most cities, children and youngsters are also highly mobile. Conversely, pre-school children and the retired elderly are less mobile (Table 13.2)

Table 13.2 *Mobility and age, São Paulo, 1997*

Age group	Trips/day
0–4	0.58
4–7	1.43
7–11	1.95
11–15	2.08
15–18	2.25
18–23	2.18
23–30	2.18
30–40	2.33
40–50	2.08
50–60	1.63
> 60	1.03

Source: CMSP, 1998

Specific conditions may alter such patterns. For instance, when children have to work as well as going to school their mobility increases significantly. As stated by Turner and Kwakye (1996, p162) for Accra in Ghana, 'children and older members are seen as resources to be used to allow those with the highest potential to maximise their income for the household's benefit'. Children work for household security and sanitation – including rubbish disposal at long distances – and by selling and trading for the elderly, which requires walking throughout the neighbourhood, and also semi-illegal activities such as roadside trading. The latter activities free the elderly from travel discomfort. Children's presence at home depends on school hours; sometimes families may have to sacrifice the schooling of their children to attend to household needs.

Mobility and gender

The role of women is especially relevant. As stressed by Peters (1998, p12) 'Major differences in the basic mobility needs of women and men are grounded in the gender-based division of labour within the family and the community'. In most cases, out-of-home working activities are ascribed mostly to adult males and home activities mostly to female adults. The first consequence of this task division is that females are less mobile than males in most societies (Table 13.3). A corresponding figure is that of immobility, expressed as the percentage of people not making trips; in São Paulo, 42 per cent of females are immobile as compared to 31 per cent of males. Further, when income is considered, female immobility is always higher, varying from 56 per cent in low-income households to 29 per cent in high-income households.

Table 13.3 *Mobility and gender, several cities*

City	Trips/day	
	Men	**Women**
Delhi (India)[1], 1990	1.13	1.08
Bamako (Mali)[2]	3.7	2.4
Hanoi (Vietnam)[3], 1995	2.3	2.4
Oagadougou (Burkina Falso)[4]	4.2	3.1
São Paulo (Brazil)[5], 1997	2.0	1.7

Sources: (1) Sharma and Gupta, 1998; (2) Diaz Olvera et al, 1997; (3) Cusset, 1997; (4) Cusset and Sirpe, 1994; (5) CMSP, 1998

The second consequence is that women usually walk more than men and use less motorized transport. In Hanoi, women make 54 per cent of daily trips by foot, as compared to 38.7 by men; in Ouagadougou, corresponding figures are 56 per cent and 33 per cent (Cusset, 1997). In Delhi, private modes are mostly used by men, while bus and walking are used mainly by women (Sharma and Gupta, 1998). In Hanoi, motorized mobility rates for men and women are, respectively, 1.3 and 0.7 trips per day (Cusset, 1997).

The role played by women has to be analysed also in the light of their age. With young females, some mobility restrictions occur when schooling activities conflict with cultural characteristics or the economic expectations of the parents. In Bamako (Mali), the mobility conditions of boys attending school is better than that of girls, because the investment in the schooling of boys is seen as more profitable (Diaz Olvera et al, 1997). This is a common situation. Similar restrictions occur in rural Iran, where some fathers do not allow their daughters to attend schools with male teachers (Hallak, 1977); conversely, in the countryside of the southern Brazilian states, the wealthiest in the country (although with relatively low average incomes), girls and boys attend rural schools according to their proportion in the total population (Vasconcellos, 1997c).

Finally, cultural and religious constraints are also important. In some African societies, cycles are unacceptable for women because of the physical exposure implied. In traditional Muslim families wives are not allowed to leave home except for certain purposes, and some household tasks are performed by other household members. Also, in Muslim cities such as Dakha, the social seclusion of women makes it difficult for them to share crowded buses with men (Peters, 1998, p14). It is important to emphasize that current task divisions and cultural and religious constraints are always submitted to external forces of change. As analysed by Mankouch (1997) in Arab countries, the traditional way in which families are organized is constantly challenged by changes brought about by urbanization, industrialization and schooling. The patriarchal family is no longer the sole reference point, because the role of the women is changing quickly through participation in the regular work market. This brings new needs and aspirations. A direct impact on transport demand is that such changes require many more out-of-home trips by women, which may 'put an end to the spatial invisibility of the female gender'(p210) which characterizes such countries. Another consequence is the tendency to female motorization when new income sources become available. Such characteristics have been subject to increasing analysis by experts.

Mobility and ethnicity

Ethnicity impacts on mobility either through physical or economic differentiation. With the former, different ethnic groups are physically isolated from each other, either by direct or indirect forces. Within developed countries, ethnicity has deeply impacted on mobility in the US, due to the physical separation of black and white people which prevailed until the 1960s, and its impact on the use of transport means. In all developing countries, social and economic differences interact with ethnic differences impacting on mobility characteristics. The most radical case of class and ethnic mobility differences is that of South Africa. As Cameron (1998) has shown, there is a clear difference between the use of transport modes according to ethnic communities in Pretoria; while the use of the car accounted for 6 per cent of daily trips for black people, the corresponding figure for the white community was 84 per cent. This measure was also higher for the other 'non-white' groups – 37 per cent for 'coloured' people and 75 per cent for Indians.

Mobility and culture

Mobility is also influenced by cultural norms and historically based perceptions about transport modes. The most relevant case is that of the pedestrian trip as compared to the bicycle trip in low-income cities. For instance, in Hanoi (Vietnam), walking is considered painful as opposed to the bicycle, which is extensively used by people for carrying passengers and loads. This reflects to a certain extent the lack of money to buy another bicycle, but it is also related to social traditions and is facilitated by the low average weight of the population. Conversely, walking is a very important mode in Ouagadougou (Cusset, 1997).

In addition, in some African cities, the use of a bicycle is seen as a sign of poverty and it is often culturally constrained or even prohibited (Peters, 1998), which may artificially increase the number of walking trips. Another important case, although less common, is the prejudice against public transport that stems from income differences and the related perception of the 'right' modes for each social group or class. Such prejudice may arise especially within newly formed middle classes with newly acquired access to automobiles or motorcycles.

Mobility and disability

Disabled people are less mobile for obvious reasons. While in wealthier societies they receive special attention to support their minimum travel needs (ECMT, 1999) in developing countries there is seldom any support available. Undoubtedly handicapped persons form the most mobility-deprived social group in developing countries, even more deprived than the poor. In addition to physical barriers and inadequate infrastructure, they face cultural barriers related to their families not being willing to exposure their handicapped relations in public. The discussion about how to overcome such broad limitations is one of the most conflicting in transport policies, deeply related to the concept of equity, as discussed in Chapter 18.

Mobility and travel strategies: time and space budgets

The time spent by people while travelling (the time budget, or TB) is a powerful tool to analyse people's use of transport modes and their interaction with space, having been studied by several scholars including Zahavi (1976) and Hagestrand (1987). TB varies with several individual characteristics. When measuring the time spent by household, TB increases with income. In São Paulo, people in low-income households spend 107 minutes per day as compared to 289 minutes per day in high-income households (CMSP, 1998). However, when measuring the individual trips, TB seem to remain fairly constant at around 60 to 80 minutes, regardless of geography, transport modes and income (Zahavi, 1976; Schafer, 1998). In São Paulo, TB for mobile individuals varies from 86 to 102 minutes per day. The reasons for such discrepancies vary. When family budgets are considered, higher-income families use more time travelling, demonstrating that they have to 'invest' more to ensure their reproduction. They also invest more in the total distance travelled. In São Paulo, daily distance travelled per household increases from 16km in low-income families to 62km in high-income ones. If just mobile people are considered, distances increase with income, from 6.6km for low-income people to 16.6km for high-income people, reflecting their use of private motorized transport (CMSP, 1998). This demonstrates that high-income people use much more road space per day than low-income people (see Chapter 14).

One possible explanation for this behaviour is that technological vehicle improvements are used by people to adjust their travel pattern, and so 'savings' in travel time are used to increasing distance travelled and people keep a constant or rising time-budget (Whitelegg, 1997). A related issue concerns the utility of travel in respect to travel time, which increases up to a point and then decreases; when decentralization occurs, people may travel further to carry out the same range of activities, getting more mobility but not more accessibility (Tolley and Turton, 1995). However, why people seek a constant travel-time expense is not clear. Marchetti (1994) proposes an anthropological explanation; since early civilization, people had defined a natural time limit to walking or travelling around, related to the physical dimensions of all human settlements, determined by the available technology in each period. Although transport technology does influence spatial coverage and hence the possible distance and time spans, it is an exaggeration to maintain that there is a 'definite' anthropological limit. Even if averages tend to fall in the range between 60 and 80 minutes, there are wide discrepancies, especially in relation to poor people living in peripheral urban areas, where a two-hour work journey is not unusual. It is therefore more accurate to say that people who make out-of-home trips, regardless of geography and income, seem to reject long trips (as a general rule) and tend to invest an amount of time that varies from one to two hours per day.

MOBILITY ISSUES

One must now ask how it is possible to reveal the social determinants that lie behind such characteristics. To accomplish this, the mobility issue has been divided into five main social issues.

The poor

The poverty issue relates to the transport problems faced by poor people. Between a fifth and a quarter of the world's population live in absolute poverty and more than 90 per cent of these live in the South. In several developing countries, people living below the poverty line constitute up to 80 per cent of the total population (UN, 1996). Even in middle-income countries such as Thailand, Korea, Mexico and Brazil, poor people constitute the majority. Inside this group are adults, children, the elderly and the handicapped of all ages, both men and women. This specific issue is the most important one. All other issues follow this in terms of policy priorities.

The main transport problems faced by the poor correspond to all the problems mentioned and analysed before, including inequities in physical and economic accessibility, safety, environmental quality, comfort and convenience. First, there is the need to live in peripheral areas, often far away from the worksite and public facilities, especially schools and medical services. Second, there is the poor – or non-existent – supply of pavements and infrastructure to enable walking and cycling. Third, there is the poor supply of public transport, or the imposition of unbearable fares; even when some funds are available, other consumption needs limit transport expenses to essential trips, such as those for working. Fourth, there is the adaptation of the circulation environment to the needs of the automobile, working against non-motorized and public transport needs. Fifth, the effects of highly polluting vehicles, either private or public.

As stressed in Chapter 2, one has to avoid a technically limited approach to the problem by complementing it with the social approach. The root of the problem lies in poverty and deprivation and the lack of political instruments to advocate and protect poor people's interests.

The children issue

The children issue relates to transport problems faced by those below 18 years, taken here as the age at which people may be legally allowed to have a licence to drive a motorized vehicle. This group corresponds up to 50 per cent of the total population in several countries. The main mobility problems faced by children are those pertaining to the pedestrian and cyclist roles, since most have to walk or cycle to school. In addition to facing all the common pedestrian-related problems, children face additional problems. The roots of the issue are related first to biological limitations at the early ages; before the age of seven, children cannot properly discern traffic noises and movements (Vinjé, 1981). For older children, restraints are linked also to the danger of using streets as cyclists, a problem again related to the adaptation of roads to fast motorized transport, producing the 'barrier effect' – a new dangerous environment is created, forcing people to avoid using streets as pedestrians or cyclists. In several developing countries, personal safety has been an increasing concern among parents, which includes the use of public transport by their children. Finally, gender-grounded differences also appear, as translated by the more rapid outdoor socialization of boys in respect to girls in most societies.

The gender issue

The gender issue, as stressed in the available literature, relates to those transport problems faced by women that are grounded on their status within society, especially in the family domain. Such problems became more evident with the feminization of labour, as a growing number of women enter the job market and need to use public transport more frequently. The social and political realm of the gender problem lies beyond the proposed scope of this book and will not be discussed here.

The main problems that derive from the typical division of tasks are multifaceted and generate an intense debate among transport planners. I believe the debate has been infused with some emotional components and that some key issues have to be carefully analysed before reaching conclusions.

First, the gender problem in transport is often believed to be confined to women, a by-product of feminist thought. Although understandable, this is an incomplete approach to the issue, since both men and women are affected by the family division of tasks. Therefore, the question that has to be asked is: Once the division of tasks has been decided, what are the actual problems faced by both genders while circulating?

As stressed by some authors (Diaz Olvera and Plat, 1997; Sharma and Gupta, 1998), gender-related transport problems (seen as female problems) are tied to the spatial supply of public and private services, related to the most frequent female needs. They are also related to the assumptions of traditional transport planning. Considering the spatial supply of services, Diaz Olvera et al (1997, p132) point out that 'more than better transport, the solution relies in reorganising the distribution of urban services in space, especially around the living space'. Sharma and Gupta (1998, p674) further acknowledge that

> *The apparent inequity in urban travel is more on account of the inad-*
> *equacies in social and gender-related infrastructure than the prevailing*
> *inadequacies in transport infrastructure. The removal of the spread of*
> *social infrastructure, such as schools, childcare facilities and a proper*
> *home-to-work relationship, will help in making quantitative and quali-*
> *tative changes to mobility standards.*

Therefore, there is a direct influence between the spatially constrained provision of public services and the ability of women to perform their duties, which is related to urban planning policies.

With transport planning, some misunderstandings also have to be discussed, to yield consistent proposals to improve women's transport conditions. First, as Peters (1998, p12) states, 'existing transport systems are not adequately geared towards the needs of women. Rather, most systems are biased towards the needs of male breadwinners'. By saying that systems are biased towards males' needs, Peters may unwittingly convey the idea that men in developing countries benefit from good transport conditions, which is seldom – if ever – the case. Peak-hour public transportation conditions in cities of the developing world are well known to be very poor, not to mention the other bad safety and environmental conditions imposed on those enacting the role of regular public transport passengers.

Second, other authors stress that in some societies the use of mechanized transport modes by women is taken to be superfluous in the light of their traditional duties, and hence walking is much more used by them than by men. It is implicit that women take part in 'non-productive' tasks and are forced to use the worst transport means. Two comments are relevant here. Initially, all 'informal', 'non-productive' activity has been considered 'inferior', regardless of gender. Millions of poor men working in the informal sector in the developing world are constantly subject to human devaluation, physical threats and exploitation. Second, in cases in which males work far away from home and female activities are restricted to nearby locations, the decision to give preference to the use of motorized modes by men is not necessarily a proof of male domination, but rather may stem from an economic decision about how to use available resources. Such a decision may arise from differences in the cost, distance and time requirements of work-related trips, as compared to shorter trips. If little money is available, it has to be used to pay, for instance, the bus fares for the longest trips, which often happen to be made by the male partner. The situation is different when both adults work or have activities far away, when the preferential use of resources by males may be the rule, revealing the gender bias.

So, what are the most important planning drawbacks and gender-related transport problems we must face? As explored in Chapters 5 and 6, actual reproduction needs and transport demand will vary according to individual and family specific conditions. If we imagine the very common case of a low-income family in which the man works away from home and the woman takes care of the children and of the household's immediate needs, the consequent transport conditions faced by them are, in the case of men:

- Submission to the poor public transport supply, with direct impacts on walking and waiting times.
- Discomfort due to overcrowding in peak-hours.
- Greater exposure to traffic congestion, with direct impacts on travel time, fatigue and productivity.
- Greater exposure to traffic pollution in highly trafficked corridors, with direct health impacts.

In the case of women, the gender issue translates into other main problems:

- Lack of adequate pavements and crossings on walking trips; the problem is aggravated when women have to cater for children.
- Lack of adequate supply of infrastructure and signing for cyclists.
- Greater exposure to traffic accidents in the roles of pedestrian or cyclist.
- Lack of adequate public transportation supply for out-of-peak trips.
- Difficulty of entering crowded public transportation vehicles, because of physical disadvantages; again, the problem is aggravated when women have to cater for children inside the vehicle.
- Sexual harassment in public vehicles.

If older children form part of the household, adult men and women have different tasks, leading to different transport needs. Escorting will be less necessary, but additional mobility may pose economic burdens on the budget. The same may be the case if a retired person stays at home most of the time. If one adult becomes unemployed and the other works far away, decisions concerning the family division of tasks and the use of available vehicle and money resources will have to be reconsidered. If the children leave home to live in another house, household time and space budgets decrease, as well as expenses and individual constraints.

The example illustrates two important issues. The disregard of transport planning for the pedestrian and cyclist is one of the major drawbacks faced by poor people in the developing world. Most fatalities in developing countries happen to the non-motorized and pedestrian roles. If women enact the role of pedestrian more frequently – which seems to be the case in most countries – they are more severely affected by the problem. Also, in the role of the cyclist, women face additional problems related to the vehicle itself. Existing bicycles are mostly made for adult males, with a structure and parts that make them difficult or embarrassing for women to ride. They are also too high for the average height of women and make it particularly difficult to ride in a long dress (Hierli, 1993). Also, females frequently have to carry water and goods, a constraining task in several countries and implying severe physical difficulties not attended to by conventional transport means.

Also, problems with public transport supply play an important role. First, supply has been historically based on peak demands because of strict economic reasoning; in most cases (before the feminization of labour), users were mostly males and recent changes in the labour market have not yet translated into changes in the service to better fit women's needs. Second, the daily activity pattern of adult women is frequently more complex than that of men, leaving few time windows in which to perform non-constrained activities (Tolley and Turton, 1995; Diaz Olvera and Plat, 1997). Traditional transport planning hardly considers such complexity, which is reinforced by the aforementioned economic devaluation of 'non-productive' activities performed mainly by women. Third, vehicle supply seldom caters for women's particular needs (Kwakye et al, 1997).Therefore, traditional planning provides inadequate vehicles and often yields a poor supply of public transport in out-of-peak hours, severely hampering the mobility of those who most need it in such periods, women.

Problems are worse when the woman lives alone with the children, which is an increasingly common pattern all over the world. In such cases, to combine working, escorting children and housekeeping tasks may become extremely difficult. In addition, the time–space limitations may impose limits on places to work and shop, creating additional problems. Traditional transport modelling assumes that the journey to work decision involves deciding first the destination and then the mode and route. This seems to fit the male's typical decision, but not female's, which may be subject to the workplace being close to home (Sheppard, 1989). This is the case when the combined inadequacies of the supply of social services (school, nursery, health) and transport reaches a critical level.

The elderly

The elderly issue in transport translates itself through difficulties in enacting the roles of public transport user and pedestrian. With the former, the problems are similar to those experienced by adult females, especially in respect to the physical difficulties in accessing public transport vehicles, due to lack of adequate stairs and crowded conditions. With the latter, the elderly experience serious problems while walking, both because of personal physical limitations and the lack of proper arrangement of streets to meet their needs and limitations. Of special concern is the time taken to traverse streets, when 'green' times are not sufficiently long to allow for a comfortable and safe crossing.

The disabled

The disabled issue in transport translates itself through difficulties in enacting all roles in traffic. The disabled experience the sum of the difficulties of all non-disabled people mentioned above, plus their own difficulties. The roots of the problem lie in both the physical or mental impairments and in the political impairment, that of not having their needs attended to by society. Among the mobility-related issues, the disabled one is the most pressing from the

Table 13.4 *Mobility problems according to social condition and active role*

Condition	Share (% pop)	Level of problem Role	Accessibility[4]	Safety[5]	Quality[6]
Poor	40–80	Pedestrian	S	S/XS	S
		Cyclist	S	S/XS	S
		Public transport	S/XS	M/L	S/XS
		Motorcyclist	L	S/XS	L
		Car driver	L	M	M/L
Children[1]	50	Pedestrian	XS	XS	S
		Cyclist	XS	XS	S
		Public transport	S	M/L	XS
		Motorcyclist	–	–	–
		Car driver	–	–	–
Adult male[2]	20	Pedestrian	S	S	S
		Cyclist	S	S	S
		Public transport	S/XS	M/L	S
		Motorcyclist	L	S	L
		Car driver	L	M	L
Adult female[2]	20	Pedestrian	S/XS	S/XS	S
		Cyclist	S	S	S
		Public transport	S/XS	M/L	XS
		Motorcyclist	L	S	M (culture)
		Car driver	L	M/L	L
Elderly[3]	10	Pedestrian	XS	XS	S
		Cyclist	XS	XS	S
		Public transport	S	M/L	XS
		Motorcyclist	L	S	L
		Car driver	L	M	L
Disabled	12	Pedestrian	S	XS	XS
		Cyclist	S	XS	XS
		Public transport	S	M/L	XS
		Motorcyclist	S	S	L
		Car driver	S	S	L

(1) under 18 years old; (2) working-age adults, between 18 and 60 years old; (3) over 60 years old; (4) accessibility to space, see Chapter 6; (5) traffic safety; (6) transport quality
XS – very severe; S – severe; M – medium; L – low

social point of view, since it reveals how far a society intends to go in discussing their rights.

Summarizing mobility issues

The analysis may now be used to summarize the main issues concerning mobility and transport in developing countries. This will be done by combining the analysis of reproduction needs, traffic roles and mobility. This is performed with the most relevant individual characteristics for the analysis: general social and economic conditions (poverty, gender, age and disability), active roles, and three traffic conditions – accessibility, safety and quality. The process is qualitative and is intended to provide a broad view of how people's conditions and roles interact with transport supply to define their use of the space.

Table 13.4 shows a wide array of conditions. For poor people in general (from 40 to 80 per cent of population), the most crucial mobility problems are related to the roles of pedestrian and cyclist (safety, accessibility and quality), public transport user (accessibility and quality) and motorcyclist (safety). If just children and youngsters are considered (50 per cent of population), very severe problems with accessibility and safety appear with the roles of pedestrian and cyclist, along with the quality of public transport. If working-age adults are isolated (40 per cent of the population), additional problems related to gender may be devised: severe accessibility problems in the roles of pedestrian and public transport user, and quality problems in using public transport. When the elderly are analysed, a similar condition is identified: severe problems of accessibility and safety in the roles of pedestrian and cyclist and severe quality problems in using public transport. Finally, when disabled people are examined, most problems become sharp, due to the often inadequate travelling environment.

There are many other ways of using the proposed framework to perform complementary analyses. Other variables could be used (cost, individual environmental impact), leading to a more detailed or more focused analysis. In addition, passive roles such as that of a resident could be examined in relation to age and gender. Further, the 'children' group could be broken down into two subgroups, to study the specific problems faced by younger people (over 14 years old) in enacting the role of an independent (non-escorted) public transport user or cyclist and also in respect to differences between boys and girls.

Transport externalities

Transport activities imply several costs and are related to the production of externalities. Main costs may be divided into internal (purchase, taxes, maintenance) and external, represented by those paid by others (office parking) or imposed on others (congestion, accidents) (Litman, 1996). In a more precise scientific definition,

> An external effect exists when an actor's (the receptor's) utility (or profit) function contains a variable whose actual value depends on the behaviour of another actor (the supplier), who does not take these effects of his behaviour into account in his decision making process. (Verhoef, 1994, p274)

As Baulmol and Oates have pointed out (1998), such a definition excludes cases when someone deliberately does something to affect someone else, that is, externality is seen as an unintended effect. Such a characteristic is stressed even further by saying that an externality exists whether or not a payment for the effect is imposed on the decision maker.

Discussions about external effects abound in the literature and I do not intend to reproduce its methodological – and highly complex – content here. What matters is to analyse the most relevant external effects of transport for the case of developing countries. The comprehension of such externalities have evolved in time, as perceived transport impacts were also becoming more clear. Table 14.1 summarizes some contributions from important sources in the last decade.

As may be seen in these sources, the list of external effects may be quite long. In addition, there is controversy over what is an 'external' transport benefit or cost (Verhoef, 1994). Some effects are direct – congestion, pollution – while others are indirect – barrier effect, visual annoyance. In most cases three main impacts have been considered: congestion, pollution and accidents, both for their visibility and their tangible nature. Pedestrians hit by cars, drivers delayed by others and people breathing polluted air are all suffering externalities, often without any sort of compensating mechanism.

Table 14.1 *External and environmental effects of transport*

Bovy, 1990	Button, 1993	Miller and Moffet, 1993	Verhoef, 1994	Litman, 1996
Air pollution	Air pollution	Energy	Congestion	Accidents
Noise	Water resources	Congestion	Accidents	Congestion
Land	Land resources	Parking	Pollution	Parking
Solid waste	Solid waste	Vibration	Noise	Land use
Accidents	Accident risk	Accidents	Parking	Land value
Energy	Noise	Noise	Resources	Air pollution
Landscape	Disruption	Air pollution	Waste	Noise
	Congestion	Water pollution	Barrier effect	Resources
		Land loss	Visual annoyance	Barrier effect
		Historic buildings	Severance	Water pollution
		Property values		Waste disposal
		Urban sprawl		

Some effects are relatively easy to measure, such as the excess time imposed by congestion on buses using a particular road, while others are difficult to measure, such as the health effects of accident and pollution, or the impact of the barrier effect on people's quality of life. An important aspect has to be emphasized in respect to developing countries. While the analysis of transport externalities is usually related to individuals – leading to individualized 'blaming' – wider processes such as the organization of the built environment and the corresponding traffic conflicts have to be addressed to better understand the issue. When heavy traffic is allowed to use a road with high pedestrian movement to alleviate congestion on parallel roads, a new built environment is created, with several negative consequences for residents and users. Such a decision will generate an externality-producing environment, hence the public authority is to be blamed first, not individuals using the street (which does not preclude measures to control the externalities).

These costs and impacts will have different relevance according to specific local characteristics, and to place priority on them is always a difficult and debatable task. I will discuss some impacts that I assume to be the most relevant for developing countries. With public or natural resources, I will analyse the use of road space and energy consumption; in respect to externalities, I will discuss the barrier effect/social disruption, air pollution, congestion and accidents. Although several other effects are important, they will not be treated here, considering their intangible nature and the lack of reliable data or information.

According to the assumptions made in the book, road use and accidents are the most important aspects in the case of developing countries. All impacts are discussed in this section, except traffic accidents, which are treated in Chapter 15.

SPACE

The space issue may be analysed considering two separate although complementary views: the physical and the symbolic space.

The physical space

One of the greatest environmental impacts of transport is on the land that is required. The use of space is a key element for analysing the equity component of urban transport. The space occupied by a person while using the public road is dependent on the transport mode, its speed while moving and, in the case of a vehicle, the time it remains parked. The total area needed by a car to park at home, in the office and at shopping areas has been estimated in the UK at 372m², which is three times that of the average home (Tolley and Turton, 1995, p284).

Many authors have already explored this issue, analysing the different space requirements of each transport mode (Brunn and Vuchic, 1993; Whitelegg, 1997). The space needed for parking and circulating is compared for four modes in Table 14.2. It can be seen that the most insatiable mode is the automobile, consuming 30 times more area than a bus and about five times that of a two-wheeler.

Table 14.2 *Space required for a peak-hour 10km, two-way working trip (9 hours)*

Mode	Space (km × m²)		
	Parking	Traffic	Total
Bus, 50 people	< 0.5	3	3
Two-wheeler	12	8	21
Car, 1.25 people	72	18	90

Source: Vivier, 1999

When comprehensive, city-wide surveys are performed, it is possible to compare the relative use of the streets by different transport modes, reflecting how road public assets are being divided among citizens. Table 14.3 shows, for several large Brazilian cities, that people using automobiles – the minority – are taking from 70 to 80 per cent of road space. When average vehicle occupancy is considered, people using automobiles are found to be consuming from 7 (Campinas) to 28 (Rio de Janeiro) times the area used by those travelling by bus.

One of the most wasteful characteristics of automobiles is that they remain parked from 20 to 22 hours per day. Space for parking may be provided in several ways, with different social impacts. First, the car owner may have a space at home, when social impact is limited to causing additional costs to the city spatial arrangement (once more space is needed for every lot and for public services such as sewage, water and roads). Second, parking space may be provided free on streets. This is by far the most common situation. Is this case, a public asset is delivered and reserved free for several hours for the

Table 14.3 *Road space used by people circulating in buses and in cars, several Brazilian cities, 1998*

City	Road area used (%)[1]		Relative area per person (evening peak)[2]
	Autos	**Buses**	
Belo Horizonte	77.2	22.7	25.6
Brasilia	90.7	9.7	15.1
Campinas	87.1	12.8	6.7
Curitiba	79.2	20.7	17.3
João Pessoa	87.7	12.2	11.2
Porto Alegre	69.6	30.3	8.7
Recife	84.5	15.4	7
Rio de Janeiro	74.3	25.6	27.6
São Paulo	88	11.9	13.1

(1) Average of morning and evening peak hours
(2) Area per person in car/area per person on bus
Source: IPEA/ANTP, 1998

person using a car. In the São Paulo metropolitan region, 54 per cent of auto trips on an average day in 1977 ended up parking freely on streets. This corresponded to 1.5 million trips, using 12 million m² of public road space (considering 8m² per parked vehicle) (CMSP, 1988). Third, the parking space may be provided by the business owner to its customers. In the São Paulo metropolitan region in 1977, 36 per cent of auto trips had free parking at office and shopping areas and just 11 per cent had to pay for parking (CMSP, 1988). Such parking provision adds more vacant space to the city structure, and is only apparently free, since costs are passed down to customers. In the US, the design of shopping centres' parking lots leaves half of the spaces vacant 40 per cent or more of the time (Cervero, 1998a).

The use of the space by social groups

The use of roads is highly dependent on the social and economic characteristics of people. When the daily space consumption of families (space budget) is computed for several income levels, large differences appear. Linear daily distances (Table 14.4) are similar for walking trips. With public transport, distances increase up to the fourth income stratum and then decrease. For auto trips distances increase with income. When distances for all modes are combined, final values increase with income; the ratio between the lowest and the highest income levels is almost 1:4.

When linear distances are multiplied by the specific personal space correspondent to each motorized mode, differences between income levels become even more pronounced. Considering that a bus has a 'shadow' area of 2.5m × 12m (30m²) and that average daily occupancy is 30 passengers, the average space used by a passenger is 1m². Considering that the automobile has a 'shadow' area of 1.6m × 4.5m (7.2m²) and that the average occupancy is 1.5, the average space used by a person is 4.8m². When such individual spaces

Table 14.4 *Daily linear family space budgets according to income, São Paulo, 1997*

Family income (R$)	Daily linear distances per mode (km)[1]			
	Foot	**Public**	**Private**	**Total**
< 250	2.2	10.4	3.2	16
250–500	2.6	19.5	5.5	28
500–1000	2.8	26.9	10.2	40
1000–1800	2.8	31.3	18.6	53
1800–3600	1.9	25.5	29.9	57
>3600	1.2	15.8	45	62

Source: CMSP, 1998
(1) Measured as straight lines between trip origin and destination

are multiplied by linear distances (Table 14.4), the ratio between the lowest and the highest income levels is 1:9 (Table 14.5 and Figure 14.1). This means that a higher-income family uses nine times the road area, per day, more than the lowest-income family (I am not considering the space needed for parking and the space differences arising from different car and bus speeds). This simple ratio shows that actual road usage is highly variable according to income (and transport mode used). The most important conclusion for policy purposes is that public road assets are not equally distributed among people and that treating road investments as democratic and 'equitable' is a myth. As explained in Chapter 16, this is one of the most powerful and important myths behind automobile-supporting policies.

Table 14.5 *Daily dynamic family space budgets and income, São Paulo, 1997*

Family income (R$)	Daily distances per mode (km×m²)			
	Public	**Private**	**Total**	**Ratio**
< 250	10.4	15.4	26	1.0
250–500	19.5	26.4	46	1.8
500–1000	26.9	49.0	76	2.9
1000–1800	31.3	89.3	121	4.6
1800–3600	25.5	143.5	169	6.5
>3600	15.8	216.0	232	8.9

Source: CMSP, 1998

The symbolic space: barrier effect and segregation

If on the one hand the differential use of private transport implies equity concerns with road consumption as a public asset, on the other a further negative effect arises with the impact of motorized traffic and especially automobiles on the built environment. Such impacts may be analysed in two ways. First, as stated before, by seeing how the use of road space is organized; second, by seeing how such organization affects social relations occurring in space. These relations may be severely affected by traffic, once people are forced to reorganize their travelling behaviour to adapt to new conditions. Main consequences

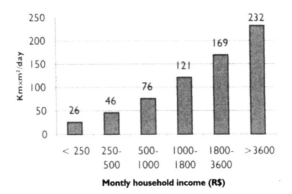

Source: CMSP, 1998.

Figure 14.1 *Daily dynamic family space budgets and income, São Paulo, 1997*

are the reduction in social interaction and in the use of public spaces (Appleyard, 1981) and the need to define strategies for reducing the risk of accidents (Hillman, 1988). This effect is labelled 'the barrier effect' (traffic severance), because traffic inhibits or prohibits social interaction and the use of non-motorized modes. Children and youngsters are especially affected by this externality while socializing and, since the very early ages are 'informed' that space does not belong to them but to motorized vehicles, this imposes a behaviour pattern that will last for their lifetime.

There is a complex relationship between built environment and transport modes. Each adapts to the other in a mutually reinforcing relationship. While this mutual influence is light when non-motorized transport prevails, it is very strong when motorized movements become dominant. As stressed by Harvey (1996, p185) quoting Lewontin, 1982, p162:

> *Organisms within their individual lifetimes and in the course of their evolution as a species do not* adapt *to environments; they* construct *them. They are not simple objects of the laws of nature, altering themselves to the inevitable, but active subjects transforming nature according to its law.*

Accordingly, there is no sense in speaking about the impact of society *on* the ecosystem, as if they were two separate entities. Therefore, when motorized transport is used by a society, a complex reorganization of the built environment occurs. Two particular conditions of such motorized traffic are relevant: the traffic mix and the traffic volume, both expressed by their consequences for safety, air pollution, noise and vibration over roadside constructions.

The traffic-related impacts profoundly shape people's behaviour, leading to reactions against an inadequate burden by those able to voice their protest or to silence by those unable to do it. Negative impacts may be attributed to all motorized means, according to their specific use. Trucks, because of their dimensions and engine power, often cause large nuisances and building vibration. Buses, when organized in heavily trafficked corridors may also cause negative impacts in respect to concentrated pollution and visual annoyance. However, the most pervasive negative influences are caused by automobiles, because of their number and their need to adapt space to survive.

The space adapted to automobile use is often large and widely dispersed, in which people inside vehicles hide themselves from others and people outside vehicles feel threatened and excluded from using the public space. This mechanism, although to a lesser extent, may also be related to the extensive use of motorcycles, as in Asian cities. Traditional transport planning, by working with highway-based transport, has contributed to isolation and the disintegration of neighbourhoods (Williams, 1998). Current trends are leading to the polarization of society into those with and without a car, with the latter being harmed mostly by the deterioration of local services that can no longer compete with car-oriented facilities (Owens, 1996). Middle- and upper-class urban spaces symbiotically linked to automobile spaces have produced urban ghettos protected from the 'outside world'. Along with strong political and economic forces, the adaptation of space to the automobile driver has contributed to the privatization of public spaces. 'The insecurity reflected in the seclusion of rich neighbourhoods and the ordeal of using public transportation shrinks public spaces and leads to a perverse kind of privatisation that spills into other spheres' (O'Donnell, 1994, p164).

As long as space is adapted to the interests of those with access to automobiles, it creates a special, isolated space that excludes or severely damages the needs of those without such access. The supposed market freedom has been serving to adapt space to the interests of a few car drivers, while denying convenient access to pedestrians, cyclists and public transport users. In this respect, cars help to create a new class of 'access poor' (Whitelegg, 1997) and isolate the poor, the young and the elderly when they are unable to drive; people without cars have no rights. As pointed out by Owens (1996, p48):

> *People want to live in attractive residential areas whilst at the same time having access to a range of jobs, services, green spaces ... such choices are denied to those without access to a car ... even when journeys are short ... the dominance of traffic and its expropriation of otherwise attractive spaces makes walking an cycling an unpleasant, if not daunting, prospect.*

As stressed on Chapter 12, profound transformations are now taking place in several developing countries which are adapting their urban space to the use of the automobile for selected groups. Such transformations are being organized at the expense of the historical urban physical tissue and of the most vulnerable road users.

ENVIRONMENT

Pollution

At a global scale, transport contributes a high percentage of total emissions, but with highly different shares between the various regions (Table 14.6).

Table 14.6 *Contributions of motor vehicles to global anthropogenic emissions of air pollutants, 1986–1987*

Pollutant	% in global emissions	Contribution by region (%)		
		OECD and Europe	East Africa and Latin America	Asia
CO_2	14	69	9	22
CFC-12	28	90	< 10	< 10
CO	10 to 54	73	11	16
NO_x	29 to 32	75	11	14
HC	47 to 49	73	12	15

Source: Faiz, 1993

Table 14.6 shows that transport contributes significant shares to global emissions and that industrialized countries play a major role in polluting the atmosphere. Conversely, developing countries contribute a minor quantity, due to their much lower level of motorization; while OECD countries have 74.2 per cent of the world's motor vehicles, Asia has 10.2, Latin America and the Caribbean 6.3 per cent and Africa 2.1 per cent (Faiz,1993). This lower motorization level also holds when per capita vehicle rates are considered; the number of vehicles per 1000 population was, in 1993, 561 for the US, 366 for OECD countries, and from 72 to just 3 for the other world regions (World Bank, 1997).

From the environmental point of view, the worst implications of present transportation and traffic policies in developing countries are traffic accidents, not air or noise pollution. However, these latter consequences are becoming especially problematic in large cities, with bleak prospects, due to both population increase and motorized transportation growth. Large cities in the developing world already produce enormous quantities of pollutants. In two mega-cities, Mexico and São Paulo, the yearly production of pollutants is, respectively, 2.3 and 1.6 million tons of CO (carbon monoxide), 555,000 and 368,000 tons of HC (hydrocarbons) and 18,800 and 48,600 tons of SPM (suspended particulate matter). Most CO and HC production comes from transport operations, while SPM also comes from industrial activities (Benitez and Roldán, 1999; ANTP/IPEA, 1998).

The first important conclusion regarding urban air pollution is that it affects everybody, regardless of social or economic conditions, because people travel everywhere.[1] However, the source of pollution is highly class-based; most of the pollution is produced by motor vehicles, especially private transport (Table 14.7).

Table 14.7 *Contribution of motor vehicles to pollutant emission, selected cities*

City	Pollutant emitted by motor vehicles (%)				
	CO	**HC**	**NO$_x$**	**SO$_2$**	**SPM**
Beijing, 1989	39	75	46	n/a	n/a
Bombay, 1992	n/a	n/a	52	5	24
Colombo, 1992	100	100	82	94	88
Delhi, 1987	90	85	59	13	37
Lagos, 1988	91	20	62	27	69
Mexico, 1994	99	54	71	27	4
Santiago, 1993	95	69	85	14	11
São Paulo, 1990	94	89	92	64	39

Source: World Bank, 1997, Table 4.2, except Mexico (Benitez and Roldán, 1999; Connolly, 1999)

Table 14.7 shows that motor vehicles are responsible for almost all CO emissions, and most HC and NO$_x$ emissions. In some cities they are responsible for most of the SO$_2$ and SPM. Contribution to SPM varies tremendously but this may be a result of computation procedures; the inventory in Mexico City attributes 94 per cent of SPM to 'vegetation and topsoil' (Benitez and Roldán, 1999; Connolly, 1999), a source not found in other inventories. When the contribution is analysed by vehicle type, important differences arise. Pollution may come from several sources, depending on the traffic mix. While in Latin American cities automobiles may play a major role (Table 14.8), in Asian cities motorcycles are more important (Table 14.9).

Table 14.8 *Contribution to overall pollution by transport mode, Mexico City and São Paulo*

City, country	Contribution to pollution (%)				
	Vehicle	**CO**	**HC**	**NO$_x$**	**SPM**
Mexico City, Mexico[1]	Motorcycles	n/a	n//a	na	n/a
	Cars	70	39	39	2.6
	Bus/trucks	30	15	32	1.5
São Paulo, Brazil[2]	Motorcycles	2	1	0	0
	Cars	78	76	25	9
	Bus/trucks	18	12	70	31

Source: (1) Connolly, 1999; (2) CETESB, 1996

Table 14.9 *Contribution to pollution by transport mode, large cities in India*

Mode	Contribution to pollution (%)
Two-wheelers	79.5
Cars	10.1
Three-wheelers	6.3
Buses	2.6
Trucks	1.5

Source: Chakravarty and Sachdeva, 1998

The concentration of pollutants is higher in heavy trafficked corridors. In a street survey in Delhi, India, Twari (1997) found excess concentration of CO, HC, lead and NO_x in several main roads. In a typical major traffic corridor in São Paulo, where cars, buses and trucks account for 94, 5 and 1 per cent of vehicles, automobiles are responsible for 98 per cent of CO, 96 per cent of HC and 67 per cent of NO_x emissions. Buses account for 58 per cent of SO_x and 28 per cent of NO_x emissions. When the actual passenger distribution is considered, figures demonstrate that most emissions are caused by people using private transport.

Pollution, environment and health

The negative effects of transport pollution on human health have long been recognized. Transport has to be seen as a public health issue, just as much as clean water and clean air (Steensberg, 1997). Most motorized-related pollutants are harmful to people's health. An important distinction, though, is between pollutants that have a direct effect on the Earth's health and those that have a strong effect on people's health. In the first category are CO_2 and other pollutants and in the second are SPM, HC, NO_x and SO_2 (and CO above certain levels).

Table 14.10 shows the estimated relative contribution of gases to global warming.

Table 14.10 *Relative contribution of gases to global warming, 1989*

Gas	Contribution (%)
CO_2	50
Methane	18
Chlorofluorocarbons	14
Tropospheric ozone	12
NO_x	6

Source: Tolley and Turton, 1995

CO_2 concentration in the atmosphere has increased from about 315 ppmv (parts per million volume) in the 1950s to about 350 ppmv in the 1980s. Although several gases contribute to global warming, the actual (final) contribution depends on the lifetime of every gas in the atmosphere and its relationships with other gases (Goldemberg, 1998). With transport and global warming, different fuels have different CO_2 emissions, with diesel giving the higher contribution per litre (Table 14.11).

Table 14.11 *CO_2 emissions per type of fuel*

Fuel	CO_2 (kg/l)
Petrol	2.406
Diesel	2.694
Methanol	1.088
Ethanol	1.503

Source: Goldemberg, 1998

At the local level, there is increasing evidence that fine particulate matter is the most health-threatening pollutant (provided that lead has been eliminated) (Gwilliam, 2000). There is a growing concern on the impact of SPM on the elderly and people with respiratory diseases. Table 14.12 shows for several cities that there is a relatively high risk of death with an increase in PM_{10} (very small particulate matter). In São Paulo, there is a 13 per cent extra risk for each 100 mg/m³ increase in PM_{10}, for those of 65 or older. A very important fact is that there is no 'safe threshold'; that is, mortality increases with any PM_{10} increase (Saldiva, 1998).

Table 14.12 *Increases in PM_{10} and relative risk of death*

City	Relative risk for a 100 mg/m³ increase in PM_{10}
Amsterdam	1.08
Athens	1.08
Birmingham	1.11
Chicago	1.08
Detroit	1.12
Los Angeles	1.05
Philadelphia[a]	1.12
Santiago	1.11
São Paulo	1.14

(a) converted from SMP assuming PM_{10}/SPM equals 0.60

Source: Schwartz, 1997

Emissions in cities

The urban and transport pattern and the type of motorized vehicles used determine the emissions pattern of a city. As Newman and Kenworthy (1999)

Table 14.13 *Emissions per capita, several cities in developed and developing countries*

Cities	Emissions per capita, per year (kg)		
	CO_2	NO_x	CO
Developed			
Amsterdam	1475	13	34
Frankfurt	2813	20	68
Houston	5193	27	241
Sidney	2588	24	207
London	1704	16	97
Los Angeles	4476	20	181
Developing			
Bangkok	1304	4	85
Jakarta	653	16	58
Kuala Lumpur	1424	11	90
Manila	529	9	68
Seoul	705	9	29

Source: Newman and Kenworthy, 1999

have extensively demonstrated, dispersed, high-income and automobile-based cities expend much more fuel and generate much more pollution than compact, low- or high-income, transit-based cities. Table 14.13 shows how great the difference in emissions may be.

Typical vehicle emissions

Vehicle emissions depend on the type of fuel, the engine technology, the engine regulation and the existence of catalytic converters. Low-standard gasoline automobiles are high producers of CO. Diesel vehicles are high producers of particulate matter, especially when there is a high sulphur content as in Brazil. Motorcycles are also worrisome, especially two-stroke ones (Faiz et al, 1996). It is estimated that two-stroke and three-wheelers emit more than ten times the amount of fine particulate matter per vehicle kilometre than a modern car (Gwilliam, 2000). In several Asian cities such as Hanoi, most motorcycles are second-hand, imported from Japan and highly polluting (Griffin, 1995). Most pollutant emissions increase exponentially with decreasing speeds. This is the main reason for congested roads being so harmful to people's health (see Table 14.14).

Table 14.14 *Speed and pollutant emissions, autos and diesel buses*

| Speed (km/h) | Vehicle emission (grams/km) | | | | | |
| | Autos[1] | | | Buses[2] | | |
	CO	HC	NO_x	CO	HC	NO_x
10	33.02	4.47	2.53	22.6	5.7	22.3
25	21.2	2.6	2.17	14.4	2.3	16.4
50	9.8	1.3	2.24	8.2	0	11.9
75	6.4	0.93	2.97	–	–	–

Source: (1) Faiz et al, 1996 (2) IPEA/ANTP, 1998

Traffic and noise

Traffic volume and composition have an important effect on noise. Heavy vehicles such as trucks and buses, and motorcycles as well, are major contributors to noise. The way vehicles are driven and the speed of travel are also important factors. Severe negative effects may be caused by railways in urban areas. The effects of noise on human health depend on the level of exposure. They can be significant, affecting concentration and productivity and causing health-damaging tensions. Extreme effects may be permanent hearing impairment, stress and insomnia (Miller and Moffet, 1993). Table 14.15 reveals that the level of noise on a collector street (100 vehicles/hour) is 17 times higher than that of a local street (6 veh/hour) and that the level of noise of a heavily trafficked arterial road (2000 veh/h) is 333 times higher.

Table 14.15 *Effect of traffic volume on noise*

Veh/hour	Noise level-Leq (1 hour) dB(A)	Estimated daily flow (veh/day)	Ratio (first level = 1)
6	51	90	1
60	61	900	10
100	63	1500	17
500	70	7500	83
1000	73	15000	167
2000	76	30000	333

Source: Certu, 1996

ENERGY

The energy consumed by a transport mode is of particular relevance to developing countries, be it fossil fuels (diesel, petrol) or from a hydroelectric origin. The computation of units of energy per distance has to be weighted by the number of people using the mode, to yield a comparative figure among different modes. Overall energy efficiency comparisons reveal that while automobiles use 2.3 to 2.6 MJ/pass-km (mega-joules per passenger-kilometre), trains use 0.6 to 1.5 MJ/pass-km and buses 0.6 to 0.8 MJ/pass-km (Goldemberg, 1998).

Table 14.16 shows, for several vehicles in Brazilian conditions, that diesel buses are still the most energy-efficient modes, closed followed by the subway. The particular relation between buses and cars shows a 1:4.7 ratio (standard bus). It must be remembered that the figures assume fully loaded vehicles – that is, with different vehicle loading, energy consumption rates will change. For example, if we compare buses and cars, Tolley and Turton (1995) show a 1:4.1 ratio for central London, Whitelegg (1993) shows a 1:3.8 ratio for Germany and Gordon (1991) shows a 1:3.4 ratio for commuting trips in the US. In extremely loaded buses, such as in Beijing, the ratio may go up to 1:9 (Newman and Kenworthy, 1999).

Table 14.16 *Energy efficiency of different transport modes*

Transport mode[1]	GEP/pass-km[2]
Articulated bus	3.2
Bi-articulated bus	3.5
Standard bus	4.1
Subway	4.3
Motorcycle	11.0
Automobile	19.3

(1) fully-loaded vehicles; (2) equivalent grams of petrol units to move 1 passenger by 1 kilometre
Source: Alqueres and Martines, 1999

Box 14.1 *The myth of the 'empty buses': the 6-4-2 rule*

Ordinary people seem to be disgusted or even ashamed when they see a bus with fewer than 50 people inside it. Automobile users always refer to this when discussing traffic issues (and congestion, of course). Even experts seem to be prisoners of the same vision. 'Inefficiency' is another word, in a scale that goes up to 'waste of public resources' or 'economic heresy'. People would like to see a crowded bus, with possibly nine passengers per m^2. Without considering now the plain injustice of submitting people to such crowded conditions, let us recall some basic figures, that I will name 'the 6-4-2' rule (for average conditions in São Paulo):

- A standard, 45-seat diesel bus with *six* passengers is occupying, per person, less public road space than the average automobile with an occupancy of 1.5 people.
- A standard, 45-seat diesel bus with *four* passengers is using less energy per person than the average automobile with an occupancy of 1.5 people.
- A standard, 45-seat diesel bus with *two* passengers is emitting less carbon monoxide, less carbon dioxide and less hydrocarbons per person than the average automobile with an occupancy of 1.5 people.

CONGESTION

For the average person, traffic congestion represents a situation where travel time along roads (vehicles) or pavements (pedestrians) is considered too high. This is a subjective measure, since the idea of what is 'too high' depends on individual opinions. A large literature attempts to give a clear definition of congestion (ITE, 1976; TTI, 1996; Maddison et al, 1996; Litman, 1996). The traditional concept is that of extra travel time, which comes out of a comparison between 'ideal' and actual values (the 'capacity' concept), implying the ideas of traffic efficiency and quality. Another economic concept is related to the cost a user imposes on others while travelling, and the corresponding search for an 'equilibrium point' (the economic concept of 'optimal' congestion).

The significance of congestion stems from two sorts of concerns. First, equity, because congestion is a sort of transport externality, in that people using the road cause delay to others. Second, environmental, since congestion with motorized vehicles implies higher energy consumption and pollutant emission.

The first congestion studies were made in the US, where the use of the automobile increased rapidly in the first decades of the 20th century. Most of the studies of that country demonstrate the enormous waste of time involved in huge congestion in major towns (TRB, 1994; TTI, 1996).[2] This book considers two other sorts of problem: that created by automobiles and affecting public transport, non-motorized vehicles or pedestrians, and that resulting from defective traffic management.

Technically, the congestion phenomenon occurs because vehicles entering a traffic stream on a particular road increase the relative travel time (minutes per kilometre) of the vehicles already travelling on the road. This impact is low when the traffic flow is small as compared to road capacity, and increases exponentially as traffic flow increases (TRB, 1985; Button, 1993). The exponential nature of travel time increase is particularly strong when traffic flow reaches the 0.7–0.8 threshold in respect to road capacity. When the flow equals capacity, the road capacity is said to be reached and flow regime starts to be highly unstable. If further vehicles enter the road, then speed and flow both decrease, causing the sort of congestion with which we are familiar. If the costs of travelling on a particular road are examined, it is possible to divide them into costs incurred by a particular driver and those imposed by him on others. The costs of making the trip (personal time, fuel) may be called the average social cost of the journey (ASC), which increases with the traffic flow. The cost imposed on others may be called the marginal social cost (MSC), and also increases with traffic flow, in an exponential way (Maddison et al, 1996). The congestion phenomenon is a clear demonstration of how actions which attend to individual interests end up producing the worst possible outcome for everyone.

This general framework was developed in the industrialized countries, particularly in the US, and is automobile-centred. Developing countries have different traffic conditions, especially the extensive use of non-motorized and public transport modes; in Asian cities, for instance, in addition to pedestrians, there may be up to eight different vehicle types using the streets at any one time, at speeds that vary in a proportion of one to five. A specific methodology for such conditions is yet to be developed.

A particular analysis of congestion that is relevant for developing countries concerns how bus traffic is affected by automobile traffic. In major cities of the developing world, increasing congestion has been damaging bus speeds and reliability. Average speeds in Bangkok, Seoul and São Paulo are, respectively, 11.5km/h, 18.4km/h and 14.5km/h (see Table 11.5). In the former socialist economies, public transport has also been severely damaged by automobile-based congestion (Pucher and Lefévre, 1996). A study of ten middle and large cities in Brazil in 1998 demonstrated that automobile-related congestion severely impacts on the bus system's efficiency and reliability.[3] For the two largest cities in the country – São Paulo and Rio de Janeiro – severe congestion imposes on bus passengers, respectively, 118 million and 80 million additional hours per year (representing, on average, about 15 minutes in peak hour). In such cases, rather than using the elegant term externality we should instead talk about expropriation of time. Extra costs imposed on bus operations are passed on to users (IPEA/ANTP, 1998).

Traffic congestion may also severely damage pedestrians. When vehicle flow is high, signal timing is based on higher signal cycles to minimize vehicle delay (Webster and Cobbe, 1966). These longer cycles imply higher red times at crossings, increasing waiting time for pedestrians. If one considers additional limits imposed on pedestrians at busy intersections – such as short crossing times to free the traffic – we can figure out how far such an externality may go. At major intersections crossing time is often so short that only the first pedestrian platoon is able to reach the opposite pavement, and the remaining pedestrians having to wait in the middle of the street, often without any physical protection such as a central reservation. This sort of priority definition is deeply embedded in the ideology of motorized transportation; people using motorized vehicles are granted priority, often with the excuse that making them wait longer would result in intolerable congestion; that is, those circulating inside metal cases are considered more important than those circulating with their own bodies.

COMBINED EFFECTS

The analysis of transport-related externalities demonstrates that transport implies high consumption of energy and natural resources, including space, and causes severe environmental problems, especially air pollution. These impacts depend on the vehicle used.

A simplified idea of the mutual causation of externalities may be derived from analysing particular characteristics of each transport mode:

- Non-motorized modes (pedestrians, bicycles) produce zero pollution but may cause accidents and congestion; bicycles consume a low quantity of natural resources and need moderate circulating and parking spaces.
- Motorized modes produce air and noise pollution, as well as accidents and congestion; may produce building vibration depending on their size and quantity; they are all related to the extensive use of natural resources and cause large waste disposal impacts; they make extensive use of road space and require large parking spaces as well.
- Electric modes (trains, subways) produce near-zero pollution while operating and zero congestion when using separate tracks; they may cause accidents to other vehicles crossing their path, when on-grade crossings exist; they are all related to the extensive use of natural resources and are large space consumers.
- All motorized modes may contribute to the barrier effect when their physical characteristics and the traffic composition or quantity affects social relations between nearby residents or users.
- Road infrastructure consumes large amounts of land and may require the extensive dislocation of people; it may cause the barrier effect/social disruption when its physical characteristics, along with traffic composition and magnitude, affect social relations between nearby residents or users; it may cause urban disruption as well; finally, it may have profound effects on land use.

When several characteristics of transport modes are put together, their relative burden on space and the environment may be easily compared. Table 14.17 shows the enormous difference between one extreme – walking – and the other – automobile transport.

When the most common motorized technology is examined – the automobile – it may be estimated that its production consumes large amounts of raw materials and energy resources – 17,700 kWh. This places high burdens on space and the environment; a car used for ten years in Europe emits 60 tons of CO_2 and 89.5 kg of NO_x and produces 26.5 tonnes of wasted material (Whitelegg, 1997). It is important to remember that in respect to pollution,

Table 14.17 *Levels of consumption and emission of different modes*

Characteristic	Car	Train	Bus	Bike	Foot
Land use[1]	120	7	12	9	2
Energy use[2]	90	31	27	0	0
CO_2 emission[3]	200	60	59	0	0

(1) m²/person; (2) grams of coal equivalent units per pass-km; (3) grams/pass-km

Source: Whitelegg, 1997

figures in developing countries are much higher due to the vehicle age, and fuel and engine characteristics.

These crude conclusions are very important to address current problems in developing countries. However, they may still be complemented by analysing the most important transport externality for these countries, now and presumably for years to come: the traffic accident.

15 TRAFFIC ACCIDENTS

CURRENT CONDITIONS

Traffic accidents are a major problem in both developed and developing countries, albeit related to different historical reasons and circumstances. The single clear, common feature is the impact caused by the use of the automobile.

In the industrialized countries, the traffic accident problem started to become serious in the first decades of the 20th century in the US, when the number of automobiles increased sharply. After the Second World War the problem became serious in most European countries, and Japan as well. In developing nations, the traffic accident problem has been increasingly serious since at least the 1970s, when several countries became dependent on motorized transportation in general and on automobile transportation in particular. It is reaching epidemic proportions.

Traffic accidents are a major public health problem. They are the leading cause of death for males aged 15–44 and the fifth greatest cause for women of the same age group. The 1999 WHO *World Health Report* estimates 1.17 million road traffic deaths and more than 10 million injured in the world in 1998. Actual figures are certainly higher than those reported, due to a failure to relate reported deaths to traffic causes and to register post-accident deaths. The number of injuries is unknown, as the drawbacks mentioned are even more severe. If we assume a 1:15 ratio between killed and injured people, and the aforementioned global number of fatalities, then we may estimate a world figure of about 18 million injured people per year. From a public health perspective, traffic fatalities have become increasingly more significant within overall fatalities. As stated by Tolley and Turton (1995, p317) 'it is inconceivable that the car would have been adopted had it been known in 1885 what we know now – that it would kill some 15–20 million people in its first 100 yea s'. When compared to diseases, road fatalities rank third on a disease ranking in 16 developing countries, after diarrhoea and tuberculosis (Punyahotra, 1979). Traffic accidents are the third most common cause of death in Europe, after cancer and cardiovascular diseases, and account for 40 per cent of all accidental deaths. 'Preventing traffic accidents … may save more years of life than medical procedures for cancer and heart diseases' (Steensberg, 1997).

If current traffic safety conditions in developing countries are already extremely serious, they will undoubtedly worsen in the near future, because of the rapid increase in the use of motorized means, within social environments that are not prepared to experience such changes. The increased use of motorized means, especially automobiles and motorcycles, has been pursued intensively by most developing countries in an irresponsible, socially unacceptable way.

Figures and rates: methodological issues

Despite the difficulties in relating accidents to possible explanatory factors – accidents are indeed a complex phenomenon – a relative idea of a country's situation can be obtained by analysing some accident figures and rates. Some of them may be misleading, as has been demonstrated by Mohan and Tiwari (1998) and care must be taken in using them. The number and diversity of motorized and non-motorized vehicles using the streets in developing countries preclude the use of traditional techniques to understand the problem. For instance, the attempt to correlate traffic conflicts with crashes or fatalities using traditional methods often fail, because the self-organization of road users leads to an 'optimization' of road use. However, as stressed by the authors, this optimization does not result in a safe traffic environment, as there is always the need to organize traffic to minimize accidents.

The most direct measure of the problem is the number of dead or injured people caused by traffic accidents. As the latter is often under-reported (or even unknown) the former is used as a standard measure of the gravity of the problem. The number of fatalities (or injured people), considered as an absolute value, may be compared to other causes of death (or injuries), acting as a powerful public health indicator. Indirect measures relate the number of accidents to some form of underlying cause or exposure to traffic conflicts; accidents may be related to the number of people living in the country or city – usually in the form of accidents per 100,000 people – or to the number of motorized vehicles or automobiles, such as the rate of fatalities per 10,000 vehicles.

The number of accidents or fatalities per population is misleading because it does not take into account the actual physical exposure of people on the streets, related to the mobility level in each condition (for example, the number and extent of trips made). The number of fatalities may be low in a very poor country or city just because people make few trips; or may be high for the same low level of mobility should the traffic environment be very dangerous.

The number of accidents per vehicle (usually automobiles) is misleading, because it does not take into account the nature and composition of different vehicles using the streets and the pattern of traffic conflicts. The problem becomes clear when data from a city such as New Delhi (India) are analysed (Mohan and Tiwari, 1998); there are seven different motorized and non-motorized vehicles using the streets, ranging in width from 0.60 to 2.60m and in speed from 15 to 100km/h, leading to a complex pattern of traffic conflicts which cannot be analysed using traditional rates and techniques.

One way of improving the analysis is to adopt as a rate the number of accidents or fatalities per vehicle or person kilometre. Although much more consistent, it is rarely used in developing countries, because in most cases there are no data available on the distances travelled by people.

Data on traffic accidents

Despite these shortcomings, the first important analysis from the social point of view is the absolute number of traffic fatalities and its relationship to population and vehicle fleet. As analysed in Chapter 2, a large number of fatalities is found in several countries, both developed and developing ones. When overall accident rates are analysed, sharp differences appear between the countries. With fatalities per population, differences are lower.

The second important analysis concerns recent trends. Between 1968 and 1985, while road accident fatalities decreased by 20 per cent in developed countries, they increased by 300 per cent in Africa and almost 200 per cent in Asia (TRRL, 1991). When selected developing countries are analysed, it is concluded that they have been experiencing high increases in recent decades. For the countries with data for the last 25-year period, increases may be as high as 564 per cent, as in China (Table 15.1). Considering recent average rates of auto ownership and population increases, the number of road fatalities in developing countries can now be expected to be 50–100 per cent higher, as compared to 1980's levels (Carlsson and Hedman, 1990). In the urban scene, figures are also worrisome (Table 15.2).

Table 15.1 *Recent trends in traffic fatalities, selected developing countries*

Country		Traffic fatalities		Change (%)
		Initial	Final	
25-year period[a]	China, 1970–1997[1]	9654	73,861	665
	India, 1971–1996[2]	15,034	69,800	364
	Brazil, 1971–1995[3]	10,692	27,886	161
13-year period[a]	Thailand, 1980–1992[4]	4493	8184	82
	South Korea, 1982–1995[5]	6110	10,323	69

(a) approximately

Sources: (1) Dianpin, 1999; (2) Mohan, 1999; (3) Denatran, 1996; (4) Tanaboriboon, 1994; (5) Soon-Chul, 1994, and Lee, 1998

Table 15.2 *Traffic fatalities in selected major towns in developing countries*

City/year	Pop[5] (1000)	Fatalities	Fat/100,000 pop
São Paulo (Brazil), 1999[1]	10,000	1683	16.8
Bogota (Colombia), 1995[2]	5600	1139	20.3
Delhi (India), 1985[3]	6700	1114	16.6
Bangkok (Thailand), 1992[4]	5900	977	16.5

Sources: (1) CET, 1999; (2) Granne et al, 2000; (3) Tiwari, 1997; (4) Tanaboriboon, 1994; (5) UN, 1996, approximate figures at the time of the accident data

A SOCIAL PERSPECTIVE: WHO HITS WHOM

The most important questions from a sociological perspective relate to who is harmed by traffic accidents and who is responsible. Early studies with data from the 1970s in four developing countries show that pedestrians, cyclists and motorcyclists (the most vulnerable roles) accounted for 56 per cent to 74 per cent of fatalities (Hill and Jacobs, 1981). This is the main difference with respect to developed countries, where the corresponding figure is 20 per cent (Guitink and Flora, 1995).

In developing countries, the share of non-motorized means (pedestrians, cyclists) and that of motorized (all forms of motor and two-wheeler vehicles) in traffic accidents vary according to fleet composition. For instance, in Asia, where motorcycles abound, they are responsible for a high share of fatal accidents, while in Latin America in general and Brazil in particular, motorcycles correspond to a small part of the fleet and pedestrians and cyclists are the most harmed by traffic accidents (Tables 15.3 and 15.4).

Table 15.3 *Condition of traffic resulting in fatalities, selected countries*

Country	Fatalities (% of total)				
	Pedestrians	**Cyclists**	**2-wheelers**	**4-wheelers**	**Other**
Developing					
Thailand, 1987	47	6	36	12	4
South Korea, 1995	42	3	10	41	3
Poland, 1992	40	9	7	44	–
East Germany, 1989	30	9	24	34	–
Malaysia, 1994	15	6	57	19	–
Developed					
Japan, 1992	27	10	20	42	1
Germany, 1993	17	9	13	59	2
Netherlands, 1990	10	22	12	55	1
Australia, 1990	18	4	11	65	–
USA, 1995	13	2	5	79	–

Source: Mohan and Twari, 1998

Table 15.4 *Conditions of traffic resulting in fatalities, selected cities in developing countries*

City	Fatalities (% of total)				
	Pedestrians	**Cyclists**	**MTW**[a]	**4-wheelers**	**Other**
Delhi (India)[1], 1994	42	14	27	12	5
Bandung (Indonesia)[1], 1990	33	7	42	15	3
Beijing (China), 1994[2]	16	39	–	45	–
Colombo (Sri Lanka)[1], 1991	38	8	34	14	6
Nairobi (Kenya)[3], 1977-94	65	3	2	30	–
São Paulo (Brazil)[4], 1999	51	1	14	34	–

(a) motorized two-wheelers
Sources: (1) Mohan, 1998; (2) Navin et al, 1994; (3) Khayesi, 1997; (4) CET, 1999

Traffic accidents affect all ages but many of the victims are young people (less than 14 years old), from 9 per cent in Argentina to 19 per cent in Korea (Table 15.5).

Table 15.5 *Traffic fatalities by age group, selected countries*

		Fatalities – % (age range)		
South Korea[1]	Argentina[2]	Brazil[3]	Thailand[4]	India[5]
18.6 (0–14)	9 (<15)	19.7 (0–14)	18.8 (0–9)	9.5 (0–14)
2.9 (15–20)	47 (15–39)	29.8 (15–24)	22.0 (10–19)	29.1 (15–29)
10.3 (21–30)	24 (40–59)	23.9 (25–34)	29.2 (20–29)	34.1 (30–44)
12.1 (31–40)	20 (>60)	18.7 (35–59)	12.9 (30–39)	19.4 (45–59)
13.1 (41–50)	–	7.3 (>60)	17.3 (> 40)	7.6 (> 59)
42.0 (>51)	–			

Sources: (1) Lee, 1994; (2) BID, 1998; (3) DENATRAN, 1996; (4) Punyahotra, 1979; (5) Mohan 1999

When such figures are adjusted for population and age group, there is often a common pattern of rates increasing with age. In Argentina, for instance, motor vehicle fatality rates per 100,000 people in 1990, adjusted for population, were about 3–4 for the group up to 14 years old, about 10 in the 'productive phase' (from 25 to 44 years old) and more than 15 for the elderly (over 65 years old). A similar pattern (although with very different figures) was identified for other Latin American countries such as Chile, Brazil, Costa Rica and Mexico (Roberts, 1997). With cities, the same pattern holds, although local social and transport characteristics may introduce differences.

Traffic fatalities and gender

In Delhi, records of 177 autopsies of road traffic victims between January 1 and May 31 revealed that there were 126 males and 21 females. Males outnumbered females for all age groups except that under 10 years (reasons are unknown) (Sahdev et al,1994). Such figures reflect a public health issue but should not be used for comparisons in transport analysis without properly accounting for the degree of exposure to traffic – distances travelled on roads – and to the type of exposure as well – the roles played while circulating. In the Americas, traffic fatality rates adjusted for age and gender population shows a common pattern: male rates are always higher then female, in a proportion of about 1 to 3 or 4. In Argentina, the male fatality rate was 12 as compared to a female fatality rate of 4; in Chile, corresponding figures were 15.6 and 4.2, and in Costa Rica corresponding figures were 19.6 and 4.8 (Roberts, 1997). Such figures still do not account for the exposure to traffic.

A better example may be that of São Paulo. Males make 2 trips per day as compared to 1.7 by women (CMSP, 1997); however, males correspond to 76 per cent of pedestrian fatalities and 86 per cent of vehicle occupant fatalities (CET, 1997), revealing a disproportionate exposure to danger.

The hidden effect: disabled people

It is often neglected that traffic accidents cause several physical damages to those who survive. Some of these effects are temporary, some are permanent. Among the latter, some people will be totally impaired, others will be partially harmed. A study made in 1990 by the Pan-American Health Association of 19 countries in the region showed that 29 per cent of deaths attributed to injury were due to intentional causes (homicides, suicides, war) while 71 per cent were due to unintentional causes. Among the latter, motor vehicles were the most important single cause (Table 15.6), with 39 per cent overall.

Table 15.6 *Causes of unintentional fatal injuries, several countries in the Americas, 1990*

Cause	Share (%)
Motor vehicles	39
Drowning	10
Falls	7
Occupational injuries	6
Burns	3
Poisoning	1
Other	34

Source: Roberts, 1997

The number of injured and disabled people generated by traffic accidents in the developing world was estimated as 18 million per year. Consequently, a large number of hospital beds are occupied by road casualties representing high social security costs in often tiny budgets. Total costs are estimated to correspond to 1 to 2 per cent of the GNP (Carlsson and Hedman, 1990).

In São Paulo, for every person killed in 1997 in traffic accidents, there were 22 injured. For every pedestrian killed there were 10 injured and for every vehicle occupant killed there were 36 injured. Among the injured, 5 are seriously injured, yielding a total of 14,000 seriously injured people every year (CET, 1997). The personal and social costs of these injuries are enormous and are aggravated by the lack of proper social security support to most of the poor people affected by the problem. Figure 15.1 shows the estimated overall consequences of traffic accidents in the city in 1995.

Vehicles involved in accidents

Motorized vehicles in general are much more damaging, because of the much higher kinetic energy involved and its harmful potential. However, actual damage depends on the mix of motorized vehicles, and the speed and behaviour of drivers. When motorized vehicles are large (trucks, buses and automobiles) or travel at high speeds (automobiles and motorcycles) danger of severe harm is much higher, especially against pedestrians and cyclists (and motorcycle drivers as well). As a general rule, in Latin America and middle-income Asian countries automobiles are more numerous than motorcycles,

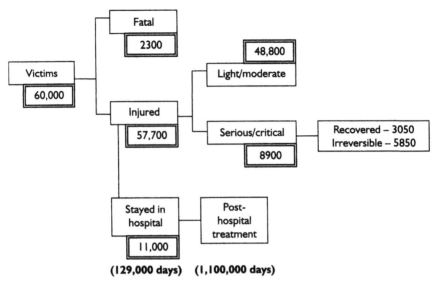

Note: Figures in 'people' (except for days, as noted); estimated values; current figures are about 20 per cent lower due to safety programmes

Figure 15.1 *Tree of social costs arising from traffic accidents, São Paulo, 1995*

while in Africa and low-income Asian countries motorcycles – sometimes along with minibuses – constitute the larger share. In a large city such as Delhi, traffic mix is very complex. Accident patterns reflect such complexity and motorized vehicles play a major role as causes of traffic fatalities: buses and trucks are involved in 58 per cent of fatalities.

When pedestrians and cyclists are analysed separately, it may be seen that 54 per cent of pedestrian fatalities and 66 per cent of bike fatalities are caused by buses and trucks. Overall, Mohan and Tiwari demonstrate that VRU – vulnerable road users, seen as pedestrians, cyclists and motorcyclists – 'constitute 77 per cent of the fatal road traffic accident victims in Delhi and that trucks and buses are involved in almost two-thirds of the crashes' (1998, p35). In Hanoi, motorbikes are responsible for 62 per cent of accidents.

This accident pattern is completely different from cities in developing countries with a high percentage of automobile usage. Table 15.7 shows, for São Paulo, that cars are involved in most traffic accidents and particularly in 70 per cent of pedestrian accidents.

Table 15.7 *Traffic accidents by vehicles involved, São Paulo, 1997*

Accident type	Vehicles involved (%)				
	Cars	**Motorcycles**	**Trucks**	**Buses**	**Bikes**
Pedestrian	70	11	6	10	3
Vehicular, damage-only	70	2	19	9	3
Vehicular, with victims	62	19	9	7	3

Source: CET, 1997

A particular concern has been arising with the non-motorized versus motor-cycle conflict in Asian cities. The increasing use of motorcycles brings extra danger for pedestrians and cyclists, such as in Hanoi; this increase 'is making bicycling and walking increasingly dangerous and unpleasant '(Griffin, 1995, p15).

The impact of the automobile: the death payroll

The increase in accidents is related to the increase in heavy or speedy motorized vehicles, especially automobiles. Relating the number of fatalities to the number of automobiles in a country with a rapidly growing auto fleet may be very useful to estimate its impact.

The increase in car use has had serious negative effects in Eastern Europe but mostly in eastern Germany. The motorization rate almost doubled between 1988 and 1992 from 225 to 415 cars per thousand people. From 1989 to 1991, traffic fatalities increased from 1784 to 3759 (111 per cent) and traffic injuries from 41,037 to 83,580 (104 per cent) (Pucher and Lefèvre, 1996). This means that the increase in the number of vehicles in this period (about 1.5 million) was related to 3950 extra fatalities and 85,086 extra injuries to people (adding 1990 and 1991 events). Although the use of the car alone may not be blamed for all problems (the whole society passed through profound behaviour changes), it is undoubtedly the main factor behind this enormous social price. Not considering the differences that would arise from making a yearly account of the fleet increase, it may be said the each additional 1000 cars in eastern Germany led to 2.6 extra fatalities and 56 extra injuries. The same negative consequence happened in other socialist countries: in Poland, the number of traffic fatalities per thousand people rose from 13.4 in 1984 to 18.1 in 1992 (Pucher and Lefèvre, 1996) and in Hungary from about 16 in the 1980s to about 24 in 1990 (Brühning, 1997). In Poland, each additional 1000 cars purchased between 1989 and 1991 is related to 1.8 extra traffic fatalities and about 27 extra injured persons (assuming 15 injuries per each fatality) (basic data from Reksnis, 1995). If we now consider China, the recent increase in vehicle fleet from 1994 to 1997 was about 6 million (2 million a year), while yearly traffic fatalities increased from 66,362 to 73,861 (Dianpin, 1999). Therefore, every new 1000 vehicles in China may be associated with 1.25 extra traffic fatalities.

In addition to these impacts, the increase in accidents was at the expense of the most vulnerable roles: pedestrians and cyclists are the most harmed in the former socialist countries, corresponding, for instance, to 40 per cent of fatalities in eastern Germany, 49 per cent in Poland and 46 per cent in Hungary (Pucher and Lefèvre, 1996).

These estimations lead us to a key issue for developing countries: how many people will die or get injured before traffic safety improves? The technical, even cynical view that 'ultimately' traffic accidents will decrease has to be firmly rejected (see discussion in Chapter 17).

ALTERNATIVE APPROACHES TO UNDERSTANDING CURRENT CONDITIONS

Early on, accidents were considered either an act of God, or an unavoidable consequence of modern life. Only when accidents became increasingly common throughout the physical space of road networks, did industrialized countries begin to realize they were facing a new phenomenon. The first major change was seeing the accident as a man-made problem. Similar to the shift in political science in the 16th century, when Machiavelli proposed that political power was not derived from God but from human beings themselves (Skinner, 1978), traffic accidents were no longer viewed with a 'fatalistic' attitude, as a question of fate, but as a consequence of human actions. Therefore, they could be prevented. The second major change that followed was seeing the accident as a public health problem, deserving special attention from the state. This status was reinforced by two combined features: traffic fatalities increased to high levels and became as damaging as contemporary illnesses such as cardiovascular disease or cancer, causing large social and economic losses to society. From a public policy point of view, the transformation of the accident problem into a vital political issue became a major factor to be acknowledged. The mobilization of society and the state around this issue led to new combined efforts in dealing with accidents. Major comprehensive, interdisciplinary programmes were implemented in several developed countries from the 1950s to the 1970s, with remarkable effect in reverting the upward tendency in the number and severity of traffic accidents.

Unlike developed countries, the accident problem in developing countries has not yet assumed the status of a social issue. Public acknowledgement of the problem is still divided into conflicting views, ranging from the 'fatalistic' to the 'unavoidable-cost-of-development' approaches. Therefore, policy decisions have entailed different and sometimes conflicting actions, pursued independently by various public agencies, with poor outcomes.

Built environment and accidents: unsafe in any place

Traffic accidents occur in man-made built environments. Both the way the city is constructed, and the way the circulation structure is formed, have a direct effect on the nature of traffic conflicts and hence the probability of traffic accidents. As stressed before, there are several difficulties in relating accidents to the possible explanatory factors. A relative idea of a country's situation can be obtained by analysing two accident rates. The first represents the *accident-propensity* of the space, by revealing how many fatalities are associated with each motorized vehicle. The second rate shows the *inequity-propensity* of the space, by revealing who is being harmed, pedestrians, cyclists, driver and/or passengers. As shown before, higher propensities are characteristic of developing countries; more people die per vehicle and, among the dead, the majority are the most disadvantaged. The case of São Paulo is notorious. In 1986 there were 1621 pedestrians killed in traffic accidents, compared to 271 in New York and 43 in Tokyo (CET,

1992). Despite some social differences, and different vehicle fleets, the figures are self-explanatory.

The actual result of this sort of spatial occupation reveals a hidden feature of the built environment in developing countries: it is *inherently dangerous* for the majority of the population. This situation derives from several factors related to the built environment. First, street systems have been either constructed or adapted to allow for greater mobility in space, implying relatively high average speeds by motor vehicles. Most of the adapted streets do not have proper pavements forcing the pedestrians to share the space with vehicles. Conditions in Bangladesh are clear,

> *Yet pedestrians have so far received very little attention compared to vehicular traffic. Moreover, pedestrian movement is restricted due to the absence and/or non-availability of designated footways and safe road crossing facilities.* (Hoque and Noor-Ud-Deen, 1994, p263)

In addition, street widening is often made at the expense of pavements, squeezing the pedestrians into the remaining space and generating large distances to be traversed. When new roads are open, they usually cross high-density pedestrian areas, changing a once pedestrian-friendly environment into a new, automobile-friendly one. Urban social networks are disrupted and remaining pedestrian movements have to face heavy traffic. The ultimate objective of this urban surgery is to insert a grid-pattern paved street system, where mobility is enhanced for those using private transport. The street is turned from a habitat for people into a habitat for cars.

Second, these new road systems require a higher level of flow optimization, ensured by proper traffic management techniques, especially one-way streets and signal coordination. Such measures tend to allow for higher speeds, further restraining pedestrian movements. As stressed by Wright (1992, p7 and p179) when criticizing the 'soft' image marketed for the car 'most realistic images of the automobile include ... the disappearance ... of the elementary right to walk safely ... [and the causation of] ... traffic accidents that kill more people than do the machines of war'.

The coexistence of high-speed motor traffic and low-speed pedestrian traffic make accidents unavoidable; this is especially problematic in areas of intense pedestrian traffic, like schools, bus stops, parks and commercial areas. The existing circulation environment turns out to be inherently dangerous and the situation is uncontrollable. As stated by Sachs (1992, p192) 'space conformed to speed destroys space conformed to the pedestrians'.

The failure to acknowledge the importance of the built environment, along with a persistent attempt to explain accidents as 'behaviour' faults, leads to faulty diagnoses about the nature of the problem and hence to less-than-optimal policy proposals. To blame pedestrians and cyclists can be called 'blaming the victim' (Irwin, 1985, p45). Moreover, the assumption that in developing countries pedestrians and cyclists are harmed more just because they happen to be more numerous does not diminish the social nature of the problem. Conversely, it highlights the violent imposition of a new automotive-based environment. In Nairobi, for instance:

> *The pedestrian is often blamed for carelessness as a road user ... the traf-*
> *fic mix creates a high probability of conflict that could easily lead to a*
> *road traffic accident. This probability gets even higher in a situation where*
> *the road users do not adhere to the traffic rules, a state of affairs that is*
> *prevalent in Nairobi. The pedestrian turns out to be a weak and disad-*
> *vantaged negotiatior when confronted with the strong motor traffic ...*
> *In the absence of adequate pedestrian facilities and in a situation where*
> *there is little regard for the pedestrian right of way, pedestrians are obliged*
> *to take risky actions to cross the roads.* (Khayesi, 1997, p6)

In addition to its hostility to the weaker pedestrian and cyclist roles, the built environment in developing countries is also dangerous for the driver. Most developing countries committed themselves to extensive road-building programmes, following the automotive-oriented development model. This investment was not followed by appropriate operational and maintenance efforts, leading to fast physical deterioration and unsafe traffic conditions. Such a risky environment poses serious questions about the attempt to place most of the blame on the human factor. The bias in analysing developing countries' accident problems has been unwittingly enhanced somehow by the influence of studies conducted in developed countries, especially in Europe, most of which emphasize the human factor as the primary cause of accidents in industrialized countries. Although disregard for traffic rules, speeding, poor vehicle maintenance and drinking and driving can be said to account for a significant part of accidents in developing countries, the built environment has a very important effect.

Ralph Nader (1965) produced a devastating report about the safety of American automobiles, called *Unsafe at any speed*. The report was 'auto-centred', compatible with an auto-oriented society, and its ultimate purpose was to force the industry to produce safer cars, so that people could continue to use them. When thinking about developing countries, one needs to change the point of view from the driver to the pedestrian and the public transportation passenger. In developing countries the travelling environment is *unsafe in any place*, especially for pedestrians and cyclists. The built environment is auto-oriented, hence speed-oriented, hence pedestrian-hostile.

Ivan Illich (1974) in his analysis of energy and equity, emphasized the mobility inequity brought about by car ownership and use. The analysis made so far shows that irresponsible use of the car results also in *safety inequity*, with the car as a device for threatening others and violently occupying the circulation space. Therefore, the irresponsible introduction of the car in developing countries, and the corresponding space adaptation measures, deeply altered the environment, generating one with dangerous new characteristics, in which the majority is being harmed.

The political and technical conditions that generate and reproduce this sort of environment are discussed ahead. This critical assessment has to be performed to supersede some misleading ways of explaining traffic accidents. Two aspects are important to emphasize before the reassessment. First, in respect to viewing accidents as externalities. Cervero (1998, p48) states that

> *most economists do not view traffic accidents as an externality ... costs are largely borne by those who willfully choose to travel ... the very act of travel suggests that they (people) generally consider net benefits to offset whatever risks.*

In the case of developing countries, this is a mistaken assumption which forgets that people travel in inadequate conditions because they have no alternative. And while travelling they cannot properly protect themselves from the savage travelling environment. In addition, the fact that some drivers pay insurance for their cars does not disqualify traffic accidents as externalities (Baumol and Oates, 1988). Second, one has to emphasize the peculiar characteristics of the 'barrier effect' and the corresponding 'avertive behaviour', as leading to a disguising effect that induces faulty diagnosis. Hillman (1988) and Whitelegg (1993) point out that motorized traffic causes an increased burden of responsibility on road users, especially parents, who take their children off the street to reduce exposure to risk. The disguising effect in respect to accidents, with relevant impact to traffic policies, is that the decrease in non-motorized traffic leads to a false conclusion that accidents have been reduced. In fact, the most vulnerable roles were forced out of roads by the most powerful roles and a new pedestrian-free circulation environment is organized to ease the flow of motorized vehicles. In the specific case of the UK, Hillman et al (1990) demonstrate how children have lost their independence to walk and cross streets, being increasingly escorted.

Traffic accidents and the political environment

In developing countries deep class divisions, translated into social, cultural, economic and political differences between people, have profound consequences for the access to transportation modes and for the use of the circulation space. As stressed in Chapter 7, democracy – in its broader sense – is weakly institutionalized. The decision-making process is highly concentrated and affected by the nature of the technocracy, with strong political commitments to the middle-class lifestyle and ideology. This results in an auto-oriented modernization strategy.

Another important consequence is that citizenship, as political consciousness about collective behaviour, is weakly developed: there is a loose apprehension of rights and duties, which is weakened still further by the bias of formal justice in societies characterized by deep class differences. Drivers and pedestrians often develop informal ways of dividing space, which either ignore or interpret differently formal traffic laws. This creative behaviour also reveals that the built environment is 'chaotic' and highlights the inefficiency of formal traffic education; there is a basic contradiction between what is proposed as adequate behaviour and what is observed in daily life. An additional element is at stake with respect to traffic behaviour; class differences are translated into assumed differences in the right to occupy space. On the one hand, people in the role of drivers actually think, as political human beings, that they have priority in occupying the circulation space. On the other hand, people in the role of pedestrians or public transportation passengers actually think, as political human beings, that they do not have priority in occupying the circulation space (it is common to see pedestrians thanking drivers who allow them to cross the street first). Formal rules giving priority to pedestrians are seldom respected. In São Paulo, it was found that only 7 per cent of drivers stop at the stop sign (CET, 1992). Hence, on practical grounds, the priority of spatial appropriation by drivers has already been established in many developing countries, although traffic laws often state the opposite. In developing countries pedestrians are 'second class citizens'. Conversely, middle and upper sectors often travel by car and park close to their destinations, minimizing their exposure as pedestrians.

Traffic accidents and the technical environment

Transport planners are not trained, much less compelled to consider safety as a priority issue. Many still see accidents as 'fatalistic' or as inevitable outcomes of development. Most are deeply committed to the auto and mobility-oriented approaches. Therefore, the provision of high-capacity facilities and free-flowing streets are primary objectives. Further, planners usually belong to established public agencies, with a long history of 'technical' work, where road building and adaptation play the central role. In most developing countries, transportation and traffic agencies have road departments but few have traffic safety departments. The technical expertise to design and build roads is highly advanced in some countries, but the expertise to analyse and address traffic accidents is poorly developed in most. As non-motorized social groups often do not have access to the decision-making process, pressures come from the well-organized, motorized groups, and the road construction sector. Therefore, the technical expertise within state agencies is comfortable in pursuing the prime objective of good roads, while treating the accident problem as a marginal, and sometimes incidental one. Conditions get even worse when traffic duties are attributed to untrained police forces, who often have to deal simultaneously with traffic engineering, enforcement and safety aspects.

Foremost for our purposes, this behaviour is reinforced because planners and engineers have no formal obligation to be responsible for the traffic safety consequences of their acts as transportation planners. Unlike structural and industrial engineers, who can be legally prosecuted for any safety consequence of their acts, transportation engineers are not in practice prosecuted for traffic accidents occurring in their jurisdiction. The built environment of roads is thought of as good, and the blame for accidents is placed mainly on humans or vehicles (Whitelegg, 1981).

Traffic accidents and the enforcement environment

The consequences of this dangerous built environment are enhanced by the poor performance of traffic police and the judicial system. There are three major problems related to police performance. First, police personnel are seldom properly qualified. Second, there is a low supply of personnel, vehicles and specialized equipment, such as radars and alcohol-measuring devices. Third, enforcement logistics give priority to parked-vehicle offences, which often have little impact on safety. This is so for several reasons: unrestricted mobility is seen as a right and policeman act accordingly, focusing on traffic fluidity; parking enforcement is easily performed on foot and is highly productive; the lack of proper equipment makes it difficult for the policeman to enforce moving vehicles and enforcement is primarily organized to enhance mobility; finally, as in Bangkok, police may have two conflicting duties, to control traffic and ensure public safety (Daniere, 1995).

Traffic accidents and the judiciary environment

The judicial process is extremely complicated and slow moving. Moreover, no penalty is imputed to most of the serious traffic offenders. Some are 'more citizens than others': a peculiar form of citizenship based on personal relations introduces a large bias in favour of those who have direct relationships to power and use them to avoid punishment. As a consequence, a socialization of the feeling of impunity reinforces poor traffic behaviour. A vicious circle is formed, with severe consequences for traffic safety. Within this environment, formal traffic laws are often disregarded and traditional traffic education becomes nonsensical and counterproductive.

UNDERSTANDING CURRENT CONDITIONS

The preceding chapters have examined a wide array of urban transport conditions in developing countries, as a result of the economic, political technical and social development of recent decades. The objective of this chapter is to summarize the most important conclusions.

I decided to select a method which splits data and information according to analytical dimensions. I have identified ten dimensions: structural, political, ideological, economic, institutional, technical, technological, operational, social and environmental. While the first eight dimensions reveal how policies are formulated and implemented, the last two reveal the actual results of such policies. Several dimensions cross each other in fruitful ways and I will explore such crossovers whenever it appears convenient.

The structural dimension

Structural factors characterize the process of economic and social development in developing countries. Although profoundly impacting on transport conditions, solutions to minimize or overcome such structural factors fall outside transport policies.

It is well known that income disparities in developing countries are enormous, with most wealth owned by 5 to 15 per cent of people, who usually own 50 per cent of national income, while the lower 50 per cent of people own just 5 to 15 per cent of total income. In 1990, between a fifth and a quarter of the world's population still lived in poverty, without adequate food, clothing and shelter. More than 90 per cent of these lived in the developing countries. Between 1980 and 1991 the annual average change in per capita income was negative for the regions of sub-Saharan Africa, the Middle East, North Africa, Latin America and the Caribbean (N'Dow, 1997). Asia had the highest number of poor people but the fastest growth in urban poverty was occurring in Africa (Barry and Kawas, 1997). Apart from this unbalanced wealth, unemployment and sub-employment in highly unstable informal activities is already high and increasing in most places.

World population total in 1990 was estimated at 5.3 billion (UNCHS, 1996). Urban population was concentrated in Asia (44.5 per cent of world total), followed by Europe (22.8 per cent) and Latin America and the Caribbean (13.8 per cent). There were already 281 cities with more than one million inhabitants. Between 1950 and 1990, urban population as part of total population increased from 41.6 to 71.4 per cent in Latin America and the Caribbean. In Asia, urban population share between 1950 and 1990 varied from 11 to 26.2 per cent in China and from 12.4 to 30.6 per cent in Indonesia. In Africa, similar variations were 10.1 to 35.2 per cent in Nigeria and 31.9 to 43.9 per cent in Egypt. Not a single country in Asia, Latin America and Africa escaped an increase in its urban population share in the period.

This immense and continuing migration process is caused by several factors, among them persistent poverty and enormous regional economic imbalances, which attract or force people to move to cities. African cities appear to be unable to accommodate recent growth and their ecological sustainability is in jeopardy. In Arab countries, urban population was small in the 1950s – about 30 to 40 per cent in most cases – and increased rapidly in the 1970s, when most countries reached urbanization levels above 60 per cent. In some cases – such as Tunisia and Morocco – strong ties to European colonial powers created a dual spatial structure, in which a new urban pattern was superimposed onto the existing one, characterized by cellular organization into quarters, narrow streets and linearly organized bazaars. In other cases – such as Egypt and Jordan – the funds that support the economy are not generated by the indigenous economies but by international subsidies and remittances from people working abroad. The consequences are a strong concentration of the population in central cities – up to 50 per cent of Jordan's population in the case of Amman – lack of adequate housing and infrastructure, overcrowding, the separation of families, and the depletion of the local labour force, attracted by foreign opportunities. In the 'oil' states, the inhospitable terrain and the high level of urban services brought by increasing state wealth attracted large numbers of people, up to a point when 80 to 90 per cent of the population live in cities. An important aspect is that in several cities almost 90 per cent of the people was comprised of migrants, with few rights and subject to spatially based ethnic segregation: 'ethnic ghettos became increasingly institutionalised ... [and] ... develop their own social and commercial services' (Abu-Lughod, 1996, p201).

Some Asian countries encounter similar processes. In Indonesia, the rural production system has been changing into an urban job market; from 1971 to 1990, urban population increased more than 5 per cent a year, moving from 17.2 to 30.9 per cent of total population, while employment in the service sector quadrupled, reaching the 71.6 per cent level of total employment (with the informal sector playing an important role). The concentration of inhabitants in the island of Java has been increasing through the occupation of new transport corridors radiating out from large urban areas. This diffuse urbanization has been increasing long-distance daily commuting to large cities, which adds to the 'circular migration' of poor rural people working in the urban informal market (Hugo, 1996). India, although remaining a 'rural' country, saw its urban population increase from 17 per cent in 1951 to 25.7 per cent in 1991, when the country already had 296 cities with more than 100,000 people and 53 cities of over half a million people, in which infrastructure and transport problems are severe (Mohan, 1996). In China, which is also still a 'rural' country, recent economic changes have intensified rural–urban migration and 'temporary migrants' (those without official permission) were estimated to account in the late 1980s for 10 to 30 per cent of total population in the largest towns. This intense migration caused severe problems for urban infrastructure and transport (Chen and Parish, 1996).

In Latin America, the process of 'fast, massive, violent and non-reversible' urbanization (Henry and Figueroa, 1987) was followed by attempts to either support better life conditions in large towns through major investments, or limit urban and demographic expansion. When considering urban transport issues, two particular features of this urban development process must be emphasized: the socio-spatial segregation and the different distribution of public services. With the former, large income and cultural differences led to the physical separation of wealthy groups, the middle classes and the poor, although mixed land-use patterns may also be found. Of special interest is the long-lasting process of occupation of peripheral areas by increasing numbers of poor migrants. With the latter, public investments were driven by the uneven distribution of political power, generating sharp differences in the availability of public goods such as schools, hospitals, roads and public transport, with a direct impact on mobility and travel patterns.

This physical transformation had definite impacts on transport demand. While pre-automotive cities allowed for unlimited consumption of space by any person, modern cities began to spread over larger areas, making it more difficult to rely on non-motorized means of transport. Recently, as cities experienced an even more rapid growth of population, this has created average distances that cannot be walked or cycled. Therefore, the dependence on motorized transport means is inevitable in medium and large urban areas. This dependence requires motorized transport to be accessible, in physical and economic terms. Therefore, accessibility inequities were generated and a question remains about the possibility of restoring equity (Hagerstrand, 1987).

The specific characteristics of capitalist development further complicate the issue. Land speculation, weak public planning controls, and the spatial segregation of social groups and classes all work to generate social clusters, highly differentiated by income and social characteristics, with the poorest layers furthest away from the central areas. Ethnic and religious factors may translate into further spatial differences.

The political dimension

The political dimension reveals the failure of the political system to ensure a democratic representation of the conflicting interests of social groups and classes in the formulation of transport and traffic policies. In addition to highly centralized states, in which decisions are taken by a limited elite, most developing countries that have more open political regimes still suffer from a lack of adequate means of political representation. They are not institutionalized democracies but fragile democracies, deeply biased in their decision-making processes. As shown in Brazil, besides being controlled by an economic and political elite, the decision-making process favours the middle-class sectors, which have direct and indirect means of influencing policy outcomes. Other important agents also interfere, such as the highway and the automotive industry lobbies, and foreign interests. As the main fuel for capitalist modernization is social mobility, the middle classes pursue this mobility fiercely. They see the automobile (and the motorcycle to a lesser extent) as one of the main tools for their efficient social reproduction. Consequently, a symbiosis between middle classes and automobiles is formed. In addition, the economic role of the middle classes inside the capitalist economy places them in a politically conservative position, which leads to reaction against apparent threats to their reproduction. Therefore, political and social conditions generate auto-oriented transport and traffic policies, and middle-class cities – where space is adapted to the middle class enacting the role of auto driver – mushroom everywhere. Consequently, other social groups in general, and public transport users in particular, are kept away from the decision-making process, and are often subject to insufficient and unreliable transport supply. Social movements to support public transport are weakened by the fragile democratization environment, by political repression, and by public transport being just one among several deprivations experienced by poor people. Citizenship is poorly developed as people have defective knowledge on rights and duties and deficient means to influence state policies.

The ideological dimension

The ideological dimension reveals how the automobile-adapted space has turned out to be a model to be pursued. Several views of the automobile – freedom, privacy, pleasure – are called upon to justify the planners' submission to the idea of the auto as a natural human desire and hence to the appropriateness of investing public money in constant road expansion. The socially and economically constrained demand for cars is transformed into something natural and the planners' role is then seen as that of providing peoples' desires. Consequently the urban, economic and transport policies promoted in developing countries have been shaping the contemporary space in a way that reinforces the need for the car, while making non-motorized and alternate public transport means impractical.

The investment in road expansion is supported by two instruments: the use of forecasting techniques to reproduce current conditions, and the use, in appraising transport projects, of travel–time–benefit estimates based on differential wage rates between car and public transport users, therefore helping to perpetuate current inequalities. The ideological dimension also operates when defining the supply of public transport services. Investments in roads are believed to correspond with the public interest while investments in public transport are often left to the market. Public transport provision is subject to permanent instability, with recurrent 'cycles' in which public and private providers change positions. On the one hand, the attempt to leave public transport to the market often leads to unsafe, uncomfortable and unreliable services. On the other, public irresponsibility and corporativism may harm the public interest.

The economic dimension

The economic dimension relates first to the fiscal crisis of the state, which hinders the support of efficient public transport systems and distributive social policies. The crisis is only partly genuine; large transport infrastructures, which rely on public investments, are becoming less feasible and subsidies to special groups are subject to increasing opposition; conversely, large amounts of public resources are used to support road infrastructure, based on the myth that they are democratic, equitable investments. Second, the crisis is related to the continued poverty of most of the population, which lowers general mobility, prevents people from having access to convenient public transport and limits access to space and to social services. Both problems have sustained a continuous crisis in the supply of adequate public transport means and have consequently been supporting transport deregulation and privatization proposals, which often do not bring the supposed benefits. However, transport conditions continue to be inadequate.

The institutional dimension

The institutional dimension reveals that the attempt to coordinate policy efforts faces many obstacles. Few cities have agencies in charge of such duties. Technical resources are rare. Technical requirements and the time span for implementing actions for each area conflict with each other. Agencies overlap in their jurisdiction and conflicts around common issues are frequent. The problem is also serious in metropolitan areas, where coordinated efforts are essential to ensure the implementation of large-scale transport systems.

The technical dimension

The technical dimension is related to the implementation of traditional techniques generated in developed countries without proper adjustment to developing countries' conditions, and to the functionalistic approach to road use. Transport planning and traffic management rely on supposedly neutral and scientific approaches, which have been serving to generate an unequal distribution of accessibility. The rationale of the transport planning process is conservative, as it proposes solutions to accommodate present tendencies, without questioning the factors that shape transport demand; planning is reduced to a mere surrender to the results of forecasting exercises. The lack of reliable data and the use of imported and/or simplified model procedures do not reproduce or simulate trip behaviour properly. Only a few experts decide which data are included and how to manage them. This sort of procedure is made possible by the image of technology as a symbol of modernity, and the closed character of the political system; it is also fostered by the alliance between local expertise, local industry lobbies and foreign interests and pressures. Moreover, no one is accountable for the consequences of these actions; one must wait some years to evaluate the forecasting exercises, and there is always a possibility of explaining any deviation from the forecasted figures by a set of unexpected social and economic changes. These problems, coupled with high rates of demographic, social and economic changes, lead to forecasting activities that generate absurd results, supporting the provision of large road structures to be used by minorities, often with clear excess capacity. Planning based solely on peak demands particularly harms women's travelling needs. Traffic management is highly influenced by the myth of neutrality, using technical tools that avoid social and political considerations, and pursuing the distribution of the circulation space supposedly to the benefit of 'everybody'. It ends up providing a circulation space in which the weakest are severely harmed to allow efficient conditions for private transport. The most striking proofs of this irresponsible adaptation are the lack of proper pavements, the generation of high accident rates – especially those affecting the most vulnerable – and the lack of priority treatment for public transport.

The technological dimension

The technological dimension is related to the commitment to the automotive development model in a way that operates *against* non-motorized and public transport systems. Walking has been neglected as a form of transport, local transport means have been constantly disregarded and even banned, buses have been treated as a market problem and railways have been dismantled, while the automobile – and motorcycles in several places – have received special attention as representing 'legitimate' desires pertaining to society as a whole.

The technology to support walking does not exist. If something is deemed to be 'democratically' distributed among developing countries it is certainly the unsafe, inconvenient and uncomfortable conditions of the role of pedestrian. Pedestrians are treated as second-class citizens by current transport and traffic planning and the result of such treatment is indelibly imprinted on space.

The technology to support non-motorized transport such as the bicycle is also poorly developed. The problem becomes critical where motorized transport is being increasingly supported. NMVs are also affected by unfavourable regulation, especially taxes, import duties, fuel taxes, licensing and financing. Such regulations have been used in many places to either restrain or ban NMVs. Lack of integration facilities to public transport also deeply affects the convenience of using bicycles.

The technology to support buses – the most used public transport mode in developing countries – also does not exist. Vehicle technology is appallingly poor; most vehicles are old private cars, adapted trucks with benches or low-quality microbuses. Even large, standard diesel buses such as those used in Brazil are mostly adapted vehicles. Bus terminals barely deserve such a denomination, being physical points in space where vehicles and passengers try to find each other. Users have no information source on services other than their relatives and friends who have managed to find out routes and timetables, or small, handmade plates hanging on the windshields of trucks and microbuses that are supposed to provide public transport. High-quality priority treatment on roads is rare, confined to a few bus corridors implemented in some large cities.

The operational dimension

The operational dimension relates to the instability of the supply of public transport and to the irregularity of traffic conditions. Public transport is permanently subject to instability, due both to the market approach to the business and the never-ending struggle between fare levels and expected revenues. In addition, traffic management is highly skewed towards automobile traffic fluidity, paying little attention to the circulation needs of public transport users. Public agencies in charge of public transport have no monitoring systems and information on public transport performance is seen as a luxury. Conversely, efficient traffic management and monitoring techniques have already been developed to support automobile traffic and clearly ITS – intelligent transport systems – are included in the agenda of several large cities that intend to 'modernize' their traffic for the wellbeing of all.

The social dimension

The social dimension is the first to capture the results of prevailing urban, transport and traffic policies in developing countries. It reveals several inequities.

Accessibility inequity

The most radical statement concerning inequity in access was made by Illich (1974): energy and equity are strongly related and the increase in energy provided by motorized transport has a profound negative impact on equity. Social and economic differences are heightened when people become 'prisoners' of the transport industry. Mechanized transport allows people to increase their speed and hence expands the number of destinations which can be reached; it dramatically increases the consumption of both space and the facilities demanded. Considering the unequal distribution of circulation means, the ability to consume space is highly biased towards those with access to private transport. The 'radical monopoly of motorized transport' created a new form of inequity, giving the dominant classes another means of exercising power over space; accessibility became a scarce good, demanding the purchase of 'public transport kilometres' (Illich, 1974, p45).

Access time inequity

This concerns the differential time needed to get access to public transport means, as opposed to private motorized transport. The access time to public transport may be five to six times higher than the access time to automobiles, and this increases in peripheral areas.

Speed inequity

This refers to differential speeds while travelling on vehicles (fluidity conditions). In non-congested cities, the difference between cars and buses can be 200 per cent, with buses travelling at 20km/h and cars at 60km/h. In more congested cities – as in most large cities in contemporary developing countries – the mean speed of cars can still be double that of buses. Although part of the difference stems from the operational constraints of the bus, much comes from both automobile-related congestion and the inefficiency of bus operation, both related to disregard for the needs of the majority.

Comfort inequity

This relates mainly to the conditions of pavements for most pedestrians, the differential passenger density inside buses and automobiles, and the possibility of travelling seated. The actual conditions of public transport demonstrate that especially in peak-hours comfort is far from acceptable. Crowded buses and trains are a daily reality experienced by millions of people. Women, elderly, the disabled and children are especially harmed. This inequity is directly related to supply conditions – seats provided per hour – which is itself related to the overall operational costs.

Cost inequity

This relates to people having no affordable transport means to use under minimum safety and comfort conditions. Absolute expenses with transport increase with income, as higher-income families are more mobile and use faster or more expensive modes; however, low-income families expend a much higher share of their income on transport than higher-income ones.

Space appropriation inequity

This relates to different modes having highly distinct spatial consumption rates. On the one hand, most people use roads in the role of pedestrians, cyclists or public transport users and consume low quantities of space. Conversely, a few use roads in the role of auto drivers and consume several times more space per person. Therefore, while middle and upper sectors can actually consume the circulation structure efficiently (from their point of view) most people cannot, unless adequate pavements and convenient and affordable public transport are provided. Consequently, criticisms of public transport subsidies are illogical in the face of the externalities caused by private transport and the large subsidies provided to ensure its dominance.

The environmental dimension

The environmental dimension concerns the continued degradation of the urban quality of life. It is represented by high traffic accident rates, increasing pollution, disruption of urban space and the 'barrier effect'. It comprises two inequities. *Safety inequity* relates to differential risk exposures when using streets; the most vulnerable – pedestrians and cyclists – are the most affected. *Environmental inequity* relates to the fact that a few people produce most of the pollution, which will impact on all. Automobiles – and motorcycles – are responsible for most transport-related emissions. Historical and architectural heritages are destroyed, due to extensive road and transport infrastructure

Box 16.1 *The alliances sustaining inequity*

Several political alliances lie behind the implementation of urban transport policies in developing countries. Some of them are especially relevant because of the negative results they yield. They may be divided according to their internal or mixed nature. Internal alliances are those constructed around political and economic interests occurring inside the country. Mixed alliances are those occurring between internal and external interest groups. Five main alliances operating in developing countries to sustain inequity may be identified:

1   The *ideological* alliance, linking the elite, middle classes and state technocracy in devaluating and discrediting non-motorized and public transport and praising private transport.
2   The *technical* alliance, linking internal or foreign interest groups and the state technocracy, involving the use of questionable technical procedures to justify inadequate or unreasonable transport and traffic proposals.
3   The *technological* alliance, joining internal or foreign interest groups, local elite and the state, involving the regulation, purchase or use of inadequate or unnecessary transport equipment and means.
4   The *automobile* alliance, joining middle classes, the automotive industry and the state technocracy in promoting automobile-adapted spaces.
5   The *corporativist* alliance, joining some public agencies and their employees, in appropriating public resources for their benefit without public consent.

construction. The 'barrier effect' represents a pervasive, although disguised, impact, which has been affecting residential and living spaces, because of motorized traffic. Main consequences are the reduction in social interaction and in the use of public spaces and the need to define strategies for reducing the risk of accidents. Children and the elderly are especially affected.

THE MYTHS WHICH SUSTAINED TRADITIONAL INTERVENTION TECHNIQUES

The use of the aforementioned procedures and intervention techniques in developing countries – urban, transport and traffic planning – was based on pre-established assumptions which reflected the dominant thinking in developed countries. Several of these assumptions are debatable and some became accepted without discussion. Identifying these myths is therefore essential.

Some myths and counter-arguments

Myth

What happened in developed countries is always good for developing countries, and consequently the way developed countries have managed urban transport and their technical knowledge on the issue has to be imitated.

Counter-argument

Developed countries have gone through varying historical development processes, with different outcomes. Some are important for developing countries, others are not. Technical knowledge in the North is indeed highly developed, but it is based on its specific needs. Developing countries should therefore select what is to be used on the basis of their specific development processes and needs.

Myth

Investments in the social and economic reproduction of the elite and middle-class sectors are the most efficient because their effects are spread all over society and economy (the 'trickle-down' effect).

Counter-argument

The reality in developing countries contradicts this assumption. After decades of economic modernization, most developing countries present immoral social and economic differences between social groups and classes. The priority adaptation of urban space to the reproduction needs of the middle classes has given this inequitable process a physical expression, which limits or bans the enacting of roles by other social groups.

Myth

Urban, transport and traffic planning are rational, neutral methodologies which define optimal solutions for general wellbeing.

Counter-argument

These techniques are used by political human beings, with values and expectations, inside political environments where convergent, conflicting or contradictory interests cross each other. Only the dominant sectors have effective, permanent ways of influencing policy decisions. Therefore, neutrality is a myth, because decisions will distribute benefits and disbenefits unevenly. Furthermore, the idea that decisions promote general wellbeing is also illusory; decisions follow pressures and serve, also, the planner's interests.

Myth

Investments in streets and roads are self-justified, since they are collective resources whose benefits will be equally distributed.

Counter-argument

The actual distribution of roads between users will depend on their access to transport modes. People with access to private transport may use such infrastructure extensively while those relying on public transport or non-motorized means are denied the same use. Those using private transport consume much more space than those walking or using public transport. This myth is the main instrument for propagating current inequities, especially when used along with the rejection of public transport.

Myth

Public transport is a service like any other, and has to be paid for by those who use it to ensure economic equilibrium. Hence, transport services have to be operated at maximum efficiency, subsidies being a form of waste and social injustice.

Counter-argument

Public transport is a very special sort of service. It is vital for social and economic life. Transport infrastructure deeply affects urban development and economy. Attachment to strict economic efficiency leads to overcrowding and discomfort. The apparent 'inefficiency' of seated-only bus transport reflects in fact service quality and is much less harmful to society than road system inefficiency and automobile inefficiency. While subsidies to public transport systems are often termed wasteful, automobile subsidization via road construction, free parking and free externality causation is hardly acknowledged.[1]

Myth

Demand, as captured by technical surveys, reflects free consumer choices. The objective of transport planning is to respect such choices and provide the means to support them. Therefore, the increase in automobile use is both a free choice and a natural consequence of development, and should be supported by road construction and adaptation.

Counter-argument

The surveyed demand reveals only possible demand considering physical, social and economic conditions. This demand would be different if conditions were different. Therefore, increased automobile use, besides its utility, reflects the relative conditions of transport modes, which favour automobile use with several sorts of subsidies. Seeing increased automobile use as a free consumer choice is not just technically wrong but also environmentally and socially unfair and inadequate. Accordingly, automobile demand is not an outcome of 'progress', it is an outcome of the complex relationship between prevailing spatial and transport conditions and the reproduction needs of selected social sectors.[2]

Myth

Automobile-oriented space provides freedom and choice to society.

Counter-argument

Automobile space provides freedom and choice only for selected groups who have access to it, and reduces or denies freedom and choice to the majority who rely on walking, cycling and using public transport. It also disrupts social life. Along with the myth of road investment, it proposes that a future benefit will be obtained by everybody once economic development makes cars affordable to all, which is obviously a fantasy for most people in the developing world. In the extreme and increasingly common case of severe congestion, automobiles end up denying freedom even to their owners.

Myth

Social development requires increasing mobility, and it should be a transport planning objective to provide as much mobility as possible.

Counter-argument

Higher mobility does not necessarily represent better living conditions. What matters is the accessibility to desired destinations, which can be obtained with less movement, provided there is compatibility between the physical distribution of destinations and available transport means.

Myth

The right to circulate at will is a fundamental right and transport and traffic policies should never restrain it.

Counter-argument

The right to circulate refers to the person, and not to the vehicle. The mere possession of a vehicle does not entitle anybody to unlimited use of roads, since they are shared public assets, and their use may cause externalities that have to be controlled. Therefore, transport and traffic policies may restrain the circulation of any vehicle, conditioning it to collective needs.

Myth

Traffic accidents are the inevitable outcome of progress; in most cases, they occur because of people's irresponsible behaviour.

Counter-argument

Traffic accidents are caused by many factors related to people, vehicles and the road. However, the built environment in developing countries plays an essential part. This environment favours the occurrence of accidents, since it was organized to ensure comfort for the automobile driver, which enhances high speeds all over the space. Severe conflicts between motorized traffic and pedestrian traffic are a widespread phenomenon and are mostly impossible to solve in the existing travelling environment, leading to permanently high accident rates. New road construction and adaptation contribute to the situation.

Myth

Disrespect of formal traffic laws is a proof of people's ignorance and lack of civility.

Counter-argument

Disrespect derives from the absence of formal education for traffic and from the confusing travelling environment, which requires a special interpretation of traffic conflicts and the way the space can be negotiated. Deficient signing and illogical road and intersection geometry also lead to a defensive strategy to lower the probability of accidents (however ineffective). A special informal 'traffic culture' is developed, which coexists with the formal one.

Myth

Transport projects must be evaluated as private investments, using economic rates of return (ERR).

Counter-argument

ERR evaluations are controversial because they calculate benefits according to people's different salaries, transforming improvements for automobile users into highly attractive investments as compared to those directed at public transport users. They incorporate market-based wage differences which are incompatible to an equitable understanding of the use of public money. In addition, computations seldom consider in a proper way negative impacts such as accidents and pollution, the congestion inflicted by automobiles, and community severance caused by undue traffic.

Myth

Economic development increases equality. Therefore, road investments and incentives to the automobile industry are always very important.

Counter-argument

The experience of developing countries demonstrates that economic development seldom implies more equality. Development can be pursued while inequality remains unaltered, by benefiting selected sectors. Investment in road construction and new automobile factories does not necessarily lead to economic development or increased economic output, let alone improved income distribution.

TENDENCIES

If current conditions in developing countries are worrisome, which are the trends for the near future?

The profound economic and social changes fuelled by the globalization process tend to affect urban transport conditions in developing countries.

Capitalism itself passes through a profound restructuring, with the spatial and time reorganization of production processes (flexible production), the strengthening of capital vis-à-vis labour, the division and weakening of labour movements, the increase of the female work force and almost universal state intervention to deregulate markets and dismantle the welfare system (Castells, 1999). This reorganization has four main objectives: the capitalist logic of profit-seeking in capital–labour relations; to increase capital and labour productivity; to create a global production apparatus and market, using all available profit opportunities; and to ensure productivity gains and competitiveness inside local economies, often against welfare principles and the public interest.

This reorganization has been changing the geography of power, by creating new economic centres, dismantling traditional ones and generating 'black holes of human poverty', in both rich and poor areas (Castells, 1999, p24). It is highly dynamic and is also restrictive, creating exclusion areas. While Western Europe and North America were responsible for 50.7 per cent of global industry production in 1988, Africa, Latin America and the Middle East were responsible for just 4.7 per cent; it is clear now that the new economic world centre is being created in the Asian-Pacific region, with Japan as the main leader, China as the rapidly growing economy, and several newly industrialized economies, mainly South Korea, Singapore and Taiwan. Extreme poverty and deprivation will probably continue in several parts of the world, as part of an income concentration process and strict economic adjustment plans. The most problematic areas are those in Latin America and particularly Africa, where subhuman conditions will prevail in the near future, forming the 'fourth world' (Castells, 1999); 'one thing is clear: the relative conditions of black Africa, already not enviable, are prone to worsen even more' (Diaz Olvera et al, 1997, p121).

These powerful transformations will have profound impacts on demographic and social conditions. With increasing rural–urban migration, a large number of cities will be unable to accommodate growth and will face severe infrastructural and environmental problems. Urban physical changes will have definite impacts on transport demand, increasing the amount of trips and tending to greater congestion on public transport vehicles. The dependence on motorized transport means will seemingly increase in medium and large urban areas and accessibility inequities will worsen, as will social and ethnic segregation.

The increase in the informal job market and the feminization of labour may introduce important changes in people's use of time and also in household task division, with a direct impact on travel demand.

The political dimension also reveals worrisome tendencies. On the one hand, the 'delegative' democracies that have been replacing authoritarian regimes do not seem likely to become more representative in the foreseeable future. On the other hand, many developing countries continue to face disruption of their political systems because of internal conflicts or external forces. Therefore, true democratic representation of the conflicting interests surrounding transport and traffic policies does not seem likely in the near future. In addition, the restrictive educational system will continue to select those who have access to relevant positions in the state and in the private sector, therefore restricting the decision-making process to specific social sectors. Income concentration will generate additional middle classes, who will continue to have privileged access to policy decisions, which influence investments that ensure their social and economic reproduction. Consequently, as long as private motorized transport continues to be seen as vital for such reproduction, the construction of automobile-based spaces will continue to be fostered and the support for motorcycle use will increase. Although environmental concerns will play a vital role in limiting policy choices, the highway and automotive industry lobbies will exert increasing influence as neoliberalist ideology spreads throughout the developing world. Therefore, middle-class cities will continue to be organized and social movements tend to be fragmented, local and ephemeral, related mainly to basic cultural or religious identities. However, the strengthening of citizenship brought about by inherent economic conflicts may oppose such tendencies to some extent.

The ideological dimension is illustrated by an increasing anti-statism and a deteriorating public sector (O'Donnell, 1994). There is also an ideological conflict between the automobile-supporting ideology and increasing environmental concerns. Such concerns may limit the extent to which space may be adapted to the automobile and will exert increasing pressure on motorcycle use, especially in medium to large Asian towns. With public transport the conflict may be less severe, since neoliberal proposals have been succeeding in promoting privatization and deregulation in a once publicly controlled and regulated environment. The 'cycles' of transport supply may enter a phase in which private, deregulated (or lightly regulated) operation will dominate. However, the clear negative effects of such forms of supply may lead to reactions in the medium term, generating open, reactive and perhaps violent social movements in some cities.

The economic dimension will continue to be important because of the persistent fiscal crises of the state, which may worsen in the near future in several countries, as recently happened with Russia, Mexico and Thailand. The non-adherence of capitalist modernization to equity concerns will not change. Consequently, pressures against public investments will increase and reactions against all sorts of subsidies will be enhanced, further restraining the implementation of equitable urban transport policies. Poverty will persist for most of the population, limiting mobility and accessibility.

On the institutional side, efforts to organize technical agencies or to coordinate policies will be affected by pressures to dismantle existent public agencies and to lessen public planning capability. This tendency may be opposed in the specific case of large cities, where chaotic urban transport conditions are found to be hampering economic development and the interests of dominant groups. However, strong political conflicts are occurring in large metropolitan areas such as Bangkok, Mexico City and São Paulo.

The use of traditional techniques generated in developed countries resists change. Technocrats and politicians seem to be trapped in available methodologies, which are being propagated more easily now through advanced modelling and computing techniques. In addition, the symbolism of 'technical perfection' and 'scientific neutrality' seems difficult to overcome. This is strengthened still further by the closed decision-making process and the alliance between local expertise, local industry lobbies and foreign interests which will be fostered by globalization. Rapid social and economic changes and the lack of adequate data may persist for a long time in most places, making it difficult to analyse conditions. Increasing use of private motorized transport by the middle classes will reinforce the use of traffic management techniques to support space adaptation for their convenient use. However, the strong attachment to current practices may be affected by the increasing environmental and social concerns – including the gender issue – that have been forging alternative approaches and introducing additional variables to the planning exercise. Future practices may also be affected if the development of democracy and citizenship forces the state to open the decision-making process to alternative external participation.

The neglect of pedestrians and cyclists seems difficult to overcome in the near future, because of the deepness of the ideological prejudice against all non-motorized means, and also the deficiencies of the political representation process. A conflict with vehicle technology seems highly probable, related to the aforementioned increasing environmental concerns. It may to a certain extent counterbalance the aforementioned prejudice. While private motorization will increase, other, more environmentally friendly modes tend to be increasingly supported. This movement started in Asia ten years ago and is getting stronger, as more people and institutions support the proposals. Although this movement may affect public transport technology – in the form for instance of electric modes replacing private transport – a similar conflict between private and public transport seems less probable, since privatization and deregulation proposals have been succeeding in transferring the issue to the market sphere. Therefore, bus technology will probably be confined to poor-quality vehicles and facilities in the foreseeable future, should current practices and approaches remain. However, should democracy and citizenship develop in some countries, better public transport will be demanded; these movement will be stronger if poor people's income increases, because mobility will increase.

On the operational side, the supply of public transport may continue to be subject to instability, because of deregulation tendencies and a lack of investment. The aforementioned difficulty in organizing public agencies will negatively affect the organization of priority treatment for public transport and control of the quality of services.

In the social dimension, several interrelated tendencies may be expected.

Motorization is expected to increase in most countries. Major increases in auto ownership may be expected in large countries such as China, India and Brazil, and increases in motorcycle ownership may be expected throughout Asia. 'As incomes increase, the poorest people in countries like India and China will be able to own bicycles and those who own bicycles today may opt to buy motorcycles when they become richer' (Mohan and Twari, 1998, p31). In large Vietnamese cities, although bikes are still dominant, motorized two-wheeler transport may surpass them because of transport and fiscal policies (Cusset, 1997).

Following the recent increase in auto ownership, a higher portion of daily trips have been made by cars. In Latin America, auto trips between 1986 and

1990 increased from 17 per cent to 34 per cent in Buenos Aires and from 18 per cent to 21 per cent in Santiago (Figueroa, 1999). The same phenomenon may be expected in all countries where car ownership is on the increase.

Increased motorization is expected to lead to worse safety and environmental problems. With respect to safety, the occupation of the built environment by motorized vehicles without proper safety measures will lead to increased traffic accident figures. The impact will not be confined to fatal accidents but will also produce a much greater number of injured and disabled people. If we consider the estimated figure of 1 to 2 extra fatalities for each new 1000 cars (see Chapter 15), for every 1 million new cars we could expect from 1000 to 2000 extra fatalities, from 3000 to 6000 extra permanently disabled people, and from 15,000 to 30,000 extra injured people. If one imagines an increase of 10 million new cars per year in the developing world, the resulting accident figures are self-explanatory. Although the problem tends to be severe all over the developing world, large countries such as China, India and Brazil deserve attention for their prospective figures. The Chinese case may represent one of the most significant global problems of the future. It was estimated that the climbing fatality curve would peak at 180,000 fatalities per year, with 3.6 million injury accidents (Navin et al, 1994b, p53). Developing countries, in the words of Whitelegg (1997, p145), 'will also come to have the dubious distinction of sharing this most recent manifestation of freedom and economic progress from the world's car manufacturers'. However, increased traffic accidents and severance may fuel social movements to protect the quality of life, especially in residential areas violated by undue traffic.

With respect to congestion, the increase in auto use in major cities of the developing world is already causing a rapid increase in travel times. Increased congestion will foster reaction from automobile users, who will continue to exert both hidden and open pressures on traffic authorities to improve conditions.

Table 16.1 *Recent traffic speed decreases in major towns*

City	Period	Speed (km/h)	
		Before	After
Beijing (China)[1]	1980–1985	28.2	15.6
São Paulo (Brazil)[2]	1984–1997	28.2	19.3
Seoul (Korea)[3]	1980–1994	30.5	23.2
Shanghai (China)[4]	1985–1995	19.1	14
Warshaw (Poland)[5]	1988–1994	30	14–20

Notes and Sources: (1) Hayashi et al, 1998; ring roads, non-weighted average calculated by the author, using source data for each ring; (2) CMSP, 1998; evening peak, outbound direction; (3) Kim and Gallent, 1998; (4) Lu and YE, 1998; (5) Pucher and Lefèvre, 1996

As stressed before, most important for our purposes is that congestion has been having a major impact on bus operations. The attempt to improve bus speeds will face opposition in most places because it requires reclaiming scarce road space for buses, against automobile-based interests.

Increased motorization will also lead to increased pollution. The World Bank estimates that by 2010 CO_2 emissions will be five times higher than in

1986, with the main increases located in the former Soviet Union, China, centrally planned Asia and other developing countries (World Bank, 1996). Especially worrisome is the increase in automobile use in large countries such as China and India; should this reach a modest rate of 300 cars per 1000 population, the consequences for air pollution and space consumption are unsustainable (Whitelegg, 1993). Also disturbing is the expected increase in pollution from increased use of motorcycles because they are less environmentally friendly vehicles. The problem is expected to be very serious in Asia.

There has been some debate about how the information revolution will affect transport demand. For Castells 'there is no structural and systematic relationship between the diffusion of informational technologies and the overall change in the level of employment' (Castells, 1999, p284). Recent research suggests that the home-worker, contrary to initial beliefs, will not constitute a large proportion of the workforce. Most studies show that telecommunication 'substitutes for rather than stimulates trip making', making average daily distances decrease. However, most activities are not suited to home-working and many workers do not want to be out of the office (Cervero, 1999a). What seems to be more probable is the decentralization of the workplace, because regional offices working with computer networks may keep workers distributed in the space. New telecommunication services seem to be used to organize trips better rather than replacing them (Bieber et al, 1992). Also, internet shopping seems to be a complement to traditional shopping activities. Although it is important to analyse tendencies in the developing world, differences between them preclude any conclusive survey. In some countries with developed industry and a relatively large middle class, the telecommunication 'revolution' may cause a change in the daily travel pattern; however, in most developing countries significant changes are unlikely. What seems to be much more relevant is the change in the labour market – the size of the informal market, the feminization of labour – and income level and distribution.

These tendencies reveal that urban transport problems in the developing world may worsen significantly in a few years. Recalling the reasoning used previously, cities in the developing world may evolve from one type to another with severe social and environmental impacts. Increased motorization trends will be the main factor in these negative impacts, should the same political conditions and technical approaches prevail.

PART 4
PROPOSALS

17 POLICY ASSUMPTIONS AND PRINCIPLES

INTRODUCTION

The urban transport crisis faced by developing countries requires a radical change in the transport planning process. This change is the result of a long effort made by planners, scholars and organizations from both developing and developed countries to point out the drawbacks of traditional techniques and approaches. This movement has also being fuelled by the emergence and the strength of the environmental movement, which emphasizes new equity concerns. Finally, the globalization process has been placing further emphasis on the need to address international and North–South relationships, and the related equity issues. We are now in the middle of a process in which

> the critical mass of opinion and social change that has become evident in the last few years of the twentieth century ... [will produce] ... a new set of arrangements of space, time and energy and a new relationship between people and places. (Whitelegg, 1997, p5)

Such powerful movement towards change will face enormous obstacles, but the contradictions inherent in the new form of internationalized economic development carry the possibilities of generating the necessary conditions to support the reassessment of prevailing principles and the building of a more equitable urban space.

The 'critical mass' movement has also affected important players at the global level. The World Bank, who played an essential role in exporting traditional methodologies to the developing world, long ago recognized that new approaches were needed to deal with prevailing conditions in developing countries. In a document issued in 1975, the Bank acknowledged that the situation in the developing world was alarming in respect to transport and traffic conditions. It recommended that the main issue was to provide minimum accessibility to basic services, within limited resources. The report also advanced a proposal to decrease the need for transport by considering new transport–urban pattern relationships, along with broad objectives of the rational use of transport facilities and institutional/operational coordination. Later, other reports proposed alternative technical measures (Linn, 1983) and recognized the inappropriateness of using the traditional four-step modelling process in developing countries, suggesting its replacement with simple, adapted modelling procedures (Bayliss, 1992). This latter report followed others issued in several parts of the world, criticizing the traditional approaches as inadequate for use in the developing world (Dimitriou, 1992). This positive movement has recently been followed by documents adding new proposals, infused by neoliberal approaches to privatization and deregulation and structured according to three 'sustainability' objectives: economic and financial, environmental, and social (World Bank, 1996). These recent proposals represent, to a certain extent, a retroactive movement, which may lead to undesirable outcomes in developing countries if not properly evaluated.

The principles that support traditional techniques have to be replaced by others, better able to support new socially and environmentally sound transport policies. These changes are also necessary to ensure adequate decisions about the deregulation and privatization of transport services, which need to confront the central issues of equity and efficiency. In addition to these changes in the planning process, the organization of the travelling environment and the relationship between the state and the private sector in supplying urban transport have to be carefully analysed.

TRANSPORT, ECONOMIC DEVELOPMENT AND EQUITY

Public assets and transport

Transport is a vital component of any society. It ensures communication, integrates space and activities, induces or guides investments and urban development, and is an essential input to the economy. Transport relies on infrastructure availability. In developing countries, infrastructure is still deficient in most cases and suffers from critical, continuing problems of maintenance and repair. It is estimated that developing countries invest US$200 billion a year in new infrastructure and that many improvements have been generated, providing for instance better water and sanitation services (UN, 1994). However, average supply and access conditions are very poor for most. The most important investments are therefore those directed at improving the existing infrastructure. This implies choosing between alternative investments and hence deciding who is going to benefit.

The lack of investment or maintenance has profound negative impacts. It was estimated that US$12 billion spent on proper maintenance would have saved US$45 billion in road reconstruction in Africa in the 1980s (UN, 1994). In Latin America:

> *The maintenance of negative net investments rates in many areas of the public sector ... [caused] a severe deterioration of the public infrastructure ... particularly in health, education and transport. The deterioration of public services was followed by an immense waste of resources.* (Fanelli et al, 1994, p113)

With urban transport, the main infrastructure problems are related to pavements, roads, railways and subways, and terminal facilities.

Priority investments

Given the availability of scarce resources in developing countries and the equity issues related to the use of public money, a crucial decision concerns the placement of investments. This question separates into two more, concerning the social sectors deserving priority investment and the type of infrastructure that should be supported.

Discussions about which social sector to support first revolve around a decision between 'rich' and 'poor'. Traditional economics has long supported investment in wealthier sectors as the best way to ensure permanent development for all. Consequently, traditional transport economics has for long favoured investments on automotive-based spaces.

As stressed on several sections of the book, deep social and economic differences in developing countries translate into different access to transport modes and to space. Most people are transport deprived – hence socially deprived – in some way. Therefore, the priority social sector is that formed by the large number of poor people and not the wealthier sectors. The need to invest in the poorer sectors of society has ever been voiced but rarely accepted by dominant economic thinking, a challenge that becomes even more striking in the present neoliberal times. The reaction arises, on the one side, from several cases of clear misallocation of public resources, due to mismanagement or corruption. On the other side, it arises from deeply embedded economic beliefs related to the 'trickle-down' effect, when investments in the middle to upper income sectors are believed to diffuse down through strata of society, benefiting the poorer in the middle term. Such proposals are supported also by the use of aggregate statistics on growth, which masks inequity effects among social groups and ends up reinforcing the same trickle-down approach (Roqué, 1996). As stressed by Howe (1996, p10), 'the disappointing results of the past four decades has largely discredit such theory'. Indeed, average conditions in developing countries after decades of development put a philosophical and moral limit to such proposals.

As with the gender issue analysed in Chapter 13, poverty results from a complex association of factors that lie beyond the transport issue. However, transport conditions have a direct relationship to individual wealth, in a mutually reinforcing circle. Poverty may stop people from using transport and hence from having access to convenient destinations (the same may happen when transport is deficient). For example, poor children do not have the money to use buses to get to schools, and they remain poor because of a lack of education (among other factors). Therefore, the claim about transport having a major effect on poverty only in an indirect way – by increasing economic efficiency in the long term (World Bank, 1996) – is inaccurate. Although the solution to structural poverty lies beyond transport policy, adequate transport planning and provision may minimize or eliminate some of the crucial barriers faced by the poor or deprived. The key word is accessibility in its wider sense, ensuring that people have the opportunity to access space and services under safe, convenient and comfortable conditions.

As for the relation between transport investments and poverty, it should be remembered that transport is an essential element in ensuring the social and economic reproduction of all people. Furthermore, public transport is essential for most, because access to private transport is limited to the few. In addition to macro-economic and social functions, transport has an additional purpose: it is a vital asset for fuelling social and cultural life. To damage or restrain it may threaten the continuity of the social system and severely harm the very notion of citizenship and the sense of belonging to a community or society. The problem is especially serious with poor people; as described by Kane (1997) for Dakar, several spatial, economic and logistic constraints limit access to space and activities, mainly the social gathering that is so important to local culture. There is still a tense relation between such needs and production, which is reflected in the time spent on each one. In practice, the need to be selective restricts the space used to some areas, the others being unknown. Such limited conditions lead to frustration and impair important social and cultural activities.

When considering alternative, socially driven transport investments it is useful to compare them with the results of traditional forms of investments. Investing in the wealthier sectors has proved inequitable, environmentally harmful and dubiously efficient, however appealing affluent lifestyles may be. The organization of the automobile-based travelling environment and the recent making of middle-class cities demonstrate it very crudely. Space conformed to cars creates multitudes of access-deprived people, destroys space for human interactivity, causes death and injuries to many, implies high use of natural resources and energy, and severely damages the environment. When private motorization reaches a point where road capacity is unable to cope with demand, inequity, inefficiency and externality impacts become unbearable. Two questions naturally come out of the astonishingly irrational, congested environments of cities such as Bangkok and São Paulo: What for, and for whom? The result of the provision of more road space for cars, compatible with traditional approaches and consistently supported by dominant thinking, are frustrating, although the thinking remains extremely resistant to available evidence.

Therefore, the main proposal is to invest primarily in the poorer sectors and to do it now, to decrease inequalities immediately and not in a future that the market, supposedly, will take care of. In 1998, after four decades of economic 'development', 33 per cent of Brazilian people (50 million) still lived under the poverty line and among them, 40 per cent (21 million) lived under the line of extreme poverty (indigence). Although there is definitely a relationship between economic development and the possibility of reducing the number of poor people, the effect is very slow; in Brazil, it is estimated that a 3 per cent annual increase in the per capita income would produce a 1 per cent decrease in poverty, meaning that it would take 25 years of continuing growth at this pace to reduce the number of people under the poverty line from the current 33 per cent to 15 per cent (Paes de Barros et al, 2000). 'For neoclassical economists and technologists who believe that the trickle down philosophy simply must be given more time to work, one can respond only by stating that we have waited long enough' (Roqué, 1996, p190). This should not be seen as naive, although it is clear that powerful opposing forces have to be faced and strong political support has to be gathered to make it work. Further, priority investment in poor and deprived sectors must be followed by investments in other economic areas which are found to be relevant to the economy and society as a whole. As stressed by Draibe (1993, p44)

> *reduction of poverty is strategic for development in the sense of giving poor people access to economic activities and allowing them to participate in society in a more productive way.*

When devising practical actions, some essential clarifications must be stressed. First, the concept of poverty is relative and complex and varies in time and space; it has to be seen not only in terms of the quantity of money available but also in terms of the purchasing power. Second, poverty is not homogeneously distributed and differences between poor people preclude a general policy towards poverty and transport (Diaz Olvera et al, 1997). Third, differences between poverty and deprivation have to be clarified. While the former may be seen more in quantitative terms, relating to lack of material resources (including money), the latter is more qualitative and relates to a lack of access to economic opportunities, social services and interaction; that is why the concept of poverty generated in wealthy countries cannot be used in poor ones, because of the radically different conditions of urban infrastructure and accessibility, and the role of informal markets; in practice, the use of a narrower concept leads to an underestimation of the poverty phenomenon (Satterthwaite, 1995). Therefore, one should associate mobility impairment with poverty and accessibility impairment with deprivation.

Proposals must distinguish between needs related to the strict physical reproduction of people and needs related to ensuring social and economic relations (Diaz Olvera et al, 1997). Transport investments may affect both in different ways; subsidies to bus fares may improve mobility but they will be useless if there are no schools or jobs available or if the opening hours of public services are incompatible with people's work-constrained time schedule.

The decision to invest in poorer groups also raises concerns about the distributive policy consequences. The Pareto optimality rule is always called upon to justify care in investing public money. To follow the Pareto optimality rule – that no one should be worse off than he or she was before – assumes that the status quo should be maintained, which appears to treat everyone equally but is fundamentally conservative (Sheppard,1989). Therefore, developing countries should consider using public resources to invest in alternative social sectors. This may be accomplished by either transferring resources from road investments to the non-motorized or public transport areas, or reorganizing the use of road space in favour of the most numerous roles enacted in traffic. Both investments may harm some people – conflicting with the formal Pareto rule – but they must take place if we want to change our current conditions.

Decisions on investment should consider the overall effect on social sectors and on road users as well; the objective is to improve the efficiency of the transport means that are most important for the majority, including the road. There are two crucial infrastructural investment targets. First, pavements and pedestrian facilities, to ensure safe, convenient and comfortable walking. Second, the building or adaptation of roads in a way that ensures that space will be used primarily by the most numerous mechanized roles, cyclists and public transport passengers.

An additional target could be proposed: that of organizing the circulation structure to optimize overall efficiency, subject to the two aforementioned priorities.

The support of public transport

Support of public transport is clearly a priority target in developing countries. In addition to convenient supply, two forms of support are especially important here: subsidies, and physical and operational integration.

As a general principle, public transport operation should be financially self-sustaining through fares (coverage of infrastructure costs is a different issue). Most bus systems in developing countries survive on their own, while mass rail transit does not. When self-sustainability is not possible and services are considered essential, external resources have to be used. One possibility is subsidization. Subsidies are an important form of social investment and of intervention in the transport market. There are two sorts of subsidies. The first is direct, applied to the service or to users themselves: monetary subsidy, in the form of reduced fares, tax exemptions, low-interest loans, or the coverage of operational deficits. They can also be provided as 'cross'-subsidies, when adult riders pay for the deficit caused by cheaper student tickets, or short-distance riders support long-distance ones. They can also occur as structural subsidies, in the form of street and terminal building. The second form of subsidy is indirect, when competitive modes and services are penalized to protect a specific service.

If we take the social approaches proposed before, subsidization is justified for one single and clear reason: it provides minimum services to the most needy, who otherwise could not afford to pay for them in market-oriented transport operations. This includes the poor in general, women in particular situations, the elderly, students, disabled and geographically isolated people. Several implicit assumptions underlie subsidization: subsidies will not be used elsewhere (UNCHS, 1992); demand is elastic with respect to fares – that is, lower costs will increase patronage; the mode being subsidized is not less environmentally friendly than competing modes; and most of the new demand will come from less efficient modes, particularly the automobile (CEPAL, 1988). The first condition is very important, since subsidies received by the operators themselves can end up supporting inefficiency or private accumulation. Also, experience has demonstrated that some subsidies are ultimately appropriated by higher income levels, in terms of more trips, or longer trips; studies argue that sometimes very poor people can actually get only a small part of the subsidies.[1] The second condition holds because demand is elastic, although not very.[2] In addition, there is a limit beyond which fare reduction will no longer push up demand. The third condition generally holds because bus and rail transport are more environmentally friendly than automobile transport. The last assumption, however, has to be analysed taking a wider political approach. It assumes that subsidies are efficient when most of the transferred demand comes from automobiles, which are a less efficient mode. This condition is tailored to developed countries, where most may choose between private and public transport and planners are always trying to convince travellers to choose public transport or to keep using it. If we accept this condition, then all subsidized public transport in developing countries should be terminated at once. As analysed in Chapter 12 it is very difficult in prevailing conditions to promote trip transfers from private to public transport. But the main reason for this assumption being unreasonable is that the assumption itself is nonsensical in the developing world where there is no choice. If subsidies are to be seriously approached in developing countries, their prime objective must be to provide services to those whom the market would ignore. The attempt to attract automobile trips is a secondary objective (although relevant in some cases).

Critics of the public regulation of services often argue that privatization has one winner: the taxpayer, because the state no longer has to provide subsidies to maintain services. This is true in the case of subsidies related to overstaffing, managerial and operational inefficiency or revenue leakage – all unacceptable conditions already discussed in Chapter 11. But this is not true when subsidies are related to social needs considered relevant by society. One must also remember the huge subsidies provided to automobile users, even in low-income countries.

Subsidies have to be considered an *investment*, provided that they are explicitly targeted as a part of a specific programme, they actually reach the targeted groups, and they are not used to support inefficiency. In developing countries, this can represent the difference between life and death, or being integrated into the economic and social life. 'The alternative to poor subsidy policies is not a "no-subsidy policy" but rather a more efficient one' (Fanelli et al, 1994, p115). Public transport is a public issue, affecting several important social and economic dimensions in any society. It should not be primarily market-driven.

Conflict between these two approaches is inescapable. Recent attempts to reconcile them revealed again how intricate the issue is. The framework proposed by the World Bank (1996) to reorganize public transport in developing countries is a clear example. The proposal states that this endeavour should be subject to three sorts of sustainability: economic and financial, environmental, and social. Economic and financial sustainability refer to services being cost-effective and responsive to changes in demand, implying privatization and deregulation; environmental sustainability refers to decreasing threats to life and health, and to the environment; and social sustainability refers to increasing the poor's access to jobs, education and healthcare, reducing gender bias and improving non-motorized transport. The framework itself is difficult to sustain because social sustainability is not necessarily compatible with economic and financial sustainability. How to reconcile the need to provide access to jobs and opportunities for poor people with the need to ensure that public transport is cost-effective (and also safe and comfortable)?

Service integration is another way of supporting public transport. It may be provided in physical or financial forms. Physical integration entails the organization of a space in which passengers may change between different modes or services; financial integration is provided by creating combined tickets. The forms complement each other but may be provided separately. The issue of physical integration is of paramount importance for the social and political approach to urban transport because it challenges the myth that roads are equitable investments. As discussed before, although built with public resources roads are not consumed equitably or collectively. Unless car users pay the cost of this private appropriation of public resources, the only way of minimizing the inequity is to provide a widely integrated public transport system that mimics the spatial penetrability of private transport. This implies additional costs that have to be covered by society, subject to the aforementioned public control.

Non-motorized transport and the economy

When analysing urban transport in developing countries, an additional important social issue arises: that of the impact of transport policy decisions on the informal sector which relies on non-motorized transport services.

While the reasons for dealing with poverty are essentially humanistic and directed at reducing unacceptable inequalities, the reasons for treating the informal sector are also economic. Increases in motorization rates are threatening labour-intensive forms of transport which provide employment opportunities to people (Etherington and Simon, 1996; Williams 1998). Therefore,

> *focusing on the urban poor is important not only on humanitarian grounds, but also on economic ones because of the significant role played by the urban informal sector in the overall productivity of a city.* (Werna et al, 1996, p201)

This challenge, although difficult to face, is inescapable because of the historic, cultural and macro-economic constraints and the large number of people who rely on informal activities.

As with the aforementioned mutually excluding opposition between 'rich' and 'poor', another opposition – between 'formal' and 'informal' activities – permeates the debate. With urban transport, philosophical and practical concerns run through discussions on whether to support or ban the informal sector by allowing motorized transport to replace it. The principle of 'appropriate technology', based mainly on the ideas of Schumacher (1974), has prompted actions by transport experts and non-governmental groups concerned with equity issues in developing countries. The key proposal is to support local technologies and the large economic network that depends on them. From the point of view of justice and equity, these proposals are pertinent and correct. However, their short- and long-term impacts have to be better analysed.

The issue concerns comparing the macro-economic results of alternative transport policies. While non-motorized transport provides a large number of direct and indirect jobs, motorized transport is expected to push up overall productivity and may have diversified impacts on the economy as a whole. With employment, as pointed out by Reprogle (1992) for Bangladesh, although the motorized and non-motorized transport sectors had similar economic assets, the former employed about 90,000 people and the latter about 3 million people. With productivity, the higher average speeds provided by motorized transport have been argued to be beneficial. However, considering the trade-off between speed and spatial coverage – resulting in a seemingly constant travel-time budget throughout societies – higher speeds are 'needed' when longer distances are run, and longer distances are run when higher speeds are feasible. Therefore, increased average speeds are not necessarily 'better' and in fact generate several negative impacts, as sensibly pointed out by Illich (1974). With the overall economic impact on economy, there can be no denying the motor industry's large chaining effect; however the extent to which such impacts compensate for the loss of jobs in the existent informal economy is not clear.

The two more relevant practical cases for developing countries are, in order of overall impact, the replacement of non-motorized transport by buses (small or large) and the choice, within an already motorized public transport system, between large or small buses. With the former, the crucial problems are the large displacement of workers, the negative safety and environmental results that come out of motorization and higher speeds, and the need for extra resources to pay for oil (and parts) imports. With the latter, the most relevant issues are related to employment, road-space consumption and traffic performance.

There is no single recipe for dealing with the variety of situations that may be found throughout the developing world. Overall impacts on employment, income generation and economic output have to be compared, along with broader social and environmental consequences. The most adequate decision probably lies in the middle, with changes in transport technology being analysed according to both their broader, long-term effects on economy and the short-term effects on society.

TRANSPORT, SUSTAINABILITY AND EQUITY

General approach

The definition of sustainability in the 'Brundtland Report', issued in 1987, lies in current development which does not compromise the ability of future generations to meet their needs. This definition has been criticised for its imprecision (Steensberg, 1997) and for not defining what is to be sustained: the natural system (environmental capital), human activities or economic growth. Ecological sustainability, social sustainability, economic sustainability and community sustainability have all sprung from it (Mitlin and Satterthwaite, 1996).

One problem with the definition concerns the word 'needs'. First, as Whitelegg (1997) points out, 'needs' have been reconstructed in consumer society to mean 'wants'; second, it is not possible to know now what future generations' needs will be, making it difficult to define a framework for action.

This reassessment of sustainability is also grounded in the experience of developed countries and the increasing concern about the need for significant changes in dealing with the developing world. Part of this criticism is based on a broader, holistic view of a global society. The pattern of development that was followed by the most wealthy countries is not ecologically sustainable, because it is based on the vision of development as high economic growth, with few concerns about redistribution and the impact of environmental costs on other people (Mitlin and Satterthwaite, 1996):

> *The resources consumed and greenhouse gases emitted to support even the cleanest of Northern cities are, on a per capita basis, far larger than those associated with the poorer cities of the South.* (McGranahan et al, 1996, p108)

In wealthy countries such as the US and Canada, as Wright recalls,

> *as long as petroleum can be kept readily available and at a low price, they have little incentive for change and little reason to perceive that US involvement in Middle Eastern crises as a consequence of their own lifestyle.* (1992, p162)

As pointed out by Whitelegg (1993), it is much easier to continue to live in the same way and wait for technological developments to provide society with clean cars than to lower the consumption of energy and goods:

> *Sustainability is a very convenient concept because it allows us to defer facing the unthinkable: that maybe we ought to consume less and shift consumption and wealth to third world countries reversing the traditional flow of benefits.* (p7)

High levels of consumption in wealthy countries are partly supported by the extensive use of natural resources from less developed nations, often leading to destruction of the environment; therefore, there is a huge 'ecological footprint' attached to such consumption patterns. This is the internationalization of externalities. Therefore, the word 'sustainability' is inadequate because some of the best examples of 'sustainability' are societies whose conditions we do not want to 'sustain' or replicate. An alternative definition proposes sustainable development as 'improving the quality of life while living within the carrying capacity of supporting systems' (Whitelegg, 1997). This concept offers a new agenda that implies at least three important decisions: to care for the Earth's health in the long term, to impose limits on human activities, and to accept that several features that surround the issue have an essentially social nature, rather than an economic one.

The case of developing countries

The intensification of global production and consumption will impose environmental burdens that threaten human health. Although developed countries are responsible for most current environmental problems,[3] uncontrolled development and increased motorization in the developing world – especially in large countries such as China, India, Brazil and Indonesia – may further increase local and global environmental problems.

The concentration on ecological sustainability, focusing either on sustaining the resource base or limiting human activities that disrupt global cycles, tends to ignore the poverty dimension of the problem (Mitlin and Satterthwaite, 1996). There are two different agendas: the 'green' agenda, linked to global problems such as global warming, ozone layer depletion, deforestation and exhaustion of non-renewable resources; and the 'brown' agenda, which deals with water and air pollution, lack of basic services and green areas, solid waste and poor housing (Ducci, 1996). Therefore, any sustainability agenda has to include another pattern of resource distribution. This critical thinking on development has come from questioning the aforementioned 'trickle-down' assumption and is also grounded on a different view of development and its impacts. Although very important for understanding current development inequities and for guiding developing countries in searching for alternative forms of development, such approach has to be complemented by broader, macro-economic views of what should be done to face poverty, deprivation and inequity. Development demands social changes, not 'sustainability in the sense of keeping them going continuously' (Mitlin and Satterthwaite, 1996, p27). Sustainable development in developing countries cannot be achieved until poverty and inequality are addressed.

What should we 'sustain' in developing countries?

To the aforementioned question about what is to be sustained, one should add a vital question for developing countries: We should provide sustainability for whom? If this question is not asked, we remain prisoners of a superficial, politically naive vision of the issue, as if everybody affected by environmental problems were equal and as if general sustainability targets such as 'economic sustainability' would be equally beneficial or relevant to all people. Automobile-based cities in wealthy countries such as the US are plainly sustainable from the point of view of car owners, provided enough road space and fuel are ensured. The new 'middle-class' cities being organized all over the developing world will provide the same conditions to new middle-class sectors should adequate inputs be secured; meanwhile, those relying on non-motorized and public transport modes will face unsustainable conditions. Therefore one has to ask whose sustainability has to be pursed, which implies digging inside every society and analysing the relative transport conditions faced by different social groups and classes.

What, then, should we sustain in developing countries, and for whom? First, we should sustain *life*, for everybody but mainly for those most at risk. Life is being directly threatened by two impacts of motorization: traffic accidents and pollution. As stressed in Chapter 14, pollution and accidents have been mentioned as transport-related externalities, but pollution has been receiving more attention, because of the strength of the environmental movement and of its relevance for the developed countries, who to a certain extent have already solved their traffic accident problems. For instance, Tolley and Turton (1995, p187) state that

> *environment problems in particular have become of central concern: indeed, one could make a strong case for arguing that they are the most critical issues facing cities in the twentieth century.*

Even comprehensive proposals to deal with developing countries' problems emphasize pollution and neglect safety: one of the four proposals made by the United Nations Habitat conference is 'human settlement development strategies that integrate transport, land-use planning and the environment to reduce emissions, shorten trip distances and reduce the overall demand for travel' (Williams, 1998).

However, seen as social problems, pollution and traffic accidents are very different in respect to their impacts and their relevance for developing countries. The first difference relates to their spatial occurrence. In metropolitan areas, as a rule, transport-related air pollution affects everybody, regardless of social and economic characteristics; traffic corridors are used daily by both public and private transport and polluted areas are also major employment and activity areas, shared by everybody.[4] In small or medium-sized cities however, the importance of the problem can be much reduced. As a result, most people are actually pollution-free. Conversely, traffic accidents are present throughout all the circulation environments, regardless of city size or the class of road.

The second difference relates to who is affected, and by whom. Both automobile pollution and accidents may be seen as class-based phenomena, in the sense that the few with access to cars or motorcycles cause damage to the majority who walk, or use bicycles or public transport means. However, the pollution also harms the driver who causes it, even if its effects may be softened by drivers being less exposed to traffic in some instances than pedestrians and transit riders. Conversely, the nature of traffic accidents in the developing world – most fatalities are pedestrians and cyclists – is a one-sided affair: the most vulnerable are the most harmed and few (if any) damage is inflicted on the car driver. Deficient traffic enforcement and legal procedures aggravate the problem, because unsafe and irresponsible driving are hardly punished.

The third difference relates to the social impacts. While vehicle pollution can theoretically affect anyone – especially those with respiratory diseases – research has shown that the increases in mortality associated with air pollution seem to affect mostly physically vulnerable people, especially elderly people with coronary or respiratory diseases (Saldiva, 1998). Conversely, traffic accidents affect all ages and are direct causes of death or injury.

The fourth difference refers to the different impacts expected in the future. Even considering that a rise in the number of automobiles is expected to occur in the developing world, the number of automobiles per person will still remain much lower than in wealthy nations. In addition, a large part of the population will live in small- to medium-sized towns. Finally, emission control programmes are increasingly being adopted in large cities. Consequently, the air pollution problem will still leave a large part of the population pollution-free in the foreseeable future and can be expected to have a reduced importance in large cities. Conversely, the increase in the number of vehicles, and especially automobiles, is expected to cause a large increase in traffic fatalities, and in injured and disabled people. Therefore, although both problems are relevant, traffic accidents are the most severe environmentally related impacts in the developing world. Traffic accidents are indeed a grave collective problem, with immediate, direct and long-lasting severe effects on millions of people. It deserves appropriate priority treatment. The acceptance that accidents are the major problem is the next step to be pursued, if actual changes are to be achieved.

Second, we should sustain *equitable life*. Equity is being directly threatened by transport-related inequities such as accessibility, comfort, space and energy consumption, and urban disruption and severance. Third, we should sustain the *physical environment*, which is being threatened by air pollution, noise and urban disruption. Fourth, we should sustain *natural resources*, such as land, water and energy sources. These are being threatened by the automobile-based space and the lifestyle that it supports.

To ensure that sustainability conditions are achieved, a profound reassessment of principles and a corresponding change in the organization of urban space and the travelling environment are required. As for planning, cities need integrated answers to the problems of unemployment, education, housing, culture and transportation, implying coordinated urban policies. They need to define new forms of political participation and reach compromises between the public and private sectors (Borja, 1996). As for transport, the agenda for sustainability should include, as priorities, reducing urban disruption, traffic severance, accidents, pollution and energy consumption. Such an agenda should result in practical actions like emphasizing accessibility rather than mobility and reducing the need to travel.

Policy constraints

When devising new approaches to support decisions, it is important to consider some policy constraints, to avoid proposing inadequate, unrealistic or inequitable policies. The main constraints are:

- deep social and economic political differences between social groups and classes, coupled with unemployment and under-employment, a pervasive informal market and poor citizenship;
- the highly conflicting nature of the use of streets and pavements, with a complex pattern of coexistence between pedestrians, vehicles and vendors;
- the political nature of transport and traffic policies and the political pressures that emanate from diverging interests, with highly unbalanced access to the decision-making process;

- the differentiating nature of capitalist development, physically expressed by spatial segregation and by social differences in use of transport means and space;
- the household as a basis for a social reproduction, influencing transport strategies and demand; and
- the increasing concern with environment and equity.

PRINCIPLES FOR TRANSPORT POLICIES IN DEVELOPING COUNTRIES

It is now possible to analyse principles underlying transport and traffic policies. Four principles are proposed: accountability, social progressiveness, equity and sustainability.

Accountability refers to the right to participate in policy decisions and to evaluate the results. It denies the supposed intellectual and technical superiority of experts, and democratizes access to decisions. Planners, bureaucrats and technocrats should have an ethical and formal obligation to open up the decision-making process to the whole society. This does not mean that all decisions, regardless of their nature, must be submitted to a vote by all concerned. Rather, it refers to the organization of open and fluid channels for communication and control, operated by democratically selected groups and agents. 'High energy methodologies', of which transport models are a prime example, are antithetical to participatory processes and should be put under public control (Healey, 1977). Those who have the power should be accountable. Moreover, an open decision-making process does not mean that technical skills and knowledge are useless and that politicians should take care of everything. The great challenge for new planners is to work on both sides, the technical and the political, and this requires a new understanding of their work.

The second principle is *social progressiveness*. This argues against both trickle-down theory and the surrender of planning to forecasting techniques used to reproduce current conditions. It proposes the detection of inequalities and inefficiencies in present transport and traffic systems – to design solutions to decrease or eliminate them in the present, rather than the hypothetical future – and that investments should be directed primarily to the most deprived social sectors. The central task is to detect and fill existing accessibility and equity gaps (Moseley et al, 1977). Forecasting techniques are not assumed to be conclusive instruments, used to generate supposedly scientific foundations that will justify vital decisions. Instead, the new principle requires planners to be more modest and to use short-term forecasting simply as a way of identifying approximate trends and 'ceilings' to the amplitude of the analysis. It also requires the use of simplified models adapted to local conditions (Willumsen, 1990). Thus, instead of asking how present trends can be accommodated in the future, the planner should concentrate on some fundamental initial questions: How was the present built environment organized? Who can use it and under what conditions? How can equity gaps be filled now?

The third principle is *equity*. It relates to the targeting of transport and traffic policies to ensure an equitable appropriation of space, from the standpoint of accessibility, safety and environmental protection. To better understand the issue, it is necessary to discuss the concept of equity and its relation to transport. Equity is a complex concept that bears several meanings. By equity I mean a situation in which people are granted satisfactory living conditions and opportunities in respect to socially accorded services (for instance education, health and access to the city), irrespective of their individual physical, economic, social, religious or ethnic characteristics. It is different from equality, which represents the mere equalization of a right. Equality occurs when equal coverage of bus services in a neighbourhood in terms of space and time is ensured or when an equal right to vote is granted to all. Conversely, equity implies the consideration of the specific characteristics of people. The spatial and temporal coverage of bus services may be equal but not equitable once individual differences among people – age, gender, income, physical conditions – may interfere in their ability to use such services; the formal right to vote may be violated should adequate transport means for the disabled and the poor not be provided. Therefore, inequitable conditions may end up denying access to formally 'equal' rights. An equitable condition is therefore superior to a formally equal one and the search for equity in transport is inevitably a difficult task for planners in developing countries, for both political and economic reasons.

This involves submitting the prevailing efficiency paradigm to equity requirements. This does not mean neglecting efficiency, but it does mean considering it differently; instead of asking what the most efficient way of ensuring the highest mobility is, we should ask about the most efficient way of ensuring the equitable appropriation of space.

The right to participate in activities implies a right to transport, seen as a means to certain ends. This right can be understood as pertaining to two major dimensions of contemporary life. First, it can be said to pertain to the sphere of social citizenship (Marshall, 1975) and the related rights to economic and social wellbeing; as Button stresses (1982, p55): 'Just as everyone in a civilised society is entitled to expect a certain standard of education, medical care etc, so they are entitled to enjoy a certain minimum standard of transport provision.' Second, it can be said to pertain to the world of capitalist economic relations. Most transport needs are generated and shaped by the dominance of capitalist relations of production, the physical separation between working and living, the promotion of a segregated space and the commodification of social relations, implying monetary payment for an increasing number of previously free services.

The political acceptance of the right to transport varies according to the characteristics of each society and its understanding of equity and welfare. As analysed in previous sections, this right has been permanently denied to most people in developing countries. It is not just physical displacement per se that is often denied but also, and as importantly, *equitable* displacement, ie displacement that ensures adequate access to necessary activities.

Welfare analysis implies considering different approaches to the concept of the welfare state. The extensive debate on the issue will not be replicated here; I will use instead an interesting comprehensive classification provided by Furniss and Tilton (1977). The classification identifies three sort of states: positive, social security and welfare. Positive states are based on liberal political theory and limit public intervention to the minimum needed to ensure economic efficiency and to protect individuals from market failures. They reject totally the right to transport, unless emergency conditions appear (war, energy shortage). Social security states are also based on liberal political theory but they accept public intervention to ensure minimum conditions to selected services; the right to transport is accepted in a limited sense, which places clear limits for instance on subsidization. Welfare states see social wellbeing in selected areas as more important than economic efficiency; accordingly, the right to transport is accepted, whatever the costs (although efficiency is not disregarded at all). When the period 1945–1989 is scrutinized, one may identify different types of states around the world. While Reagan's US and Thatcher's UK may be seen as positive states, other European countries may be seen as having either social security or welfare states. In the developing world, conditions are highly variable. Excluding the large number of countries that cannot be said to have organized states at all because of extreme poverty or political disruption, most of the remaining may be seen as social security states, because few have the resources or political institutions to support a welfare state. Recent privatization and deregulation tendencies have been pressing many countries in the developing world towards 'positive' states, in which state support is directed to ensure productivity gains and competitiveness.

Accordingly, the discussion of the right to transport implies the discussion of the access to transport services. The first approach, within the liberal perspective, is that of limiting access to solvent demand. This approach is at the centre of all recent proposals of transport privatization and deregulation. The second approach postulates that transport conditions should be equally distributed. This is just apparently equal, because it conveniently hides deep exclusion impacts, as with the myth of roads as democratic investments of public resources. Further, this approach does not consider using transport investments to change inequitable accessibility conditions. The third approach is that of access according to needs. This is closer to the concept of equity but it raises important questions about what is a 'need', and to what extent unsatisfied needs should be attended to. Answering these questions requires a careful analysis of transport demand, identifying both manifested and suppressed demand. Considering these three approaches, corresponding paradigms for public intervention in the transport sector may be devised (Dunn, 1981). First, the laissez-faire paradigm, associated with the positive state; this works only with the solvent demand, and is left to the market. Second, the regulatory paradigm, associated with the social security state, works with both manifested and suppressed demands and defines rules for allocating public resources in specific cases. Third, the interventionist paradigm, associated with the welfare state, works with both demands and organizes a comprehensive intervention plan.

The most important consideration at the highest policy level is that the prevailing market paradigm, which leaves all decisions to the market as a superior tool for allocating resources, must be replaced by a social paradigm, in which transport is an essential tool for ensuring the right to access and the achievement of broader social goals (Dunn, 1981). In more general terms, the prevailing efficiency paradigm is to be replaced by an equity paradigm, as a consequence of an ideological commitment to reducing social problems (Healey, 1977). The proposal does not imply neglecting efficiency but rather approaching it from a different perspective. Hence, policies should not limit proposals to manifested demand but should instead investigate the suppressed demand and also differences in accessibility. Both normative views of accessibility (minimum levels) and comparative views (differential accessibility) may be followed. Although no rigid patterns are suggested, it is possible to postulate that some minimum, general accessibility conditions may already be devised for developing countries. These include access to work, school and medical services; also, maximum desirable travel times and family expenses, and minimum comfort conditions.

Obviously, the extent to which suppressed demand, inequalities and inequities will be addressed will vary according to economic conditions and political arrangements within each developing country. Those with very low income levels and few economic resources will face larger difficulties than those with higher economic and technological resources.

Table 17.1 *Approaches to the right to transport*

Political approach	Underlying paradigm	How transport supply is seen	Demand that is considered	Impacts
Liberal	Free market; laissez-faire	Only if payment of all costs is ensured by users	Manifested	Limited spatial accessibility; services limited to solvent demand; exclusion of large sectors; emphasis on economic efficiency
Social security	Regulation and definition of minimum conditions	When payment of costs is ensured by users and also with few selected subsidies	Manifested and part of suppressed	Higher accessibility; partial exclusion of users; higher average costs
Welfare State	Intervention to ensure social objectives	Subject to payment but considering users' economic capability and constraints	Manifested and most of suppressed	Enlarged spatial accessibility; small or null exclusion of users; higher overall cost; emphasis on social efficiency

As for the circulation system, it is seen as a collective asset to be shared by all. No one has the right to circulate at will, regardless of others' needs and interests.

Misuse of collective space was made possible by automobile-oriented policies and is unprecedented in human history (Illich, 1974). Mere possession of a vehicle entitles a person to occupy far more space and to threaten others' lives almost without punishment.[5] The circulation structure should prioritize the most numerous and vulnerable roles, which in developing countries are indisputably the pedestrian, the cyclist and the public transport passenger. This need not entail eliminating private transport, but will require submitting it to others' needs and interests. The alternative proposal does not presuppose an immobile society, but a society in which the required mobility can be achieved safely and conveniently by all, rather than just by selected groups. Moreover, the mere provision of circulation infrastructure does not mean that it can be used collectively. The long distances in ever-larger cities make it impossible to use this infrastructure by walking. Thus, if collective motorized means are not provided at affordable prices, with highly integrated modes and services, streets end up being just private means of consumption for those who have access to automobiles or motorcycles.

Box 17. 1 *Sorry, the market did not agree with your public transport proposal*

The myth of roads as equitable and democratic investments is powerful in supporting the reproduction of inequities. However, to be completely successful, it has to be managed alongside the attribution of responsibility for public transport to the market. In addition to the two most important theories about the demise of public transport in the US – the 'conspiracy' theory (automotive industries buying street-car companies to close them afterwards) and the 'consumer sovereignty' theory (the automobile as a superior good, selected by a free and enlightened consumer to replace public transport as an inferior good) – a third explanation, less quoted, has much to offer to developing countries. It explains how the myth of road investments as promoting the wellbeing of all was used in the US to support the largest road investment in human history (Barrett, 1983), while public transport was left to market forces. Transport planners in developing countries have been proving good pupils. The conservative city government in São Paulo applied between 1994 and 1997 US$2 billion to build new expressways and tunnels, for the "wellbeing" of all (12.5 per cent of the four-year total budget). One of the major undertakings was a 2km tunnel under Ibirapuera Park, costing US$300 million and serving 60,000 auto users per day (see Box 19.1). The irony surrounding the venture is that at the same time the city bus-corridor plan, that would benefit 600,000 people at the same cost as the tunnel, was given to the market to solve. Private transport operators did not agree to give private properties as warranties for loans, banks refused to lend money, and the corridors are still not built. The market did not agree and we will have to wait for another chance. But don't worry, public money was judiciously used and the tunnel is already there for the wellbeing of all of us.

Another proposal relates to safe circulation as a right. It is difficult to advocate this principle, given its obviousness. But it is worth emphasizing because built environments in developing countries, far from ensuring this right, are on the contrary natural producers of accidents. Thus the crude view of accidents as the 'inevitable costs of development' must be firmly rejected. The same rejection applies to the blind importing of methodologies and assumptions from industrialized countries, where conditions are very different. The technologies developed in these countries were very effective in dealing with post-war accident problems and can be considered when organizing policies for developing countries. However, the use of these technologies must be submitted to an analysis of actual conditions in the developing world, thus ultimately defining the path to follow. The clearest example is the over-weighting of human factors as causes of accidents, in accordance with the experience of industrialized countries, whereas the built environment in developing countries is itself highly accident-prone.

Environmental quality must also to be seen as a right. Environmental quality refers both to an accident-controlled space and to acceptable levels of noise, air pollution, urban disruption and traffic severance. These reflect the conditions faced by both mobile roles (pedestrian, passenger, driver) and immobile roles (resident, worker), meaning that the space for living, working and circulating should be environmentally friendly. This implies that efficiency must be subjected to safety and environmental needs and that living spaces should be free from undue environmental disturbances.

The fourth principle is *sustainability*. This is the only principle focused on the future, as a guide to generating sustainable conditions for society. In practical terms, it means that instead of searching for the modes of highest efficiency regardless of their environmental impacts, it is necessary to ask what is the most environmentally sound and sustainable way of ensuring an equitable and safe appropriation of space. This principle does not neglect efficiency, but instead of dealing with limited technological efficiency, it embodies the broader notion of social efficiency by representing the levels of technical efficiency within which broad social and democratically determined objectives are being achieved.

The equity and sustainability principles can then be translated into a final single question: What is the most efficient, environmentally sound and sustainable way of ensuring an equitable appropriation of space? This question carries a positive answer to Hagerstrand's (1987) question, mentioned earlier, about the possibility of restoring equality (and equity).

Answering this basic question has a very important political meaning for developing countries. It indicates that it is not sufficient to search for environmentally sound and sustainable means of transport, because equity is the prime goal. It is better to have an equitable and environmentally unfriendly space than an environmentally friendly but inequitable space. While the former can in the short term lead to a change of course to ensure sustainability – as political power is more democratically distributed – the latter can be 'frozen' in an unequal situation with few opportunities for change. This is the current situation in some developing countries that have been pursuing automobile emission controls as a priority, while most of the people remain subject to fatal traffic accidents and poor transport conditions. The same can be said of policies that provide hidden subsidies to private transport while labelling public transport subsidies as unacceptable. In practical terms, a policy to ensure equity of access and safety in developing countries, coupled with restrictions on automobile use, is far more consistent and politically valuable. Developing-country planners should be aware of not falling into the traps laid by traditional approaches. The improvements in people's life in developing countries should not made to depend on biased policies, but should instead be promoted inside a broader sustainability framework, based on equity principles.

Table 17.2 *Proposed principles and related questions*

Principle	Traditional question	Proposed question
Accountability	Which are the best technical tools to support transport and traffic policies?	Which are the most democratic ways of using technical tools to support transport and traffic policies?
Social progressiveness	How may transport demand tendencies be provided for in the future?	How were urban and travelling environments built; who may use them and under which conditions; and how can equity gaps be filled now?
Equity	Which is the most efficient way of ensuring the highest mobility?	Which is the most efficient way of ensuring the equitable appropriation of space?
Sustainability	Which are the technological alternatives to ensure the highest mobility?	Which are the most efficient, environmentally sound and sustainable means of ensuring the equitable appropriation of space?

18 Proposals for Urban Planning

Proposals for urban transport policies in developing countries will be depicted according to the three broad intervention techniques analysed in Chapter 8 – urban planning, transport planning and traffic planning – and considering the principles suggested in Chapter 17 – accountability, social progressiveness, equity and sustainability. Before specific proposals are summarized, a tentative typology of cities in developing countries will be proposed and comprehensive views of the planning process will be addressed.

The following discussion will face an important obstacle – the large variations in the characteristics and dimensions of cities in the developing world. It is neither sensible nor possible to try to outline an agenda that fits every situation. The objective is to provide a set of possible solutions whose final combination will be defined by those addressing the specific problems of their cities.

TYPOLOGY OF CITIES IN DEVELOPING COUNTRIES

The data presented in the preceding sections provide the basis for constructing an initial typology of cities in the developing world, in respect to transport characteristics.[1] This typology is important to better understand current and future conditions in such cities. The typology is based on two major characteristics: the public versus private nature of transport (the political classification), and the non-motorized versus motorized nature of transport (the environmental classification).

The political classification reveals how society uses available transport modes according to either a more publicly driven or an individualistically driven propensity. Societies may organize their travel needs using mostly public modes – most often buses and their variations – or, conversely, mostly individualized modes, such as bicycles, motorcycles or cars. The importance of this distinction relies on the impact on personal accessibility and comfort. The environmental classification reveals how actual transport use may be more or less environmentally friendly, in respect to space and energy consumption, safety, pollution, urban disruption and the barrier effect. Societies where non-motorized means are dominant are more environmentally friendly than those using more motorized means. The importance of this distinction relies on the impact on the use of public resources and on the production of externalities, which implies equity concerns.

There is some degree of interrelation between those two classifications, as well as internal differences. For instance, transport individualization may be environmentally friendly (bicycle) or unfriendly (motorcycles and cars). Motorization based on public transport has fewer pollution impacts and energy consumption per person than that based on motorcycles or automobiles. Motorization based on motorcycles is more dangerous for the user than that based on automobiles, but the opposite may be the case in respect to their relative impact on non-motorized transport (depending on traffic mix and speed distribution). Also, the size of the city and the pattern of the circulation structure may introduce additional differences; in large non-motorized cities accessibility may be deficient for some, and in cities with low road supply and a complex pattern of traffic conflicts, pollution and severance may be high. Four types of cities may be initially devised:

1   Non-motorized cities: cities where walking and bicycles are the dominant modes. Accessibility is usually high for most but comfort may be severely damaged. Implies low consumption of road space per person, low accident severity, no pollution impact and close-to-zero energy use; urban disruption, the barrier effect and traffic severance are often absent.
2   Lightly motorized cities: cities where lightly motorized means such as motorcycles and three-wheelers already play an important role. Accessibility is usually high for most but comfort may be low. Entails moderate consumption of road space per person, moderate to high accident severity (depending on the motorcycle–pedestrian conflict), moderate energy consumption and high pollution impact; urban disruption is low (less pressure on road expansion) but the barrier effect and traffic severance may be high.
3   Public-transport-motorized cities: cities where motorized means such as trucks, buses and minibuses already play a major role. Accessibility and comfort are usually low (depends on public transport time and spatial coverage and vehicle conditions). Implies low consumption of road space per person, moderate traffic accident severity (depending on average speeds and pattern of traffic conflicts) and middle to low energy consumption and pollution impacts per person; urban disruption may be high if road expansion is pursued, and the barrier effect and traffic severance may also be high.
4   Automobile-motorized cities: accessibility and comfort are usually high for car owners (except in congested cities) and low for others; entails high consumption of road space per person, high traffic accident severity, high energy consumption and high pollution impacts; urban disruption, the barrier effect and traffic severance are high and may in some cases reach unbearable levels.

A tentative joint classification is provided by Table 18.1. It refers to current, average conditions faced by people living in each type of city, rather than to idealized conditions. It must be emphasized that social impacts refer more specifically to conditions faced by individuals (internal impacts); environmental impacts refer to conditions produced by individuals using each transport mode and impacting on others (external impacts). Non-motorized cities have positive impacts on accessibility for most, but comfort levels may be low, because of the deficient infrastructure and poor traffic conditions for pedestrians and cyclists. Conversely, motorized cities where automobiles are dominant provide high accessibility and comfort for car owners. Although comprehensive conclusions may not be proposed, general tendencies may be identified in respect to modes. With social impacts, accessibility is high both for non-motorized and private modes and decreases for public transport, because of the manifest deficiencies in supply and operation; comfort is low for both non-motorized and public means and high for private means. With environmental impact, non-motorized and public modes have much lower impacts than private means.

Table 18.1 *Typology of cities in developing countries with respect to dominant transport modes and related impacts*

City type	Impact							
	Social (internal)				Environmental (external)			
	Access	Comfort	Safety	Use of space	Pollution	Energy	Disruption	Barrier
Non-motorized	P	N	P	P	P	P	P	P
Lightly motorized	P–I	I–N	P–I	P–I	I	I	I	I
Motorized (public)								
Non-motorized user	P–I	N	P	P	P	P	P	P
Public transport user	N	N	P–I	P	P–I	P	P–I	P–I
Motorized (private)								
Motorcycle user	P	P	N	I	N	I–N	I	I–N
Automobile user	P	P	I–N	N	N	N	N	N

P – positive impact; I – intermediate impact; N – negative impact

Based on such analyses, it is possible to propose a broad qualitative classification of cities in the developing world. Following Illich's approach (1974) it considers that the introduction of motorized means creates inequity and generates environmental damages. One may identify firstly two extremes:

1 Environmentally friendly and equitable: non-motorized cities.
2 Environmentally unfriendly and highly inequitable: automobile-motorized cities.

In between, we may find additional cases. For instance, both lightly motorized cities and highly motorized cities with public transport and trucks are environmentally unfriendly, to a degree that will vary with the actual impacts of motorized vehicles, which in turn will depend on the traffic mix and the vehicle emission patterns. For instance, extensive use of motorcycles may lead to high pollution levels as in some Asian cities, while a high use of medium-quality diesel buses may yield tolerable pollution levels, as in most Brazilian cities. Equity impacts may also differ: while motorization with public transport may be more equitable – in terms of space consumption, accident propensity and traffic severance – that with motorcycles (or with a large percentage of trucks) may be inequitable considering the same variables.

Main questions for developing countries

The fundamental question for the future of cities in developing countries is how to accommodate or drive growth to ensure higher social and economic equity and more equitable accessibility and transport conditions. With the former, solutions rely mostly beyond the transport agenda – income distribution, better housing, educational and health conditions – although transport policies and social policies interfere with each other. With the latter, urban, transport and traffic policies may be worked out to change current conditions and to help in achieving the objectives. In this respect, two practical transport problems may de identified:

1   How to deal with the transferring from non-motorized means to motorized ones, either public or private? With the former, the move towards using public transport may be seen as driven more by increasing travelling distances, related to spatial or land-use changes. With the latter, two possibilities appear: the move towards using motorcycles, a major policy issue in Asia and Africa and probably in Latin America in the near future, should the motorcycle industry succeed in easing access and use of vehicles with the help of governments; and the movement towards using automobiles, a process that has been happening in most developing countries.
2   How to deal with transferring from public transport to private modes, especially the automobile? This is a major issue in most medium to large cities of the developing world and is going to be increasingly pressing in the near future.

The relevance of the first question lies in the breaking of the 'motorization' threshold. Society moves from a low-speed, often integrated space to a high-speed space, with a increasing propensity to spatial and social disintegration. I will call this the first 'Illich threshold', when energy (and environmental) inequity is introduced for the first time within society. The relevance of the second question lies in the individualization of transport, when society moves from a public means to a private one. I will call this the second 'Illich threshold', when energy (and environmental) inequity is further enhanced.
    These questions logically give rise to others:

3   Should we transfer people using non-motorized means to buses and trains? This question pertains to non-motorized cities, mostly found in Asia and Africa; one of the most visible and pressing case is for instance that of Beijing.
4   How to promote a shift from individual motorized means to more environmentally friendly ones? The question divides into two others, relating

to transferring trips to non-motorized or to public transport means. This question pertains to all cities in the developing world.

5 Should we promote denser urban spaces to improve public transport efficiency or should we adapt it to urban sprawl, by offering alternative, new services? This question also pertains to all cities in the developing world.

The relevance of the third question relates to environmental and efficiency issues concerning mainly the relative overall use of energy and space of both transport models; equity issues concerning the relative individual use of energy and space are less important because both models – non-motorized and public – rank high in this respect. The relevance of the fourth question relates to all issues, comprising environmental and equity concerns, since differences between social classes or groups play a vital role. The relevance of the last question relates to overall equity, environmental and energy concerns but also to the debate on the supposed inevitability of urban sprawl and increasing car use with increasing wealth. As Newman and Kenworthy (1999) have stressed, there are no reasons to believe in such 'predestination', which is reinforced by the increasing concern about the environmental and energy negative impacts of urban sprawl; I would add that conditions in developing countries further limit such a tendency, since most will not have access to automobiles in the foreseeable future. However, as Cervero (1998a) has pointed out, there are important lessons to draw from the transit metropolis, which has adapted to market pressures in several ways in order to keep public transport systems alive. This is an important warning for those developing countries where higher relative incomes, coupled to deficient public transport services, have supported increased private motorization to a point that threatens equity and sustainability and the survival of public transport as a public service.

General challenges for cities may now be summarized. Non-motorized cities, where pedestrian and bicycles are dominant modes, have a special need to protect and enhance such modes, while minimizing the possible negative impacts of motorization. Lightly-motorized cities face the challenge of how to accommodate increasing motorcycle use or rather decrease it. Heavily public-transport-motorized cities face the challenge of improving accessibility and environmental conditions and avoiding transferring trips to private transport. Heavily automobile-motorized cities – better called 'automobile threatened cities' (Wright, 1992) – face an immense challenge, that of minimizing environmental and inequity conditions that become extreme.

It is important to emphasize when devising proposals that motorization per se should not be considered totally negative. It corresponds to technological developments embedded in society's changing path and may produce either positive or negative impacts, depending on how it is handled. The 'ideal city' (if such an idea may ever be conceptualized) is not that of a 'walking' city but instead that of a city where most people have equitable transport conditions and access to space and opportunities, in a sustainable way.

Proposals for dealing with current and future problems may now be analysed.

PLANNING PROCESS

Comprehensive views

As discussed in Chapter 9, drawbacks of traditional planning techniques became apparent in the 1970s and led to attempts to develop improved methodologies. Many authors have tried to summarize the new achievements and organize broad alternative frameworks. Two broad frameworks and a more restricted one will anchor the following discussions.

First, Dimitriou's (1990 and 1992) alternative framework, while largely based on the Indonesian case, is a relevant contribution to other developing countries. It follows an integrated approach to urban development, called integrated urban infrastructure development programming (IUIDP), as a tool for policy, planning and management. Five main objectives are proposed:[2] first, to generate 'developmentally effective' urban transport planning, combining national goals and local activities, implying planning transport as a support for urban development and not planning for urban transport alone; to improve the productive potential of cities and to provide for the basic needs of its inhabitants and for the absorption of migrants; to improve social life and the distribution of opportunities, by decreasing poverty and deprivation; to promote increased accessibility to, and responsiveness of, the public sector administration in urban affairs; and to improve the physical environment by promoting adaptative urban spatial arrangements, which can accommodate cultural and social identities and needs.

Crucial to the framework are parallel assumptions regarding accessibility, transport technology and modelling techniques. With accessibility, it is assumed that planning will work to accommodate the basic needs of the majority of the population, by improving access to work, school and recreational activities and hence decreasing the gap between the 'increasingly mobile affluent and the immobilized poor'. With transport technologies, the proposal stresses the need to better utilize available transport systems and idle resources before additional resources are called upon. It also emphasizes the need to use simple models for travel demand and forecasting, adapted to local conditions. Finally, the framework emphasizes the need to disaggregate goals and benefits according to targeted socio-economic groups and particular geographical areas; this implies that policies will not mechanically generate 'positive results for everybody', an assumption found in some traditional studies. These proposals break with several of the negative characteristics of traditional methodology and clear the way for more equitable and environmentally sound transport policies. However, an implicit criticism is that the IUIDP is suggested as a new framework that it is not intended to replace the existing planning activities, but rather support a dialogue with them: these must also change, otherwise the whole process will not yield the desired results.

A framework that may partially fill this gap is provided by May (1991), focused on a more practical metropolitan case. The starting point is the acknowledgement of the client's (city's) view of the city it aims to be in the future. Two basic questions are: What sort of city is desired? And: How can transport contribute to it? These are vital questions, for they imply collectively imagined scenarios (including the 'do-nothing' one) and the submission of transport policy to the achievement of broader goals, as in Dimitriou's proposals. Although based on the experience of UK cities, under different political, economic and social conditions, most suggestions can be generalized successfully.

The framework presents some problems. The first relates to the initial question: Who is entitled to define what type of city is desired? In long-established institutionalized democracies like the UK, various social groups and agents may be called upon to represent different views in a collective discussion. In addition, there are established and more open mechanisms of mediating decision-making processes. Both characteristics ensure more democratic results when compared to similar attempts in weak democracies like those of developing countries (whenever they exist). Hence, the use of the method in such countries will face weakly institutionalized democratic procedures, and rather concentrated decision-making processes. This may cause an initial major bias that will affect its final results. If no conditions are created to effectively open the decision-making process, outcomes will mainly represent the views of dominant sectors and again induce the reproduction of current conditions.

A second drawback relates also to the first question and refers to the implicit vagueness of the desired qualities for the city. Unless these qualities are defined more precisely, and disaggregated by target groups, virtually any broad policy will appear able to provide ways of achieving them. A third problem refers to how transport can contribute to the achievement of the desired qualities for the city's future. As stressed earlier in the book, the complex relationships between land-use, travel patterns and transport supply hinder rigid forecasting and modelling procedures. It is virtually impossible to accurately anticipate these relationships and their outcomes, making it difficult to justify the use of expensive intellectual efforts. Even May explicitly acknowledges the uncertainties that have to be faced when forecasting land-use, population, and demand, and states that even transport supply is uncertain. Moreover, complementary suggestions to improve the traditional UTPS procedures further complicates the achievement of sound proposals, because they legitimize a process that has been proven inappropriate even in developed countries. While the proposals to change the decision-making environment, to replace the traditional question (What is the best mode to replicate the same city?) by a more socially consistent one (What city is desired?), and to disaggregate objectives and impacts according to targeted groups, are indeed important contributions, the continued reliance on forecasting and modelling exercises weakens the overall proposal by submitting outputs to an hypothesized and unaccountable future.

Another proposal was advanced by Wright (1992), focused on infrastructure and service selection. After examining the relevant features of the urban setting, existent transport systems and its users in respect to apparent deficiencies, the method should search for alternatives that provide better transport characteristics[3] and that are within the financial limitations of the public sector and transport users. After checking for coherence, the method has to search for less expensive ways of providing similar performance. The final decision is taken by the public authority, which chooses between the technically appropriate options. This proposal has the advantages of avoiding unreliable forecasting exercises and the mere reproduction of present conditions, and of working to 'fill the gaps' in the short term, considering financial constraints; however, it does not define how public authority will choose between the options, leaving space for traditional, closed decision-making exercises.

From the aforementioned proposals and analyses some initial conclusions may be drawn. The central objective of a comprehensive planning process has to be to generate decisions to provide equitable transport conditions and spatial accessibility and to organize space and transport systems for sustainability. Technically, this implies planning transport and traffic as a support for urban development and not planning for urban transport or traffic alone. Politically, it implies the refusal to submit urban growth to market forces, the abandonment of long-term forecasting exercises as constraints to policy decisions and the rejection of the trickle-down assumption; investing in improving equity and attending to the needs of the majority of people are the priority objectives instead. The proposal implies that planning has to interfere with market forces when needed, to control externalities and avoid the generation and reproduction of inequities. In addition to equity reasons, this proposal has macro-economic and environmental objectives, related to the efficiency of the urban economy and its sustainability as a human habitat. A consequent need is that transport planning has to be compatible with urban and traffic planning. This may be ensured either at the technical level – by assuring connected proceedings and methodologies – or at the institutional level, by joining corresponding agencies and expertise. Each city or region has to find its specific way of facing the challenge.

The institutional challenge

As stressed in Chapter 8, one of the most serious problems in developing countries is uncoordinated policy, affecting urban, transport and traffic issues. The challenge has to be confronted in steps by separating small, medium and large cities, and metropolitan areas. In small to medium-sized cities, policy coordination may be achieved by defining one single public agency to deal with urban, transport and traffic issues. In large cities, separate departments for each area may be operationally necessary, but this division should not hinder a comprehensive approach to the urban problem. Care must be taken also in respect to a very unfavourable situation, in which traffic experts are granted too much power, restricting public action to limited traffic-related objectives such as traffic fluidity; this is especially dangerous in middle-class-dominated cities. Key to achieving success is systematic training on both the social and technical aspects of related policies. Difficulties may also emerge from local financial or technical restrictions; city consortiums may be an alternative, by defining resources to be shared by all, such as planning tools, specialized personnel, technical equipment and vehicles.

With metropolitan areas, the challenge is even greater, as clearly demonstrated by the aforementioned examples of Bangkok, Mexico City and São Paulo. The coexistence of multiple levels of power – federal, regional, local – and the strong power often attributed to mayors render negotiations around common policy issues very complicated. There is no single solution for such political conflict other than pressing for an open decision-making process and for broad forms of social control over public decisions. Western-type metropolitan arrangements such as those of Munich (Cervero, 1998a) are not transferable to most developing countries considering the widely different political culture. An indirect way of ensuring compatible policies is to involve all government levels in comprehensive planning efforts. The joint discussion of problems and objectives may create a positive environment for proposing common strategies.

Comprehensive planning proposal

Although no rigid framework may be suggested, one way of redirecting the planning process would be by organizing it according to the following steps:

- Planning agencies have to analyse the city as a built environment and must use expertise from several origins, blending social sciences and technical sciences; urban, transport and traffic planning have to be exercised jointly.
- The planning process has clearly to define the way society and organized groups will be included in the decision-making process.
- Technical and social data have to be gathered in a way that illustrates the social and economic life of the city, combining land-use and travel information; data have to reveal actual transport and traffic conditions of accessibility, safety, fluidity, comfort, environment and cost.
- All people involved with planning tasks, including social representatives, should evaluate current conditions and identify positive or negative conditions, which externalities are being generated, who is responsible and who is suffering their consequences.
- Two questions must them be asked: What city (or transport system) do we have? And: What city (or transport system) do we want to have in the short to medium-term? The desired future situation must be represented by quantitative and qualitative objectives related to the aforementioned transport and traffic conditions and the analysis of externalities; plausible scenarios may be drawn with the most relevant and discernible variables.
- Transport and traffic alternatives that support the idealized future situation are then evaluated; the analysis has to combine social, technical and economic characteristics and impacts, according to the aforementioned variables. Impacts have to be analysed considering the relevant roles (resident, pedestrian, cyclist, public transport user, car or motorcycle driver, truck driver) and their relative weight; with large projects, simple modelling techniques, adapted to local conditions, should be used to compare outputs among different proposals vis-à-vis the adopted scenarios.

- Selection of alternatives should be based on clearly defined social and economic objectives, on economic and financial feasibility (not precluding socially accorded subsidies) and on institutional capability to implement and monitor them; extreme care must be taken when placing monetary values on time (if it is considered necessary), by considering the equity-related impacts implied in using public resources.
- An implementation plan must be defined for the selected alternative, concerning legal support, institutional responsibility, investment flow, means of social control, intermediate evaluation procedures and impact assessment.

URBAN PLANNING ACTIONS

At the urban planning level, actions would have to pursue two objectives. First, with accessibility and equity, they would comprise the humanization of space and its reappropriation by the majority of people; key related actions are the redistribution of road space, support to non-motorized and public transport means, and the restraint of private transport, especially the automobile. Second, with environment and energy, they would involve decreasing average distances and reducing the use of motorized transport; key related actions are the change in land-use and density and again support to non-motorized and public means.

The search for both objectives would ultimately involve a profound physical transformation of existent space, requiring a high level of land-use control – which conflicts with the statutes of private property and a free land market – and the challenging of the preferential right to use space ascribed to car users, which may face strong opposition. These actions may be labelled 'structural' for they would generate, in the middle term, a change in travel patterns and hence in transport demand and supply (more practical measures are discussed ahead). Measures may be divided into two groups: urban development and urban renewal.

Urban development

The first level of measures involves interfering with the urban development process through land-use and fiscal regulation, targeting a medium-term transformation of space. The physical inheritance of cities poses considerable obstacles to such reorganization, both as a historical/cultural asset which cannot be affected and as a physical stock of buildings and infrastructure which cannot be altered at affordable cost. Hence, what seems to be feasible is to combine efficient, creative land-use rules in new development areas with a change in land-use rules in areas which are already facing transformations related to market forces.

With the former, public agencies are better able to interfere and impose conditions that ensure broad objectives are met. One important although difficult case is that of peripheral, low-income residential development, where private investments are driven by the low price of land, implying large and sometimes insurmountable problems in providing adequate public transport and other public services. With the latter, as cities in the developing world are permanently changing, there are several opportunities to submit these changes to new relationships between land-use and transport by creating special mechanisms to redirect development. In both cases, the guiding principle would be to organize the built environment to generate shorter distances and less dependence on motorized transport and, also very important, to avoid generating unsustainable conditions for non-motorized or public transport.

One special case is that of new traffic generators. Because transport demand is directly related to land-use and density, major constructions such as commercial centres, universities and industries may profoundly impact on the travelling environment and place unbearable pressures on existing transport infrastructure and services. The opening of such new facilities must be submitted to urban planning and transport agencies, to identify potential excess transport demand that will not be accommodated by the existing infrastructure, and to either impose changes on the project or charge investors for the additional costs transferred to society.

These efforts may be followed by parallel fiscal actions concerning vacant areas and the appropriation of benefits from transport infrastructure. Uncontrolled urban growth creates empty spaces that are often used for speculation. These spaces increase overall urban costs and preclude more efficient social uses. One of the objectives of planning has to be the definition of fiscal punishments for such areas or fiscal incentives for using them according to combined land-use and transport projects. In addition, land-value benefits arising from new transport infrastructure are not charged to the beneficiaries. Although international experience clearly demonstrates that are several obstacles to defining values and targeting payers (Nigriello, 1993), developing countries should face the problem by defining legal ways of reappropriating, as public funds, a part of the benefits generated.

Land-use restrictions and mandatory investments for new traffic generators may face opposition from several sectors, but urban changes may also be beneficial to some. Changes will face resistance from those with previous land-use rights, whose economic actions are dependent on the maintenance of the status quo. In addition, they will have to be negotiated inside the state, where conflicting interests will play a major role in defining practical limits. Despite these resistant forces, supporting forces will also be present, especially segments of the real state and construction sectors, along with financial capital, which will see investment opportunities in the new situation. Also the transport sector can be convinced to join the new built environment profitably.

Urban restructuring entails two essential decisions concerning land-use zoning and urban density. With land-use zoning, results are controversial. The experience of automobile-dominated societies such as the US, which has a rigid separation of urban functions by zoning, coupled to low-density suburbs and a high-density CBD, has led to extensive road building, high energy consumption and inequitable access. European experience is different, with much higher urban densities (Pucher and Lefévre, 1996; Bovy, 2000), favouring the use of non-motorized and public modes. In developing countries, part or even most of the urbanized area is formally illegal. Defining rigid land-use zoning is not only ineffective but also unrealistic in most cases. In addition, specific economic and social characteristics forge mixed uses that are highly adapted to the fabric of community life. In view of the larger objective of decreasing the need for motorized travel, to reinforce or induce mixed land-uses appears to be the most convenient policy. With density, the positive relationships between higher densities and higher use of public transport, and lower densities and high energy consumption, have been clearly demonstrated (Newman and Kenworthy, 1989 and 1999). Despite being mostly based in industrialized countries, the results clearly show that higher densities, coupled to car restriction measures, decrease energy consumption and increase the use of public transport, even in wealthy societies. Hence, denser urban spaces and automobile restraint techniques are clearly very important objectives for urban planning in developing countries. In addition to facilitating the use of public transport by middle-class sectors, denser cities lead to decreased public transport costs, because the patronage per unit of distance increases.[4]

Urban renewal

The second level of measures relates to spatially confined projects concerning urban renewal. Urban renewal occurs when public agencies and the private sector promote changes in deteriorated areas or in those areas where the travelling environment has collapsed (extreme congestion and inefficiency). Developing countries have plenty of opportunities for such investments but they require a complex bargaining process to overcome the opposition of land owners and to convince private partners to join the venture. Of special relevance here is the relationship between transport investments and growth. As stressed by Cervero (1998a) in analysing several large cities, there is evidence to suggest that public transport distributes rather than creates growth. Hence, urban renewal projects – and new public transport developments as well – require that urban investments are already committed to the generation of synergy and that the new transport infrastructure is delivered just prior to the upswing in urban growth. A particularly important example is that of depressed, formerly railway-served areas in large cities. The increase in motorization – both private and public – coupled to disinvestment in railways has created large, deteriorated areas along railway paths. Some of them are still vacant, because old industrial and retail buildings were abandoned. The renewal of such areas would require changes in land-use rules to attract new investments, to generate high-density occupation and a high-level transport demand, such as in the Japanese case (Cervero, 1998a). It would also require the revitalization of railway services to provide adequate quality. Such combined efforts would yield large social, economic and environmental benefits, fostering the reorganization of the built environment in fruitful ways.

Another form of urban renewal is the organization of car-free zones. The most common example is the pedestrianization of downtown areas, widely adopted all over the world. The restraint of cars frees the way for non-motorized roles, providing a reappropriation of the space that increases safety and comfort. It faces two operational problems. In the short term, these proposals tend to be successful, because some building owners and businessmen see them as a revitalizing change. Public opinion seems also to be in favour, as such areas are a civilized urban environment. In addition, as they are often well served with alternative transport modes – especially taxis, buses and subway – and as nearby private parking supply flourishes following the closing of the central area, most auto users find a way to accommodate the prevailing trips. However, the elimination of direct automobile access has often important middle-term impacts, changing the nature of activities, rent levels and land value. This is directly related to class conflicts and their physical expressions in the built environment, because spaces where automobiles are no longer allowed appear as spaces where higher income and also middle-class sectors are consequently 'not allowed'. Hence, many pedestrianized areas end up being 'poor people' areas and face later pressures to reopen to cars, as an attempt to invert the process and ultimately recover previous land values.

Box 18.1 *The rise and fall of a pedestrian area*

In São Paulo, a downtown pedestrian area was implemented in September 1976, in the middle of the oil crisis. Despite having to go through long negotiations with owners and businesses – most of central bank activities were held there, as well as the stock market and law-related activities – it was a large area, and was favoured by public opinion. The new conditions worked with little opposition until the end of the 1980s, when structural economic changes began to threaten its long-term survival. As a consequence of economic modernization, and the spatial specialization of the city, two other large business and service centres developed, attracting most new investments. In addition, the daily use of the pedestrian areas by mostly low-income workers – transferring from public transport modes or walking between their job location and shopping/eating places – generated land-use changes that adapted the supply of services to low-income demand. Hence, rents decreased steadily as a result of decreased capital interest, and land values also experienced sharp decreases. These changes forged the association of local businesses – among them important bank and financial activities – to propose a 'revitalization' plan, which included the reopening of a significant part of the streets to automobile access. Part of the renewal plan was accomplished but the two other competing centres seem to be increasing faster. Harvey's prophecy about capital having an inherent need to search for new accumulation spaces proved correct (Harvey, 1990).

TRANSPORT PLANNING PROCESS

Main suggestions to guide transport planning activities in developing countries are summarized below. They complement the proposals to guide the planning process depicted in Chapter 18.

- The decentralization of power, to allow regional and local governments to guide the process. While federal government should establish only national urban transport goals, regional and local governments should be entitled to define transport and traffic policies within their jurisdiction. This is in opposition to the tendency towards organizing large metropolitan agencies, a solution that appears attractive at first. However, although transport coordination is indeed important at the metropolitan level, it can be better ensured by strengthened local authorities. As long as local authorities have open and democratic decision-making processes, and have to discuss common issues at the metropolitan level, negotiations about metropolitan coordination will yield better results for society.
- The opening of all public agencies involved with transport planning to the inspection of society. Public accountability is irreplaceable as a democratizing tool and is urgently needed in developing countries, to control both the interference of dominant sectors in the state agenda, and planners' decisions. This requires a 're-empowerment' of society (Friedman, 1992), where political parties and social organizations will play a vital role. It also requires, as previously stressed, new behaviour from the planners themselves.[1]
- The replacement of traditional procedures organized to reproduce the present situation by new procedures and models capable of identifying and minimizing the existent accessibility and equity gaps. This effort will entail the analytical replacement of fixed categories such as 'cars' and 'passengers' by the roles played in traffic ('pedestrians', residents', 'drivers'). It also requires the analysis of time and space budgets, related to social, cultural and economic conditions of households, as a complement to individualized trips. It requires stopping the unrestricted transferral of models from industrialized countries and the developing of new simplified models, adapted to developing countries' conditions (Neto, 1990; Dimitriou, 1992). Forecasting exercises with a span greater than ten years

should be made just for speculations about possible long-term 'ceiling' limits; for spans up to ten years, forecasting should be carefully exercised along with plausible scenarios. These new models will have to include non-motorized and public transport modes as essential targets for planning, and should be much more operationally driven, constructed to better analyse how different operational schemes work (a curbside bus lane compared to a median bus lane). The corresponding change in the evaluation side would be the submission of the time-savings rationale to the accessibility–equity rationale, as a superior way of evaluation.

- The combination of transport and urban planning activities, to better control their interaction and generate travel exchanges less dependent on long distances and motorized transport. It requires both the reorganization of the set of agencies dealing with urban planning, transport planning and traffic management, and the generation of new university curricula, in which these fields would be addressed jointly. The objective is to prepare planners and engineers to be transport policy managers.

TRANSPORT MODES

The complex nature of transport and traffic systems in developing countries naturally raises the question of which modes should be used. The decision concerning the modal mix for a city depends on several social, economic, environmental and technological factors (Reprogle, 1994; Wright, 1992). Some important factors are the patterns of land use vis-à-vis the physical arrangement and the capacity of the road system, the technological profile of existent vehicles, the current and projected environmental impacts, and existing and expected investments in transport infrastructure and vehicles. This wide variation precludes rigid proposals and policies have to be tailored to specific conditions.

Vehicles have different characteristics concerning cost, capacity, fuel consumption, comfort and safety, which influence the user's choice and impact on the environment in different ways. If we follow the approach proposed by Wright (1992), transport modes present very different characteristics from the points of view of society and the user. While non-motorized modes (walking and cycling) display superior individual and social performances (energy efficiency, environmental impact and cost), public transport presents intermediate performances and private transport lower ones. These conclusions match with those of Chapter 18, concerning the average impact of different city types in developing countries. Vehicles also present large variations in their comparative performance and impacts: Wright adds that no mode gets perfect grades on all proposed attributes, as cycling may be too dangerous in some places, walking long distances is not reasonable, transit may be inflexible and the car may be highly polluting.

The capacity of different transport modes is better expressed by the number of people that can transported per hour, per length of road. Actual capacity also depends on the speed of the vehicle (TRB, 1985). Some general figures are provided in Table 19.1.

Table 19.1 *Transport mode carrying capacity (interrupted flow)*

Mode	Speed range (km/h)	Capacity range (pass/hr/meter)
Walkway	3–4	3609
Bicycle	10–16	1000–1750
Cycle – rickshaw	6–12	500–1500
Motorcycle (1 person)	15–40	500–1000
Car (1.5 person)	16–24	140–250
Minibus	10–25	500–1500
Regular Bus	10–25	1000–6000[1]
Tram	10–30	1000–6000

(1) Busways with vehicle overtaking and high performance operation
Source: Wright (1992) for walking and cars; author's computation for busways, based on Brazilian figures; Kitamura et al (1994) for the others, with approximate values, deduced from the graphics provided in the paper. Rounded figures in all cases

Figures demonstrate that walking has a very high performance and, with vehicles, public modes have far more capacity per road width than private motorized transport.

Walking

As stated by Wright (1992, p179):

> *to be able to walk in safety in one's surroundings is an elementary human right ... transport systems deny us that basic right ... the result is that we are all transformed to some degree into handicapped persons.*

This approach is so deeply embedded that it is able to make highly qualified experts construct road infrastructure without pavements.

The most profound change would have to came from a reappropriation of the circulation space in favour of the most numerous and vulnerable roles. Such reappropriation may be pursued through both incremental and radical strategies. In an incremental approach, several improvements may be provided by traffic management techniques, mainly minor physical adaptations, which do yield large benefits when the built environment is 'savage', as is the case in most developing countries. In a radical approach, the entire travelling environment would have to be changed. Some of the most important measures are:

- *The building of pavements.* Traditional transport and traffic planning has come to a point where 'network' is a word restricted to vehicle infrastructure, revealing the underlying principle that the motorized driver is the single 'productive' role in society. Unlike vehicle road capacity, literature on pavement capacity is almost null, which is not surprising at all. In developing countries, one should ask first where the walking network is and how it is functioning. Hence, the building of pavements is the first prime investment. Their construction on roads with important traffic flows should be a governmental responsibility. Pavements must avoid slippery conditions and must provide adequate capacity to ensure comfortable travelling conditions.

- *The use of road humps or the narrowing of intersection approaches* close to pedestrian areas, to control the speed of approaching vehicles and reduce the possibility and severity of accidents.
- *The lighting of pedestrian crossings*, to make pedestrians visible to drivers; this may be complemented by road humps.
- *The treatment of pedestrian needs at intersections.* Intersections are treated by conventional traffic engineering as vehicle conflicting points, hampering the road system's capacity. Attention has to be given to pedestrian needs.
- *The building of intermediate islands* in large crossings, to provide safe waiting spaces.

Such measures should also consider the needs of special pedestrians, like the disabled. This includes freeing pavements from excessive and dangerous obstacles, creating dropped kerbs at pedestrian crossings, installing special signs and audible and tactile signals for the visually impaired (ECMT, 1999).

Bicycles

For many people, bicycles are the only means of mechanized transport, because even low-priced or subsidized public transport may be cost-prohibitive for them. It is clear that cyclists have to be provided with adequate safety, comfort and efficient circulating conditions and have to be conveniently integrated into public transport.

Space organization to accommodate bicycles can be accomplished in varying ways, ranging from conventional signing to dedicated infrastructure such as bike paths or bikeways. Three typical situations may be devised. First, when bicycles constitute the majority of vehicles in the traffic stream. In such cases the basic role conflict is between pedestrians and cyclists, which does not imply severe negative impacts. Traffic organization is related more to efficiency, to improve comfort for both modes. Additional problems may occur if bicycle traffic exceeds road capacity, as in many Asian cities. The second situation occurs when bicycles are numerous but have to share road space with motorized traffic, such as in Beijing or Delhi. Conflicts are much more severe, implying high accident risks. In such cases the best proposal seems to be organizing a dedicated infrastructure for bicyclists, like those already existing in Chinese cities and those recently proposed in Delhi (IIT, 1999). While Chinese cities often provide plenty of space, finding adequate space may be difficult in other cities, raising conflicts over road appropriation by different motorized roles. The third situation occurs when bicycles are a minor part of traffic volume inside a motorized travelling environment. This is the most difficult to deal with, since space domination by motorized modes imposes political restrictions on the reorganization of the travelling environment. This is the case in most large cities with higher average incomes.

The recurrent attempt to draw on European experiences is tempting and provides insightful ideas. However, unless the profound cultural and political differences are acknowledged, conclusions will be misleading and proposals may be frustrated by reality. In most developed countries the role of cyclist (and pedestrian) is accepted as a part of citizenship, along with the corresponding right to use road space safely and comfortably; in developing countries actual conditions are very different. The same political prejudice attached to the role of pedestrian affects the role of cyclist in most places. Although in China the numerical dominance has given it a strong position to protect its needs, in most developing countries the role of cyclist is being threatened by the new motorized roles that are being enacted by those with higher incomes. Hence, to ensure separate spaces or dedicated infrastructure to cyclists is not an easy task and compares to similar problems with public transport.

Practical difficulties reveal the extent of the challenge. The complex traffic mix causes a myriad of conflicts. The implementation of bicycle priority measures has to be followed by proper enforcement, or people using motorized transport will violate the space or recapture the lost space. In any case, essential measures are the provision of adequate signing and pavement conditions, the treatment of conflicts at intersections and space integration through network arrangements, in the very same way as that proposed for public transport. With physical integration between bicycles and public transport, key aspects seem to be protection against theft and parking prices. Integration is especially important for short trips from 1km upwards, when walking starts to be less attractive.

Public transport

Regulation

As proposed in Chapter 11, the 'business' of public transport cannot be analysed taking a strict economic approach. The nature of the service and its broad urban, social and economic impacts require it to be seen as an essential public service, whose evaluation comprises diversified aspects. It follows that regulation and monitoring by the public sector is inescapable. A question remains about how to perform such public duties ensuring social and economic efficiency.

Public and private roles have to be defined according to the specific conditions of each particular situation. Historically closed markets that have entered the 'irresponsible cycle' may require flexible regulations, while more open markets that have entered the 'savage cycle' may require tougher regulation. High economic differences between the social strata, as well as low-density settlements may command special attention to ensure the provision of non-profitable services. In practice, regulation has to be defined considering several factors such as current transport conditions, existent transport means, average income of users as compared to average costs, institutional capability of the state, the level of organization of the private sector and its managerial capability. The key issue is how to ensure proper services by private operators, by creating mechanisms to foster quality and productivity, to avoid collusion and to limit congestion, accidents and air pollution.

There are basically three mechanisms. The first is the organization of geo-graphically defined areas, where operators with market exclusivity are responsible for all services, both the essential (mandatory) and the comple-mentary, defined according to market sensibility. The second is the auctioning of routes in areas of high demand, as suggested by Koprich (1994), as a way of replacing the undesired 'street competition' by the 'auctioning competi-tion'. The third is to contract out services which will be paid according to selected parameters, like distances run and/or passengers transported, pro-vided all the conditions previously mentioned still hold. In all cases only a strong public agency, capable of monitoring services, can avoid the pre-bid-ding counteractions from existent operators,[2] inefficiency and the adoption of irregular or illegal profit-seeking measures at the expense of service qual-ity and reliability. Also in all cases, subsidies may have to be considered.

The 'public responsibility' proposal has to be tempered by reality. Many cities in developing countries are so poor that society barely can afford to have a few, adapted, unsafe and uncomfortable vehicles. These particular condi-tions have led some scholars to pessimistic conclusions. While Cervero (1998a, p390) states that 'crowded and sometimes tattered vehicles are a necessary evil in the Third World paratransit marketplace in order to keep fares low', Gómez-Ibáñez and Meyer (1991, p21) put it more roughly by saying that

> in essence, the developed countries can afford the luxury of relying on publicly owned and heavily subsidised urban buses more easily than their less developed counterparts ... by contrast, the developing world, of ne-cessity, has had to be more imaginative and innovative.

To submit public transport to comprehensive public scrutiny in such de-prived social environments is unrealistic. However, the proposal remains a general guide, for when the economy allows better public transport means to be used and society manages to better organize itself through democratic representative public agencies. The proposal is based on the principle that if we want to change urban transport conditions in our countries, public transport has to be considered a public service and public control has to be seen as a superior form of guiding and protecting the public interest. The solution for incompetent or corrupted states is not the dismantling of the state but its reorganization according to democratic principles, under so-cial control. The 'virtuous' cycle (Figure 19.1) portrays the most important characteristics of the proposed form of public responsibility for public trans-port. After government and society have defined the desired characteristics of the service (spatial accessibility, technology, cost and comfort) and in-centives to productivity are outlined, the private sector is contracted to provide services and starts to be controlled by both public agencies and society representatives. Control leads to permanent reassessment and adap-tation of services to improve performance and ensure economic sustainability, subject to subsidies that are considered necessary.

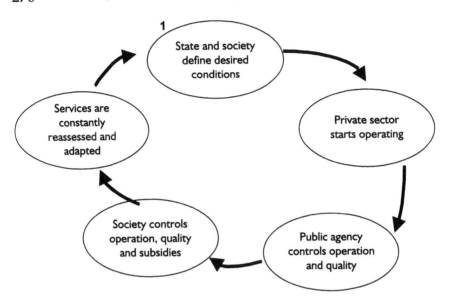

Figure 19.1 *The 'virtuous' public transport supply cycle*

Infrastructure supply

The change in public transport supply can be effected by connecting three main policies. First, it can be accomplished physically, by providing new infrastructure such as busways, terminals, connected bikeways and pedestrian areas. Second, it can be done operationally, by reorganizing spatial and time supplies of public transport services. Third, it can be performed economically, by developing a fare structure that would facilitate the use of the system and its connection to other transport means.

The search for the 'best' mode and the incentive to mode competition has to be replaced by the search for the best complementarity of modes (Proud'homme, 1990). Varying physical, historical and social conditions require the provision of varying transport networks. There is no single mode which could be considered ideal for any situation (Lindau, 1992). The differences in cost and performance of the various modes have been extensively analysed and will not be replicated here.[3] It is sufficient to emphasize that every mode has a role to play according to prevailing conditions and that there are broad 'validity areas' where a certain mode is superior to others.

The role of 'heavy' modes has to be carefully analysed. Major transport infrastructures such as suburban trains and subways have been suggested either as an improvement to transport quality and speed, or as a congestion-relief measure. The former is indeed true in most developing countries, especially regarding vehicle quality and service reliability, because available bus services are unsatisfactory. Consequently, the better image of subways is reflected in users' opinion.[4] However, speed cannot be counted as a prime advantage: subways run at average speeds of 30–35km/h, while properly operated busways can operate at 25km/h at much lower costs. In addition, door-to-door travel time can be high when walking and transfer times inside subway stations are taken into account. In respect to the second advantage, however, there is no evidence that subways have reduced congestion, for the released space was seemingly taken up by suppressed automobile demand (Fouracre and Gardner, 1994). Hence, new heavy transport modes may be considered important in large cities only when the use of lighter modes is already exhausted. This occurs only when a combination of high population density, long average distances and low road-reserve-capacity occurs, making it difficult to provide a good level of service through road public transport. In these cases, heavy systems can act as a reorganizing tool, leading to a broad rearrangement of the entire public transport supply.

Despite their importance in these circumstances, heavy modes are expensive, and they often involve urban disruption. Developing countries seldom have the required economic resources. Even if they are available and economic and social costs are tolerable, major transport systems require proper connections to feeder systems for their survival. Hence, there is a need for comprehensive planning, where every mode finds its proper space and where major systems serve as the 'spines' of a city-wide system. In developing countries, the opposite is very much the case. In fact, major transport systems are often planned and provided before the existent bus or rail systems are properly operated to their full capacity. The case of São Paulo is very clear: the subway system was superimposed over an already existent network of suburban trains and local and regional bus lines, which were kept operating at very low levels of service. Although being one of the most efficient metro systems in the word, the superimposition highlighted a technological gap between modern and obsolete systems that could be avoided by complementary investments in the other systems. It is important to emphasize that large transport systems always symbolize progress and are used by politicians and planners to justify high investments. To some extent, these images are shared by users, especially when alternative bus systems are inadequate. A 'lighter' form of rail transport is the LRT – light rail transit. It has been used in industrialized countries (Europe and North America) and is now being promoted in developing countries. Lindau (1992) makes a comprehensive summary of LRT characteristics, concluding that experiences so far reveal that no LRT has carried more passengers than bus-based operations, especially in the light of operational constraints. This is a very important conclusion for developing countries, which are more prepared to operate standard buses. Construction and operation costs vary remarkably according to the system, increasing with the carrying capacity and the need to build underground structures. While busways and LRT have kilometre costs in the US$2 to 7 million range, rail and subway costs range from US$50 to 100 million per kilometre (Armstrong-Wright, 1986). Average cost per passenger-km will vary with patronage and operation costs, but buses usually present lower average costs than rail.

With buses, the most promising form of mass transport is the busway, in the form of median bus lanes or exclusive tracks. Busways are more efficient than conventional bus lanes, yielding average speeds of around 20–25km/h, as opposed to 15km/h achieved with curbside lanes. They are able to carry up to 26,000 passengers per hour in each direction, as in the case of Porto

Alegre, Brazil; carrying capacities of 20,000 pass/hour are very common in some Brazilian cities (Lindau and Willumsen,1990; UNCHS, 1992; ANTP, 1998). However, busways present some operational and safety problems that have to be addressed. First, if not properly designed and operated, they will produce the same performance as curbside lanes. Moreover, badly planned busways can in fact worsen pedestrian safety conditions, due to the need to provide many crossings, which will be used in unsafe conditions. In addition, busways require a space seldom available in developing countries, except in newly occupied areas. In practical terms, the attempt to implement busways in narrow streets has been leading to the operation of a sub-optimal facility, frequently at the expense of pedestrian or vegetation space. Hence, best results can be achieved only when large streets exist, provided that conflicts with local traffic are properly handled to the benefit of bus users. This was the case in Curitiba, Brazil, where the first comprehensive busway network was implemented in the 1970s. The existent street system allowed the inclusion of busways with few impacts on traffic fluidity and with a proper adjustment for pedestrian safety.

In addition to these problems, busways face other challenges related to their specific physical and operational arrangements. Busways represent the reorganization of bus supply into 'transport corridors', as 'trunk' lines operated by larger buses are supported by feeder bus lines. It has a fundamental 'rational' appeal. The rationale for trunk operation lies in some clear advantages (Szasz, 1985). It makes supply and demand compatible along the corridor, reducing costs in respect to free operation; it allows the use of larger and more energy-efficient buses; it decreases the need for bus stop spaces downtown, a severe constraint in many cities; when demand is high, it is possible to break down supply according to specific OD patterns, with high gains in travel time for certain groups. However, as Szasz acknowledges, trunk line operation presents some drawbacks. First, from the user's point of view, the best transport is door-to-door transport and most users dislike transferring between buses: in Curitiba, approximately two-thirds of the then existent bus lines had their routes changed and were connected to terminals located on the new trunk lines. The feeder bus has to manouvre while approaching the terminal, adding up to 0.5 kilometres to the overall distance. In addition, the time spent transferring is a major problem for users.[5] If this is true for well-operated corridors, it is much more true for badly operated ones. Finally, large terminals may require an additional one or two minutes to find the proper trunk bus. It is estimated that transfers can add up to ten minutes to the travel time. Therefore, busways have to be properly designed and operated to compensate. Despite these problems, busways remain one of the most promising operational measures for developing countries, deserving not only careful technical consideration but applied research to improve their effectiveness.

Bus service organization

In addition to infrastructure considerations, the organization of public transport services is also essential. Such reorganization may be seen as driven by two objectives: to ensure adequate transport for the majority and to transfer trips from automobiles to buses. The former is the most relevant for developing countries, since buses are the most important public mode for most. The latter is important in cities where the automobile already plays an important role or is expected to cause problems in the near future.

Service organization should be based on the expansion of the surface transport network using available streets, followed by efficient operational and surveillance work. This depends on an increased number of vehicles and crews, a better spatial and time coverage and the implementation of a variety of priority schemes. Services have to be diversified to cope with different demands, using the best vehicle for each case. It assumes high-quality online information to users, now available at much lower costs. It also presupposes new comfortable conditions for vehicles and access points. Finally, it involves the organization of better transfer conditions between motorized public transport and non-motorized transport, especially the bicycle.[6] They have to be friendly systems. This reorganization can rely on many transport means, properly integrated and complementary, operated either by public or private agents, as long as the objectives of equality, sustainability and efficiency are met. One of the greatest challenges – in addition to ensuring adequate service for the poor in general – is to make gender-sensitive projects that ensure better public transport supply for women, especially in respect to personal safety, ease of physical access and services tailored to their specific travel needs (Peters,1998). Another challenge is to provide better access and use conditions for the disabled.

As with public control, different conditions in cities will define which proposals are viable, in the light of institutional capability, technological needs and resulting costs. On the technical side, the adaptation of the circulation space to bus travel presents no technical problems for a generation of transport planners and traffic engineers who managed to ensure good traffic conditions to millions of automobiles. But it does present political obstacles

Box 19.1 *The devaluation of public transport: the negative pedagogy*

Public transport has been subject to a campaign of destabilization. For the minority with access to private transport this prejudice is reinforced in daily life. The increase in motorization fuelled by social, spatial and economic constraints is always called upon to prove that people desire private transport and, consequently, do not desire public transport. This movement is deeply embedded in the ideology of individualization as an expression of liberty and progress, which disqualifies anything that is 'public' and qualifies everything that is private, especially the isolated life inside the metal case of the automobile (and maybe in a room, alone with the computer). The negative pedagogy of public transport was first developed to an extreme in the US and is now a permanent, pervasive movement in most developing countries. In practice, the world of public transport is permanently shaped to demonstrate clearly that those who belong to it are second-class citizens. It is a programmed ordeal that constantly challenges people's psychological limits. Buses are appallingly bad, users are denied proper information and are carried like cattle, having to dispute space with people in automobiles. When complaints are raised, a common answer is that 'well, at least these poor people can get to work and make their living'.

of large magnitude, because it relies to a large extent on a political commitment whose viability is doubtful. This reorganization would have to be supported economically, for it will generate lines and services that will not pay for their operational costs; it will also have to be done at the expense of private transport's space and speed.

Fares and system financing

The organization of new fare systems is a necessary complement to the reorganization of public transport. The fare system should be based on five main assumptions and objectives (OECD, 1985). First, economic efficiency, in the sense of getting the most benefit from available resources. Second, cost recovery, implying that as a principle revenues should be sufficient to cover costs. Third, social equity, meaning both that costs and benefits should be fairly distributed among users and non-users and that convenient transport is available to those who need it. Fourth, administrative convenience, so means to collect revenues are not too costly, time consuming or inconvenient to both suppliers and consumers. Finally, coordination of services, in the sense of sharing responsibilities among all transport-related agencies. The same broad set of objectives is assumed by Strambi and Novaes (1992), who also provide a general framework for the definition of fare policies. In practical terms, it is important to distinguish clearly the fare level – the monetary value attached to the service – from the fare structure, which is the differentiation of fares according to social groups or services. International experience shows that most fare structures are highly complex, embodying several different fares. This is not surprising, considering the different patterns assumed by transport services and the social policies usually applied to differentiate fares between social groups (students, elderly, poor). As previously stressed, the economic problem related to public transport subsidies is in fact a political problem. Therefore, according to this view, highly expensive road systems can be maintained empty 20 hours per day, but buses can never be allowed to run with fewer than 60 passengers.

In addition to new fare schemes, integrated fare operation has also to be encouraged. Long trips requiring mode interchange are increasingly necessary in large towns. Any transfer implies economic and personal costs, which interfere with modal choice and demand. Hence, implementing system-wide integrated fares increases average speed and comfort. Recent developments in communication greatly improved the rapidity and reliability of revenue control, at lower costs. These special schemes face only two major problems. In systems with human fare collection, electronic collectors may cause unemployment, as has been discussed recently with the Brazilian bus system. Also, when the system is operated by a large number of firms, there are problems with revenue accountability and distribution among them.

One of the most promising ways of dealing with the financing problem is to charge part of transport costs to two external sources: those sectors benefiting from a good transport system and those imposing externalities on public transport. With the former, industrial, service and commercial sectors may be charged, to raise resources to finance public transport, as happens with the French *'versement-transport'*. In a more direct form, employers may be charged part of the transport costs of their employees, as with the Brazilian *vale-transporte* (ticket voucher). With the latter, road pricing schemes may be imposed on automobile users (see discussion ahead).

Box 19.2 *Are you ready for a bus ride?*

When trying to travel in a city you do not know, you will have to compare different modes. With buses, you will probably face the following conditions:

- There is no information on services.
- There are no pavements and/or no bus stop.
- When buses are coming they have no identification or route signing.
- If you miss a bus you never now when the next will come and which one will come.
- When the (supposedly) right bus arrives, entering is often difficult and becomes an ordeal for women with children or luggage and for the elderly or disabled.
- Inside the bus, finding a seat is almost a joke.
- The bus interior is dirty, noisy and uncomfortable; if deregulated minibuses are used, passengers must bend their heads to avoid being compressed by the vehicle roof.
- Travelling is problematic in the face of reckless driving and delays due to irregular automobile parking and congestion.
- When approaching the desired area, the crowd has to be overtaken to get to the door; if turnstiles are used for fare collection, there is the second obstacle to overcome.
- Getting off the bus, pavements may not exist and you have to face vehicles on the road.

With cars, city maps display routes, roads are paved, guiding signs are provided on main intersections, radio informs about traffic conditions, enforcement does not exist and the space is all yours.

Are you ready for a bus ride?

Motorcycles

Motorcycles are and will remain a key issue in Asia and Africa and will probably be a major problem in Latin America in the near future. The continued use of motorcycles is a challenge for most developing countries because of three aspects: accidents, pollution and transport individualization. Corresponding restrictive policies are controversial because they may also harm poor people for whom motorcycles are the only efficient transport mode (Gwilliam, 2000).

With accidents, there is very little to do, because the vehicle itself is dynamically dangerous for driver and passenger. Education and enforcement on safety devices may improve safety records but the nature of the technology renders accidents inevitable to a certain extent. In the US, fatality rate per passenger-kilometre is still 45 times higher than that of the car (Wright,

1992). The correct decision from the point of view of safety would be to ban motorcycles in their current form, but such a decision seems unrealistic. With pollution, although several improvements have been made (Gwilliam, 2000), the use of old, low-performance vehicles and the rapid increase in the new fleet will certainly add considerably to pollution problems in urban areas. With individualization, the increasing use of motorcycles reflects the same search for motorized mobility that is understood as essential by higher-income sectors and implies long-term effects: as recalled by Craig Townsend[7] the building of roads also offers the potential for mobility (albeit more dangerous) to low-income households who can afford cheap motorcycles, and this in turn builds a form of popular legitimacy for road expansion decisions.

Vehicle engineering

Bicycles are a highly stabilized technology, used all over the world. The major problems with bicycles are the unsuitability for some users and the conditions of purchase and use. Technical changes are needed if bicycles are to be more women-friendly. With purchasing, much of the problem is related to duties and taxes and the lack of a local industry. One of the important measures is to improve local or regional industry, especially in Africa; as suggested by Howe (1994, p8)

> *the first requirement ... is ... efficient mass production for the poor masses ... why should there not be Chinese bicycle factories in ... [sub-Saharan Africa] ... the way there are Japanese car factories in Europe and the USA?*

However, bicycle production involves using a large number of parts, requiring a network of small contractors to produce them, which poses many practical difficulties for developing countries (Hierli, 1993).

Adapted vehicles such as motorized rickshaws also present serious safety and comfort drawbacks. Although avoiding inherently unsafe motorcycle conditions by having an elongated rear axle, body structure and parts are incompatible with minimum safety standards. It was found that such vehicles are not safe for the driver, passengers or pedestrians, even at low impact speeds of 15 to 20km/h (IIT, 1995). As with motorcycles, the most judicious measure would be to ban them. However, they may be improved by technological changes and, if used in low-speed, low-conflict travelling environments, they may play an important role as a light form of public transport.

Public transport vehicles in the developing world are mostly defective, adapted vehicles. There is an urgent need to improve them. Several developing countries already use more advanced buses but a greater improvement has still to be made. Such improvements have to include better vehicles – with safer structure and parts, less noise and more comfort – and better conditions for women, children, the elderly and disabled people. Environmentally related improvements must also be pursued, like new forms of energy and fewer emissions. With energy, the use of electricity and CNG (compressed natural gas) seem promising in some cases (UN, 1993) as well as hydrogen. With emissions, the main target is to reduce particulate matter emissions.

With cars, vehicle engineering is also important but to a much lesser degree when compared to other areas. Several developing countries have already incorporated the most important safety devices – belts, emergency lights, special windshields, more efficient brakes – and pollutant emission restrictions have been increasingly adopted. However, the major problem with the automobile is not its physical features but its irresponsible use – especially in respect to poor maintenance conditions, unacceptable speeds and disrespect for pedestrians – and its space and energy consumption. Further physical improvements are less important than changes to such socially irresponsible use.

Vehicle emission control

The change in vehicle technology and equipment to decrease average emissions may yield interesting results, although in some contexts the increase in vehicle ownership and use may compensate for such a decrease. In Brazil, the launch of a federal programme in the 1980s gradually reduced average emissions from all vehicles manufactured in the country. Both CO and HC emissions were lowered to less than 10 per cent of the pre-1980 levels.

Road construction

Road construction and expansion has been the cornerstone of automobility policies. Most now agree that 'you can't pave your way out of congestion' (Cervero, 1998a). In developing countries, unrestricted proposals for automobile-based road expansion are absurd in the face of the poverty and

Box 19.3 *Now we have our green tunnel*

Within the 2 billion-dollar investment in road expansion made in São Paulo by the conservative city government between 1994 and 1997 (city annual budget is about US\$4 billion), there was a tunnel under the Ibirapuera Park, in the wealthiest part of the city. The tunnel, a two-kilometre, four-lane facility built in two separate structures, cost at least US\$300 million (the government has disclosed dubious figures). It links two important arterial roads and tries to overcome the physical impediment caused by the park. As with other road investments, it was directed to serve middle-class automobile users, who had elected the conservative government; as with other road investments, it did not help to alleviate the increasing city congestion and generated extra traffic to keep the nightmare alive. At both tunnel entrances there is a sign: 'No trucks or buses allowed, except CNG buses' (compressed natural gas). When the tunnel was opened for traffic, there were 30 CNG buses in the city, among a fleet of 11,000 and none was using the tunnel, a situation that persists today. Insult was added to injury. But we do have our 'green' tunnel; we are an 'environmentally friendly city' and may finally 'dive' into the globalization era with our cars.

deprivation of most people, the unequal consumption of road space and also considering the need to invest according to socially driven objectives. As pointed out by Kim and Gallent for Seoul (1998, p90):

> *The construction of arterial roads, traffic tunnels, urban expressways and improved parking facilities has proven to be a double-edged sword; whilst it reduces traffic congestion in the short term, over the long term it increases the potential for higher rates of car ownership and generates a greater volume of road traffic. The apparent futility of this investment is only matched by the social inequality which it accentuates ... 70% of passengers in Seoul remain dependent on public transport and investments in facilities for car-owners does little to improve transport services for the majority of Seoul's population.*

Therefore, all road expansion projects should be submitted to detailed scrutiny about who is going to benefit, how every role will be affected and how the future road space will be consumed.

INSTITUTIONAL ORGANIZATION

Traffic problems faced by cities in developing countries pose challenges for those willing to face them. However, pessimistic views should not discourage planners. In most cases traffic management can be successfully accomplished by using relatively small groups of technicians and simple tools, at reasonable costs. Planning may be based on a knowledge of local problems, acquired through a small set of surveys, which may be performed on a regular basis. Should traffic authorities organize clear objectives and coordinate efforts with the urban planning and transport planning teams, results may be surprisingly good.

Crucial to success is the gathering of basic data. It should concentrate on traffic conditions through both a social and a technical approach, as detailed in preceding sections. A possible list of relevant data and information is:

*   Travel habits: OD patterns, modal choice, trip purposes and social and economic household characteristics.
*   Travelling environment: land use and major traffic generators; pavement and road system physical and operational characteristics; traffic volumes and traffic mix.
*   Travelling conditions: safety, accessibility, comfort, fluidity and cost for all modes and roles.

Actual work may be exercised by linking efforts in several areas. First, planning, which entails understanding travel patterns and traffic conflicts, identifying problems and devising possible solutions. It is a crucial step that the analysis of roles and conflicts should be exercised to unveil how road space is divided among social groups and classes, how externalities are generated and who suffers their consequences. Second, devising possible solutions, with the community or users' participation, and defining their technical characteristics. Third, implementation, which requires defining the strategy to change the travelling environment and to communicate changes to users. Extreme care must be taken; the use of roads is based on acquired habits and people compelled to change them may present unpredictable reactions, generating an unsafe transition. Fourth, operation and surveillance, which entails ensuring proper human and material resources to verify daily, in the field, how the transition is being made and which adaptations may be needed. Fifth, enforcement, to instruct people and punish persistent offenders. Finally, assessment, to verify how initial objectives are being met.

The use of more sophisticated technologies has to be limited to specific situations where expected benefits are clearly higher than incurred costs, and where maintenance and operation capacity has already been ensured.

PRIORITY ACTIONS

Safety

Traffic accidents are the most relevant environmentally related transport problem in developing countries and should receive priority attention. The status of traffic safety is already changing from that of a problem to that of an *issue*. A larger number of people are increasingly denying the 'fatalistic' explanation and accepting human and environmental causation as more appropriate. However, many areas remain where the traditional view is still dominant. Therefore, no unanimity can be expected in the utilization of resources to deal with traffic accidents. In addition, the democratization of political institutions is recent and partial, and power concentration remains high, fuelling the construction of auto-oriented spaces. In this respect, the 'collective irresponsibility' for traffic safety, produced by the direct and indirect actions of political and economic dominant groups (Portugal and Santos, 1991), may be seen as a determined development project which emphasizes selective economic growth, irrespective of social costs. Finally, the built environment presents accident-prone physical characteristics. Possible elements of change are:

- *Viewing safe environments as a right.* To travel in a safe built environment should be considered a right protected by traffic codes and regulations. This right should be guaranteed by traffic authorities with the condition that travellers behave adequately. In Brazil, this is the main rationale adopted by the new Traffic Code issued in 1998.
- *Viewing accidents as environmentally related.* Accidents are a product of several factors, of which the built and the travelling environments are the most important. This represents a radical change in prevailing views to the problem. Accidents are an environmental problem and, more specifically, a built environment problem. This new view challenges the urban pattern pursued so far, as well as the appropriation of the space by motorized transport, especially the automobile. Accordingly, traffic accidents should be monitored in exactly the same way as physical and biological environmental problems – air and water pollution – through either independent public or private agencies, or community associations.
- *Viewing accidents as multidisciplinary phenomena.* Accidents deserve a multidisciplinary approach and treatment with the coordination of efforts by public and private agencies. This approach was placed at the centre of all the national road safety plans of developed countries (SWOV, 1993).

- *Generate social controls over engineers and planners.* Engineers and planners in charge of traffic safety should be responsible for the safety aspects of their decisions. The 1988 Brazilian constitution created a special public function to control policy impacts, independent from the executive power.[1] With transport, Brazilian engineers and planners now have to present environmental impact studies before proposals can be submitted for technical review. This obligation has led to a profound change in the profession's way of thinking and acting. The same effect has to be pursued with traffic safety. Two measures are important. First, public sectors in charge of environmental surveillance should include traffic safety in environmental auditing. Second, all transport and traffic projects should be preceded by a safety audit, to ensure proper safety conditions for the proposed infrastructure and services. All travelling environments should be evaluated regularly in respect to their traffic safety performance.

The citizenship pact: the humanization of space

A structural approach to urban transport problems requires the rebuilding of the travelling environment. The best way of achieving the objective is by organizing changes grounded in voluntary shifts of people's behaviour, as part of an understanding of the traffic problems sustained by all. Working with traffic conflicts experienced by local people in their daily lives is the best way of triggering a consciousness about the mutual interference of roles and the citizenship issues evolving around such conflicts. Change has to come from an organized discussion at the local level, based on a comprehensive review of how road space is divided and used and how people are interacting while enacting roles. Intervention has to be based on building a travelling environment where priorities are clearly seen as favouring the most important roles and which is consequently respected by all. The proposal differs from the traditional 'traffic calming' projects: it is directed at changing consciousness and behaviour, not just circulation patterns. It is focuses on the *humanization of space*, grounded in a *citizenship pact*. Main phases may be described as follows:

- Equity and environmental audit, through the analysis of how people interact while enacting roles. The key variables to be used are accessibility, space consumed by role, traffic severance and traffic conditions concerning safety, comfort, cost and pollution. The analysis has to combine travel patterns with land use, identifying main traffic generators (schools, medical care, shops). Interviews may complement information on suppressed demand, identifying traffic conditions that hamper the circulation of people, especially children, women and the elderly.
- The analysis of current conditions has to be performed along with the local population, public staff in charge of public facilities, shop owners and public transport and taxi drivers, benefiting from the discussion of how everybody interacts in their roles while using roads.
- The proposal of a new travelling environment must follow. It comprises first the definition of the physical characteristics of the circulation infrastructure –

pavements and roads – and of the circulation pattern, meaning how each role may use public space and which roles will be favoured or restrained.

- The new travelling environment has to be physically defined by signs, signals and additional traffic devices. They must be visible and clear and define in an unequivocal way whom the public space belongs to.
- Should the plan be approved by the community, implementation has to be discussed jointly. Discussion has to concentrate on how people should behave while enacting their roles in the new travelling environment, to build a 'behaviour consensus' within the community: the citizenship pact. The participation of traffic police in discussing the pact is essential.
- Once implemented, the travelling environment has to be monitored jointly. Community representatives may perform the job on a shift basis. However, care must be taken to not hinder or replace the legal duties of the traffic police: the role of the community has to be limited to enforcing social behaviour and adherence to the citizenship pact. Monitoring results must translate into permanent reassessment of the plan, discussed in public meetings.

Space humanization represents a profound change in current conditions. Many political, economic and physical obstacles will be faced. However, all may be overcome. Car drivers may be harmed by changes in circulation patterns, parking policies and speed limits. Shop owners may be affected by changes in truck loading and unloading operations or by limits imposed on customers. However all may be benefited directly while enacting other roles and indirectly through the benefits acquired by their families. Therefore, careful marketing efforts are essential to reverse initial opposition. These efforts must be based on enhancing the positive social and environmental impacts of the proposed changes for all.

The humanization of space is intended to yield several additional positive results:

- To raise people's awareness of space and equity issues, while seeing themselves and others negotiating road space in their neighbourhood.
- To find a practical way of channelling the collective desire to improve safety and quality of life, that is already embedded in most people.
- To achieve a genuine behavioural change, able to reduce conflicts and accidents and to improve quality of life.
- To form a comprehensive 'traffic safety mentality', grounded in the concept of citizenship.
- To eliminate or minimize the contradiction between formal education for traffic and actual behaviour on roads.
- To establish new habits generating a potential for disseminating a new way of using space.

As stressed before, these changes would entail a profound transformation of prevailing approaches, also requiring a parallel policy regarding land use. Considering the structural obstacles, this strategy has to be followed carefully. Ultimately, the production of a safe and equitable circulation space in developing countries depends on the achievement of a democratic society and the reduction of social and economic discrepancies, which cannot be considered as a short-term possibility. Therefore, the major factors that can induce both strategies in the short term are the pursuit of equity and the desire to improve quality of life, the latter directly related to the environmental movement. Such factors may lead to a physical change in space in the middle term that will ultimately form a safer and more equitable travelling environment.

Box 20.1 *Cynical thinking on traffic accidents*

When faced with increasing accident figures in developing countries, some experts mention the developed countries' experience, saying that accident rates will 'gradually reduce' as motorization increases. This cynical thinking means that developing countries have to pass through the problem until 'time' takes care of it. It is implicit that motorization is a good in itself and that thousands of people will have to die, get injured or disabled, until the situation comes to a 'normal statistical level'. This is simply outrageous.

Priority of public transport

Few cities in developing countries have effective bus priority treatment. São Paulo, the largest city in Brazil (10 million inhabitants) has 11,000 buses operating on 2000km of main roads and just 43km of bus priority lanes, of which just 16km are busways (CET, 1997).

Improvements in the operational performance of public transport are the main objective. The most common measure is the curb-side bus lane. However, international experience in general (UNCHS, 1992) and Brazilian experience in particular, demonstrates that curb-side bus lanes present severe operational problems in conflicting travelling environments. The first is curb-side activity such as loading, unloading and access to lots. A second problem is parking enforcement, especially when the bus lane crosses middle-class commercial areas. The third problem is bus congestion itself, when the number of buses is high (more than 90 standard buses per hour) and there is no extra lane to overtake. Signal coordination is also difficult due to capacity restraints related to high traffic volumes. As most roads are narrow, the physical 'reserve capacity' is often very low,[2] yielding no operational space for good signal coordination (unless an extremely high level of congestion is imposed on general traffic, which is operationally undesirable and politically difficult). In view of these problems, the overall results of most bus lanes in São Paulo were very poor, with small benefits compared to the whole bus cycle.[3] If properly operated and enforced, curb-side bus lanes can carry from 5000 to 8000 passengers per hour, per direction. If overtaking space and better infrastructure is provided, capacity increases up to 20,000 passengers per hour (Lindau and Willumsen, 1990). A similar operational scheme is the organization of bus platoons. One of the first experiences in the world was organized in São Paulo, in 1977, at the Nove de Julho corridor, which yielded excellent results while the enforcement and operational efforts remained effective (Szasz, 1977).

Contraflow bus lanes have some advantages, especially the decrease in travel time due to short-cuts and the self-enforcing impact on irregular parking. However, they tend to be more dangerous for pedestrians, due to the odd nature of circulation patterns and the difficulty in ensuring clear signing. Hence, their implementation should always be subject to a careful study of the safety and operational aspects.

Busways, as previously analysed, may increase bus speeds by up to 30km/h, depending on the frequency of intersection and signal densities and provided good operational conditions are ensured. Table 20.1 shows that speeds in busways may vary significantly; the Brazilian busways in the table perform better because they have good physical and operational conditions. The table also reveals that deficient operation may significantly decrease busway speeds down to even lower levels than that of curb-side lanes.

Table 20.1 *Bus speeds on busways, several cities*

City (country)	AM speed	PM speed
Abidjan (Ivory Court)	12.8	8
Ankara (Turkey)	12	10.4
Istambul (Turkey)	14	11.3
B Horizonte (Brazil)	24.6	29.3
Curitiba (Brazil)	21	21.3
P Alegre (Brazil)	22.7	17.8

Source: Armstrong-Wright, 1993

While extensive signal coordination is hardly achievable on major roads, other measures have large potential benefits. Priority at intersections and left-turn special movements can be easily implemented with the new technologies available today. Pavement and smoothing of road surfaces – especially to eliminate potholes or drainage ditches – may considerably improve passenger comfort. The adoption of a set of physical and operational improvements can yield significant results in terms of increased overall speed, reliability and quality of service. The final objective is to organize a comprehensive bus system, with high service quality and operating between 20 and 25km/h (up to 30km/h should special conditions occur), in standard and special routes, where priority schemes will be provided. It has to be properly designed, implemented and operated, using operational and enforcement teams. Again, this is no problem for technical people used to ensuring good fluidity conditions to automobile traffic.

Finally, improving bus performance also helps to reduce pollution, since at speeds around 25km/h, easily attainable in urban areas, buses produce fewer emissions, especially CO, NOx and PM.

The division of space

When current road traffic mix in developing countries is considered, it is clear that one of the most difficult tasks will be to arrive to a fair and safe division of road space. Key to the safety problem is the division of motorized and non-motorized traffic; key to the equity problem is also the split between public and private transport; key to the efficiency/capacity problem is the traffic mix itself. Table 20.2 shows that the share of motorized transport in cities may vary tremendously, from a minimum of 12.8 per cent (Shanghai) to a maximum of 97.8 per cent (Chiang Mai).

Table 20.2 *Share of motorized and non-motorized vehicles, selected cities in developing countries*

City	Vehicle proportion (%)	
	NMV	**Motor vehicles**
Shanghai (China)	87.2	12.8
Hanoi (Vietnam)	64.3	35.7
Kanpur (India)	55.7	44.3
Phnom Penh (Cambodia)	52.1	47.9
Dhaka (Bangladesh)	51.8	48.2
Metro Manila (Philippines)	33.8	66.2
Surabaya (Indonesia)	15.6	84.4
Penang (Malaysia)	6.5	93.5
Chiang Mai (Thailand)	2.2	97.8

Source: World Bank, 1995

The mixed-mode nature of the traffic stream will continue to exist and may worsen in several places, because of the use of new vehicles or of increasing motorization. Three general principles may be followed:

1 Road space has to be divided primarily according to the number of people, and not vehicles. This challenges current approaches that use capacity methodologies based on vehicles (in fact, automobiles).
2 Road space has to be divided in a way that ensures the safest traffic mix possible.
3 Road space has to be divided in a way that yields the least environmentally harmful traffic mix possible (which also implies efficiency).

These three principles reflect the same essential concern behind the question raised in Chapter 17: Which are the most efficient, environmentally sound and sustainable means of ensuring the equitable appropriation of space? Working with the three principles in the wide array of cities in the developing world will lead to several combined possibilities. They have to be weighted locally, considering for example existent modes, their safety conditions, and their space, energy and environmental impacts. In some places the best mix will be based on a predominance of non-motorized means while in others the best mix will be based on the coexistence of non-motorized and public motorized means.

In other instances truck or automobile traffic may have to be subject to special analysis. On some roads physically separated paths such as pedestrian areas, bikeways or busways may have to be provided to ensure safety or efficiency objectives.

An important point refers to the question proposed in Chapter 18, about whether or not we should transfer non-motorized trips to public transport. Some modelling exercises have shown that NMVs in roads with mixed traffic cause a large impact on overall traffic speeds even at low proportions, and that with intermediate proportions, such as 30 per cent, traffic speeds stabilize at a low level (Hossain and McDonald, 1998). Such findings support the proposal to ban NMVs, to bring large benefits for the remaining motorized traffic, because speeds and passenger-carrying capacity would increase, without changing the current traffic mix. This would be done by ensuring a smoother traffic and by transferring NMV passengers to public transport modes. Although appealing, such a proposal has to be analysed in the light of broader objectives, related to social and economic impacts and to how existent roles will be affected. Should the final results benefit the majority without access to private transport they should be supported, provided that NMV users – and those dependent on the NMV business – are compensated in some way. Conversely, should users of private transport be the main beneficiaries, the proposal has to be questioned.

Box 20.2 *Road-capacity analysis and the contradiction between two distinct speed-worlds*

When analysing road capacity and signal timing, two different speed-worlds are inherently included in the reasoning: those of pedestrians and vehicles. While the former involves speeds around 3 to 5km/h (about 1m/s on average for a physically able person), the latter involves speeds that may go up to 80km/h in main arterial roads. Such extreme speed differences lead to an insurmountable conflict: to ensure proper crossing times for pedestrians may drastically increase vehicle waiting times and queue lengths. Signal cycle length is directly related to the 'dead time' caused by yellow and 'all-red' intervals, and inversely related to the volume-to-capacity ratio, the latter at an exponential rate (Webster and Cobbe, 1966). When longer pedestrian crossing times are introduced to protect pedestrian interests, signal cycle increases, which may affect vehicle delays and queue lengths up to a point when physical (blocking of nearby intersections) or political (drivers' acceptance) limits are approached. The priority granted to mobility of motorized modes, grounded in structural political and economic constraints, leaves no space for alternative approaches on how to treat such conflicts and the result is fairly obvious for those working in developing countries. Even in developed countries, the conflict has often a similar answer, as stressed by Whitelegg's concept of traffic management's 'theft of time' (1997). Once again, Illich's (1974) energy inequity postulate reveals itself, now through a space-constrained phenomenon.

Changing auto use

Modal change

Another fundamental objective relates to diverting private transport trips to public transport means. Although important, the question has to be placed on its proper position in the scale of priority actions. In developing countries the prime objective is to provide mobility, accessibility and safety for the majority of people who rely on public transport. However, many transport engineers in these countries consistently spend time and effort thinking about how to convince auto users to shift to public transport. Except for large cities and highly congested motorized travelling environments, this effort is a waste of time, and feeds both frustration and a wrong approach to the problem of the tenacious use of the automobile: it appears to be a mere result of 'selfish behaviour' by auto users, when actually it is dependent on a complex set of factors.

Improving bus services to attract auto users is a very difficult task. Deficiencies in public transport supply and the complex pattern of daily travel activities of middle-class people make the car (or the motorcycle) the most convenient mode. For buses to attract auto users they have to be organized as convenient and friendly systems, as close as possible to the advantages of the automobile system. As stressed by Bovy (2000, p17) 'in a context of competition between individual and collective forms of mobility, advances made in car use ... need to be matched by equally spectacular and efficient advances in public transport ease of use'.

Considering the obvious difficulties in promoting such a shift to existent public transport means, the most common solution has been the provision of special bus services, with more sophisticated vehicles and fewer stops, running through high- and middle-class neighbourhoods. São Paulo has an unfavourable experience with such services, while Porto Alegre and other Brazilian cities have successfully implemented a minibus system (ANTP, 1998). The difficulties should not lead to pessimistic conclusions. Cities in the developing world are permanently subject to changes in their built environments. Economic changes in the increasing importance of the tertiary sector, although requiring out-of-peak trips and hence enhancing private transport convenience, also generate new market segments which could be properly approached with alternative transport means. Such special services may be very appealing for instance to the segments of the middle classes that face difficulties in using the car for several trips or in having two cars, and to trips linked to delivering services to customers. In any case, the attempt to transfer trips from auto to public transport will fail if not planned in a wider context that considers land use changes and encouraging walking and cycling (Whitelegg 1997; Bovy, 2000).

A particular concern is at stake here. It has been proposed that such new services should be provided by informal transport, as the most efficient means of transferring trips from the car to public transport (Cervero, 1998a). There is no denying of the attractiveness and convenience of small, comfortable buses to convince car drivers to shift. However, as previously proposed, this suggestion should not lead to transport deregulation, because all public transport services should be regulated and monitored by public authorities.

Public transport as a public service has to face future economic and urban tendencies. A question immediately arises: Considering the tendency towards urban sprawl and motorization, how should we treat public transport? A large, detailed and comprehensive survey revealed how cities adapted to preserve a relatively high share of public transport trips (Cervero, 1998a). The conclusion was that cities have accepted sprawl as inevitable and tried to provide services that best adapt to the environment; it follows logically that instead of trying to organize public-transport-friendly environments, what we ought to do is to adapt it to the environments people supposedly like to live in. The assumption is adequate for devising a strategy to cope with the alarming increase in low-efficiency urban occupation patterns, because provision of adapted, efficient bus services is clearly a powerful way of attracting auto users. However, the broad assumption has three drawbacks. First, it is grounded in the Western tendency to urban sprawl shaped by wealthier sectors, and assuming that this tendency applies to developing countries is controversial. Second, it neglects the rising environmental concerns that are pressing for more compact, less energy-consuming cities, including in developed countries. Third, it again neglects the main objective of transport planning in developing countries, which is to provide adequate transport for captive users, before trying to attract auto users.

Car pooling

Car pooling is another measure extensively mentioned in the literature and intensively pursued by some transport planners. It is used in several developed countries (especially in the US), as a freeway congestion-relief tool. In developing countries, it has a very limited importance, for several reasons. First, it proposes an irrational decision to automobile owners: the individualized use of the car allows efficient trip-chaining which is eliminated if the person joins a car-pool programme. Second, car-pooling programmes require a certain scale of combined origins and destinations, and surveillance capability, which can be found only in large enterprises. Third, it depends on fixed-hour work schedules, which are not consistent with the duties and needs of the higher middle-class sectors. Fourth, it may have a very limited social impact because most people in developing countries just do not have access to automobiles; it is clearly not a priority action.

Traffic restraint

Traffic restraint measures impose restrictions on people's travelling activities, thereby directly impacting on their reproduction needs. Hence, they always face an immediate reaction, depending on the level of restriction. May (1986) provides a comprehensive description of restraint measures, classified according to their physical, regulatory, delaying and fiscal natures. Physical restrictions can occur in the form of spatial restrictions (traffic cells, pedestrian areas) or parking restrictions. Regulatory measures are related to time restrictions (prohibiting/inhibiting traffic in downtown in peak hours).

Delaying restrictions refers to artificial organization of bottlenecks to discourage traffic. Finally, fiscal measures concern taxation of car ownership, parking charges and road pricing. These measures can be taken in a isolated or combined form. Some of the most important to developing countries are discussed ahead.

Entry restrictions are often created to protect neighbourhoods whose roads had been previously opened to cross traffic as part of a plan to generate new linkages and improve overall fluidity. With the increasing problems of disturbance, speeding, noise and accidents, residents tend to pressure traffic authorities to prohibit or divert crossing traffic. Consequently, traffic cells are organized, requiring a decision about which streets should remain open to allow minimum circulation conditions. The discussion about the final layout often raises strong controversy, causing many schemes to be abandoned. Space reorganization – the aforementioned citizenship pact – intends to overcome part of the problems faced by traditional 'traffic calming' projects.

Daily restrictions to car traffic are often adopted as licence plate-limiting access: the odds-evens plate scheme is easy to understand and enforce and has been adopted in several cities, such as Mexico, Caracas, Athens, Lagos and São Paulo. In Lagos, the scheme yielded positive results in the first phase (up to six months after implementation) such as higher use of buses, less use of automobiles, more car-pooling activities and speed improvement. However, the method was found to be a failure, since many people ended up finding ways of circumventing the limitation. These were either legal – entering the restricted area before the time limit, adopting longer routes leading to unrestricted entries or changing an inconvenient second car to a convenient one – or illegal, by manipulating the licence plate, or even bribing policemen (Ogunsanya,1984). The case of São Paulo is more encouraging, although detailed surveys were not performed. In 1996 an all-day restriction was imposed on 20 per cent of the fleet in the metropolitan area, on a five-day shift basis, and a 95 per cent compliance was observed (violators could be fined). It is estimated that the overall daily reduction in the CO emission was 1171 tons and that 40 million litres of fuel were saved. Other effects were an average increase of 20 per cent in traffic speed and a decrease of 40 per cent in congestion during peak hours. Beginning in 1998, restrictions were limited to peak hours in the city of São Paulo and nearby congested cities. Compliance was again high (about 90 per cent) although final traffic volume reduction was found to be 12 per cent, mostly because of people rearranging their travel schedules (CET, 1998). The problems can be avoided by proper enforcement and by more adequate planning, in order to reduce the possibilities of fraud or undesired circumvention.

Parking restriction is one of the most powerful mechanisms to restrict the use of cars, because micro-accessibility is directly affected. When parking facilities are abundant micro-accessibility is optimal and the use of the car is exercised to its fullest extent: one of the most important mechanisms included in the auto-oriented traffic policy in São Paulo was the provision of 20,000 short-term paid curb-side parking spaces close to businesses and commercial areas, along with the availability of an enormous quantity of free street parking spaces. Conversely, when parking is restricted, micro-accessibility is highly damaged, impacting on auto attractiveness. However, parking restrictions can be easily circumvented by parking illegally (when enforcement is deficient), by parking nearby (often disturbing residential parking) or by using private parking supply, which may flourish as a market response to restrictions. The latter case poses a serious policy problem when parking restrictions are intended to diminish the flow of automobiles into a certain area.

Driver behaviour: intersection conflicts and speeding

The control of dangerous intersections that do not warrant traffic signals may be performed through the use of special devices like the mini-roundabout. These devices are highly cost-effective, resulting in safety. With speed control, good results may be achieved both by traffic devices such as road humps and by electronic means such as radars. Road humps such as those in the UK have proved highly effective in reducing speeds to the 20km/h level, at relatively low costs. However, extreme care must be taken to ensure they are properly designed and installed, with adequate advertising, otherwise severe accidents may be caused. Electronic speed detectors have become more accessible to traffic authorities and are a powerful tool in decreasing average speeds: in São Paulo, their use on major expressways has decreased the number of speed violators from 60 to 5 per cent (CET, 1999).

Enforcement

As previously analysed, the enforcement of traffic regulations is poorly exercised in developing countries, because of low availability of personnel, vehicles and equipment, and of most grave offenders never being punished. Hence, as a general rule, traffic polices should be provided with adequate resources, should be submitted to a different logistic and should see their actions resulting in actual punishment.

The provision of adequate human and material resources requires a policy decision on training personnel and ensuring proper conditions for them to exert their activities. There are both political and economic problems. On the political side, in several cases enforcement is ascribed to military personnel, both for historical reasons related to the dominance of authoritarian political regimes and for practical reasons, of economy of scale in using police resources. This generates a resistance to change and especially to a civilian-driven enforcement effort. On the economic side, a well-trained and organized enforcement corporation will require budget commitments that would have to compete with other requirements. To be effective, the reassessment of logistics requires a true change in mentality, besides material support. Presently, enforcement is concentrated mostly in one single sort of offence – irregular parking – and the entire system is directed to facilitate mobility. This needs a radical change. Enforcement should be directed to safety-harming offences, especially aggression towards pedestrians, speeding and drinking and driving, and vehicle maintenance conditions.

Finally, the actual punishment of offenders is almost null, which feeds a feeling of non-punishment and hence improper behaviour. The violent nature of space appropriation, where pedestrians and cyclists are the most harmed, further stresses the inequity faced by the most vulnerable roles. Political conditions in most developing countries pose formidable obstacles to changing the situation. In addition to the normal slowness of judicial procedures, corruption is a rather common form of solving the problem, backed by a highly stratified society, where income and personal relationships are related to the power of avoiding punishment (Da Matta, 1987). Despite these difficulties, improvements can be made to the judicial system. One of the most interesting attempts to change the situation is the organization of faster judicial procedures, in specialized trial courts.

Education

Education has been considered one of the main pillars of traffic management, in addition to engineering and enforcement. It is given high priority in industrialized countries, especially among children and teenagers. Consequently, developing countries have been importing some educational techniques and have also been giving them a formal priority. This seems to be not only a 'modern' civilized attitude but also one that receives strong support from the public and the media. Unfortunately, a critical analysis shows that the results are meagre, because traffic fatalities are still a major social problem. As may be deduced from previous suggestions, the proposition is to concentrate efforts in two areas: traffic management and enforcement. These are the areas where benefits can be gained in the short term. Hence, education is somehow placed in a secondary position, which does not diminish its relevance as a structural, middle-term action.

The problem with education for traffic is related to a basic contradiction between what is taught and what is observed in daily life. Despite traffic regulations formally assigning priority to pedestrians in respect to drivers, in practice the opposite is very much the truth. While traffic codes define a clear priority rule for intersections without any signing, drivers negotiate space according to relative speeds, street width or just tradition. Hence, people develop an informal way of negotiating space, that either ignores or interprets differently the formal rules. This behaviour signalizes a defensive (or aggressive) strategy, necessary to diminish life risks and to improve efficiency in circulation. Educational efforts in these political and cultural environments is doubtful, not to say nonsensical: it is much less efficient than it is supposed to be and is in fact counterproductive. Therefore, the maintenance of formal traffic education in such environments is contradictory. Education will be indeed very important for children and youngsters provided it is related to the elimination of the inconsistency between theory and practice and the reappropriation of the space by the most numerous and vulnerable roles. The only way of doing it is combining traffic education with major changes both in enforcement logistics and in space reorganization. Education will be effective and meaningful only when people feel that proper behaviour will be rewarded and improper behaviour punished. Education will be socially valuable only when the circulation space reflects, like a mirror, the priority given in the law to the most vulnerable roles.

Road pricing

It is sometimes argued that the undercharging of automobile costs has been compensated for by subsidizing public transport, as a 'second best' solution (Gómez-Ibáñez and Meyer, 1991). If subsidies are interpreted as a way of attracting auto users to public means, this explanation is inadequate, because the main objective of transport planning in developing countries is not to attract auto users to public transport but instead to provide the captive population with adequate accessibility conditions. Conversely, if the 'second best' solution is interpreted as an actual mechanism to compensate most people, it can be taken more seriously. However, even in this case, the relevance of externalities generated by private transport and the maintenance of poor conditions for public transport attest that the compensation is far from sufficient: automobiles continue to generate much more negative externalities in traffic accidents, air pollution and congestion than the irregular, inconsistent (and sometimes non-existent) public transport subsidies can compensate for.

The rationale for road pricing has been intensively debated. It is based on a market approach to road use, considering that costs incurred by cars are not paid entirely by their users. These externalities can occur in the form of accidents, congestion or pollution, and road pricing analysis is more often restricted to congestion. The technical explanation for road charging is extensively explained in the literature and will not be replicated here.[4] In the case of a congested network, it is assumed that prices actually 'charged' to consumers will be below real costs, for users will be generating costs for others that are not paid for, resulting in an inefficient use of roads. If the user had been charged for these externalities, the actual flow would be lower and prices would equal costs, restoring the best equilibrium. Despite the widespread acknowledgement of this inequity in the distribution of transport costs, few governments implement road pricing schemes. The world-famous Singapore case is the single comprehensive example so far (in addition to the pilot Hong Kong and London proposal). However, its specific geographical and political conditions precludes its straightforward transferral to other countries.

The failure to implement road pricing is based on two main reasons, the first technical and the second political, the former being actually the 'perfect excuse' for avoiding the latter. On the technical side, any attempt to promote road charging would inevitably involve complex (and rather subjective) computations to avoid unfairness (May, 1986) and would lead to considerable operational difficulties: constrained by additional costs, drivers will try to use parallel roads, increasing or creating traffic severance and the 'barrier effect'. Diverted traffic may also damage or destroy existing road surfaces, especially if trucks change their routes.

On the political side, the acknowledgement of this clear inequity has been followed by the implicit avoidance of any concrete measure because it would be politically unacceptable in present conditions. The proper charging of private transport could cause the entire transport system to blow up. The impacts on the US, for instance, could reach an unbelievable scale. Even in developing countries with already high numbers of automobiles such as Brazil, Mexico or Indonesia the impact would be enormous. Road charging could cause a large impact on the automobile economy, raising complaints and opposition from the most powerful sectors in society, including the middle class and the automotive workers themselves. The reaction can be based both on economic reasons related to the overall impact of a reduction in automobile usage and on political reasons related to the liberal views of freedom to circulate.

Therefore, the best and also feasible actions seem to be a combination of localized road pricing – where route diversion and negative impacts may be minimized – parking and time/space restrictions to automobile traffic and effective bus priority schemes.

PART 5
CONCLUSIONS

21 Conclusions

Current urban transport conditions in developing countries result from a large set of social, economic and political factors. Improvements in these conditions depend on several changes, both outside and inside the limits of urban and transport policies.

Urban transport conditions remain highly inadequate and inequitable for most of the population. Traditional procedures, along with political and technical alliances, have been generating transport systems that propagate an unfair distribution of accessibility and reproduce inequities. Private transport has often benefited, and non-motorized and local public transport means have been neglected. These problems have been aggravated since the 1980s, because of economic restructuring and the fiscal crises of the state, which increase poverty and deprivation and prevent the organization of an adequate supply of public transport means for most people. There are no reasons to believe that the private sector alone will be able – or interested – to ensure transport services that fit the needs of the majority of the population, because equity does not belong in the agenda of economic modernization.

Problems and inequities concerning transport and traffic conditions in developing countries can be attributed first to structural factors, such as intense and uncontrolled urbanization, persistent poverty, fragile democracies, closed decision-making processes, poor citizenship, inequitable economic development and the denying of education for most. Second, they may be related to urban and transport policies themselves, especially to two historical processes: the dominance of private transport and the submission of public transport to a market approach. The dominance of private transport lies behind safety, environmental and space inequities. The market approach to public transport precludes a social approach and translates into deficient accessibility and quality: to deny access to space is a means of maintaining the historical exclusion of most.

Transport is not an end in itself. The 'end' has to be the equitable appropriation of space and the corresponding access to social and economic life. Structural changes depend on factors beyond the direct influence of urban and transport polices and require enhanced democracy and citizenship, extensive access to education and healthcare, increased wealth for the poor and better income distribution. Practical changes will have to be pursued inside a highly conflicting political arena and within a economic globalization process whose impacts will be extensive and severe. State structure and functioning are very different between developing countries, implying

different possibilities of pressing for changes; cultural and religious constraints may pose further obstacles. The attachment of the bureaucracy and
the technocracy to the interests of the elite and middle class may be
countervailed by pressures from organized groups and by the inherent conflicts and tensions that emerge from the increasing desire for equity and quality
of life. A particular positive aspect is that the feasibility of new solutions may
benefit also from the emergence of the environmental movement – and its
impact on the way urban transport is seen – and from the urban transport
crisis itself, which may help to support alternative policies that were never
adopted before or that have been facing opposition. Increasing equity concerns may be used to oppose negative effects.

The planning process will have to be changed, to develop new forms of
driving and controlling urban growth, to address non-motorized and public
transport as priority means, and to define restraints on the undesirable use of
private transport.

The book suggests that the major challenge – in addition to the mentioned
structural changes – is to modify roadway building and use, by reassessing
them according to social and equity concerns and ensuring safety and priority to the most numerous and vulnerable roles. Negative externalities caused
by motorized transport in general and automobiles in particular should be
controlled, such as traffic accidents, congestion, pollution, urban disruption
and traffic severance. The final objective of all these actions is to revert the
actual privatization of roads caused by the adaptation of cities to the selected
sectors that may use the automobile and to consequently recapture roads as
public assets.

In addition to changes in the planning process and in the use of roads, the
relationship between the state and the private sector in supplying public transport has to be carefully analysed. Recent trends towards deregulation and
privatization need to confront the central issues of equity and efficiency. The
role of the public sector in regulating and enforcing public transport operation has to be preserved and used primarily to ensure that the transport needs
of the majority are fulfilled, that public transport works in support of the urban social and economic life, and in accordance with equity and efficiency
objectives. The regulatory environment should be flexible, to provide services
better suited to the market, and should be tailored to stimulate mode diversity
and physical and operational integration, to attract automobile users. Regulation should also include fare subsidization whenever necessary, for those
who otherwise would not be attended to by the market. Contrary to viewing
them as wasteful, they should be considered as an investment, provided they
can be controlled by society, actually reach the target groups and are not used
to support inefficiency.

For all these changes to be accomplished it is vital that the crucial alliances
that have been maintaining and reproducing inequities be opposed. A particular points is at stake: however important external interests may be, in most cases
the alliances within internal forces – the state, the elite, the bureaucracy, commercial and financial interests – are the main obstacle to be overcome.

Finally, it must be stressed that the large differences between developing
countries will naturally lead to different choices regarding specific solutions,

which have to be decided by those social and political forces dealing with the issue in any particular case.

In view of the widely disparate conditions of developing countries, it is difficult to summarize the main concepts and proposals. The following list intends to overcome the obstacle, by mentioning those that could be generalized:

- People have the right to an equitable life, which implies an equitable access to social, cultural, political and economic opportunities, which in turn implies an equitable access to space.
- Roads and sidewalks are public assets that must be shared by all according to social and equity parameters; a key change refers to dividing road space according to the number of people, and not vehicles, in a way that ensures the safest and the least environmentally harmful traffic mix possible.
- Public transport should be seen as an essential public service to ensure the equitable access to space, social life and economic opportunities. It has to be subject to society and public control. Although uncontrollable growth, poverty and society disorganization may lead to a precarious public transport provision, efforts should be made to reach a superior form of provision as soon as adequate conditions are met.
- Safety has to be treated as the most important transport-related environmental problem, which further enhances the importance of changing the travelling environment, as opposed to working primarily with pollution-reduction actions; it has to be treated accordingly, by physically reorganizing the built environment and by reassessing traffic management principles, education and enforcement logistics.
- Scarce financial resources have to be properly used; developing countries should invest in reducing the waste of resources by improving maintenance of the available infrastructure, stopping supporting inefficient or inequitable investments, transferring investments committed to automobile-based road expansion to more equitable investments on non-motorized and public transport and charging or controlling private transport for related externalities.

The most important measures are summarized below. They were selected according to their relevance to change present conditions and not for their political feasibility, which will vary according to specific conditions. These actions could concentrate the efforts of planners, politicians and social groups committed to the desired changes.

Political and strategic measures

Decentralize the decision-making process.
Implement social control over planners.
Integrate planning activities.
Define public regulation of public transport, under society's control.
Define comprehensive financing for public transport.
Define automobile restraint measures and externality charging.

Planning procedures

Drive land use towards social interaction and less motorized transport.
Address primarily the needs of the poor, women and children.
Complement analysis of individual trips with household travel activity.
Replace analysis of vehicles with analysis of roles – 'equity anditing'.
Develop new operational transport-modelling techniques.
Replace long-term with short-term limited forecasting.
Complement cost–benefit with equity/accessibility analysis.

Non-motorized and public transport

Ensure high-quality infrastructure and circulation for non-motorized modes.
Ensure high-quality operation of the public transport system.
Implement effective bus priority infrastructure and operational schemes.
Ensure integration of non-motorized and public transport means.
Develop new services to cope with varying demands.
Develop new vehicles, especially bicycles and public transport vehicles.
Develop more environmentally friendly fuels and new forms of energy.

Traffic management

Reorganize the travelling environment in favour of the most numerous roles.
Develop education and citizenship for those using roads.
Implement speed and conflict control devices.
Reorganize traffic enforcement towards safety.
Submit projects to equity and safety auditing.
Implement efficient traffic management.
Create fast judicial procedures for major traffic offences.

While pursuing these objectives and applying such measures, planners in developing countries should be aware of the essential tension inherently imbedded in our challenge: that between equity and efficiency. This conflict has coexisted with humanity for a long time and was fuelled in the modern era by economic modernization and the generation of profound social differences between people. Traditional approaches and the ideological principles attached to the current globalization process are pressing again for efficiency as the prime objective. While a liberal approach calls for efficiency even at the expense of equity, the alternative approach calls for equity as the prime objective, provided a minimum efficiency, socially accorded, is ensured. The latter is our path. Although complex, it is as simple as that.

NOTES

CHAPTER 1

1 'Black box' ethics refer to systems, procedures or techniques that only those who developed them can understand easily.

CHAPTER 3

1 For the early impact of the car in the US, see especially Rae (1971) and Flink (1972); for more recent studies see Wachs and Cramford (1991), Miller and Moffet (1993), ITS-UC (1997) and Vuchic (1999).
2 See especially Whitt (1982), Yago (1983), Sawers (1984), Barrett (1983) and Sachs (1982).
  For detailed information on the debate, see Castells (1976), Lojkine (1976),
3 Preteceille (1981), Saunders (1979) and Pahl (1977b).

CHAPTER 5

1 The commodification of social relations refers to activities and services that were free, but have started to charge. This radically changes the relationship between the state (as the regulator), the private sector (as the supplier) and the consumer.
2 Despite efforts to arrive at a precise distinction between individual and collective consumption, many authors doubt that such a distinction is possible, because it cannot cover all the nuances of consumption. First, reproduction is accomplished in other spheres, for example in family, religious or community spheres (Preteceille, 1981); second, consumption occurs within a complex web of public and private actions, and individual, family or class restraints can make it difficult to find a watertight definition of collective or individual consumption (Ball, 1986); third, some consumption is compulsory (education, some health services), introducing new difficulties into the analysis. See also Castells, 1977; Pahl, 1969; Preteceille, 1986 and Theret, 1982.

CHAPTER 6

1   The ITE, formerly Institute of Traffic Engineers, is the largest organization of this kind in the world. It was founded in the US in 1930 and has remained one of the main sources of technical procedures.
2   The first special class of traffic engineers graduated from Harvard University in 1926, by which time the US already had a fleet of 24 million vehicles. See Soares, 1975.
3   The conflicts between automobile, taxi and truck drivers are also analysed by Falcocchio and Cantilli (1974, p108) but with only a limited approach.
4   Buses are noisy, and they emit black fumes that are aesthetically displeasing. In middle-class neighbourhoods, buses may be regarded as an 'inferior' form of transport, and the presence of a bus route may drive down house values.

CHAPTER 8

1   This section is partially based on my paper published in *Transportation Quarterly Journal* (Vasconcellos, 2000), with permission from the Eno Foundation.

CHAPTER 9

1   Pas argues that this fundamental change represents a paradigm choice in Kuhn's terms (1970), unlike the other changes to the modelling process (improved statistical efficiency, and the incorporation of a consideration of comfort, convenience and safety.
2   The four steps are explained in detail in Stopher and Meyburg (1975), Hutchinson (1974) and Kanafani (1983).
3   Lewis et al argue that 'a transport planning failure occurs when there is a clear gap between demand and supply and it would have been economically (or socially) justified to provide extra capacity'. As an example, they discuss the opening of the M25 (London's orbital motorway), which was found to be heavily overloaded at its opening.

CHAPTER 10

1   In Singapore, the average journey duration is ten minutes, and the average distance is 740m (Olszewski and Tan, 1999).

CHAPTER 11

1   In Lima in 1984, there were 1391 formal vehicles and 14,837 informal vehicles, of which 6868 were 'pirate' vehicles. See ILD, 1990, pp49–50.
2   The logic of the market is so compelling that service inequities arise even in the poorest communities. In Accra, Kwakye et al (1997, p10) stress that while 'there is no obvious differentiation in fares between services to

higher- and lower-income communities ... there are differences in quality ... *trotos* (minibuses) that service the squatter settlement of Tsui-Bleoo
in the Teshie area are very old and in a state of poor repair'.

3 The Brazilian bus industry manufactures between 12,000 and 15,000 buses
per year.

4 'Predatory' refers to both 'dumping' operations and arrangements between
operators to restrict entry to the market. 'Uncompensated cost increases' refers to fare compensation and artificially maintained low fares.

5 Cervero points out that, in the case of Mexico City, unrestricted paratransit
emerged following the opening of a metro system in 1969, and it soon
became clear that laissez-faire conditions in such a large city were leading to chaos (Cervero, 1998a, p392).

6 The voucher is limited to those working in the formal job market, and is
used by about 50 per cent of public transport passengers (NTU, 1998).

CHAPTER 12

1 This section is largely based on my paper 'The demand for cars in developing countries' (Vasconcellos, 1997b) and is reproduced courtesy of
Elsevier Science.

2 In economic terms, there are no easy ways to identify the middle classes.
I will take 'middle class' to refer to those whose monthly income is higher
than 15 minimum salaries. In São Paulo, this accounts for about 25 per
cent of the population.

3 Average personal income is US$400 a month and private schools cost
about US$300 per month. The number of children attending public schools
in São Paulo increased by 38 per cent between 1978 and 1990, but the corresponding increase in private school attendance was 122 per cent (SEADE,
1991).

4 For example, trips to the beach (50 miles away) are regularly made by more
than 100,000 cars at the weekends, rising to 250,000 at carnival time and
during long weekends. See DERSA, 1992.

5 The chaining capability of the car plays an important role. For the three
highest income levels, the car accounts for between 40 and 80 per cent of
chained trips.

6 Vuchic is quoting Weyrich and Lind, 1996.

CHAPTER 13

1 In a survey of 757 households in Niamey, Niger, in 1996, 45 per cent were
'nuclear' families, 48 per cent were extended and 7 per cent consisted of
only one person (Diaz Olvera et al, 1999).

2 In Bamako in Mali, the mobility of the rich households is slightly lower
than in the poor households, although motorized mobility still rises with
income. This seems to be the result of the employment patterns of the higher-
income earners, who tend to stay in the office all day (Diaz Olvera et al,
1997).

CHAPTER 14

1   The only exception is the opportunity that middle- and higher-income groups have to own houses in the country, or to take holidays from the polluted environment. Working in heavily polluted environments obviously affects everyone equally.
2   All major metropolitan areas in the US experience high levels of congestion on existing expressways – it is estimated that 1.2 billion passenger-hours are wasted per year (TTI, 1996). Costs in the whole country are over US$100 billion per year (an 11 per cent increase over total travel time costs) (Litman, 1996).
3   The study adopted the 'capacity' concept and used local traffic data, international studies and the experience of local transport planners to define volume–speed relationships and overall congestion parameters.

CHAPTER 15

1   This part of the paper is based largely on my paper 'Reassessing traffic accidents in developing countries', published in *Transport Policy* and with permission from Elsevier Science (Vasconcellos, 1995).

CHAPTER 16

1   Vuchic (1999, p189) gives the example of the debate in the US, in which the use of public money for public transport modes is called 'an outlay of taxpayers' money', while its use to support roadway construction is called 'investment', and the provision of subsidized parking spaces is called 'customer service'.
2   The myth of car-use as an inevitable consequence of wealth has been explored in detail by Newman and Kenworthy (1999).

CHAPTER 17

1   See Kranton (1991) and UNCHS (1992).
2   For data on the elasticity of demand for public transport, see for instance Oum, Waters and Yong (1990).
3   For instance, CO_2 emissions per capita in 1992 were 19.3 tonnes in the US, 9.78 in the UK and 0.88 in China (Whitelegg, 1993).
4   Richer people can escape pollution through weekend breaks, but during the working day everyone is affected.
5   Whitelegg (1997) shows very clearly how this ideology quickly changes into the assertion of a 'human right'. In Germany, people reacted against the imposition of speed limits with the slogan 'free travel for free citizens'. As Whitelegg points out, there was no corresponding campaign to assert children's rights to use the streets safely.

CHAPTER 18

1 Reprogle (1992) outlines an interesting discussion on non-motorized cities.
2 Dimitriou provides the policy objectives, implict economic roles and the performance criteria separately; I hope that I have combined them faithfully here.
3 Wright takes Lancaster's approach (1966), which emphasizes the intrinsic characteristics of transport modes and vehicles, and not the modes and vehicles themselves.
4 A study of medium-sized towns in the state of São Paulo showed that, in the case of cities with 600,000 inhabitants, a four-fold increase in the population density leads to an average public-transport cost that is 2.7 times lower than that which is to be found in circular-type cities, and 4 times lower than in linear cities. See Ferraz et al, 1991.

CHAPTER 19

1 The city of Porto Alegre in Brazil has been organizing a highly transparent public discussion around public policies since 1993. The process revolves around four main issues: economic development, urban development and reform, transport and urban circulation, and city financing.
2 This was the case in Chile, where the first auction was opposed by operators. It also happened in the state of São Paulo, where the state government tried to auction off intercity bus services in 1989. The bidding was opposed by operators and has yet to take place.
3 See Vuchic, 1979 and Armstrong-Wright, 1986.
4 Several surveys in São Paulo have shown that users prefer the subway to current low quality bus services.
5 Transfer time, like waiting time, is much disliked by passengers.
6 A general framework is provided by Wright (1992). The African case is discussed by Howe (1994) and the Asian case by Rao and Sharma (1990) and Reprogle (1992).
7 Personal communication.

CHAPTER 20

1 The Public Ministry is a relatively independent public agency in charge of all public issues. Under the 1988 constitution it was accorded the surveillance of environmental problems. It can therefore take action against anything that harms the public environment.
2 Reserve capacity (RC) refers to unused capacity (Webster and Cobbe, 1986). In most large developing world cities the RC is low.
3 Most bus lanes yielded a net gain of 1–2 minutes on a journey time of 30 to 40 minutes.
4 See Button, 1982, Bayliss, 1992 and Greene et al, 1997.

References

Abercrombie, N, and Urry, J (1983) *Capital, labour and the middle classes*, George Allen and Unwin, London.

Abras, K A (1999) 'Estimation and assessment of cost allocation models for main transit systems operating in Cairo', *Transport reviews*, vol 19, no 4, pp353–375.

Abubakar, I (1998) 'The implementation of an urban transportation policy: the Triple Decker project' in *Urban transport policy*, Freedman and Jamet (eds), Balkema, Netherlands, pp979–986.

Abu-Lughod, J (1996) 'Urbanisation in the Arab world' in J Gugler (ed), *The urban transformation of the developing world*, Oxford University Press, pp185–208

Akapko, A M (1998) 'The role of the city of Lomé in urban transport' in *Urban transport policy*, Freeman and Jamet (eds), Balkemna, Rotterdam, pp517–521.

Akinbami, J F K and Fadare, S O (1997) 'Strategies for sustainable urban and transport development in Nigeria', *Transport policy*, vol 4, no 4, pp237–245.

Alford, PR and Friedland, R (1985) *Powers of theory: capital, the state and democracy*, Princeton University Press, US.

Alquéres, C A and Martines, G L (1999) 'As relações entre o conforto, a capacidade, o desempenho e o consumo no planejamento de sistemas de transporte', paper presented at the Caracas Clatpu meeting, December.

Amin, S (1992) 'Can environmental problems be subject to economic calculations?' *World development*, vol 20, no 4, pp523–530.

ANFAVEA – Associação Nacional dos Fabricantes de veículos automotories (1997) *Boletim Estatístico*, São Paulo.

ANTP – Associação Nacional de Transportes Públicos (1997) *Anuário estatístico dos transportes*, São Paulo.

ANTP – Associação Nacional de Transportes Públicos (1998) *Transporte humano, cidades com qualidade de vida*, São Paulo.

ANTP/IPEA (1998) *Melhoria do transporte urbano com a redução da deseconomias*, Instututo de Pesquisa Econômica Aplicada, Brasília.

Appleyard, D (1981) *Livable streets*, University of California Press, US.

Armstrong-Wright, A (1993) *Public transport in Third World cities*, TRL, London.

Arruda, J B Furtado (1996) 'Valor do tempo de viagem para avaliação de projetos de transportes no Brasil: um estudo crítico-comparativo', *Transporte em transformação*, CNT/Makron Books, São Paulo, pp52–71.

Atkins, S T (1986) 'Transportation planning models – what the papers say', *Traffic engineering and control*, September 1986, pp460–67.

Bacha, E L and Klein, H S (1989) *Social change in Brazil: 1945–1985, the incomplete transition*, University of Mexico Press, US.

Ball, M (1986) 'The built environment and the urban question', *Environment and planning D: society and space*, vol 4, pp447–64.

Banjo G A and Dimitriou H (1983) 'Urban transport problems in Third World cities: the third generation', *Habitat International*, no 7, pp99–110.

Barat, J (1985) 'Integrated metropolitan transport – reconciling efficiency, equity and environmental improvement', *Third World planning review*, vol 7, no 3, pp242–261.

Barat, J (1991) 'Transportes urbanos no Brasil: diagnóstico e perspectivas', *Planejamento e políticas públicas*, no 6, Brasilia, pp75–96.

Barat, J (1992) 'Sistemas de remuneração pela produção no serviços de transporte coletivo', *Revista dos transportes públicos*, no 57, pp5–25.

Barge, C and Chesnais, M (2000) 'Accessibility and mobility in Cairo: the challenge of public transportation', *IX Codatu proceedings*, pp707–712, Mexico City.

Barrett, P (1983) *The automobile and the urban transit*, Temple University Press, US.

Barrett, R (1988) *Urban transport in West Africa*, World Bank technical paper no 81, Washington DC.

Barry, N and Kawas, C (1997) 'Putting the poor at the centre of urban strategies' in *Cities fit for people*, Uner Kirdar (ed), UN, New York, pp232–245.

Basu, J (1997) 'The underground railway system in Calcutta,' *World transport planning and practice*, vol 3, no 3, pp42–46.

Baumol, W J and Oates, W E (1988) *The theory of environmental policy*, Cambridge University Press, UK.

Bayliss, B (1992) *Transport policy and planning – an integrated analytical framework*, Economic Development Institute of the World Bank, Washington DC.

Bell, D D and Kuranami, C (1994) 'Nonmotorized vehicles in Hanoi and Phnom Penh: existing situation and options for improvement', *Transportation research record* 1441, pp93–100, Transportation Research Board, Washington DC.

Benitez, B N and Roldán, S L B (1999) 'Transporte y medio-ambiente: la experiencia de la ciudad de Mexico', Clatpu, Caracas meeting, December, pp227–233.

Bernard, Jean-Claude and Julien, N (1974) 'Pour un analyse des transports urbains', *L'archit11ure d'auhourd'hui*, no 172, pp98–104.

Bhattacharyya, D (1995) 'The throttling of a transport system: Calcutta tramway', *World transport policy and practice*, vol 1, no 3, pp23–27.

Bhattacharyya, D (1997) 'Unco-ordinated public transport: Calcutta style', *World transport policy and practice*, vol 3, no 3, pp38–41.

BID – Banco Interamericano de Desarrollo (1998) *Seguriad vial en America Latina y el Caribe*, Washington DC.

Bieber, A, Massot, M H and Orfeul, J P (1992) *Questions vives pour une prospective de la mobilite quotidienne*, INRETS, France.

Blanchard, R D (1976) 'Transportation and the new planning: towards a synthesis', *High speed ground transportation journal*, vol 10, no 1, pp14–30.

Bonsall, P (1996) 'Can induced traffic be measured by surveys?', *Transportation*, vol 23, pp17–34.

Borja, J (1996) 'Cities: new roles and forms of governing' in *Preparing for the urban future – global pressures and local changes*, M Cohen et al (eds), Woodrow Wilson Center, Washington DC, pp242–263.

Boschi, R R (1987) 'Social movements and the new political order in Brazil', in Wirth, Nunes and Bogenschild (eds), *State and society in Brazil, continuity and change*, Westview Press, US.

Bovy, P (1990) *Transport and the environment: a tentative overview of issues in cities of developed and developing countries*, Swiss Federal Institute of Technology.

Bovy, P (2000) 'Integrated planning and transport development for more sustainable mobility', UITP meeting on mobility, Mexico City, April.

Brasileiro, A (1999) 'Rede integrada e viação diante do modelo urbanístico de Curitiba', in A Brasileiro and E Henry (eds) *Viação ilimitada – ônibus das cidades brasileiras*, Cultura Editores Associados, São Paulo, pp457–490.

Brasileiro, A and Henry, E (1999) 'Secretaria de Viação, fabricação e promoção do sistema ônibus brasileiro' in A Brasileiro and E Henry (eds) *Viação ilimitada – ônibus das cidades brasileiras*, Cultura Editores Associados, São Paulo, pp47–118.

Brühning, E (1997) 'Injuries and deaths on the roads, an international perspective' in T Fletcher and A J McMichael (eds) *Health at the crossroads, transport policy and urban health*, pp109–121, Wiley, London.

Brunn, E C and Vuchic, V (1993) *Time-area concept: development, meaning and applications*, TRB, Transportation research record 1499, Washington DC.

Buchanan C (1963) *Traffic in towns*, Her Majesty Stationery Office.

Button, K J (1982) *Transport economics*, Heinemann, UK.

Button, K J (1993) *Transport, the environment and economic policy*, Edward Elgar, UK.

Calfee, J and Winston, C (1998) 'The value of automobile travel time: implications for congestion policy', *Journal of public economics*, 69, pp83–102.

Câmara, A P R (1994) 'Rio de Janeiro public transport provision' in X Godard (ed) *Les transports dans les villes du Sud*, Karthala-Codatu, Paris, pp31–46.

Cameron, J W M (1998) 'Transport contribution to urban restructuring', in *Urban transport policy*, Freeman and Jamet (eds), Balkema, Netherlands, pp245–252.

Carbajo, J (1993) *Regulatory reform in transport: some recent experiences*, The World Bank, Washington.

Carchedi, G (1975) 'On the economic identification of the new middle class', *Economy and society*, no 4, pp1–86.

Cardoso, F H (1977), *O modelo Politico brasileiro*, Rio de Janeiro, DIFEL.

Carlsson, G and Hedman, K-O (1990) *A systematic approach to road safety in developing countries*, World Bank report INU 63, Washington DC.

Carlstein, T, Parkes, D and Thrift, N (1978) *Human activity and time geography*, Edward Arnold, UK.

Carnoy, M and Levin H M (1985), *Schooling and work in the democratic state*, Stanford University Press, US.

Casas, L G (1999) 'Los corredores de la modernidad: movilidad y planificación urbana en Caracas', Clatpu Caracas meeting, pp55–60.

Castells, M (1975) *Lotte urbane e potere politico*, Marsilio Editori, Italy.

Castells, M (1976) 'Is there an urban sociology?' in C G Pickvance (ed) *Urban sociology: critical essays*, St Martin's Press, New York.

Castells, M (1977) *The urban question, a marxist approach*, MIT Press, US.

Castells, M (1999), *A sociedade em rede*, vol 1, Paz e Terra, São Paulo.

CEPAL (1988) 'Regulamentação e subvenção do transporte coletivo urbano: argumentos a favor e contra', *Revista dos transportes públicos*, no 41, pp29–55.

CERTU – Centre d'études sur les réseaux, les transports, l'urbanisme et les construction publiques (1996) *Plains de déplacements urbaines*, France.

Cervero, R (1998a) *The transit metropolis – a global enquiry*, Island Press, US.

Cervero, R (1998b) 'Paratransit, the gap fillers', *Habitat debate*, vol 4, no 2, pp8–9, The United Nations Centre for Human Settlements, Nairobi.

CET – Cia de Engenharia de Tráfego (1978) *Transporte por ônibus contratado*, Boletim Técnico 18, São Paulo.

CET – Cia de Engenharia de Tráfego (1983) *Nivel de carregamento do sistema viário principal*, São Paulo.

CET – Cia de Engenharia de Tráfego (1985) *Probus*, São Paulo.

CET – Cia de Engenharia de Tráfego (1992) *Acidentes de trânsito*, São Paulo.

CET – Cia de Engenharia de Tráfego (1997) *Corredores de ônibus, volumes e velocidades médias 1995* (internal report), São Paulo.

CET – Cia de Engenharia de Tráfego (1998) *Operação horário de pico, relatório de avaliação*, São Paulo,

CET – Cia de Engenharia de Tráfego (1999) *Acidentes de trânsito, estatística preliminar*, São Paulo.

CETESB, Cia de Tecnologia de Saneamento Ambiental (1996) *Relatório de qualidade do ar no Estado de São Paulo*, São Paulo.

Chakraborti, D (1997) 'Calcutta in pollution perspective', *World transport policy and practice*, vol 3, no 3, pp15–23.

Chakravarty, A K and Sachdeva, Y (1998) 'Sustainable urban transport policies for developing countries' in Freeman and Jamet (eds) *Urban transport policy*, Balkema, Netherlands.

Chapin, F S (1974) *Human activity patterns in the city: things people do in time and space*, Wiley, London.

Chen, X and Parish, W L (1996) 'Urbanization in China: reassessing an evolving model, in J Gugler (ed), *The urban transformation of the developing world*, Oxford University Press, UK, pp61–90.

Chichilnisky, G (1997) 'The costs and benefits of benefit–cost analysis', *Environment and development economics*, 2, pp202–206.

Chojoh, U (1989) 'Learning from medium and small sized bus services in developing countries: is regulation necessary?' *Transportation research A*, vol 23, no 1, pp19–28.

CMSP – Cia do Metropolitano de São Paulo (1987) *Pesquisa origem – destino 1987*, São Paulo.

CMSP (1998) *Pesquisa origem – destino 1987*, São Paulo.

Cohen, M (1996) 'The hypothesis of urban convergence: are cities in the North and South becoming more alike in an age of globalisation?' in *Preparing for the urban future – global pressures and local changes*, M Cohen et al (eds), Woodrow Wilson Centre, Washington DC, pp25–38.

Connolly, P (1999) 'Mexico City: our common future?', *Environment and urbanization*, vol 11, no 1, pp53–78.

Cusset, Jean-Michel (1997), 'Mobilité deux roues et politique de transport à Ouagadougou et à Hanoi' in *Mobilité et politiques de transport dans les villes én développement*, INRETS, France, pp87–104.

Cusset, Jean-Michle and Sirpe, G (1994) 'La mobilité apportée par le sustème deus roues. Les cas de Ouagadougou', in X Godard (ed) *Les transports dans les villes du Sud*, Karthala-Codatu, Paris, pp187–206.

Da Matta, R (1987) 'The quest for citizenship in a relational universe' in Wirth, Nunes and Bogenschild (eds), *State and Society in Brazil, continuity and change*, Westview, US.

Daniere, A G (1995) 'Transportation planning implementation in cities of the Third World: the case of Bangkok', *Environment and planning: government and policy*, vol 13, pp25–45.

Darbéra, R (1993) 'Deregulation or urban transport in Chile: what have we learned in the decade 1979–1989?', *Transport reviews*, vol 13, no 1, pp45–59

Datta, S (1990) 'Class dynamics, subaltern consciousness and the household perspective: a new approach to Third World urbanization' in Datta, Satya (ed) *Third World urbanization: reappraisals and new perspective*, Swedish Council for Research in the Humanities and Social Sciences.

Datta B C (1998) 'Comparative transport profile of mega cities in India for strategic transport planning', in *Urban transport policy*, Freeman and Jamet (eds), Balkema, Netherlands, pp157–164.

Davis, D E (1994) *Urban leviathan – Mexico City in the twentieth century*, Temple University Press, US.

Dear, M and Scott, A J (1981), *Urbanization and urban planning in capitalist societies*, Methuen, US.

De Boer, A (ed) (1985), *Transport sociology*, Amsterdam.

de la Haye, I (1980) *Marx and Engels and the means of communications*, International General, US.

Deloucas A (1983) 'Macro-micro relationships and in depth research in activity/travel behaviour' in P Jones (ed*) Developments in dynamic and activity based approaches to travel analysis*, Avebury, UK, pp75–98.

DENATRAN – Depto Nacional de Trânsito (1996) *Acidentes de trânsito no Brasil*, Brasília.

DERSA – Desenvolvimento Rodoviario SA (1992) *Estatistica de transito rodoviario*, São Paulo.

DETRAN – Departamento Estadual de Trânsito (1997) *Frota de veículos do município de São Paulo*, São Paulo.

Dianpin, Z (1999) 'Road accidents in People's Republic of China', *IATSS review*, vol 23, no 2, pp114–5.

Diaz Olvera, L, Plat, D and Pochet, P (1997) 'Les mobilités quotidiennes deux pauvres à Bamako et Ouagadougou' in *Mobilité et politiques de transport das les villes en développement*, INRETS, Paris, pp119–134.

Diaz Olvera, L and Plat, D (1997) 'Confisquée, partagée, consensuelle. La voiture à Ouagadougou' in *Mobilité et politiques de transport das les villes en développement*, INRETS, Paris, pp213–226.

Diaz Olvera, L, Plat, D and Pochet, P (1999) *La mobilité à Niamey. Premiers resultats de l'enquête-ménages*, research report, LET, France.

Dimitriou, H (1990) 'Transport problems of the third word', in G A Banjo and H T Dimitriou (eds) (1990), *Transport planning for Third World cities*, Routledge, US, pp50–83.

Dimitriou, H (1992) *Urban transport planning – a developmental approach*, Routledge, London.

Domencich, T A and McFadden, D (1975) *Urban travel demand – a behavioural approach*, North-Holland/American Elsevier, Netherlands.

Doulet, Jean-François (1997) 'Espace urbain, mobilité et développement de la voiture en Chine' in *Mobilité et politiques de transport das les villes en développement*, INRETS, Paris, pp185–198.

Draibe, S M (1993) 'A natureza social de investimentos em transporte de massa: o exemplo da região metropolitana de São Paulo', *Revista dos transportes públicos*, pp37–58.

Ducci, M H (1996) 'The politics of urban sustainability' in *Preparing for the urban future – global pressures and local changes*, M Cohen et al (eds), Woodrow Wilson Center, Washington DC, pp264–298.

Dunleavy, P J (1986) 'The growth of the sectoral cleavages and the stabilization of state expenditures', *Environment and planning D: society and space*, no 4, pp129–144.

Dunn, James A Jr (1981), *Miles to go*, MIT Press, US.

Du Pont, P and Egan, K (1997) 'Solving Bangkok's transport woes: the need to ask the right questions', *World transport policy and practice*, vol 3, no 1, pp25–37.

Dupuy, G (1978), *Urbanisme et technique, chronique d'une marriage du raison*, Centre de Recherche d'Urbanisme, France.

ECMT – European Commission of Ministers of Transport (1999*) Improving transport for people with mobility handicaps*, OECD Publications, Paris.

Etherington, K and Simon, D (1996) 'Paratransit and employment in Phnom Penh: the dynamics and development potential of cyclo riding', *Journal of transport geography*, vol 4, no 12, pp37–53.

FABUS – Sindicato das Empresas Encarroçadoras de Ônibus (1997) *Estatísitca de produção*, São Paulo.

Fainstein, S (1997) 'Justice, politics and the creation of urban space', in Merrifield and Swyngedouw (eds) *The urbanization of injustice*, New York University Press, New York.

Faiz, A (1993) 'Automotive emissions in developing countries – relative implication for global warming, accidification and urban air quality', *Transportation research A*, vol 27, no 3, pp167–186.

Faiz, A, Weaver, C S and Walsh, M (1996) *Air pollution from motor vehicles*, The World Bank, Washington DC.

Falcocchio, J C and Cantilli, E J (1974) *Transport and the disadvantaged*, Lexington Books, US.

Fanelli, J M, Frenkel, R and Rozenwurcel, G (1994) 'Growth and structural reform in Latin America: where we stand' in *Latin American political economy in the age of neoliberal reform*, Smith et al (eds), Transaction Publishers, US, pp101–126.

Ferraz, A C P, Silva A N R and Felex, J B (1991) 'Custo do transporte público x tamanho e forma das cidades', *Revista dos transportes públicos*, vol 13, no 52, pp17–21.

Figueroa, O (1985) 'Diagnostico general del transporte urbano en America Latina', in E Henry and O Figueroa (eds), *Transporte y servicios urbanos en America Latina*, INRETS/CIUDAD, Quito.

Figueroa, O (1990) 'La desregulation del transporte colectivo en Santiago: balance de diez años', *Revista EURE* XVI (49), pp23–32.

Figueroa, O (1991) 'La crise de court terme des transports en commun: l'experience de San Jose du Costa Rica', *Recherche transports securite*, no 31, pp47–56.

Figueroa, O (1997) 'La voiture dans les systèmes urbains en Amérique Latine', in *Mobilité et politiques de transport das les villes en développement*, INRETS, Paris, pp227–242.

Figueroa, O (1999) *Politicas nacionales de desarollo y politicas secoriales de transporte urbano. Coherencias y contradicciones*, Clatpu Caracas meeting, Caracas, December.

Figueroa, O et al (1993) *Transports, tramways, technologie – splendeur et decadénce des tramways en Amerique Latine*, INRETS, Transport transfert development no 6, Paris.

Figueroa, O and Pizarro, A (1998) 'Santa Cruz de la Sierra urban public transport system, urban structure and netwrok restructuring,' in *Urban transport policy*, Freeman and Jamet (eds), Balkema, Netherlands.

Flink, J J (1972) 'Three stages of American automobile consciousness', *American quarterly XXIV*, vol 4, pp451–473.

Fouracre and Gardner (1994) 'Mass transit in developing countries', *Journal of advanced tansportation*, vol 27, no 3, pp251–260.

Friedman, J (1992) *Empowerment – the politics of alternative development*, Blackwell, US.

Furniss, N and Tilton, T (1977) *The case of the welfare state*, Indiana University Press, US.

Gakenheimer, R (1993) 'Land use/transportation planning: new possibilities for developing and developed countries', *Transportation quarterly*, vol 47, no 2, pp311–322.

Gakenheimer, R (1999) 'Urban mobility in the developing world', *Transportation research A 33*, pp671–89.

Garcia, L I and Ocàna, R V (1992) 'Metrobus: Caracas y Santiago, dos experiencias alternativas,' paper presented at the Buenos Aires Clatpu meeting.

Ginsburg, N (1992) *Divisions of welfare, a critical introduction to comparative social policy*, Sage, UK.

Godard, X (1990) 'Concurrence ou reglementation?', in R Proud'homme (ed), *New perceptions and new policies, Urban transport in developing countries*, CODATU Jakarta Conference, Paradigme, Paris, pp209–22.

Godard, X (1997) 'La mobilité dans les villes en développemen, repères comparatifs' in *Mobilité et politiques de transport das les villes en développement*, INRETS, Paris, pp135–142.

Goldemberg, J (1998) *Energia, meio ambiente e desenvolvimento*, Edusp/Cesp, São Paulo.

Goldsmith, W W and Blakely, E J (1992) *Separate societies: poverty and inequality in US Cities*, Temple University Press, Philadelphia Pa.

Gómez-Ibáñez, J and Meyer, J (1991) *Going private – the international experience with transport privatisation*, The Brookings Institution, Washington DC.

Goodwin, P B (1981) 'The usefulness of travel budgets', *Transportation research A*, no 15, pp97–106.

Gordon, D (1991) *Steering a new course – transportation, energy and environment*, Island Press, US.

Gottdiener, M (1993) *A produção social do espaço*, EDUSP, São Paulo.

Gough, I (1979), *The political economy of the welfare state*, Macmillan, England.

Gould, A (1981) 'The salaried middle class in the corporatist welfare state', *Policy and politics*, vol 9, no 4, pp401–18.

Granne, Y H, Hills, B L, Walteros, E P and Peréz, S H (2000) 'Road safety in urban Santa Fé de Bogotá', Codatu Mexico conference proceedings, Balkema, Netherlands, pp905–911.

Greene, D L, Jones, D W and Delucchi, M A (1997) *The full costs and benefits of transportation*, Springer, US.

Grieco, M, Turner, F and Kwakye, E A (1994) 'A tale of two cultures: ethnicity and cycling behavior in urban Ghana', *Transportation research record*, no 1441, pp101–07, Transportation Research Board, Washington DC.

Griffin, J (1995) 'Hanoi, Vietnam: bicyclists facing competition from motorcycles', *Sustainable transport*, winter 1995, pp14–15.

Gueye, B and Bamas, S (1994) 'Systèmes de déplacements dans les villes moyennes dÁfrique. Cas de Bobo et Boaké', in X Godard (ed) *Les transports dans les villes du Sud*, Karthala-Codatu, Paris, pp339–352.

Gugler, J (1996) 'Urbanisation in Africa south of the Sahara: new identities and conflicts', in J Gugler (ed), *The urban transformation of the developing world*, Oxford University Press, UK, pp211–52.

Guitink, P and Flora, J (1995) 'Non motorized transportation in transportation systems: back to the future?', paper presented at the Transportation Research Board 74th conference, Washington DC, January.

Gunn, H et al (1996) 'Estimation de la valeur marginale du temps de transport', *Recherche transport securité*, no 52, pp45–57.

Gunnarsson, S (1995) 'Problems and needs of pedestrians', *IATSS research*, vol 19, no 2, pp47–57.

Gunnarsson, S (1996) 'Traffic accident prevention and reduction – review of strategies', *IATSS research*, vol 20, no 2, pp6–14.

Gwilliam, K M (2000) 'Pollution from motorcycles in Asia: issues and options', *World Bank infrastructure notes*, transport sector, no UT-8, Washington DC.

Hagestrand, T (1970) 'What about people in regional sciences?', *Papers of the Regional Science Association* no 24, pp7–21

Hagestrand, T (1987) 'Human interaction and spatial mobility: retrospect and prospect' in P Nijkamp and S Reichman (eds), *Transportation planning in a changing world*, Gower/European Science Foundation, Netherlands.

Halder, D (1997) 'Transport predicament in Calcutta', *World transport policy and practice*, vol 3, no 3, pp24–30.

Halfani, M (1996) 'Marginality and dynamism: prospects for the sub-Saharan African city', in *Preparing for the urban future – global pressures and local changes*, Cohen, Michael et al (eds), Woodrow Wilson Center, Washington DC, pp83–107.

Hallak, J (1977) *Planning the location of schools – an instrument of educational policy*, International Institute of Educational Planning, UNESCO, Paris.

Harvey, D (1982) *The limits to capital*, University of Chicago Press, US.

Harvey, D (1985) *The urban experience*, John Hopkins, US.

Harvey, D (1990) *The condition of postmodernity*, Blackwell, Oxford.

Harvey, D (1996) *Justice, nature and the geography of difference*, Blackwell, US.

Hasenbalg, C A and Silva, N V (1987) 'Industrialization, employment and stratification in Brazil' in Wirth, Nunes and Bogenschild (eds), *State and society in Brazil, continuity and change*, Westview, US.

Hathway, G (1985) *Low-cost vehicles – options for moving people and goods*, Intermediate Technology Publications, UK.

Hayashi, Y, Yang, Z and Osman, O (1998) 'The effects of economic restructuring on China's system for financing transport infrastructure', *Transportation Research A*, vol 32, no 3, pp183–195.

Healey, P (1977) 'The sociology of urban transport planning – a socio-political perspective' in D Hensher (ed) *Urban transport economics*, pp119–227.

Henry, E and Figueroa, O (eds) (1985), *Transporte y servicios urbanos en America Latina*, INRETS/CIUDAD, Rio Quito.

Henry, E (1993) 'Redes e empresas de transporte – viagem de ônibus pelas cidades brasileiras', *Revista dos transportes públicos*, no 58, pp31–60.

Henry, E (1997) 'Tacubaya – La Paz/1968–95 x 190 kilomètres = 4,5 millions ed Mexicans/jour' in *Mobilité et politiques de transport das les villes en développement*, INRETS, Paris, pp143–160.

Henry, E (1999) 'Os funis, um esquema analítico. Da produção simples do serviço à empresa capitalista', in A Brasileiro and E Henry (eds) *Viação ilimitada – ônibus das cidades brasileiras*, Cultura Editores Associados, São Paulo, pp373–400.

Henry, E and Kuhn, F (1996) 'Mass transit system, metro and variants: Mexican lessons and others' in *Urban transport policy*, Freeman and Jamet (eds), Balkemna, Netherlands.

Hierli, U (1993) *Environment limits to motorization – non-motorised transport in developed and developing countries*, SKAT, Switzerland.

Hill, B L and Jacobs, G D (1981), 'The application of road safety countermeasures in developing countries', *Traffic engineering and control*, vol 22, no 8/9, pp464–68.

Hill, M and Bramley, G (1986), *Analysing social policy*, Edward Elgar, England.

Hillman, M (1983) 'The wrong turning: twenty years on from Buchanan' in *Built enviroment*, vol 9, no 2, pp104–112.

Hillman, M (1988) 'Foul play for children: a price of mobility', *Town and country planning*, October, pp331–332.

Hillman, M (1997) 'Health promotion: the potential of non-motorized transport' in Fletcher and McMichael (eds) *Health at the crossroads – transport policy and urban health*, Wiley, London, pp177–186.

Hillman, M and Whaleey, A (1979) *Walking is transport*, Policy Studies Institute, vol XLV, no 583, London.

Hillman, M, J Adams and J Whitelegg (1990) 'One false move: a study of children's independent mobility', Policy Studies Institute, London.

Hook, W (1994a) 'Role of nomotorized transportation and public transport in Japan's economic success, in *Nonmotorised transportation around the world*, TRR 1441, Washington DC, pp108–15.

Hook, W (1994b) *Counting on cars, counting out people*, Institute for Transportation and Development Policy, paper no I-0194, New York.

Hook, W (1998) 'UP in smoke – Jakarta: a city in crisis', *Sustainable transport*, no 8, pp14, 20–21.

Hoover, J H and Altschuler, A A (1977) *Involving cities in metropolitan region transportation planning*, US DOT.

Hoque, M D and Ahmed, Noor-Ud-Deen S (1994) 'Problems of urban transport and traffic management in Bangladesh: an overview of key aspects', X Godard (ed) *Les transports dans les villes du Sud*, Karthala-Codatu, Paris, pp257–267.

Hossain, M and McDonald, M (1998) 'Modelling the impacts of reducing non-motorised traffic in urban corridors of development cities', *Transportation research*, vol 32, no 4, pp247–60.

Howe, J (1994) *Enhancing non-motorized transport use in Africa – changing the policy climate*, working paper IP-6, IHE Delft, Netherlands.

Howe, J (1996) *Transport for the poor or poor transport?*, working paper IP-12, IHE Delft, Netherlands.

Howe, C (1992) *Political ideology and class formation*, Praeger, US.

Hugo, G (1996) 'Urbanisation in Indonesia' in J Gugler, *The urban transformation of the developing world*, Cambridge University Press, Cambridge, pp133–83.

Hutchinson, B G (1974), *Principles of urban transport system planning*, England.

IBGE – Instituto Brasileiro de Geografia e Estatística (1990) *Pesquisa nacional por amostra domiciliar*, Rio de Janeiro.

IIT – Indian Institute of Technology (1995) *The work done*, New Delhi, India.

IIT (1999) *Road designs for improving traffic flow – a bicycle master plan for Delhi*, New Delhi, India.

ILD – Instituto Libertad y Democracia (1990) *El transporte urbano de pasajerows en Lima*, Editiones El Virrey AS, Lima, Peru.

Illich, I (1974) *Energy and Equity*, Harper and Row, US.

IPEA/ANTP (1998) *Redução das deseconomias urbanas com a melhoria do transporte público*, relatório final, Brasília.

Irwin, A (1985) *Risk and the control of technology*, Manchester University Press, UK.

ITE – Institute of Transportation Engineers (1976) *Transportation and traffic engineering handbook*, Prentice Hall, US.

ITS-UCD (1997) *The annualized cost of motor-vehicle use in the US, 1900–1991: summary of theory data, methods and results*, University of California at Davis.

Jamarillo, S (1993) 'El desenvolvimiento de la discussion sobre la urbanizacion Latinoamericana: hacia un nuevo paradigma de interpretacion' in S Jamarillo and L M Cuervo (eds) *Urbanizacion Lationamericana – nuevas perspectivas*, Escala, Colômbia.

Jones, P M (1983) 'The practical application of activity-based approaches in transport planning: an assessment' in S Carpenter and P M Jones (eds) *Recent advances in travel demand analysis*, Gower, UK, pp56–78.

Kanafani, A (1983), *Transport demand analysis*, US.

Kane, C (1997) 'Pour un novelle approche de l'étude de la mobilité des populations à Dakar', in *Mobilité et politiques de transport das les villes en développement*, INRETS, Paris, pp105–18.

Kane, C and Seck, A (1996) *Mobilité et pauvreté à Dakar, analyse exploratoires* (rapport intermédiaire pour le compte du Ministére de la Coopértion, sus la diretción de Xavier Godard), INRETS, France.

Kenworthy, J R (1995) 'Automobile dependence in Bangkok: an international comparison with implications for planning policies', *World transport policy and practice*, vol 1, no 3, pp31–41.

Kenworthy, J R (1997) 'Automobile dependence in Bangkok: an international comparison with implications for planning policies and air pollution' in Fletcher and McMichael (eds) *Health at the crossroads – transport policy and urban health*, Wiley, London, pp215–34.

Khayesi, M (1997) 'Livable streets for pedestrians in Nairobi: the challenge of road traffic accidents', *World transport policy and practice*, vol 3, no 1, pp4–7.

Kim, K S and Gallent, N (1998) 'Transport issues and policies in Seoul: an exploration', *Transport reviews*, vol 18, no 1, pp83–99.

Kitamura, C, Bell, D D and Winston, B (1994) 'Planning non-motorized vehicles – balancing transport modes in Asian cities', *The wheel extended*, no 90, pp11–16.

Kitamura, R, Fujii, S and Pas, E (1997) 'Time-use data, analysis and modelling: toward the next generation of transportation planning methodologies,' *Transport Policy*, vol 4, no 4, pp225–235.

Koprich, D F (1994) 'The modernization of Santiago's public transport: 1990–1992', *Transport reviews*, vol 14, no 2, pp167–185.

Koster, J H and Gerwin, H (2000), 'Formal and informal public transport performance assessment: Nairobi case study', IX Codatu conference proceedings, Mexico City, pp307–313.

Kowarick, L (1979), *A espoliação urbana*, Paz e Terra, São Paulo.

Kowarick, L (1991) 'Ciudad y cidadania, Metropolis des subdesarollo industrializado', *Nueva sociedad* 114, July–August.

Kranton, R E (1991) *Transport and mobility needs of the urban poor, an explanatory study*, World Bank discussion paper, report INU 86.

Kubota, H and Kidokoro, T (1994) 'Analysis of bicycle-dependent transport systems in China: case study in a medium-sized city', in *Nonmotorized transport around the world*, TRR 1441, TRB, pp11–15.

Kuhn, T S (1970) *The structure of scientific revolution*, University of Chicago Press, US.

Kulkami, S D (1998) 'Urban road passenger transport in Indian mega cities,' in *Urban transport policy*, Freemand and Jamet (eds), Balkemna, Netherlands.

Kuranami, C, Winston, B P and Guitink, P A (1994) ' Nonmotorized vehicles in Asian cities: issues and policies', *Transportation research record*, no 1441, pp61–67, Transportation Research Board, Washington, DC.

Kwakye, E A, Fouracre, P R, Ofusu-Dorte, D (1997) 'Developing strategies to meet transport needs of the urban poor in Ghana', *World transport policy and practice*, vol 3, no 1, pp8–14.

Lancaster, K (1966) 'A new approach to consumer theory', *Journal of political economy*, no 74, pp132–157.

Lee, J (1998) 'Road accidents in Korea', *IATSS research*, vol 22, no 2, pp124–125.

Lefevbre, H (1979) 'Space: social product and use value' in J Freiberg (ed) *Critical Sociology: European Perspective*, Irvington Publishers, New York.

Lewis, S, Cook, P and Miné, M (1990) 'Comprehensive transportation models: past, present and future', *Transportation Quarterly*, vol 44, no 2, pp249–265.

Lewontin, R (1992) 'Organism and environment' in A Plotkin (ed) *Learning, development and culture*, Chichester.

Lindau, L A (1992) 'Sistemas de transporte urbano de média capacidade: uma análise comparativa enfocando as tecnologias VLT e ônibus', paper presented at the VI conference ANPET.

Lindau, L A and Willumsen, L G (1990) 'Allocating road space to vehicles: the experience of Brasil' in H Proud'homme (ed) *Nouvelles perceptions et nouvelles politiques, transport urbain dans les pays en developpement*, Paradigme, Paris, pp127–142.

Linn, J (1983), *Cities in the developing world, policies for their equitable and efficient growth*, World Bank, Washington DC.

Litman, T (1996) *Transportation cost analysis: techniques, estimates and implications*, Victoria Transport Policy Institute, Vancouver, Canada.

Lojkine, J (1976) 'Contribution to a marxist theory of capitalist urbanization' in C G Pickvance (ed), *Urban sociology: critical essays*, St Martin's Press, New York.

Lu, X M and Ye, G X (1998) 'Situation and policy of transportation in Shanghai at turning of the century', in *Urban transport policy*, Freeman and Jamet (eds), Balkemna, Netherlands, pp149–55.

Lupo, A, Colcord F and Fowler E P (1971), *Rites of way – the politics of transportation in Boston and the US city*, Boston, Little Brown and Company, US.

McGranahan, G, Songsore, J and Kjellén, M (1996) 'Sustainability, poverty and urban environmental transitions', in C Pugh (ed) *Sustainability, environment and urbanisation*, Earthscan, London, pp102–34.

Mackie, P and Preston, J (1998) 'Twenty-one sources of error and bias in transport project appraisail' *Transport policy*, vol 5, no 1, pp1–7.

McShane, M P, Koshi, M and Lundin, A (1984) 'Public policy toward the automobile: a comparative look at Japan and Sweden', *Transportation research A*, vol 18 no 2, pp97–109.

McShane, W R and Roess, R P (1990) *Traffic engineering*, Prentice Hall, US.

Maddison, D, Pearce, D, Johansson, O, Calthrop, E, Litman, T and Verhoef, E (1996) *The true costs of road transport*, Earthscan, London.

Magdaleno, I P, Rios, H V, Moret M, Arias, Z P, Gatorno, A G and Fernándes, A G (1999) 'Investigatión de la movilidad de la población residente en la ciudad de la Habana', paper presented at the Clatpu meeting in Caracas, December.

Mandon-Adolehoume, B (1994) 'Secteru prové et service public: résultats et perspectives', X Godard (ed) *Les transports dans les villes du Sud*, Karthala-Codatu, Paris, pp127–147.

Mankouch, S (1997) 'L' automobilie dans les métropoles du Maghreg, motorisation et pratiques demobilité en voitures particulières' in *Mobilité et politiques de transport das les villes en développement*, INRETS, Paris, pp199–212.

Marcano, E E (1981) 'Caracas: producción del espacio urbano para el consumo del automóvil', *Revista urbana* 3, pp139–156, Caracas.

Marchetti, C (1994) 'Anthropological invariants in travel behavior', *Technological forecasting and social change*, vol 47, pp75–88.

Marshall, T (1975) *Cidadania, classe social e status*, Zahar, Rio de Janeiro.

Martins, J A (1992) *Uma analise critica do relatorio Buchanan: as contradicoes teorico-metodologicas e o 'mito' da escassez*, Rio de Janeiro, VI National meeting, ANPET.

Martins, L (1985) *Estado capitalista e burocracia no Brasil pós-64*, Zahar, Rio de Janeiro.

Matouk, A and Abeille, M (1994) 'La crise des transports urbains à Alger. La part du cadre institutionnel et réglentaire' in X Godard (ed) *Les transports dans les villes du Sud*, Karthala-Codatu, Paris, pp114–26.

Maundner, D A C and Mbara, T C (1994) 'The effects of ownership on the level of stage bus public transport provision in Harare, Zimbabwe', in X Godard (ed) *Les transports dans les villes du Sud*, Karthala-Codatu, Paris, pp59–71.

May, A D (1986) 'Traffic restraint: a review of the alternatives', *Transportation research*, vol 20, no 2, pp109–21.

May, A D (1991) 'Integrated transport strategies:a new approach to urban transport policy in the UK', *Transport reviews*, vol 11, no 3, pp213–47.

May, N and Ribeill, G (1976) 'Les precesses revendicatifs en matiere de transports urbains', *La Vie Urbaine*, vol 2/3/4, pp9–20.

Merlin, P (1985), *Les politiques des transports urbains*, La documentation francaise (no 4797), Paris.

Mikulik, Josef (1998) 'Road accidents in the Czech Republic', *IATSS research*, vol 29, no 1, pp132–34.

Miller, P and Moffet, J (1993) *The price of mobility – uncovering the hidden costs of transportation*, Natural Resources Defense Council, US.

Ministerio de Transporte y Comunicaciones (1982), *Dados sobre transporte en Caracas*, Caracas.

Mitchel, R and Rapkin, C (1954) *Urban traffic, a function of land use*, Columbia University Press, US.

Mitlin, D and Satterthwaite, D (1996) 'Sustainable development in cities', in C Pugh (ed) *Sustainability, environment and urbanisation*, Earthscan, London, pp23–62.

Mohan, D (1999) 'Road accidents in India', *IATSS research*, vol 23, no 1, pp2–3.

Mohan, D and Twari, G (1998) 'Traffic safety in low-income countries: issues and concerns regarding technology transfer from high-income countries' in *Reflections on the transfer of traffic safety knowledge to motorising nations*, Global Traffic Safety Trust, Australia, pp27–56.

Mohan, R (1996) 'Urbanisation in India: Patterns and emerging policy issues', in J Gugler (ed) *The urban transformation of the developing world*, Cambridge University Press, Cambridge, pp93–131.

Molinero, A (1991) 'Mexico City metropolitan area case study', *Built environment*, vol 17, no 2, pp122–37.

Moseley, M J, Harman R G, Coles O B, and Spencer, M B (1977), *Rural transport and accessibility*, University of East Anglia, UK.

Nader, R (1965) *Unsafe at any speed: the designed-in dangers of the American automobile*, Grossman, US.

Navin, F, Bergan, A, Qi, J and Li, J, (1994a) 'Road Safety in China', *Transportation research record*, no 1441, pp3–10, Transportation Research Board, Washington DC.

Navin, F, Bergan, A, Qi, J (1994b) ' Fundamental relationship for roadway safety: model for global comparisons', *Transportation research record*, no 1441, pp53–60, Transportation Research Board, Washington DC.

N'Dow, W (1997) 'An urbanising world', in *Cities fit for people*, Uner Kirdar (ed), UN, New York, pp27–49.

Neto, U (1990) 'Modelos simplificados de planejamento de transportes de passageriso: uma necessidade de curto prazo nos países em desenvolvimento', *Revista da ANPET*, no 3, pp69–83.

Newman, P W G and Kenworthy, J R (1989) *Cities and automobile dependence: a sourcebook*, Gower Technical, Australia.

Newman, P W G and Kenworthy, J R (1999) *Sustainability and cities – overcoming automobile dependence*, Island Press, US.

Ngabmen, H (1997) 'Crise des transports colletifs et stratégies d'adaptation: le cas de Yaoundé' in *Mobilité et politiques de transport das les villes en développement*, INRETS, Paris, pp171–184.

Nigriello, A (1993) 'Transporte coletivo: a experiência internacional em fontes não convencionais de financiamento', *Revista dos transportes públicos*, no 61, pp79–90.

Nijkamp, P and Reichman, S (1987) *Transportation planning in a changing world*, Gower / European Science Foundation.

NTU – Associação Nacional das Empresas de Transportes Urbanos (1998) *Transporte público urbano; crise e oportunidades*, Brasília.

Nunes, E (1991) *El gobierno en la ciudades de tamano medio en Brasil: los casos de Marilia y Piracicaba in Municio y Democracia*, Ediciones Sur, Chile.

O'Connor, J (1973) *The fiscal crisis of the state*, St Martin's Press, New York.

O'Donnell, G (1988) 'Democracia delegativa?' *Novos estudos*, CEBRAP, vol 31, pp25–40, Sao Paulo.

O'Donnell, G (1994) 'The state, democratisation and some conceptual problems (A Latin American view with glances at some post-communist countries)' in *Latin American political economy in the age of neoliberal reform*, Smith et al (eds), Transaction Publishers, US, pp157–80.

OECD (1985) *Coordination urban transport planning*, Paris.

OECD (1986) *OECD road traffic research: a synthesis*, Paris.

Ogunsanya, A A (1984) 'Improving urban traffic flow by restraint of traffic: the case of Lagos, Nigeria, *Transportation*, no 12, pp183–194.

Offe, C (1981) 'Capitalismo avançado e welfare state' in F H Cardoso and C E Martins, *Politica e Sociedade*, no 2, Cia Ed Nacional, São Paulo.

Olszewski, P and Tan, Cher-Sin (1999) 'The use of walking as a mode of travelling', Singapore, paper presented at the 78th Transportation Research Board Meeting, Washington DC, January.

Oppenheim, N (1995), *Urban travel demand modelling – from individual choices to general equilibrium*, John Wiley and Sons, US.

Orfeuil, J P (1994) *Je suis l'automobile*, Editions de l'aube, Paris.

Orrico, Rômulo D and Santos, E Medeiros (1996*) O mercado de transporte público urbano por ônibus: que contestabilidade?*, COPPE-UFRJ, Rio de Janeiro (working paper).

Ortúzar, J de Dios, Ivelik, A M, Malbran H and Thomas A (1993), 'The great Santiago origin-destination survey: methodological design and main results, *Traffic engineering and control*, vol 34, no 7/8, pp362–368.

Ortúzar, J de Dios (1997) *Valor del tiempo en evaluacion de proyectos: el dilema Chileno*, 1997, Chile.

Oulalou, T Z (1994) 'Bilan de la privatization du transport collectif urbain au Maroc (Cas de Casablanca)', X Godard (ed) *Les transports dans les villes du Sud*, Karthala-Codatu, Paris, pp161–172.

Oun, Tae H, Waters W G II, and Yong, J S (1990) *A survey of recent estimates of price elasticities of demand for transport*, World Bank technical paper S 359, Washington DC.

Owens, S (1996), 'I wouldn't start from here: land use, transport and sustainability', *Transport and the environment*, Bryan Cartledge, University of Oxford, 1996, pp45–61, UK.

Pacheco, R S V M (1985*) L'offre et l'utilization des transports colllectifs a la peripherie de Sao Paulo*, Institut d'urbanisme de Paris, Université de Paris XII (thesis).

Paes de Barros, R, Ricardo H and Rosane M (2000) 'Evolução recente da pobreza e da desigualdade: marcos preliminares para a política social no Brasil', *Pobreza e Política Social*, Cadernos Adenauer no 1, pp11–30, São Paulo.

Pahl, R E (1969) 'Urban social theory and research', *Environment and planning*, vol 1, pp143–153.

Pahl, R E (1977a) 'Managers, technical experts and the state: forms of mediation, manipulation and dominance in urban and regional development' in M Harloe (ed) *Captive cities – studies in the political economy of cities and regions*, John Wiley, UK.

Pahl, R E (1977b) 'Collective consumption and the state in capitalist and socialist societies' in R Scase (ed) *Industrial society, class, cleavage and control*, St Martin's Press, New York.

Pas, E I (1990) 'Is travel demand analysis and modelling in the doldrums?' in P M Jones (ed) *Developments in dynamic and activity-based approaches to travel analysis*, Averbury, UK, pp3–27.

Peters, D (1998) 'Breadwinners, homemakers and beasts of burden', *Habitat debate*, vol 4, no 2, pp12–14, The United Nations Centre for Human Settlements, Nairobi.

Pierce, D W (1997) 'Benefit–cost analysis, environment, and health in the developed and developing world', *Environment and development economics*, no 2, pp210–214.

Plowden, S (1972) *Towns against traffic*, Andre Deutsch, UK.

Plowden, S (1980) *Taming traffic*, Andre Deutsch, UK.

Pochet, P and Cusset, J-M (1999) 'Cultural barriers to bicycle use in West African cities', *IATSS research*, vol 23, no 2, pp43–50.

Portelli, H (1977) *Gramsci e o bloco histórico*, Paz e Terra, Rio de Janeiro.

Portugal, L S and Santos, M P S (1991) 'Trânsito urbano: a violência e seu conteúdo político', *Revista de administração pública*, vol 25, no 3, pp185–97.

Portugalli, J (1980) 'Distrbution, allocation, social structure and spatial form: elements for planning theory' *Progress in planning*, vol 14, no 3.

Poulantzas, N (1975) *Classes in contemporary capitalism*, New Left Books, London.

Preteceille, E (1981) 'Collective consumption, the state and the crisis of capitalist society' in M Harloe and E Lebas (eds), *City, class and capital*, Holmes and Meyer, US, pp1–16.

Preteceille, E (1986) 'Collective consumption, urban segregation and social classes', *Environment and planning*, vol 4, pp145–154.

Preteceille, E and Terrail, J P (1985) *Capitalism, consumption and needs*, Blackwell, UK.

Proud'homme, R (1990) 'Urban transport in developing countries: new perspectives and new policies' in *Transport urbains dans le pays en developpement, nouvelles perspectives, nouvelles politiques*, Paradigme, France, pp13–28.

Pucher, J and Lefévre, C (1996) *The urban crisis in Europe and North America*, Macmillan, UK.

Pucher, J (1999) 'Transportation paradise: realm of the nearly perfect automobile?', *Transportation Quarterly*, summer 1999 (book review).

Punyahotra, V (1979) *Road traffic accidents in developing countries*, Thailand, National Research Council.

Qian, J and Tanaboriboon, Y (1994) 'Chinese pedestrians and their walking characteristics: case study in Beijing', *Transportation research record*, no 1441, pp16–26

Quinet, E, Touzeny, L and Triebel, H (1982) *Économie des transports*, Economica, Paris.

Quium A S M Abdul (1995) 'Road accidents in Bangladesh', *IATSS research*, vol 19, no 1, pp102–103.

Rae, J B (1971) *The road and the car in American life*, MIT Press, US.

Rao, M S V and Sharma, A K (1990) 'The role of non-motorised urban travel' in G A Banjo and H T Dimitriou (eds) (1990), *Transport planning for third world cities*, Routledge, US.

Reichman, S (1983) *Les transports: servitude ou liberte?* Presses Universitaires des France, Paris.

Reksnis, M (1995) 'Road accidents in Poland', *IATSS research*, vol 19, no 1, pp100–101.

Replogle, M (1992) *Non-motorized vehicles in Asian cities*, World Bank technical paper 162, Washington DC.

Replogle, M (1994) 'Bicycles and cycle rickshaws in Asian cities: issues and strategies', in X Godard (ed) *Les transports dans les villes du Sud*, Karthala-Codatu, Paris, pp207–224.

Ribeiro, S K and Balassiano, R (1997) 'CO_2 emissions from passenger transport in Rio de Janeiro', *Transport policy*, vol 4, no 2, pp135–39.

Rimmer, J (1978) 'Redirections in transport geography', *Progress in human geography*, vol 2, no 1, pp76–100.

Rivasplata, C (1992) 'Un analysis comparativo de la movilidad en Buenos Aires y San Francisco', Clatpu Buenos Aires meeting, Buenos Aires.

Roberts, D (1997) *Mortality from unintentional injury and violence in the Americas: A source book*, Pan American Health Organisation, Washington DC.

Roqué, J A (1996) 'The social dimensions of technological change: reshaping cities and urban life' in *Preparing for the urban future – global pressures and local changes*, M Cohen et al (eds), Woodrow Wilson Center, Washington DC, pp171–199.

Rosenbloom, S (1991) 'Why working families need a car', in M Wachs and M Crawford (eds) *The car and the city – the automobile, the built environment and daily urban life*, University of Michigan Press, US.

Sachs, W (1992) *For love of the automobile*, University of California Press, US.

Sahdev, P et al (1994) 'Road traffic fatalities in Delhi: causes, injury patterns, and incidence of preventable diseases', *Accident analysis and prevention*, vol 26, no 3, pp377–84.

Saldiva, P H (1998) *Poluição atmosférica e saúde, uma abordagem experimental*, Grenepeace, São Paulo.

Sanánez, J C and Da Silva, F G (1999) 'Impacto de la congestión de tránsito en el sistema metrobus', Clatpu Caracas meeting, pp262–67.

Santos, E M and Orrico, R D (1996) *O mercado de transporte público urbano por ônibus: que contestabilidade?*, Clatpu Curitiba meeting, April.

Sattherthwaite, D (1995), 'The underestimation of urban poverty and of its health consequences', *Third World planning review*, vol 17, no 4, iii–xii.

Saunders, P (1979) *Urban politics – a sociological interpretation*, Hutchinson, London.

Sawers, L (1984) 'The political economy of urban transportation, an interpretative essay' in W K Tabb and L Sawers (ed), *Marxism and the metropolis, new perspectives in urban political economy*, UK.

Schafer, A (1998) 'The global demand for motorised mobility', *Transportation research*, vol 32, no 6, pp455–477.

Schteingart, M (1996) 'What has and has not changed since Habitat I: A view from the South' in Cohen et al (eds) *Preparing for the future – global pressures and local forces*, Woodrow Wilson Center Press, US, pp66–80.

Schumacher, E F (1974) *Small is beautiful: economics as if people mattered*, Abacus, London.

Schwartz, J (1997) 'Health effects of air pollution from traffic: ozone and particulate matter' in Fletcher and McMichael, (eds) *Health at the crossroads – transport policy and urban health*, Wiley, UK.

SEADE – Fundação Estadual de Análise de dados (1991) *Anuário estatístico do Estado de São Paulo*, São Paulo.

Sen, J (1997) 'The left alliance and the unintended city: is a civilised transition possible?', *World transpot policy and practice*, vol 3, no 3, pp31–37.

SETRA – Service D'études techniques des routes et autoroutes (1973*) Carrefours a feux*, Ministére de L'equipément et du Logement, Paris.

Sharma, A K and Gupta, S (1998) 'Women's mobility in Indian cities' in Freeman and Jamet (eds), *Urban transport policy*, Balkemna, Rotterdam, pp669–674.

Sheppard, E (1989) 'Modelling and predicting aggregate flows' in S Hanson (ed) *The geography of urban transportation*, The Guilford Press, US, pp100–128

Shimazaki, T, Hokao, K and Mohamed, S S (1994) 'Comparative study of transportation modal choice in Asian countries', *Nomotorized transportation around the world*, Transportation Research Record no 141, pp71–83, Transportation Research Board, Washington DC.

Sit, V F S (1996) 'Beijing: urban transport issues in a socialist Third World setting (1949–1992)', *Journal of transport geography*, vol 4, no 4, pp253–273.

Skinner, Q (1978) *The foundations of modern political thought*, Cambridge University Press, Cambridge, UK.

Small, K (1992) *Urban transportation economics*, Harwood Academic Publishers, Philadelphia.

SMT – Secretaria Municipal de Transportes (1978) 'Transporte por ônibus contratado', *Boletim técnico CET 18*, São Paulo.

Soares, L R (1975) *Engenharia de Tráfego*, Almeida Neves, Rio de Janeiro.

Spencer, A H and Andong, W (1996) 'Light rail or busway? A comparative evaluation for a corridor in Beijing', *Journal of transport geography*, vol 4, no 4, pp239–251.

Steensberg, J (1997) 'Future directions in policy and research: a public health perspective', in *Health at the crossroads*, Fletcher and McMichael (eds), Wiley, UK, pp311–24.

Stone, T (1971), *Beyond the automobile*, Prentice Hall, US.

Stopher, P R and Meyburg, A H (1975) *Urban transportation modelling and planning*, Prentice Hall, US.

Strambi, O and Novaes, A G (1992) 'Elementos de uma política tarifária para o transporte público: nível e estrutura tarifária', VI Nacional Conference, ANPET, proceedings, Rio de Janeiro, pp315–28.

SWOV – Institute for Road Safety Research (1993) *Towards a sustainable safe traffic system in the Netherlands*, Netherlands.

Szasz, P (1977) Nove de Julho bus convoy, *Boletim técnico CET 18*, São Paulo.

Szasz, P (1985) 'Integração de linhas tronco – desvantagens', V Congresso Nacional de Transportes Públicos, São Paulo.

Tanaboriboon, Y and Qian, J (1994) 'Chinese pedestrians and their walking characteristics: case study in Beijing', in *Nonmotorized transport around the world*, TRR 1441, TRB, pp16–26.

Tanaboriboon, Y (1994) 'Road accidents in Thailand', *IATSS research*, vol 18, no 1, pp86–87.

Tanaboriboon, Y, Chadbun, C W, Ruengsorn, D and Suriyawongpaisal, P (1999) 'Analysis of traffic accidents through hospital's trauma registry records,' *IATSS research*, vol 23, no 1, pp115–24.

Tarrius, A (1989) *Anthropologie du mouvement*, France, Transport et Communications no 27, Paradigme.

Theret, B (1982) 'Collective Consumption, capital accumulation and the urban question: conceptual problems raised by Lojkine's work', *International journal of urban and regional research*, no 6, pp345–71.

Thompson, E P (1967) 'Time, work-discipline, and industrial capitalism', *Past and Present*, no 36, pp57–97.

Thompson, J M (1977) *Great cities and their traffic*, Victor Gollancz, London.

Tolley, R and Turton, B (1995) *Transport systems, policy and planning, a geographical approach*, Longman, UK.

Town, S (1981) The sociologist's perspective on transport in D Bannister and P Hall, *Transportation and public policy planning*, Mansel, London, pp30–33.

Trani, E (1985) *L'aggravation des conditions de deplacement domicile-travail dans la Region Metropolitaine de Sao Paulo*, Institut d'Urbanisme de Paris, Université de Paris XII (thesis).

TRB – Transportation Research Board (1985), *Highway Capacity Manual*, Washington DC.

TRB (1994) *Curbing gridlock – peak-period fees to relieve traffic congestion*, Washington, DC.

TRRL – Transport and Road Research Laboratory (1991), *Towards safer roads in developing countries*, UK.

TTI – Texas Institute of Technology (1996) *Quantifying congestion, final report*, US.

Turner, J and Kwakye, E (1996) 'Transport and survival strategies in a developing economy: case evidence from Accra, Ghana', *Journal of transport geography*, vol 4, no 3, pp161–168.

Twari, G (1997) 'Issues in planning for heterogeneous traffic: the case study of Delhi' in Fletcher and McMichael (eds) *Health at the crossroads – transport policy and urban health*, Willey, London, pp235–242.

UN – United Nations (1989) *Urban Transport development, with particular reference to developing nations*, New York.

UN (1992) *The impact of subsidies, regulation, and different forms of ownership on the service quality and operational efficiency of urban bus systems in Latin America*, Economic Commission for Latin America and the Caribbean, New York.

UN (1993) *Energy efficiency in transportation – alternatives for the future*, New York.

UNCHS – United Nations Centre for Human Settlements (1992) *Strategic options for public transport improvements in large cities of developing countries*, Tata Consultancy Services, Bombay, India.

UNCHS – United Nations Centre for Human Settlements (1996) *An urbanising world, global report on human settlements*, Oxford University Press, Oxford.

Vasconcellos, E A (1995) Reassessing traffic accidents in developing countries, *Transport policy*, vol 2, no 4, pp263–270.

Vasconcellos, E A (1997a) 'The making of the middle class city' *Environment and planning A*, vol 29, no 2, pp293–310.

Vasconcellos, E A (1997b) 'The demand for cars in developing countries' *Transportation research A*, vol 31, no 3, pp245–258.

Vasconcellos, E A (1997c) 'Rural transport and access to education in developing countries: policy issues', *Journal of transport geography*, vol 5, no 2, pp127–136.

Vasconcellos, E A (2000) 'Urban transportation and traffic policies: the challenge of cohexistence in developing countries', *Transportation quarterly*, vol 54, no 1, pp91–100, winter.

Vera, A G (1999) 'De la ciudad del automovil a la ciudad congestionada,' Clatpu Caracas meeting, pp15–24.

Verhoef, E (1994) 'External effects and social costs of road transport', *Transportation research*, vol 28, no 4, pp273–287.

Vicente, O, Lamadrid, A, Arcusin, S, Turco, N and Brennan, P (1992) 'La evolución de la movilidad de los habitantes de Buenos Aires', ANPET Nacional Conference, proceedings, Rio de Janeiro, pp760–772.

Villoria, O G, Toshinori, N and Rene, Val Teodoro (1997) 'Raising the quality of public transportation services through innovative regulatory policies in Metro Manila', *IATSS research*, vol 21, no 1, pp97–103.

Vinjé, M P (1981) 'Children as pedestrians: abilities and limitations', *Accident analysis and prevention*, vol 13, no 3, pp123–35.

Vivier, J (1999) 'Comparaison des coûts externes du transport public et l'automobile en milieu urbain', *Transport public international*, vol 48, no 5, pp36–39.

Vuchic, V R (1979) 'Urban passenger transit modes' in Gray and Hoel (eds) *Public transportation plannning, operations and management*, Prentice Hall, US, pp68–97.

Vuchic, V R (1984) 'The auto versus transit controversy: toward a rational synthesis for urban transportation policy', *Transportation research*, vol 18, no 2, pp125–33.

Vuchic, V R (1999) *Transportation for livable cities*, Rutgers University, Center for Urban Policy Research, US.

Wachs, M and Cramford, M (1991), *The car and the city – the automobile, the built environment and daily urban life*, University of Michigan Press, US.

Weber, M (1991) 'The joy of the automobile' in M Wachs and M Crawford (eds) *The car and the city*, University of Michigan Press, US.

Webster, F V and Cobbe, B M (1966) *Traffic signals*, Ministry of Transport, technical paper no 56, Her Majesty's Stationery Office, London.

Werna, E, Bule, I and Harphma, T (1996) 'The changing agenda for urban health', in *Preparing for the urban future – global pressures and local changes*, M Cohen et al (eds), Woodrow Wilson Center, Washington DC, pp200–221.

Weyrich, P M and Lind, W S (1996) *Conservatives and mass transit: is it time for a new look?*, Free Congress Foundation and American Public Transit Association, Washington DC.

White, P R (1990) 'Inadequacies of urban public transport supply' in G A Banjo and H T Dimitriou (eds) *Transport planning for third world cities*, Routledge, UK.

Whitelegg, J (1981) 'Road safety: defeat, complicity and the bankruptcy of science', *Accident analysis and prevention*, vol 15, no 2, pp153–160.

Whitelegg, J (1993) *Transport for a sustainable future: the case for Europe*, Belhaven Press, London.

Whitelegg, J (1997a) *Critical Mass – transport, environment and society in the twenty-first century*, Pluto Press, London.

Whitelegg, J (1997b) 'Sustainable transport solutions for Calcutta', *World transport policy and practice*, vol 3, no 3, pp12–14.

Williams, B (1998) 'The missing link – towards sustainable urban transport', *Habitat debate*, vol 4, no 2, pp4–5, The United Nations Centre for Human Settlements, Nairobi.

Willumsen, L G (1990), 'Urban traffic modelling with limited data' in G A Banjo and H Dimitriou, *Transport planning for Third World cities*, Routledge, US.

Winner, L (1977), *Autonomous Technology*, MIT Press, US.

Whitt, J A (1982) *Urban elites and mass transportation – the dialectics of power*, Princeton Press, US.

WHO – World Health Organization (1999) *World health report*, Geneva.

Whol, M and Martin, B V (1967) *Traffic system analysis for engineers and planners*, MacGraw Hill, US.

Wise, E (1994) 'Road accidents in South Africa', *IATSS research*, vol 18, no 1, pp84–85.

World Bank (1975) *Urban transport*, sector policy paper, Washington DC.

World Bank (1986) *Urban transport systems – guideline for examining options*, World Bank technical paper, no 52, Washington DC.

World Bank (1994) *World development report, infrastructure for development*, Washington DC.

World Bank (1995), *Nonmotorized vehicles in ten Asian cities*, Washington DC.

World Bank (1996) *Sustainable transport – priorities for policy action*, Washington DC.

World Bank (1997) *World resources, a guide to the global environment*, Washington DC.

World Bank (1998) *Global road safety strategy* (draft), Washington DC.

Wright, C (1992) *Fast wheels, slow traffic – urban transport choices*, Temple University Press, US.

Wright, E O (1976) 'Class boundaries in advanced capitalist societies', *New Left review*, vol 98, pp3–41.

Wu, W (1996) 'Economic competition and resource mobilization', in Cohen et al (eds), *Urban future – global pressures and global forces*, Woodrow Wilson Center Press, US.

Yago, G (1983) 'The sociology of transportation', *American sociological review*, vol 9, pp71–190.

Yanaguaya, W (1993) 'The use of UK transport models in developing countries', *Traffic engineering and control*, vol 34, no 10, pp476–479.

Zahavi, J (1976) Travel characteristics in cities of developed and developing countries, World Bank staff working paper no 52, Washington DC.

INDEX

For Product Safety Concerns and Information please contact our EU
representative GPSR@taylorandfrancis.com
Taylor & Francis Verlag GmbH, Kaufingerstraße 24, 80331 München, Germany

www.ingramcontent.com/pod-product-compliance
Ingram Content Group UK Ltd.
Pitfield, Milton Keynes, MK11 3LW, UK
UKHW021622240425
457818UK00018B/689